THE TRAVEL BOOK

A JOURNEY THROUGH
EVERY COUNTRY IN THE WORLD

The Story of The Travel Book

Most travel journeys take in just a country or two, but the journey you're about to embark on incorporates every country on earth. In this book you'll find evocative glimpses of every single country in the world, from Afghanistan to Zimbabwe, from the postage-stamp-sized Vatican City to the epic expanse of Russia.

To actually visit all the countries in this book would require several passports and a suitcase of plane tickets, or it can be simulated with a turn of these pages. Highlighted by some of the finest photography in the world, *The Travel Book* offers a glimpse of each country's perks and quirks: when to go, what to see, how to eat it up and drink it in, and ways to immerse yourself in the life and the land. What results is a grand snapshot of our diverse and kaleidoscopic world rather than an encyclopedic reference. It's a book that unashamedly views the planet through the prism of the traveller, focusing on places for their beauty, charm or singularity, even if this does sometimes conflict with defined political or geographical borders.

MATT MUNRO // JONATHAN GREGSON // ERIC LAFFORGUE // PHILIP LEE HARVEY

The Country Conundrum

A country count can be an arbitrary thing. As a starting place we've used the United Nations' list of 193 member states. Every one of these countries features in the book, but we've also built on the list to include foreign dependencies, whether they be self-governing or not, that are popular traveller destinations. Thus you'll find Caribbean islands (Anguilla, Cayman Islands, Guadeloupe, Martinique, Puerto Rico, Turks & Caicos, Virgin Islands), Atlantic islands (Bermuda, Falkland Islands) and Pacific islands (Cook Islands, Guam & Northern Marianas, New Caledonia, Pitcairn Islands, Tahiti & French Polynesia). There are the two great land masses of Antarctica and Greenland, which are too large and fascinating to leave out of any true world guide. There are disputed lands such as Tibet and Taiwan, and recognisably unique regions such as Hong Kong, Macau and French Guiana. We've also divided the United Kingdom into its component parts – England, Scotland, Wales and Northern Ireland – to recognise their individual appeal and their rich and distinctive histories and cultures.

At the book's end you'll find an additional 11 places of interest, chosen by Lonely Planet's founder and chief frequent-flyer Tony Wheeler. These bonus destinations are small dependencies that still hold great attraction, whether it be the smoking cigar of Montserrat or that little piece of Britannia on the Mediterranean, Gibraltar. In total, you can read about 230 countries and destinations. It's exhausting just to think about.

The Structure

The Travel Book follows the most straightforward of formats – A to Z – rolling through the alphabet of nations. From a traveller's perspective, a country's might and power aren't necessarily relative to its fascination and appeal, and we've tried to capture that, giving equal weight to every country regardless of whether it has had 15 minutes or 15 centuries of world fame – the likes of South Sudan and Suriname are as noteworthy here as the superpowers of the US and China.

The book's guiding philosophy is to present a subjective view of the world from Lonely Planet's perspective, looking below the surface to show a slice of life from every country in the world. Entries evoke the spirit of each place by appealing to the senses – what you might see and feel, what kind of food and drink might flavour your visit, and which books, music or films will help prepare you for the experience. You'll find the events, objects and people that are central to each country's identity and you'll find curious, little-known facts.

Photos are paramount to capturing and sharing the spirit of a place and its people, and images in this book have been chosen to weave stories of their own. Cliched icons and picture-postcard views have been avoided in favour of photos that tell of life in its myriad forms – at work, at play, at worship, laughing, singing, relaxing, dancing or just surviving – in order to bring you countries, not brochures.

You may never visit all *The Travel Book*'s destinations, but if it's true, as Aldous Huxley once wrote, that 'to travel is to discover that everyone is wrong about other countries', then to read about them all is to find out if you are right.

We hope this new edition of *The Travel Book* inspires a world of travel.

Best time to visit
April to June and September to October – with all visits highly dependent on the political weather

Top things to see
- A modern and stable society tentatively emerging from the ruins of war in historic Kabul
- The dizzying 800-year-old Minaret of Jam, adrift in the central mountains
- The skyline of Herat's medieval old city, punctuated by its mighty citadel and thicket of minarets
- The blue domes of Mazar-e Sharif's Shrine of Hazrat Ali, Afghanistan's holiest pilgrimage site
- The Panjshir Valley, with its rushing river and neat villages and orchards

Top things to do
- Contemplate the ruins of the giant Buddha statues amid the serene Bamiyan Valley
- Trek with yaks across the Pamir Mountains in the Wakhan Corridor
- Dip your toes in the blue mineral waters of the Band-e Amir lakes
- Feel a sense of peace in the rehabilitated Nilma Gardens, laid out in the classical Mughal style
- Haggle for Afghan carpets at their source with Pashtun, Uzbek and Turkmen traders

Getting under the skin
Read: Eric Newby's witty *A Short Walk in the Hindu Kush*, a genuine classic; Rory Stewart's *The Places In Between*, an excellent post-Taliban travelogue
Listen: to *qataghani* wedding songs and spiritual *qawalis* (Sufi religious chants), now enjoying a revival after the music-free years of the Taliban
Watch: *Osama*, directed by Siddiq Barmak, which tells the story of a girl assuming a male identity to work in Taliban-era Kabul
Eat: fat Kandahari pomegranates; sweet grapes from the Shomali Plain; and (according to Marco Polo) the best melons in the world
Drink: *chai sabz* (green tea), drunk scaldingly hot at a traditional teahouse

In a word
Salaam aleikum (Peace be with you) – a ubiquitous greeting and blessing

Trademarks
Beards and turbans; Burqa-clad women; rebels with rocket launchers; lapis lazuli mountains; desert fortresses; intricately woven rugs; opium poppies; traditional hospitality to guests

Random fact
The lapis lazuli gemstones used to make Tutankhamun's death mask were mined in northeastern Afghanistan

1. Widows eating a meal at the Poultry Development for Women Project, Kabul

2. Making naan bread at a street stall in Kabul

3. The evocatively empty niche of the ancient Large Buddha of Bamiyan, destroyed by the Taliban

CAPITAL KABUL // POPULATION POPULATION 31.1 MILLION // AREA 652,230 SQ KM // OFFICIAL LANGUAGES DARI & PASHTO

Afghanistan

If we were judging just on aesthetics, Afghanistan would be near the top of any list of must-see Asian destinations. Picture its attractions: mosques and fortresses straight out of *Arabian Nights*, spectacular mountains scarred by desert winds, ancient ruins that speak of centuries at the crossroads of Asia, and a culture as timeless and enigmatic as the desert itself. In the 1960s, this was an essential stop on the hippy trail to India, but decades of war derailed the Afghan dream. Visiting Afghanistan today is possible, but only for hardened travellers who don't mind dodging militants and drones to reach Afghanistan's forgotten treasures.

A CAPITAL TIRANA // POPULATION 3 MILLION // AREA 28,748 SQ KM // OFFICIAL LANGUAGE ALBANIAN

Albania

After decades of isolation from the rest of Europe under harsh communist rule, Albania emerged in the early 1990s, blinking, as it finally entered the modern age, and it has been on a rollercoaster ride of change ever since. Endowed with incredible natural beauty, including some of Europe's most impressive mountains and miles of beautiful beach, the 'land of the eagles' has become an open secret among backpackers wanting to escape the crowds elsewhere in Eastern Europe. From its vibrant markets to its picturesque museum towns, Albania extends a warm welcome, raising a weather-beaten fedora and a shot glass of raki in honour of visitors.

Best time to visit
April to October

Top things to see
- Historic Berat, a near-perfectly preserved Ottoman town of whitewashed houses climbing up a hillside
- The serene ruins of ancient Butrint, lost deep in the forest with a lakeside setting
- Bustling Tirana, Albania's sprawling and fast-paced heart, full of museums, cafes and shopping
- The mountain top town of Gjirokastra, with its imposing views, looming castle and grand Ottoman mansions

Top things to do
- Discover your own beachside idyll on the spectacular beaches and coves of the Ionian coast
- Jump aboard the daily ferry on Lake Koman for a trip into Albania's mountainous interior
- Do the spectacular day trek between the villages of Valbona and Theth
- Plunge into the bottomless, blue glassy depths of the Blue Eye Spring

Getting under the skin
Read: *Chronicle in Stone* by Ismail Kadare, a boyhood tale set in Gjirokastra; *Land of Eagles* by Robin Hanbury-Tenison, a horseback odyssey through modern Albania
Listen: to the entwined vocal and instrumental parts of traditional southern Albanian polyphony
Watch: Gjergj Xhuvani's *Slogans*, a wry look at the hardships of life in a mountain village during the communist era
Eat: Eat roast lamb in the mountains or freshly caught fish along the coast; *byrek* is the quintessential Albanian fast food: layered pastry filled with cheese, potato or minced meat
Drink: raki (aniseed-flavoured grape brandy) as an aperitif; or *konjak* (cognac) as an after-dinner tipple

In a word
Tungjatjeta (Hello)

Trademarks
Mountains; prickly minarets in mountain villages; the double-eagle flag; bunkers

Random fact
The Albanian language is unrelated to any other in Europe and is thought to derive from ancient Illyrian

1. Mountain lakes glisten in the Albanian Alps

2. The crystal clear waters of the Ionian Coast

3. An Ottoman-era bridge at Mes, north of Shkodra

Best time to visit
November to April

Top things to see
- The Casbah in Algiers, arguably North Africa's most intriguing medina
- Djemila's Roman ruins, beautifully sited in the Mediterranean's hinterland
- The stunning pastel-coloured oasis towns in the M'Zab Valley on the Sahara's northern fringe
- A spectacular sunrise from atop barren mountains deep in the Sahara at Assekrem
- Tassili N'Ajjer's open-air gallery of rock art from the time before the Sahara became a desert

Top things to do
- Sip a cafe au lait in Algiers' French-style sidewalk cafes then dive into the Casbah
- Dream of Algeria's Roman and Phoenician past at the charming old port of Tipaza
- Discover the hidden treasures of Tlemcen's extraordinary Arab-Islamic architecture
- Sleep amid the sand dunes of the Grand Erg Occidental
- Explore the Tassili du Hoggar, with some of the Sahara's most beautiful scenery

Getting under the skin
Read: *Sands of Death* by Michael Asher, a page-turning true account of epic 19th-century Saharan battles; Jeremy Keenan's *Sahara Man: Travelling with the Tuareg*, which takes you deep into the Tuareg world
Listen: to *King of Rai: The Best of Khaled*, for Algeria's best-loved musical (and most danceable) export
Watch: Gillo Pontecorvo's *The Battle of Algiers*, a searing portrayal of the 1954–62 Algerian War of Independence, with Algiers' Casbah playing a starring role
Eat: chickpea fritters, couscous and lamb tajine spiced with cinnamon
Drink: three servings of strong tea around a Tuareg campfire

In a word
Salaam aleikum (Peace be with you)

Trademarks
The Sahara's biggest sand seas; rai music; the 'End of the World' (the literal translation of Assekrem); Tuareg nomads; Roman ruins along the Mediterranean Coast; civil war in the 1990s

Random fact
Some of France's most famous names were born in Algeria, including Edith Piaf, Albert Camus, Yves Saint-Laurent and Zinedine Zidane

1. A Tuareg man creates a piece of traditional silverware

2. A showcase of Islamic architecture, the medieval palace of the Mechouar in Tlemcen

3. The fantastical landscape of the Hoggar Mountains in the central Sahara

A · CAPITAL ALGIERS // POPULATION 38 MILLION // AREA 2,381,740 SQ KM // OFFICIAL LANGUAGE ARABIC

Algeria

Until recently, Algeria was the great barrier to travel in North Africa, leaving a hole the size of Africa's second-largest country in the travellers' map of the continent. But Algeria has made a stunning return to peace. Security can be patchy (the Kabylie region and all border areas are considered unsafe and you should check government travel advisories for travel elsewhere), but its catalogue of attractions – from wonderfully preserved Roman ruins in the north to the extraordinary Saharan landscapes and oasis towns of the south – may even surpass the better-known charms of Morocco and Tunisia.

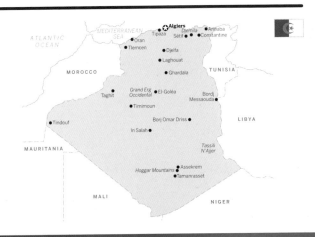

A CAPITAL ANDORRA LA VELLA // POPULATION 85,458 // AREA 468 SQ KM // OFFICIAL LANGUAGE CATALAN

Andorra

Racing down snowy pistes, sleeping snug between ice-hotel walls and splurging in some of Andorra's 2000-plus low-tax shops is how most think of this principality neatly wedged between France and Spain in the eastern Pyrenees. Fewer know about its history (which harks back to the 9th century), its fascinating people, the cobbled core of Andorra la Vella, the country's only town, or its secret hoard of thermal spas that soothe weary limbs. The absence of an airport means Andorra never gets the attention it deserves, but jet into Barcelona in neighbouring Spain or Toulouse in France and this intriguing mini-nation is just a couple of hours' drive away.

Best time to visit
Mid-December to early April for skiing; June to September for hiking

Top things to see
- The cobbled streets and hidden squares of Andorra la Vella's quaint historic quarter
- Three near-pristine valleys – each justifies a one-day hike, at least
- The stunning mountain scenery of Grandvalira, the largest ski area in the Pyrenees
- The Museu del Tabac in Sant Julià de Lòria, a fascinating tobacco-factory-turned-museum
- Historic Casa de la Vall in Andorra la Vella, built in 1580 as a home for a wealthy family, now housing Andorra's parliament

Top things to do
- Ski the winter slopes of Soldeu at the heart of Grandvalira
- Wallow in toasty-warm mineral water at Europe's largest spa complex, Caldea, in Andorra la Vella
- Join the dusk-time crowds on the rooftop of Plaça del Poble, Andorra la Vella, oohing and aahing over valley views
- Hike the 112km Grand Route de Pays (GRP): seven days of hut-to-hut tramping across the roof of Europe

Getting under the skin
Read: *A Tramp in Spain: From Andalusia to Andorra*, a travelogue by Englishman Bart Kennedy, who tramped, knapsack on back, to Andorra in 1904
Listen: to something classical by the National Chamber Orchestra of Andorra directed by top Andorran violinist Gerard Claret
Watch: *Nick* (Outlier) a thriller from Spanish director Jose Pozo about a teen trying to solve a murder he witnesses in the sleepy mountains of Andorra
Eat: hearty mountain fare – think *trinxat* (bacon, potatoes and cabbage) or traditional *escudella* (a cockle-warming chicken, sausage and meatball stew)
Drink: mulled red wine laced with lemon, apple, raisins, cinnamon and cognac after a day on the slopes

In a word
Hola (Hello!)

Trademarks
Skiing; shopping; smuggling; the Pyrenees

Random fact
In the 1980s a 2km glacier still slumbered in the Andorran Pyrenees; today it's completely gone and glacial lakes are all that remain

1. Nestled in an autumn-hued valley is the Sanctuary of Meritxell

2. Rustic architecture in the mountainous region of Encamp

3. Futuristic architecture at the Caldea Spa Complex in Andorra la Vella

1. A rainbow of sun shelters on a beach in Namibe

2. Children practise surfing with home-made boards near Luanda

3. The looping road to Lubango

A CAPITAL LUANDA // POPULATION 18.6 MILLION // AREA 1,246,700 SQ KM // OFFICIAL LANGUAGE PORTUGUESE

Angola

Angolans are fighters – but they are lovers, too. The latter fact has been lost on the world's press, who have long labelled this African nation a haven of havoc, broadcasting stories of its civil wars, blood diamonds, wasted oil revenues and starving people. For those who visit, however, it's the love that they'll remember. Whether it's an unquestioning love of God, an enthusiastic embrace of romance or an unwavering desire to dance like there is no tomorrow, the passion of Angolans is intoxicating to observe. More sobering is the rising cost of living in the capital – Luanda has been the world's most expensive city for expats since 2013.

Best time to visit
June to September during the cooler dry season

Top things to see
- The crumbling art deco and neoclassical facades in the coastal town of Namibe
- Miradouro de Lua, a rusty-topped Martian-like rock formation that drops dramatically to the Atlantic
- The horizon-topping dunes of Parque Nacional do Iona
- The enigmatic Himba tribes that inhabit the nation's southern fringe

Top things to do
- Join *Cristo Rei*, Angola's version of Rio's *Cristo Redentor,* and stare down over the city of Lubango
- Get your hot hands on a surfboard and ride the cool Atlantic swells – they are some of Africa's best
- Ride the rebuilt Benguela railway from Lobito to the Congo's fringes

Getting under the skin
Read: *Angola: The Weight of History* by Patrick Chaba for an understanding of the social and political evolution of the country since breaking free from Portuguese rule
Listen: to the sensual and romantic rhythms of *kizomba,* a modern evolution of the country's traditional *semba* music
Watch: *Rostov-Luanda,* a documentary hinged on a Mauritanian's journey to find a friend in Angola
Eat: *calulu de peixe* (fish stew)
Drink: *galãos* (white coffee) – Angola has historically been one of the world's largest producers of the bean, and locals love drinking it with milk

In a word
Tudo bom? (How's things?)

Trademarks
Blood diamonds and *garimpeiros* (diamond diggers); oil; civil war; landmines; beautiful beaches

Random fact
Although polygamy is illegal, it is common due to the civil war creating a shortage of men

CAPITAL THE VALLEY // POPULATION 15,754 // AREA 102 SQ KM // OFFICIAL LANGUAGE ENGLISH

Anguilla

The sun sets over the sea, leaving striations of orange amid the gently rippling azure waters. You lean back against the warm sands of a dune, letting an 'ahh' escape from your mouth as your back finds the perfect position. Artfully wrecked old wooden boats perch on the sand, and soon you're hearing the ever-mellow strains of reggae, played by some of the Caribbean's most renowned musicians. It's just another evening on Anguilla, one of the region's smallest islands and one that takes every holiday cliché (perfect white sand, rum, reggae, turquoise waters) and distils them down to perfection. Go for a stroll, chat to some locals, find your own beat.

Best time to visit
December to May when hurricane threats and humidity levels are low

Top things to see
- Shoal Bay, everything a Caribbean beach should be
- Prickly Pear Cays: Anguilla distilled down to milky white nubs of sand amid the cyan sea
- Meads Bay, an idyllic mile-long crescent of blinding white sand
- Wallblake House and St Gerard's church, glimpses of 18th-century plantation life
- Sandy Ground, the appropriately named cluster of the island's languorous nightspots

Top things to do
- Sail the perfectly azure waters – it's the number one local sport
- Hide out in Junk's Hole, an especially intimate beach on an intimate island
- Carefully plan your day so that you do nothing at all; Anguilla means relaxation
- Dive the 1772 wreck of the *El Buen Consejo*
- Jam to the beat of the Dune Preserve, where local reggae legends play amid wrecked boats and, yes, dunes

Getting under the skin
Read: *The Night of the Rambler* by Montague Kobbé – an exciting reimagining of the 1967 Anguillan revolution
Listen: to Bankie Banx, a celebrated Anguillan singer-songwriter known as a reggae pioneer
Watch: one of the *Pirates of the Caribbean* movies to get in the mood
Eat: sweet, fresh local lobster and crayfish
Drink: a Dune Shine (fresh ginger, pineapple juice, bitters and rum) at the Dune Preserve

In a word
Limin' (Hanging out with friends, preferably on the beach)

Trademarks
Beaches that are great even by Caribbean standards; wild goats running amok; sailing

Random fact
Anguilla was once part of St Kitts and Nevis, but squabbles between pint-sized Anguilla and its more populous neighbours led to a mini-revolution (and a permanent parting) in 1967; it has been a British overseas territory ever since

ATLANTIC OCEAN
Scrub Island
Prickly Pear Cays
Shoal Bay
Junk's Hole
Sandy Island
The Valley
Sandy Ground
Meads Bay
Blowing Point
Anguilla Channel
CARIBBEAN SEA

1. The turquoise Cove Bay Beach

2. Wide smiles and wide-open doors welcome all to a local church

Best time to visit
November to February for 'summer'; March for marine mammal spotting

Top things to see
- Colossal icebergs and mountain reflections on looking-glass waters at Paradise Harbour
- The true grit of Antarctic exploration icily preserved at Shackleton's expedition hut
- Whales moving in for the krill at heart-breakingly beautiful Wilhelmina Bay
- Thunderous glaciers calving and penguins skittering across the ice at Neko Harbour on the continent proper
- Penguins gracefully porpoising through the sheer-sided Lemaire Channel

Top things to do
- Glide on a Zodiac under the morning's pink skies past basking Weddell seals and honking gentoo penguins
- Sail into the caldera of a still-active volcano and hang out with chinstrap penguins on Deception Island
- Gasp at the echoing 'pffft' of a humpback surfacing next to your boat then marvel at acrobatic displays of lobtailing and breaching
- Experience sensory overload – the tang of salt, the biting cold and the pitter-patter of a thousand happy penguin feet

Getting under the skin
Read: *Endurance*, a gripping account of Sir Ernest Shackleton's epic, ill-fated voyage to cross the Antarctic continent in 1916
Listen: to Rothera Station's wintering rock band Nunatak – made up of two scientists, two engineers and a field assistant
Watch: the beautifully restored footage of Shackleton's men and dogs working on the ice-beset ship *Endurance* in the 1998 film *South*
Eat: an Antarctic barbecue, set up on deck or even on the ice
Drink: an Antarctic Old Fashion: a fruity mix of 100-proof bourbon, multiflavoured Life Savers sweets and just-melted snow

In a word
The A-factor (The local term for the unexpected difficulties caused by the Antarctic environment)

Trademarks
Icebergs; penguins; freezing cold; geologists; explorers; treacherous seas; the South Pole; glaciers; seals; whales; 24-hour sunlight; global warming

Random fact
Antarctica's ice sheets contain 90% of the world's ice – 28 million cu km – holding about 70% of the world's fresh water

1. Towering other-worldly ice sculptures

2. The lunchtime crowd of gentoo penguins

3. Storm clouds loom over a lonely research station

POPULATION 4490 (SUMMER), 1106 (WINTER) // **AREA** 14.2 MILLION SQ KM

Antarctica

Snow, icebergs the size of multistorey car parks, wave-lashed seas, knife-edge mountains, ever-changing light. Stark and staggeringly remote, Antarctica and the enormousness of its ice shelves and mountain ranges make for a haunting, elemental beauty. The wildlife rules here, and breathtakingly close encounters with gentoo, Adélie and chinstrap penguins, seals and humpback whales are common. Governed by 29 nations, this continent is primarily dedicated to scientific research but it's also one of the planet's regions that's most visibly affected by global warming; as parts of the continent melt, others grow, leaving scientists to debate what it all actually means.

1. St John's Cathedral dominates its namesake town

2. Spectators enjoying exuberant carnival parades

3. Nelson's Dockyard, a cultural heritage site and marina in English Harbour

A CAPITAL ST JOHN'S // POPULATION 90,156 // AREA 441 SQ KM // OFFICIAL LANGUAGE ENGLISH

Antigua & Barbuda

Talk about opposites. Antigua is a bustling island that's home to many a commercial scheme, plus a fair number of wintering celebrities. Island marketers promote the notion that it has 365 beaches, one for every day of the year. It's a tough claim to verify, but no matter the number, these dazzling strands of sand are a sure bet, strung along the coasts like pearls on a necklace. Meanwhile Antigua's tiny sibling Barbuda is more or less an empty paradise of pink and white sand. The islands also faced very different fates during the historic hurricane season of 2017: Antigua sustained only superficial damage, while Barbuda was decimated.

Best time to visit
December to mid-April

Top things to see
- Nelson's Dockyard on Antigua, an authentically preserved 18th-century British naval base
- Old hilltop forts guarding the yachties' haven of English Harbour
- St John's, a slightly hardscrabble port town, with lively markets and an energetic hubbub
- Fig Tree Drive, reveals Antigua's prettiest tropical scenery

Top things to do
- Hop on a catamaran to cruise the coastline and snorkel the reefs
- Hit the beach on the southwest coast at sublime Ffryes, Turner's, Darkwood or Jolly Bay
- Flock to Barbuda's Codrington Lagoon, the largest frigate-bird nesting site in the Caribbean

Getting under the skin
Read: Jamaica Kincaid's novel *Annie John*, a story of growing up in Antigua
Listen: to steel pan; calypso (with its roots in slave culture); ubiquitous reggae music; and zouk, the party music
Watch: music videos shot on the islands by various big names in pop, such as Duran Duran
Eat: *duckanoo* (a dessert made with cornmeal, coconut, spices and brown sugar); or black pineapple, sold along Fig Tree Drive
Drink: locally brewed Wadadli beer; or Antiguan rums Cavalier or English Harbour

In a word
Fire a grog (Drink rum)

Trademarks
Cricket; countless pristine white-sand beaches on Antigua, and endless ones on Barbuda

Random fact
Antigua has produced some of the world's best cricketers, including Andy Roberts, Curtly Ambrose and Sir Vivian Richards

Best time to visit
March to May (autumn) for Buenos Aires,
December to March (summer) in Patagonia

Top things to see
- The soaked and ear-shattering panorama of the spectacular Iguazú Falls
- The sultry steps of tango performed on the streets
- Endangered southern right whales in Reserva Faunística Península Valdés
- The massive Glaciar Perito Moreno calve with thunderous cracks
- Stray cats and sculpted mausoleums in Recoleta Cemetery, the final stop for Buenos Aires' rich and famous

Top things to do
- Live it up till the sun comes up in Buenos Aires' bars and clubs
- Feel sporting tensions run high at a Superclásico clash between Buenos Aires footballing heavyweights Boca Juniors and River Plate
- Test run various vintages on a *bodega* (winery) tour outside Mendoza
- Ride the windy range with *gauchos* (cowboys) at a Patagonian *estancia* (grazing establishment)
- Feast on steaks and every other part of a cow at a backyard *asado* (barbecue)

Getting under the skin
Read: anything by the lyrical master of the short story, Jorge Luis Borges
Listen: to the wandering alt rhythms of Juana Molina, the tangos of Carlos Gardel and gritty classic Argentine rock such as that of Charly García
Watch: a young Che Guevara discover Latin America in *The Motorcycle Diaries* or quirky man-and-his-dog road trip flick *Bombón El Perro*
Eat: *empanadas* (pastries stuffed with savoury fillings), *alfajores* (delicious multilayered cookies) and *facturas* (sweet pastries)
Drink: maté (pronounced mah-tay), a bitter tea served in a gourd with a metal straw and shared among friends and colleagues – or a fruity Malbec red wine for something stronger

In a word
Qué copado! (How cool!)

Trademarks
Tango; maté rituals; football; the Péróns; glaciers; Patagonia; *gauchos*; grass-fed beef

Random fact
At 70kg per capita, yearly beef consumption in Argentina is the world's highest

1. Patagonia's constantly advancing Glaciar Perito Moreno

2. A *gaucho* herds cattle at Estancia El Roble in Buenos Aires province

3. Cerro Aconcagua rises over a vineyard in Mendoza

A CAPITAL BUENOS AIRES // POPULATION 42.6 MILLION // AREA 2,780,400 SQ KM // OFFICIAL LANGUAGE SPANISH

Argentina

Think big. Argentina boasts the highest Andean peak (Aconcagua) and the world's southernmost city (Ushuaia), while sparsely-populated wildernesses like Patagonia or Tierra del Fuego render the scale of the hugeness huger. Buenos Aires offers countless avenues to all-night revelry, but beyond the city limits, nature comes unabashed and boundless. The dry pastel hues of the northern desert erupt into the thunderous falls of Iguazú, the crisp skies of the lakes region and the craggy, glacier-clad south. Do as locals do: slow down, accept time is fluid, and you will draw in all manner of encounters.

CAPITAL YEREVAN // POPULATION 3.1 MILLION // AREA 29,743 SQ KM // OFFICIAL LANGUAGE ARMENIAN

Armenia

Said to have its head in the West and its heart in the East, the high rocky plateau of Armenia is a redoubt of artistry and remote beauty. At the meeting point of Europe and the Middle East, Armenians went through an often traumatic 20th century. Yet they have endured, seeking solace in their Christian faith, maintaining a fierce pride in their language, culture and homeland. Flaunting mountain passes, monasteries, walking trails, stonework architecture and the lively city of Yerevan, Armenia offers an experience steeped in culture, outdoor adventure and the timeless pleasure of slowing down to the pace of the locals.

Best time to visit
May to September

Top things to see
- Yerevan, the cultural heart of the nation, with fabulous museums, galleries and the buzzing Vernissage flea market
- Holy Echmiadzin, the seat of the Armenian Apostolic Church
- The artists' retreat of Dilijan, full of gingerbread-style houses and touted as the 'Switzerland of Armenia'
- Vayots Dzor, the southern province peppered with monasteries, walking trails, the Selim caravanserai and wine-growing Arpa Valley

Top things to do
- Slow down and tap into the fabulous street culture of Yerevan
- Clamber down to the snake pit once occupied by St Gregory the Illuminator, in Khor Virap Monastery
- Trundle through the Debed Canyon, with forested valleys, quiet villages and monasteries
- Spend the day in Goris, home of potent fruit brandies and 5th-century cave houses

Getting under the skin
Read: *Visions of Ararat* by Christopher Walker, a compilation of writings by Armenian soldiers, anthropologists and poets; or *Armenia: Portraits of Survival and Hope* by Donald E Miller, snapshots of 1990s Armenian life
Listen: to the mournful melodies of the *duduk* (traditional double-reed flute) played by *duduk* master Djivan Gasparyan
Watch: the sumptuous, poetic *Colour of Pomegranates* by Sergei Paradjanov
Eat: *khoravats* (skewered pork or lamb), so ubiquitous that lighting the barbecue is almost a daily ritual
Drink: *soorch* (gritty and lusciously thick coffee); or *konyak* (cognac), the national liquor

In a word
Genats (Cheers!)

Trademarks
Intricate stonemasonry; medieval manuscripts; communal dining punctuated with raucous toasts

Random fact
Armenia was the first nation to accept Christianity as a state religion, converting en masse in AD 301

1. Women knitting and chatting in NoratusCemetery, near Gavar and Lake Sevan

2. The *gavit*, or vestry, of the impressive Geghard Monastery in Kotayk province

3. Vahramashen Church on the slopes of Mt Aragats

A CAPITAL CANBERRA // POPULATION 22.3 MILLION // AREA 7,741,220 SQ KM // OFFICIAL LANGUAGE ENGLISH

Australia

Australia is as big as your imagination. There's a heckuva lot of tarmac across this wide brown land and the best way to appreciate the country is to hit the road. Sure, it's got deadly creepy crawlies and sharks, but they don't stop people from coming here to see its famous natural beauty – from endless sunbaked deserts to lush tropical rainforest and wild southern beaches. Scattered along the coasts, its cities blend a European enthusiasm for art and food with a passionate love of sport and the outdoors. Those expecting to see an opera in Sydney one night and spy crocs in the outback the next morning will have to rethink their geography: it is the sheer vastness that gives Australia – and its population – such immense character.

Best time to visit
Any time: when it's cold down south it's warm up north

Top things to see
- A concert, dance or theatrical performance at the country's most recognisable icon, the Sydney Opera House
- The red hues of Uluru, an awe-inspiring natural monolith that is both ancient and sacred
- Broome, where the desert meets the sea in contrasting aquamarines, rust-reds and pearl whites
- Provocative and engaging art at the world-class MONA, a museum housed in an underground lair in Hobart
- Paradisiacal beaches and an astounding underwater world as you island-hop around the Whitsundays on the Great Barrier Reef

Top things to do
- Discover Aboriginal culture, rock art and biological diversity at majestic Kakadu National Park
- Wind your way beside wild waters and craggy rock formations then whip inland through rainforests driving the Great Ocean Road
- Sip on a well-balanced shiraz or crisp sauvignon blanc in the Barossa Valley or Margaret River
- Spy 'gentle giant' whale sharks at the World-Heritage–listed Ningaloo Reef
- Tackle the waves at one of the world's hippest beach spots, Sydney's Bondi

Getting under the skin
Read: *Cloudstreet*, Tim Winton's fascinating novel that chronicles the lives of two families thrown together in post-WWII Perth
Listen: to Slim Dusty's 'Pub with No Beer', a classic Australian country tune; or the soothing Aboriginal voice of Geoffrey Gurrumul Yunupingu on his album *Gurrumul*
Watch: *Rabbit-Proof Fence*, a true story about three forcibly relocated Aboriginal girls who trek 2400km to return to their families
Eat: fresh Sydney rock oysters; barely cooked purple-red kangaroo meat; Vegemite

Drink: craft beer or any one of a huge selection of local wines

In a word
G'day mate!

Trademarks
Dangerous creatures; surfing; endless coastlines; outback pubs; barbecues; wildlife warriors; beer; Aussie Rules football; sunshine; Aboriginal art

Random fact
Great Australian inventions include the bionic ear, the black box flight recorder, the notepad and the wine cask

1. Melbourne's vibrant Federation Square illuminated at dusk

2. The estuary and rainforest of Hill Inlet on dreamy Whitsunday Island

3. A drover contemplates the Mount Mulligan range in Queensland

Best time to visit
Year-round

Top things to see
- Vienna's Christkindlmarkt (Christmas market) with a mug of mulled wine in one hand and a bag of hot chestnuts in the other
- The opulent state apartments, prancing Lipizzaner stallions and jewels the size of golf balls in Vienna's palatial Hofburg
- Salzburg, the city where music, art and architecture achieve baroque perfection
- Innsbruck's medieval heart, dwarfed by majestic snowcapped peaks
- Eisriesenwelt, the world's largest accessible ice caves deep in the heart of the mountains
- The Gothic masterpiece that is the Stephansdom, piercing Vienna's sky

Top things to do
- Revel in Vienna's extraordinary cultural extravaganza, climaxing with a performance at its celebrated opera house
- Catch a rousing concert by the Vienna Boys' Choir, at their own venue, MuTh, or the Hofburgkapelle
- Road-trip through the Hohe Tauern National Park along the overwhelmingly scenic Grossglockner Road
- Dip into one lake after another in the glassy-blue Salzkammergut lake district
- Hurl yourself on skis down the spectacular Harakiri – Austria's steepest slope – in Mayrhofen, or hobnob with the jet-set ski crowd in upmarket Lech

Getting under the skin
Read: *The Piano Teacher* (also a film), by 2004 Nobel Laureate Elfriede Jelinek, to acquaint yourself with one of the most provocative Austrian writers
Listen: to Beethoven, Mozart, Haydn and Schubert
Watch: Milos Forman's *Amadeus* for the tale of Mozart and rival composer Antonio Salieri
Eat: a bowl of soup speckled with *Knödel* (dumplings), followed by a *Weiner Schnitzel* (breaded veal or pork escalope) and sweet *Salzburger Nockerl* (fluffy soufflé)
Drink: *Sturm* (semifermented Heuriger wine) in autumn; *Glühwein* (hot spiced red wine) in winter; and coffee in a *kaffeehaus* any time of year

In a word
Grüss gott (Hello)

Trademarks
Julie Andrews and *The Sound of Music*; apple strudel; Strauss waltzes; edelweiss; Arnold Schwarzenegger; Freud; Mozart

Random fact
Vienna is the largest wine-growing city in the world

1. An Alpine church

2. Hundertwasserhaus, a colourful apartment building in Vienna

3. The hills are alive

CAPITAL VIENNA // **POPULATION** 8.42 MILLION // **AREA** 83,871 SQ KM // **OFFICIAL LANGUAGE** GERMAN

Austria

Austria is something of a film set, as lavish and decadent as a Viennese ball where old-society dames waltz, gallop and polka with new-millennium drag queens. Be it the jewel-box Habsburg palaces and coffee houses of Vienna, the baroque brilliance of Salzburg or the towering peaks that claw at the snowline above Innsbruck, the backdrop for travel in this landlocked Alpine country is phenomenal. Natural landscapes – giddy mountain vistas, dazzling glaciers and deep ravines – are as artful as a Mozart masterpiece or that romantic dance Strauss taught the world. Whether it's arts and culture you're into or scaling mountain peaks, in Austria you'll have a ball.

1. Nizami St in central Baku

2. Striated Şahdağ (Shahdag) Mountain in the Caucasus

3. Baku's architectural signature, the Flame Towers

A CAPITAL BAKU // POPULATION 9.6 MILLION // AREA 86,600 SQ KM // OFFICIAL LANGUAGE AZERI

Azerbaijan

Legend has it that Azerbaijan was the site of the Garden of Eden. Tucked beneath the Caucasus Mountains and hugging the Caspian Sea, it is where Central Asia edges into Europe, with a melange of Turkic, Persian and Russian influences contributing to its fabric. Azerbaijan offers dramatic and untouched mountain vistas, the gritty reality of Caspian oil rigs, ancient Zoroastrian temples, Bronze-Age petroglyphs and elegant caravanserais seemingly lifted straight out of the *Arabian Nights*. Modern Azeris are a passionate people who enjoy the timeless pleasures of a glass of *çay* (tea) with friends over a spirited game of *nard* (backgammon).

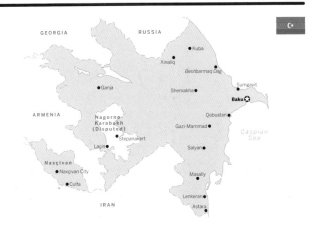

Best time to visit
May to June and September to November for pleasant weather and fewer crowds

Top things to see
- Baku's futuristic architecture, including the 'flickering' Flame Towers, the Zaha Hadid–designed Heydar Aliyev Center, and the venues constructed for the European Games
- The rusty oil derricks littering the barren landscape of the Abşeron Peninsula
- The coppersmiths of Lahic, hammering away to create the town's renowned artwork

Top things to do
- Get lost in the atmosphere of Baku's Old City, wandering the narrow alleyways around the Palace of the Shirvanshahs
- Take a horse ride into the mountains, following ancient trails with a local guide
- Marvel at ancient petroglyphs and the sputtering mud volcanoes of starkly beautiful Qobustan

Getting under the skin
Read: *Ali and Nino*, Kurban Said's epic novel about a doomed love affair between an Azeri Muslim and a Georgian Christian, set in early-20th-century Baku
Listen: to *muğam*, Azerbaijan's very own musical idiom, a traditional minstrel art form that's emotional and spine tingling
Watch: Ayaz Salayev's award-winning *The Bat*; or Samil Aliyev's *The Accidental Meeting*
Eat: flame-grilled *shashlyk* (lamb kebab)
Drink: *çay* (tea) at a traditional teahouse, or just about anywhere else in the entire country

In a word
Salam (Hello

Trademarks
Baku's Flame Towers, Caspian caviar; traditional copperware and carpets; industrial detritus of the oil industry

Random fact
'Layla', Eric Clapton's classic rock song was inspired by the Azeri epic poem *Layla and Majnun*

Best time to visit

Year-round: December to February (winter) to escape northern cold, June to August (summer) for full-on tropical heat and humidity

Top things to see

- Nassau's pirate museums and seemingly endless shopping strips
- Inagua National Park, roosting spot for untold thousands of pink flamingos
- Harbour Island, where the sands – not the birds – are pink
- Long Island, with classic pastel-hued houses and over 120km of blissfully empty beaches
- Cat Island – a peaceful refuge for traditional Bahamian culture, and the best place to hear local 'rake and scrape' music

Top things to do

- Kayak among dozens of tiny islands (cays) in the Exumas, camping when the mood strikes
- Island-hop by mail boat, the traditional links to the nation's furthest reaches
- Savour grilled conch at a beachside shack on Grand Bahama, the closest island to the American mainland
- Take the plunge at Small Hope Bay, with mysterious blue holes on-shore, and shark and reef dives in the lagoon
- Explore a shipwreck (there's at least one or two for every island

Getting under the skin

Read: Brian Antoni's *Paradise Overdose*, about the 1980s drug- and sex-addled Bahamian high life
Listen: to Tony Mackay, alias Exuma, from Cat Island; among his classic Caribbean-themed songs is 'The Obeah Man'
Watch: James Bond in action in *For Your Eyes Only*, *The Spy Who Loved Me* and *Never Say Never Again* for the Bahamas backdrop
Eat: conch (a mollusc served pounded, minced and frittered; marinated and grilled; or even raw as ceviche)
Drink: Kalik (a light, sweet lager); or a *goombay smash*, a dangerously easy-to-quaff rum punch

In a word

Hey man, what happ'nin'?

Trademarks

Casinos; luxury yachts; golf courses; tame sharks; rum punch; pirates; honeymoons; cruise ships; deserted islands

Random fact

Many Bahamians practice *obeah*, a ritualistic form of magic with deep African roots

1. Conch shells for sale in Nassau

2. A flamingo tends its nest on Great Inagua

3. The dazzling Atlantis resort, Nassau, from a peaceful distance

CAPITAL NASSAU // POPULATION 319,031 // AREA 13,940 SQ KM // OFFICIAL LANGUAGE ENGLISH

Bahamas

If you visited an island a day, you'd have over eight years of perfect adventure in the Bahamas. Some 3100 islands and islets dot the archipelago like a king's ransom of diamonds spread across a velvet cloth. Some are no bigger than a limestone spit poking above the swells; others are fully-fledged paradise islands, with swaying palms, blond sand beaches lined with sun-loungers and marinas full of luxury yachts. The Bahamas has a reputation as a luxe tourist destination, with some truly spectacular hotels and resorts, and also as a tax haven – which may explain the swanky boats anchored offshore. Nevertheless, it's easy to escape this commercial vibe, particular on the appropriately named Out Islands, or under the tropical waters, where you can swim with everything from tame reef sharks to – seriously! – pet pigs.

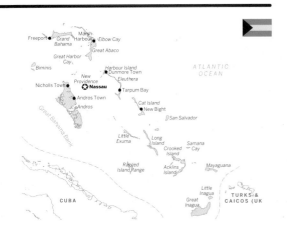

1

2

Bahrain

The smallest of all Arab countries, oil-rich Bahrain is – its Formula One Grand Prix aside – the least glitzy of the Gulf emirates and it's a fascinating introduction to the region. While the country has embraced the modern with some dazzling contemporary architecture, the past remains a presence in the echoes of the ancient Dilmun Empire and in the soulful former pearl-fishing district of Muharraq. Sadly, the turmoil of the Arab Spring sparked widespread civil unrest and a resulting crackdown. Things have quietened down a little since then but check official travel warnings before setting out.

1. Manama's distinctive skyline

2. Playtime in Bahrain

3. Al Fatih Mosque in Manama, the largest mosque in the country

Best time to visit
November to March

Top things to see
- Five thousand years of history under one roof at Bahrain National Museum
- The Portuguese-era Bahrain Fort, built on fascinating archaeological ruins
- Bahrain's National Theatre, a stunning architectural showpiece in tune with the sea
- King Fahd Causeway, an extraordinary feat of modern engineering connecting Bahrain to Saudi Arabia
- Al-Areen Wildlife Park and Reserve, where you can see 240 bird species and Arabian oryx

Top things to do
- Dive for pearls then visit the Museum of Pearl Diving to learn all about Bahrain's most exotic industry
- Watch Bahrain put on a show for the Formula One Grand Prix, which is usually held in April
- Wander amid the traditional wind towers, sandstone architecture and Manama's modern jewels of Beit al-Quran and Al-Fatih Mosque
- Explore modern Bahrain's alter ego in the Unesco World Heritage–listed 'pearling pathway' of Muharraq Island
- Spot flamingos and cormorants en masse on the Hawar Islands

Getting under the skin
Read: Geoffrey Bibby's *Looking for Dilmun*, a story of archaeological treasure-hunting and a window onto 1950s and '60s Bahrain
Listen: to *Desert Beat* by Hashim al-Alawi
Watch: *Al-Hajiz* (The Barrier), *Za'er* (Visitor) or *A Bahraini Tale*, all directed by Bassam Al Thawadi – they're the only three films ever made in Bahrain
Eat: *nekheh*, *bajelah* and *loobah* (a trio of spicy bean soups); *makboos* (rice and spices served with chicken, lamb or fish); *khabees* (a date-laden dessert)
Drink: fresh fruit juices; cardamom-infused Arabic-style coffee

In a word
Al-hamdu lillah (Thanks to God)

Trademarks
Ancient Dilmun Empire; pearl diving and natural pearls for sale; some of the Arab world's most sought-after dates

Random fact
Bahrain originally consisted of 33 islands, but that number is increasing, as is the length of its coastline, as more and more land is (somewhat controversially) reclaimed from the sea

B CAPITAL DHAKA // POPULATION 163.7 MILLION // AREA 143,998 SQ KM // OFFICIAL LANGUAGE BENGALI

Bangladesh

For years the Bangladesh tourist board used the slogan 'See Bangladesh before the tourists come', but the anticipated flood of tourists never materialised. Don't worry – the lack of tourist infrastructure is half the appeal of this fascinating Asian backwater, where rivers function as main roads and the Muslim call to prayer rings out across the paddy fields. Before 1947, Bangladesh was the eastern half of Indian Bengal; then from 1947 to 1971 it was East Pakistan. Today, this famously crowded and impoverished nation is struggling to forge its own identity in the face of challenges ranging from religious extremism to floods, cyclones and climate change. Nevertheless, visitors love Bangladesh for the way it seems to float forever in a vanished monsoon summer from the 1970s.

Best time to visit
October to February

Top things to see
- The unbelievable crowds at the Sadarghat docks in Dhaka
- Brewed leaves and pedal power in the tea estates around Srimangal
- A Royal Bengal tiger (if you get lucky) in the Sundarbans National Park
- Gleaming Buddhist stupas and Adivasi tribal culture in the Chittagong Hill Tracts
- Ocean waves breaking on the beach on tiny St Martin's Island

Top things to do
- Ride the Rocket – the paddle-wheel ferry that trundles from Dhaka to Morrelganj
- Feel the liberation of wearing a *lungi* (sarong) for the day
- Drop in on the Buddhist tribal villages dotted around serene Kaptai Lake
- Stroll barefoot along the world's longest beach at Inani near Cox's Bazar
- Experience the surreal phenomenon of a rickshaw traffic jam in Dhaka

Getting under the skin
Read: the blogs and polemic poetry of Maqsoodul Haque, Bangladesh's 'poet of impropriety', at http://tpoi.blogspot.com
Listen: to the rousing poems of Bangladesh's national poet Kari Nazrul Islam – dozens of different recordings of his works are available in Dhaka
Watch: Satyarjit Ray's Bengali classic *Apu Trilogy*; or hunt down Tareque Masud's *Matir Moina* to appreciate the growing maturity of the Dallywood (Dhaka) film industry
Eat: *ilish macher paturi* (a classic Bengali dish of *hilsa* fish steamed inside banana leaves)
Drink: *sharbat* (chilled yoghurt mixed with chilli, coriander, cumin and mint) –
the perfect accompaniment to a fiery curry

In a word
Tik aache (No problem)

Trademarks
Endless rice fields; rickshaw traffic jams; men in *lungis*; tea plantations; Buddhist hill tribes; tigers in the Sundarbans; attacks on bloggers; the political legacy of the 1971 Bangladesh Liberation War

Random fact
The national game of Bangladesh is *kabaddi*, a group version of tag where players must evade the opposing team while holding a single breath of air

1. Women tea pickers returning from the fields

2. Rickshaws, the country's main form of transport

3. Bangladeshi bangles

1. Horses love the water here too

2. Beautiful Bottom Bay, a popular picnic spot

3. A surf shop proprietor in Silver Sands

CAPITAL BRIDGETOWN // POPULATION 288,725 // AREA 431 SQ KM // OFFICIAL LANGUAGE ENGLISH

Barbados

You can drive almost all day on Barbados and never see a beach. Is that heresy in the sandy-shore-obsessed Caribbean? Not really, as this pork-chop-shaped island has a deep interior traversed by narrow, winding roads that pass through colonial backwaters, atmospheric old plantations and tiny villages where the unscrewing of a rum bottle cap is the highlight of the day. And beach bums take heart – all roads eventually lead to the coast, which is ringed with strands of white sand, each with a distinct personality. Find wave-tossed surfer havens in the east; palm-fringed bays with resorts great and small in the west. Wherever you travel around this tidy island nation, you will enjoy one of the Caribbean's most genteel cultures.

Best time to visit
February to May

Top things to see
- Barclay's Park, with miles of walks along a seashore ripe for beachcombing
- St Nicholas Abbey, which combines the beauty of a plantation estate with horrific revelations about slavery
- Hunte's Gardens, a lavish jungle oasis of flowers, trees and birds set in a tropical gulley
- Lavishly restored George Washington House, the US president's home for two months in 1751

Top things to do
- Cheer madly for your team at a cricket match
- Surf the legendary Soup Bowl on the east coast
- Get in the groove of Bridgetown, the island's capital and home to dockside cafes, appealing shops and thriving markets
- Explore the tiny coastal road to Fustic, where ages-old fishing enclaves snooze amid riots of flowers

Getting under the skin
Read: the 1953 novel *The Castle of My Skin* by Bajan author George Lamming, in which he tells what it was like growing up black in colonial Barbados
Listen: to calypso artist the Mighty Gabby, and soca artist Rupee
Watch: *The Tamarind Seed* starring Omar Sharif and Julie Andrews, a romance-cum-spy thriller
Eat: a range of dishes with African roots adapted to local produce, such as *cou-cou* (a creamy cornmeal and okra mash, often served with saltfish) and *jug-jug* (a mix of cornmeal, peas and salted meat)
Drink: world-renowned Mount Gay rum

In a word
Workin' up (dancing)

Trademarks
Cricket fanatics; elderly women in prim hats; calypso music; flying fish sandwiches

Random fact
Barbados boasts more world-class cricket players on a per capita basis than any other nation

① ②

Best time to visit
May to September

Top things to see
- Minsk, with its patina of communist architecture, kitschy clubs and top-notch ballet and opera
- The impressively restored Mir Castle, which looks like something out of a fairy tale
- The extraordinary Brest Fortress, a Soviet WWII memorial that commemorates Soviet resistance against the German invasion in the bucolic spot where Operation Barbarossa was unleashed
- Dudutki, a reconstructed 19th-century Belarusian village with craft-making exhibits, horse riding and local delicacies, including *samagon* (moonshine)

Top things to do
- Observe Europe's only surviving wild bison (the zoobr) at the wonderfully wild Belavezhskaya Pushcha National Park, the oldest wildlife refuge in Europe
- Follow the masochistic recipe for good health at a Belarusian bathhouse: sit in a steam room, beat yourself with damp twigs, dunk yourself in icy water, repeat
- Wander the atmospheric old neighbourhoods of Vitsebsk, childhood home of Marc Chagall, one of the great masters of 20th-century art
- Explore the vast swathe of marshes, swampland and floodplains of the hauntingly beautiful Pripyatsky National Park

Getting under the skin
Read: *Voices From Chernobyl*, which records the effects of the disaster on the people of the region, by Nobel prize–winner Svetlana Alexeivich
Listen: to the vaguely apocalyptic improvisations of Knyaz Myshkin, a Minsk-based band
Watch: *Dangerous Acts,* an HBO documentary detailing one theatre troupe's resistance to the dictatorship of Alexander Lukashenka
Eat: *solyanka* (meat, potato and pickled vegetable soup); and *draniki* (potato pancakes)
Drink: *kvass* (an elixir made of malt, flour, sugar, mint and fruit)

In a word
Vitayu (Hello)

Trademarks
Onion-domed churches; traditional farming villages; potatoes; snow; fur hats; monasteries; radioactive countryside (near Chornobyl)

Random fact
Many Belarusian folk-remedies involve vodka: gargle with it to cure a sore throat, wash your hair with it to alleviate dandruff and pour it in your ear to treat an earache

1. An imposing burial vault in the village of Zakozel

2. A peaceful afternoon's fishing

3. *Valour* or *Courage,* one of the massive memorials in the Brest Fortress

B CAPITAL MINSK // POPULATION 9.6 MILLION // AREA 207,600 SQ KM // OFFICIAL LANGUAGES BELARUSIAN & RUSSIAN

Belarus

Widely hailed as 'the last dictatorship in Europe', Belarus is at first glance a country that has never entirely left the USSR. But while this may be a land of Soviet-style architecture, state-run media and a centralised economy, the streets are full of modern German cars, international brands are for sale in every shop and advertising is now everywhere. Leave the archetypally Soviet capital Minsk and you'll find yourself in a charming land of forests, rivers, fairy-tale castles, Slavic tradition and warm hospitality. Indeed, Belarusians are extremely warm-hearted people who relish life's simple pleasures: weekends spent at the *dacha* (summer country house); mushroom-picking in the woods or steaming away at the *banya* (bathhouse).

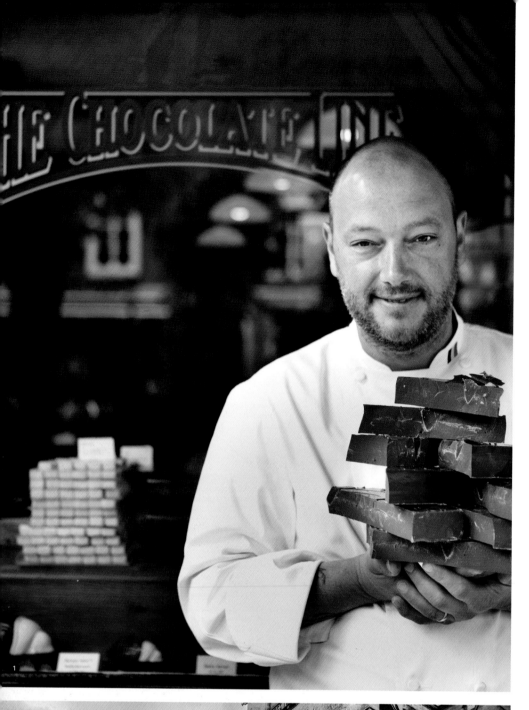

Best time to visit
May to September

Top things to see
- Brussels' guildhalls of medieval craftsmen on Grand Place
- The sobering war memorials of Flanders Fields and Waterloo Battlefield
- Galeries St Hubert, the grande dame of 19th-century shopping arcades
- Medieval Bruges with its cobblestone lanes, romantic canals and historic *begijnhof* (inner courtyards)
- Go-slow Ghent – explore it by bike
- Belgium's largest Gothic cathedral, Onze-Lieve-Vrouwekathedraal, in Antwerp, which houses four paintings by Rubens

Top things to do
- Admire a bounty of riches such as ancient Egyptian sarcophagi at Brussels' Musée du Cinquantenaire
- Expand your waistline by indulging in extraordinary pralines and truffles by prized chocolate-maker Pierre Marcolini
- Shop for fashion by local designers, fine-dine and dance until dawn in Antwerp
- Take time out in the French-speaking town of La Roche-en-Ardenne
- Peruse lengthy beer menus and sample abbey-brewed Trappist dark ales in pubs across the country

Getting under the skin
Read: two hilarity-packed chapters on Belgium by Bill Bryson in *Neither Here nor There*
Listen: to harmonica virtuoso Toots Thielemans blast the best of Belgian jazz with *Hard to Say Goodbye – The Very Best of Toots Thielemans*
Watch: *Le Silence de Lorna* (Lorna's Silence) – the grim tale of an Albanian girl growing up in Belgium – by Belgian film-making brothers Jean-Pierre and Luc Dardenne
Eat: a steaming cauldron of mussels cooked in white wine with a mountain of *frieten/frites* (fries or chips)
Drink: Trappist beer brewed by monks in Rochefort

In a word
Dag/Bonjour (Hello in Dutch/French)

Trademarks
Chocolate; beer; cafe culture; comic-strip hero Tintin; the EU; Battle of Waterloo; 1960s *chansonnier* Jacques Brel; art nouveau architecture

Random fact
Belgium's real-time linguistic divide was carved in stone in 1962 when the official line was drawn between Dutch-speaking Flanders and French-speaking Wallonia

1. Laden with treasure, one of Bruges' famous chocolatiers

2. The procession of St Waltrude's Shrine during La Ducasse festival in Mons

3. Magnificent guild houses surround Brussels' Grand Place

B CAPITAL BRUSSELS // POPULATION 10.4 MILLION // AREA 30,528 SQ KM // OFFICIAL LANGUAGES DUTCH, FRENCH & GERMAN

Belgium

There are few places that feel more in the heart of Europe than Belgium, a multilingual country smack-bang in the middle of Western Europe that Dutch-speaking Flemish in the north call België, and French-speaking Walloons in the south call La Belgique. Indeed, it's this north–south cultural and linguistic divide that makes this unusually intimate country with such dreary wet weather so unexpectedly fascinating. Amble in the shade of art nouveau architecture in its capital, Brussels; give a nod to the EU headquarters; surrender to the sweet seduction of the finest chocolate; immerse yourself in Antwerp's vibrant fashion scene and cool clubs; down a fine local beer or three; and get to know why this is what Belgians north and south call the good life.

Best time to visit

January to May (when there is less rain)

Top things to see

- The *cayes* (islands) strung out along the Meso-American Barrier Reef, the world's second-largest coral reef
- Black howler monkeys at the Community Baboon Sanctuary near Bermudian Landing
- Caracol, a vast Mayan city whose population once rivalled today's Belize, now tucked into matted jungle
- A rousing cricket match in the MCC grounds of Belize City
- Orderly and cosmopolitan Belmopan, the smallest capital city in the Americas

Top things to do

- Groove to live Punta rock, which fuses tribal Garífuna beats, soca and reggae
- Ride a speedboat from Belize City to the Northern Cayes, for the full Caribbean island experience
- Explore the narrow passages of Barton Creek Cave, an ancient sacred site for Mayan burials
- Dive the submarine canyons, cuts and blue holes of Caye Ambergris and the Northern Cayes
- Look for Big Bird – the 5ft-tall jaberoo stork common to Crooked Tree Lagoon

Getting under the skin

Read: *The Last Flight of the Scarlet Macaw*, Bruce Barcott's account of one activist making a difference in Belize

Listen: to the Garífuna rhythms, culture and politics of Andy Palacio's *Til Da Mawnin*

Watch: Harrison Ford face jungle fever in *The Mosquito Coast*, with the Belize interior standing in for neighbouring Honduras

Eat: the Belizean menu staples of rice and beans, perfect with a dash of Marie Sharp's famous hot sauce

Drink: the sweet water of green coconuts split open by machete, or traditional cashew wine at the Cashew Festival in Crooked Tree

In a word

Arright? (You alright? – the ubiquitous greeting)

Trademarks

Sandy *cayes*; coral reefs; reefers; tropical rainforests; Mayan ruins; street crime in Belize City

Random fact

As a solution to the overpopulation of the red lionfish, whose venomous spines make it all but invincible, Belize wants to commercialise this invasive Pacific species as fine cuisine – and some top chefs are biting!

1. Caracol, the largest Mayan site in Belize

2. Jaguars can be found in the country's lowland forests

3. A Mayan villager from San Antonio

4. The fringing reef and deep cave of the Great Blue Hole make a spectacular diving experience

B CAPITAL BELMOPAN // POPULATION 334,297 // AREA 22,966 SQ KM // OFFICIAL LANGUAGE ENGLISH

Belize

The Spanish weren't the only people to carve out an empire in Central America. Tiny, jungle-cloaked Belize was the site of Britain's brief colonial experiment in this tropical isthmus. The British legacy lives on in Belize's distinctive Afro-Caribbean culture, and in the lilting English spoken by most residents. Long the haunt of pirates, Belize still struggles with lawlessness, particularly in the largest town, Belize City, but inland are dense rainforests dotted with Mayan ruins, and offshore is a shimmering necklace of tropical islands, following the line of the world's second-largest coral reef. Most visitors arrive by cruise ship, stop in for the day and move on, leaving the treasures inland for more committed travellers. For the adventurous, Belize is a handy stepping stone on the overland trail to Guatemala, El Salvador and beyond.

Best time to visit
November to February (the dry season)

Top things to see
- The enduring monument to the kings of Dahomey in Abomey
- The Point of No Return memorial for countless African slaves in Ouidah, a town that is also a centre for voodoo and Afro-Brazilian culture
- Grand Popo, the loveliest palm-fringed corner of Benin's Gulf of Guinea coast
- The tranquil capital, Porto Novo, with shady streets and colonial buildings
- Dassa Zoumé, Benin's most striking terrain with rocky outcrops and lush hills

Top things to do
- Track lions, elephants and the elusive northwest African cheetah in the Parc National de la Pendjari
- Hike through the rugged northern Atakora region with a local ecotourism association
- Get an insight into local culture by learning traditional fishing at Lake Ahémé
- Dance deep into the night in Ouidah on 10 January, Benin's Voodoo Day
- Take a slow pirogue journey to the traditional bamboo stilt houses of Ganvié

Getting under the skin
Read: Bruce Chatwin's *The Viceroy of Ouidah*, which tells the story of a 17th-century Brazilian trader stranded on the 'Slave Coast'; while Annie Caulfield's taxi journey around Benin is wittily told in *Show Me the Magic*
Listen: to anything by Angelique Kidjo, Gangbe Brass Band or Orchestre Poly-Rythmo
Watch: *Angelique Kidjo: World Music Portraits*, a fascinating biopic of one of Africa's biggest stars on the international stage
Eat: *igname pilé* (pounded yam served with vegetables and meat) and *gombo* (okra)
Drink: *tchouukoutou*, a traditional millet-based brew

In a word
Neh àh dèh gbò? (How are you?)

Trademarks
Voodoo; fishing villages on stilts; an emerging ecotourism scene; singing sensation Angelique Kidjo; Oscar-nominated actor Djimon Hounsou (*Gladiator*, *Blood Diamond*, *Furious 7*)

Random fact
Almost a quarter of Benin's land area has been set aside as national parks or reserves, easily the highest proportion in West Africa

1. Motorcycle taxi drivers await passengers

2. Riding through a lush green valley

3. A ceremony is performed on Voodoo Day in Ouidah

B CAPITAL PORTO NOVO // POPULATION 9.9 MILLION // AREA 112,622 SQ KM // OFFICIAL LANGUAGE FRENCH

Benin

Small it may be, but Benin is loaded with historical significance and extraordinary sights. The country is the birthplace of voodoo, and it is still widely practiced (an official religion, in fact). Benin played a pivotal role in the slave trade for almost three centuries, with nearly a million Africans shipped from the port of Ouidah alone. And Abomey continues to hold evocative vestiges from its time as the capital of the fabled and bloodthirsty kingdom of Dahomey. Despite its tumultuous past, Benin is a success story – it is a beacon of stability, ecotourism abounds and the Beninese are among Africa's friendliest. Pick through clamorous markets, lounge on tropical beaches and watch wildlife – you'll find it easy to fall in love with Benin.

1. You'll always be welcomed with a smile in Bermuda

2. Horseshoe Bay, arguably Bermuda's most beautiful beach

3. The traditional colourful houses of Hamilton

B   CAPITAL HAMILTON // POPULATION 69,839 // AREA 54 SQ KM // OFFICIAL LANGUAGE ENGLISH

Bermuda

Rising unexpectedly from the otherwise landless central Atlantic, the British Overseas Territory of Bermuda is a lot like its eponymous shorts – casual and laid back, but with a subtle overlay of formality. Lava-belching volcanoes were responsible for creating this archipelago of 181 islands and outcrops, which is reminiscent of the Caribbean, flavoured by big servings of British and American culture. Despite its reputation, Bermuda is not really tropical – the Tropic of Cancer actually lies nearly 1000km further south, and the nearest island of the Caribbean 600km beyond that – but when you see the turquoise waters, coral reefs and pink-sand beaches, we doubt you'll mind. Set against this holiday brochure backdrop, Bermudians pay homage to their British origins with golf, croquet and lawn tennis, followed by genteel afternoon tea.

Best time to visit
Year-round

Top things to see
- Pink-sand beaches that bring a smile to the face of even the most stressed visitor
- Ancient, gnarled rubber trees in Par-la-ville Park that once entranced Mark Twain
- Colonial St George with its pastel houses, stoic churches and meandering lanes
- The harbour rhythms of Victorian Hamilton, first port of call for the Royal Bermuda Yacht Club set

Top things to do
- Dive the world's greatest concentration of shipwrecks – and more lie lost forever in the Bermuda Triangle
- Spot whales beyond the reefs of South Shore during March and April
- Play tennis on grass, just like a group of New Yorkers did in 1874, before importing the idea to America

Getting under the skin
Read: *Bermuda's Story* by Terry Tucker, the island's most highly regarded historian
Listen: to reggae, calypso and Bermuda's own *gombey*, which features groups of wildly clad men dancing in manic fashion to music that blends African and Caribbean rhythms
Watch: *The Deep*, an underwater thriller of drug lords and treasure
Eat: fish chowder
Drink: Gosling's Black Seal Rum (a dark rum); or dark 'n' stormy (a two-to-one mix of carbonated ginger beer with Black Seal Rum)

In a word
Yo Ace Boy! (Hello good friend!)

Trademarks
Bermuda shorts; pastel cottages; pink-sand beaches; the Bermuda Triangle

Random fact
Bermuda's stunning natural beauty was protected by the world's first environmental laws (dating back to the 1600s)

Best time to visit
March to May, October to November

Top things to see
- The weekend market, museums and beer and whiskey bars of Thimphu, Bhutan's only real town
- Taktshang Goemba (Tiger's Nest Monastery), squeezed into a rocky crevice and supposedly held in place by the hairs of angels
- Punakha Dzong, Bhutan's most beautiful building, set at the junction of the Mo (Mother) and Po (Father) Rivers
- Ancient 7th-century temples, sacred sites and rhododendron forests in the Bumthang valley
- Terrific Trongsa, whose enormous *dzong* (monastery fortress) once guarded the only route from the east to the west of the country

Top things to do
- Attend morning prayers and sip salted butter tea with the monks at a Bhutanese monastery
- Trek along ancient Himalayan trade routes to the sacred peak of Jhomolhari bordering Tibet
- Get caught up in the banter and the boasting of an archery tournament in Thimphu
- Spot rare black-necked cranes in the glacier-carved Phobjikha Valley
- Watch mythical beasts and fearsome monsters dance during one of the country's colourful *tsechu* (Buddhist dance festivals)

Getting under the skin
Read: *Beyond the Sky and Earth* by Jamie Zeppa or *Buttertea at Sunrise: A Year in the Bhutan Himalaya* by Britta Das, for insights into Bhutanese culture from two women who lived there
Listen: to *Endless Songs from Bhutan* by Jigme Drukpa, traditional Bhutanese folk songs accompanied by lute and flute
Watch: the stylish *Travellers and Magicians*, directed by the reincarnated lama Khyentse Norbu
Eat: mouth-melting *ema datse* (green chillies and cheese), or, if you dare, aphrodisiac *cordyceps*, a parasitic fungus that turns insects into zombies!
Drink: Red Panda beer, a delicious wheat beer brewed in the Bumthang valley; or *ara*, Bhutan's home-grown firewater

In a word
Kuzuzangbo la (Hello)

Trademarks
Gross National Happiness; archery; fluttering prayer flags; mask dances; monks and *dzongs*; rhododendron forests; a genuinely benevolent monarch; expensive daily tourist fees

Random fact
Buying cigarettes is illegal in Bhutan (as is selling plastic bags)

1. The ornate courtyard of the 12-century Tango Goemba monastery

2. Monks enjoying a well-earned break from monastery life

3. The precipitously placed Taktshang Goemba (Tiger's Nest Monastery)

B CAPITAL THIMPHU // POPULATION 725,296 // AREA 38,394 SQ KM // OFFICIAL LANGUAGE DZONGKHA

Bhutan

If the valley paradise of Shangri La exists in the material world, it will be in Bhutan. Tucked among the peaks of the eastern Himalaya, with more mountain monasteries than high-rise buildings, Bhutan is the last surviving Himalayan kingdom, clinging valiantly to its culture and traditions. Locals famously value Gross National Happiness over Gross National Product, but this historic Buddhist enclave is slowly modernising, albeit on its own terms. If you hand over the substantial daily dollar fee to travel here, you'll see locals in 15th-century traditional robes chatting on mobile phones and maroon-robed monks using high-speed broadband to connect to their congregations.

1

2

CAPITAL LA PAZ (ADMINISTRATIVE) & SUCRE (CONSTITUTIONAL) // POPULATION 10.5 MILLION // AREA 1,098,581 SQ KM OFFICIAL LANGUAGE SPANISH

Bolivia

'The beggar sitting on a heap of riches' is how Bolivia is often described. It is one of the South America's poorest nations, but the astounding diversity of its wildlife and ethnic groups gives it a cultural wealth that remains intact as traditional life in surrounding nations dwindles. This is an isolated land, with one of the world's lowest population densities and greatest topographical extremes. Andean peaks of over 6000m meet high-altitude deserts, surreal salt flats, Amazonian rainforest and the savannahs of the Pantanal. Today the Quechua, Aymara and other indigenous peoples, collectively accounting for over 50% of the population, are playing an increasingly important role in the country, and have even elected the nation's first indigenous president.

Best time to visit
May to October

Top things to see
- The breath-sapping city of Potosí and its poignant mining legacy
- The Salar de Uyuni, the blindingly white salt deserts complete with bubbling geysers and aquamarine lagoons
- The dizzying city of La Paz, dramatically set deep in a canyon and fringed by snow-covered mountains
- The astounding range of wildlife in Bolivia's Amazonian rainforest around Rurrenabaque

Top things to do
- Trek through the giddying heights of the Cordillera Real along ancient Inca routes
- Feel the adrenaline rush on a mountain-biking trek along what was once dubbed 'the world's most dangerous road'
- Boat it out to the tradition-steeped Isla del Sol, legendary island home of the Inca on the world's highest navigable lake, Lago de Titicaca
- Party the night away at Carnaval de Oruro, the nation's biggest, brightest festival

Getting under the skin
Read: *The Fat Man from La Paz: Contemporary Fiction from Bolivia*, edited by Rosario Santo, which contains 20 short stories illustrating life in Bolivia
Listen: to charango master Celestino Campos or famous Andean folk trio Los Kjarjas

Watch: *The Devil's Miner*, Kief Davidson and Richard Ladkani's award-winning documentary following two brothers working in one of South America's most dangerous mines
Eat: *salteña* (a meat and vegetable empanada); *surubi* (catfish)
Drink: the favourite alcoholic drink *chicha cochabambina*, made from fermented corn; *mate de coca* (coca leaf tea), which helps ease altitude sickness

In a word
Que tal? (How are you?)

Trademarks
Bowler hats; llamas; Andean peaks; Lake Titicaca; hand-woven shawls and blankets; *soroche* (altitude sickness)

Random fact
Many of the riches of Spain flowed from Cerro Rico above Potosí, where an estimated 45,000 tons of pure silver was mined between 1550 and 1780

1. A lonely road winds through the barren valley of Salvador Dalí Desert

2. Endless skies on the salt flats of Salar de Uyuni

3. Celebrating the colourful Fiesta de la Virgen de la Candelaria, Copacabana

Best time to visit
April to September

Top things to see
- Daredevils plunging from Mostar's bridge into the racing green waters below
- Sarajevo, the 'Jerusalem of the Balkans', a fabulous, vibrant, riverside city with cultural events and nightlife aplenty
- The castle and Ottoman-era architecture of Travnik
- The spectacular medieval Bosnian capital of Jajce, cut by the Pliva Waterfall and defended by imposing gates
- Secluded attractions such as the petite village of Vranduk, the craggy castle of Srebrenik or the ecovillage of Zelenkovac

Top things to do
- Wander the cobbled alleys, coppersmith workshops and artisanal stalls of Baščaršija in Sarajevo
- Join the pilgrims as they wait for an apparition of Mary in Međugorje, or nod at Sufi tombs in the Tekija (dervish lodge) in Blagaj
- Plummet down the Vrbas or Buna rivers on a raft or in your own kayak
- Skip up the cobbled streets of Počitelj to look out over domes, minarets, slate roofs and the Neretva River

Getting under the skin
Read: *Sarajevo Marlboro* by Miljenko Jergović, tales set during the siege of Sarajevo; or *People of the Book*, Geraldine Brooks' fictionalised tale about the Sarajevo Haggadah
Listen: to *sevdah* music, Bosnia's folk music, an excursion in harmonious melancholy
Watch: Danis Tanović's *No Man's Land* or *Grbavica: Land of my Dreams*, by Jasmila Žbanić, both poignant reflections on the Bosnian war
Eat: *zeljanica* (tasty spinach pastry); or *meso ispod sača* (lamb or kid stewed under hot coals)
Drink: the local dry red wine, Blatina; or *šljivovica* (plum brandy)

In a word
Živjeli (Cheers)

Trademarks
Copper coffee pots; mountain villages; juxtaposed mosques and churches; rafting on emerald rivers

Random fact
The black market is one of the biggest industries in the country: the 'shadow economy' accounts for more than 30% of Bosnia and Hercegovina's GDP

1. Mostar and its elegant reconstructed 16th-century Stari Most (Old Bridge)

2. The Tekija (dervish lodge) in Blagaj nestles between the cliff-face and the Buna River

3. The intricate lace of Kravice Falls on the Trebižat River

B CAPITAL SARAJEVO // POPULATION 3.9 MILLION // AREA 51,197 SQ KM // OFFICIAL LANGUAGES BOSNIAN, CROATIAN & SERBIAN

Bosnia & Hercegovina

This Eastern-European crossroads is finally enjoying a peace to match its charm and beauty. The variety of this 'heart-shaped land' is astounding: the buzzing, bohemian cafe culture of Sarajevo, doughty medieval fortresses, muezzins calling the faithful to prayer from Bosniak (Bosnian Muslim) minarets, austere architectural vestiges of Tito's Communism, and Orthodox monasteries clinging to vertiginous hillsides – it can be hard to pin down the 'true' Bosnia and Hercegovina. Ultimately, it's beyond the cities that this deeply traditional country best expresses itself, through spreading vineyards, quiet villages and a patient pace of life.

B CAPITAL GABORONE // POPULATION 2.1 MILLION // AREA 581,730 SQ KM // OFFICIAL LANGUAGE ENGLISH

Botswana

Diamonds are not forever sadly, but their legacy may just be. First discovered in Botswana by industrious termites (yes, really) in the late 1960s, the gems have allowed one of the world's poorest countries to turn itself into an international player. The government, now Africa's longest continuous multiparty democracy, has seen minimal corruption and has responsibly spent billions of dollars of mining revenue on healthcare, education and infrastructure. The good governance has also carried over to the vast tracts of sublime and unparalleled wilderness, which has ensured that the Botswanan safari industry has a wealth of iconic wildlife to wow visitors. Add to that a population of charming and peace-loving people, and tourism will always have a role in Botswana's future success.

Best time to visit
May to September (dry season) for classic safaris; November to April (wet season) for birds

Top things to see
- A procession of trunks crossing the Chobe River, each a lifeline to the elephant lurking in the depths below
- The grasses of the Central Kalahari Game Reserve coming to life with the rains
- Africa's forgotten great migration, which brings thousands of zebra into Makgadikgadi Pans National Park
- The sandstone landscape of the Tuli Block set alight by the setting sun
- San rock paintings that date back millennia, particularly in the remote Tsodilo Hills – where the natural gallery of rock formations is equally riveting

Top things to do
- Wake to sunrise on the blank, bleached canvas that is Makgadikgadi Pan
- Skirt between the reeds that line the Okavango Delta's myriad channels in a *mokoro* (traditional canoe)
- Rise before dawn to share your morning with the vast amount of wildlife in Moremi Wildlife Reserve
- Spend time understanding San culture in D'kar

Getting under the skin
Read: *Serowe: Village of the Rain Wind* by Bessie Head for an understanding of Tswana culture and village life
Listen: to Franco and Afro Musica, a 12-piece *kwasa kwasa* band
Watch: *The Gods Must Be Crazy*; or *The No 1 Ladies' Detective Agency*
Eat: *leputshe* (wild pumpkin) atop *bogobe* (sorghum porridge)
Drink: the stiff concoction from fermented marula fruit

In a word
Dumela (Hello, in Tswana) – extra marks if it's done with a 'special' handshake (place your left hand on your elbow while shaking

Trademarks
Meerkats; the Kalahari; San (aka Bushmen); the world's largest inland delta; luxurious safari camps; diamonds; free anti-retroviral drugs for citizens with HIV/AIDS

Random fact
There are more elephants in Botswana than anywhere else in Africa

1. Last light on Baines' baobabs, Nxai Pan National Park

2. Water antelopes bounding across the flooded plains of the Okavango Delta

3. San people crossing the Makgadikgadi Pans

1. The granite dome of Pão de Açúcar (Sugarloaf Mountain) towers over the Botafogo District, Rio de Janeiro

2. Deep in the Brazilian Amazon, a young Asurini do Tocantin Indian wears ceremonial dress

3. The bold and the beautiful parading Ipanema Beach, Rio de Janeiro

B

B CAPITAL BRASÍLIA // POPULATION 201 MILLION // AREA 8,514,877 SQ KM // OFFICIAL LANGUAGE PORTUGUESE

Brazil

South America's largest and arguably most seductive country is accustomed to turning heads – and not merely for its breathtaking beaches and hedonistic festivals. Today, energy-independent Brazil basks in the glow of Latin America's largest economy, not to mention the lustre of hosting the 2016 Olympic Games. Football remains a big source of pride (Brazil has won more World Cup titles than any other nation), as is the country's incredible biodiversity: Brazil is, after all, home to the greatest assortment of plant and animal life on earth. It's no wonder that locals claim *'Deus e brasileiro'* (God is Brazilian).

Best time to visit
November to April on the coast, and May to September in the Amazon and the Pantanal

Top things to see
- Ipanema Beach, Rio's loveliest and most fabled stretch of coastline
- The enchanting colonial centre of Salvador
- The thunderous Iguaçu Falls
- A football match at Maracanã Stadium in Rio, Brazil's great temple to the national addiction
- The spectacular island of Fernando de Noronha, with gorgeous beaches and world-class diving

Top things to do
- Go wildlife-watching in the Pantanal, home to the greatest concentration of fauna in the New World
- Peer out over the world's most famous rainforest from a canopy tower in the Amazon
- Ride one of the continent's most scenic train routes between Curitiba and Paranaguá
- Join the mayhem of Brazil's biggest street party at carnaval in Rio, Salvador or Olinda

Getting under the skin
Read: Oswald de Andrade's *Manifesto Antropófago* (Cannibal Manifesto), an essay on Brazilian identity
Listen: to the Afro-Brazilian rhythms of Jorge Benjor; or the bossa nova grooves of Joao Gilberto
Watch: Walter Salles' poignant, Academy Award–winning *Central do Brasil* (Central Station)
Eat: *feijoada* (black bean and pork stew); or *moqueca* (Bahian fish stew with coconut milk)
Drink: *açaí* (juice of an Amazonian berry); caipirinhas made with *cachaca* (a sugar-cane alcohol)

In a word
Tudo bem? (All's well?)

Trademarks
Carnaval; football; bossa nova; samba; beaches; the Amazon; capoeira; *favelas* (shanty towns)

Random fact
Brazilian ethanol, made from sugar cane, provides 40% of the country's fuel

B CAPITAL BANDAR SERI BEGAWAN // POPULATION 415,717 // AREA 5765 SQ KM // OFFICIAL LANGUAGE MALAY

Brunei

Hemmed in by the jungles of Malaysian Borneo, Brunei is a nation built around a single personality – the enigmatic Sultan Hassanal Bolkiah. Famous for his addiction to sports cars, the sultan presides over one of the richest nations in Asia, thanks to the vast oil fields beneath the South China Sea within Brunei's territory. Officially known as Negara Brunei Darussalam (Brunei, the Abode of Peace), this tropical sultanate is best known for its glittering mosques, its strict observance of Islam and for the traditional stilt villages in the Sungai (River) Brunei that runs alongside the capital, Bandar Seri Begawan (BSB). Less well known are the steamy virgin rainforest reserves that (at least for now) brim with wildlife, and a fledgling diving industry. However, don't expect pulsing nightlife – all bars and nightclubs were closed down when alcohol was banned in 1991.

Best time to visit
March to April for dry, warm days

Top things to see
- The gleaming gold domes of the Omar Ali Saifuddien Mosque and the Jame'Asr Hassanil Bolkiah Mosque
- The Brunei Darussalam Maritime Museum, housing more than 13,000 artefacts recovered from a centuries-old shipwreck
- Exotic fruit and local delicacies at the Tamu Kianggeh food market
- A chariot fit for a sultan (and other treasures) at the Royal Regalia Museum
- Istana Nurul Iman, the world's largest palace, and private home of the sultan (open for five days each year)

Top things to do
- Take a water taxi through the atmospheric stilt villages of Kampung Ayer
- Search for proboscis monkeys and hornbills in the dense jungles of Ulu Temburong National Park
- Eat your way around the restaurants and night-time hawker food markets of BSB
- Hike along the lichen-covered boardwalk through Peradayan Forest Reserve
- Spend a night in an Iban longhouse in Batang Duri

Getting under the skin
Read: *Some Girls: My Life in a Harem*, a memoir by American Jillian Lauren recounting her time living in the palace as a guest of the sultan
Listen: to the popular classical concerts arranged by the Brunei Music Society
Watch: local dancers performing the *adai-adai*, based on the traditional work-songs of native fishermen
Eat: *ambuyat* (a thick soup made from sago), often described as 'edible glue'
Drink: anything but alcohol, unless you bring it with you – non-Muslims are allowed to import a limited amount of alcohol for personal consumption

In a word
Panas (Hot)

Trademarks
Resplendent mosques; oilfields; jungles; water villages; sharia law; the extravagant lifestyle of the sultan; the playboy antics of Prince Jefri, the sultan's brother

Random fact
As well as owning more than 5000 cars, the sultan of Brunei has his own Boeing 747 (which he often pilots himself), kitted out as a flying palace with gold-plated bathrooms

1. The stunning golden domes of Omar Ali Saifuddien Mosque, Bandar Seri Begawan

2. Candling is a traditional Malay wedding ceremony performed before the bride meets the groom

Best time to visit
May and June, September and October

Top things to see
- The hilltop Tsarevets Fortress in Veliko Târnovo
- Jagged rocks sticking above the walled Kaleto Fortress in Belogradchik
- The 2000-year-old Roman amphitheatre in the heart of Old Plovdiv
- The bluff-top ruins looking over the Black Sea at Kaliakra Cape
- Mountain-framed Rila Monastery
- The 'UFO of Buzludzha', a surreal Soviet relic that looms over Stara Zagora

Top things to do
- Explore Thracian ruins, like the mountain-top site at Perperikon
- Walk in the fragrant Rose Valley near Kazanlak, which bursts into flower each year in May-June
- Hike up to the imposing Shipka Monument, commemorating a battle against the Ottomans and boasting an incredible mountain panorama
- Learn Cyrillic – this alphabet used in Eastern Europe and parts of Asia is a Bulgarian invention
- Search out undeveloped (or less developed) Black Sea beaches, like those south of Sinemorets

Getting under the skin
Read: about Paul Theroux's problems with eating in Sofia in his classic *Great Railway Bazaar*; Ivan Ilchev's *The Rose of the Balkans*, a recent historical overview

Listen: to traditional music with the *gaida* (Bulgarian bagpipe) or *chalga* disco music

Watch: *Under the Same Sky,* an award-winning film of the Sofia International Film Festival about a 15-year-old girl who goes in search of her father

Eat: cool *tarator* (yoghurt soup with cucumber) to beat summer temperatures; or hearty *kavarma* stews to warm up in winter

Drink: local wines that utilise local grapes like the Mavrud or Rubin, in the birthplace of the god of wine, Dionysus

In a word
Oshte bira molya (Another beer please)

Trademarks
Yoghurt; Cyrillic alphabet; Black Sea beaches; budget ski slopes; shaking your head 'yes' and nodding it 'no'; *kâshta* (traditional) taverns; pizzas with ketchup

Random fact
Bulgaria is a leading exporter of rose oil and the world's fifth-largest exporter of wine

1. Karlovo locals celebrate the Rose Festival in traditional style

2. Plovdiv glows at dusk

3. Rila monastery, an UNESCO World Heritage Site, was founded in the 10th century by the hermit St John of Rila

B // CAPITAL SOFIA // POPULATION 7 MILLION // AREA 110,879 SQ KM // OFFICIAL LANGUAGE BULGARIAN

Bulgaria

Despite its ancient ruins, sun-kissed vineyards and smorgasbord of architectural styles, Bulgaria is all too often eclipsed by famous neighbours like Greece and Turkey. But in this underrated Balkan nation you'll discover snowcapped mountains offering cheap ski slopes, the Black Sea's golden beaches, and villages with 19th-century Revival-era architecture guaranteed to inspire. Now part of the EU, Bulgaria still half looks back to traditions like sheep yoghurt stands, traditional music, ancient Thracian and Roman sites, and around 160 Bulgarian Orthodox monasteries, many of which survived 800 years living under the 'yoke' of Ottoman rule.

1. The distinctive Grand Mosque of Bobo-Dioulasso is built from clay in traditional Sudano-Sahelian style

2. Ouagadougou Cathedral: constructed from mudbrick, it houses a Roman Catholic congregation

3. A young Fulani woman from the north of the country

B CAPITAL OUAGADOUGOU // POPULATION 18.3 MILLION // AREA 274,200 SQ KM // OFFICIAL LANGUAGE FRENCH

Burkina Faso

Once named Upper Volta and forever far from the world's consciousness (despite the occasional military coup), Burkina Faso nonetheless ends up being many travellers' favourite West African country. Burkina may lack famous attractions, but the vibrant (and evocatively named) cities, thriving arts milieu, stunning traditional architecture, surprising wildlife-watching opportunities and stirring landscapes will all turn your head. And yet, it's the friendliness of the people and their sheer diversity that wins most plaudits. The Thursday market in Gorom-Gorom is like a who's who of the Sahel's peoples, Ouagadougou has its share of signposts to the once-powerful Mossi Empire, and the Lobi and Gourounsi peoples of the south rank among the most intriguing yet accessible traditional cultures in the region.

Best time to visit
November to February

Top things to see
- The tree-lined streets of Bobo-Dioulasso
- Fespaco film festival in Ouagadougou from February to March in odd-numbered years
- The colourfully painted, fortress-like houses in the heart of Gourounsi country, Tiébélé
- The waters cascading down the Karfiguéla waterfalls after the rainy season
- The 1000-year-old walls of the Ruins of Loropéni

Top things to do
- Get close to elephants with scarcely another tourist in sight at Ranch de Nazinga
- Trek amid the rock formations of the Sindou Peaks
- Wade into Ouagadougou's great restaurants, dance bars and arts scene
- Explore Lobi country, an outpost of animist culture
- Attend the Moro-Naba Ceremony, a throwback to the Mossi's golden age in Ouagadougou

Getting under the skin
Read: *Un Voyage Interieur au Burkina Faso*, a stunning photographic journey by Antoine Périgot
Listen: to *Kanou* or *Nemako* by Farafina; the eponymous *Victor Démé* from Bobo-Dioulasso's thriving live music scene; reggae by Black So Man
Watch: the prize-winning *Tilä* by Idrissa Ouédraogo or *Buud Yam* by Gaston Kaboré
Eat: *riz sauce,* rice with sauce which could be *arachide* (groundnut) or *graine* (palm oil nuts)
Drink: Brakina and So.b.bra (pronounced so-bay-bra), two locally produced beers

In a word
La fee bay may? (How are you?)

Trademarks
Fespaco, the prestigious film festival; Thomas Sankara, Africa's Che Guevara; military coups

Random fact
In the Mòoré dialect, Ouagadougou translates to 'You are welcome here at home with us'

Best time
June to September, when the skies are their driest

Places of interest
- A pyramid monument marking a small stream in Kasumo, the southernmost source of the Nile
- Chutes de la Kagera during the wet season, when torrents tumble from this waterfall
- Parc National de la Rusizi, where hungry hippos and crocs share the shoreline
- Lake Tanganyika's stunning beaches, found nowhere near the coast
- Parc National de la Kibira's rainforest, home to chimpanzees

Local customs
- The ritual dance of the royal drum – powerful and synchronised, with heroic poetry and traditional songs
- *Kivivuga amazina*, an improvisational contest of poetry by cattle herders
- Dining, drinking and dancing late into the night in Bujumbura
- *Ibikorwa rusangi*, a time for obligatory community work every Saturday from 8am to 11am
- Football – Burundians are mad about it

Getting under the skin
Read: *Strength in What Remains: A Journey of Remembrance and Forgiveness*, Tracy Kidder's Pulitzer Prize–winning novel about one man's survival of the Burundi civil war
Listen: to *Les Tambourinaires du Burundi: Live at Real World*, an amazing performance
Watch: *Gito, L'ingrat*, a story of an African intellectual's troubled return to his homeland with his French girlfriend
Eat: *impeke* (a cereal made from corn, soybeans and sorghum); patisseries; fresh fish
Drink: a cold bottle of Primus beer, one of the many churned out of the national brewery

In a word
Bwa ('Hello' in Kirundi)

Trademarks
Ethnic conflict; Les Tambourinaires; languid lakeside villages; superb inland beaches; forest-clad mountains; constitutional changes to keep the president in office

Random fact
In 2014 the country's president Pierre Nkurunziza banned jogging – he feared it was being done by groups as a cover for subversion

1. A fisherman repairing his nets on the shores of Lake Tanganyika

2. Traditional *rugos* – houses made from mud and sticks and surrounded by a cattle corral – in the region of Mugongomanga

3. A drummer dances with his drumsticks

B CAPITAL BUJUMBURA // POPULATION 10.7 MILLION // AREA 27,830 SQ KM // OFFICIAL LANGUAGES KIRUNDI & FRENCH

Burundi

A pint-sized country with a world's worth of pain, Burundi looked to be slowly emerging from the fog of its devastating civil war when political upheaval in 2015 stalled any progress. Similar Hutu-Tutsi conflicts have been soothed in Rwanda by removing historical tribal labels; Burundi chose a different path of open dialogue and good-hearted debate, which it is now struggling to follow. If this approach eventually brings stability, travellers will have the first opportunity in a generation to explore this currently off-limits nation. Its jungle-clad volcanoes offer lung-busting escapades tracking chimpanzees, while its less frenzied Lake Tanganyika beaches are perfect for soothing the soul. Encounters with Burundians are rewarding lessons in life – they prove that where there are lows, there still can be highs.

C CAPITAL PHNOM PENH // POPULATION 15.2 MILLION // AREA 181,035 SQ KM // OFFICIAL LANGUAGE KHMER

Cambodia

Insurgency and civil war kept Cambodia off the traveller trail for decades, but now that peace has returned Cambodia is catching up fast with Thailand, Laos and Vietnam. While the legacy of Pol Pot and the Khmer Rouge remains imprinted on the landscape, conflict is no longer the main tourist attraction. Today, people are as likely to come to Cambodia for seafood and boutique hotels as for wartime relics. But there is one thing that draws people above all else – the breathtaking ruins of Angkor, indisputably one of the wonders of the world. Cambodia has a beaten traveller trail – from Phnom Penh to Angkor, then down to the beaches of Sihanoukville – but increasingly, travellers are branching out to backwater market towns, remote national parks and hill tribe villages in the rugged north. Best of all, Cambodia still feels like a frontier, so bring your pith helmet and push back some travel boundaries.

Best time to visit
November to January (the dry season)

Top things to see
- Astonishing temples emerging from the jungle at Angkor
- Irrawaddy dolphins splashing in the Mekong at Kratie
- Rarely-seen Angkor-era temples in remote Preah Vihear Province
- Mist swirling around the ruins of the French hill station in Bokor National Park
- The heart-rending Khmer Rouge–era displays at Tuol Sleng and Choeung Ek in Phnom Penh

Top things to do
- Joining the incredible tide of motorcycle traffic in Phnom Penh on a wobbly motorcycle taxi
- Ride the Mekong ferry through stunning scenery between Siem Reap and Battambang
- Cheer on the racing boat crews during the annual Water Festival
- Trek through uncharted jungles in Virachay National Park
- Let the surf tickle your toes on a beach at Sihanoukville

Getting under the skin
Read: harrowing accounts of the Khmer Rouge years in Pin Yathay's *Stay Alive, My Son*; and Loung Ung's *First They Killed My Father*
Listen: to the surreal sounds of Cambodian surf rock, best exemplified by Ros Sereysothea and a generation of other artists lost in Cambodia's civil war
Watch: Roland Joffé's *The Killing Fields*, still the most powerful portrayal of the Khmer Rouge revolution
Eat: *pleah* (hot and sour beef salad) or *kyteow* (rice-noodle soup) – or bite into a deep-fried tarantula
Drink: the thick and delicious fruit smoothies known as *tukalok*

In a word
Niak teuv naa? (Where are you going?) – something

visitors are asked all the time by inquisitive Khmers

Trademarks
Angkor Wat; the mighty Mekong; Pol Pot; the Khmer Rouge; monks on bikes; maniacal motorcycle taxi drivers; fried spiders

Random fact
Pol Pot formulated his radical Marxist ideas while studying for an electronics degree in Paris

1. The ruins of the ancient temple of Ta Prohm, Ankor Wat

2. A rare red garden lizard

3. This bamboo bridge across the Mekong River to Koh Paen is built every dry season and washes away every rainy season

Best time to visit
November to February

Top things to see
- Korup National Park, the oldest rainforest in Africa and one of its most accessible
- Ebodjé, which has an even more beautiful beach than more-famous Kribi, with nesting sea turtles
- If security returns to the north, the fascinating Sahelian town of Maroua and its colourful market
- Yaoundé, arrayed across seven hills and brimful of life
- The traditional Islamic kingdom of Foumban, with a royal palace and strong artistic heritage

Top things to do
- Climb to the summit of Mt Cameroon (4095m), West Africa's highest peak
- Get off the beaten track in the traditional kingdoms of the Ring Road
- Chill on an Atlantic beach in Limbe, with the rainforest-swathed foothills of Mt Cameroon behind you
- Track elephants, giant forest hogs, buffaloes, bongos and more in Lobéké National Park
- Go truly wild in the remote and undeveloped jungles of the Dja Faunal Reserve

Getting under the skin
Read: *The Poor Christ of Bomba*, renowned Cameroonian novelist Mongo Beti's masterful account of a missionary's failures in a small village; *Cameroon with Egbert* by Dervla Murphy; Gerald Durrell's *A Zoo in My Luggage* and *The Bafut Beagles*
Listen: to Manu Dibango's *Soul Makossa*, one of Africa's most influential albums
Watch: *Afrique, Je Te Plumerai* (Africa, I Will Fleece You) by Jean-Marie Teno, an outstanding documentary about modern Cameroon
Eat: *fufu* (mashed yam, corn or plantain) with *ndole* (a bitter-leaf-and-smoked-fish sauce), or *suya* (beef cooked on outdoor grills)
Drink: Castel and 33 (beers), Guinness and milky-white palm wine

In a word
No ngoolu daa (Hello, in Fulfulde)

Trademarks
Rainforest; logging; Baka people (formerly known as Pygmies); gorillas; sea turtles; *makossa* music created and made famous by Manu Dibango

Random fact
Lake Nyos, one of two 'exploding lakes' in Cameroon, is considered the most deadly on earth – it killed around 1700 people in 1986 before efforts were made reduce its volcanic gases

1. The awesome peaks of the Mandara Mountains rise from the volcanic plain

2. A woman from northern Cameroon transports water

3. Emerging from dense rainforest, Bomana Falls in southwest Cameroon drops more than 100m

C CAPITAL YAOUNDÉ // POPULATION 23.1 MILLION // AREA 475,440 SQ KM // OFFICIAL LANGUAGES FRENCH & ENGLISH

Cameroon

Cameroon is often described as all of Africa contained within a single country, and whichever way you look at it that cliché rings true. At the crossroads of West and Central Africa, the natural world spans the full spectrum of signature African landscapes: steamy tropical beaches in the south, even steamier rainforests of the interior and the semi-deserts of the Sahelian north. Its human geography is similarly diverse: from 263 peaceful ethnic groups and a wealth of traditional kingdoms still holding sway, to the sad incursion of Boko Haram violence in the north (making that region strictly off limits to travellers). Cameroon is also the only African country to have been colonised by three European powers. The result is an extraordinary deep-immersion African experience.

Best time to visit
March to November, except in the north where winter comes early (October) and leaves late (April)

Top things to see
- Black bears, grizzly bears, moose and more in the wilds across the country
- Québec City's Old Town, a Unesco World Heritage site exuding historical romance
- The Haida Gwaii archipelago, where the rich Haida culture is thriving again
- The world-class restaurants and chic boutiques of downtown Toronto
- Newfoundland's Northern Peninsula, which blends icebergs, craggy cliffs and the odd Viking artefact

Top things to do
- Hike the craggy peaks and alpine meadows of Banff National Park
- Carve up some fresh powder at one of the Canadian Rockies' renowned ski resorts
- Sail the whale- and dolphin-filled Inside Passage along British Columbia
- Crack shells at a glorious Prince Edward Island lobster feast
- Feast on dim sum in Vancouver, where one in five residents have Chinese heritage

Getting under the skin
Read: *Selected Stories* by Nobel Prize-winner Alice Munro, largely set in rural Ontario; or Ann-Marie MacDonald's Nova Scotia epic, *Fall on Your Knees*
Listen: to Leonard Cohen, Neil Young, Broken Social Scene and Arcade Fire
Watch: *Atanarjuat: The Fast Runner*, an Inuit legend told in the Inuktitut language; or *C.R.A.Z.Y.*, about growing up gay in 1970s Québec
Eat: fresh seafood; maple syrup; poutine (French fries with gravy and cheese curds)
Drink: many superb wines from the Okanagan Valley in southern British Columbia

In a word
Eh? (bilingual and all-purpose, eg 'Nice day, eh?')

Trademarks
Moose; bears; the Rockies; Bryan Adams; maple trees; Mounties

Random fact
Every year the British Columbian town of Nanaimo holds a bathtub race, where competitors speed across the harbour in boats formed from bathtubs

1. La Citadelle and the Quebec City skyline, Quebec

2. A woman from the Siksika Nation at the Blackfoot Crossing Historical Park, Alberta

3. Early morning light on the glacier-fed waters of Moraine Lake, Banff National Park, Alberta

C · **CAPITAL** OTTAWA // **POPULATION** 34.6 MILLION // **AREA** 9,970,610 SQ KM // **OFFICIAL LANGUAGES** ENGLISH & FRENCH

Canada

You can literally lose yourself almost anywhere in Canada. The world's second-largest country has more gorgeous and remote corners than you could ever count or visit. From the glaciers of Kluane National Park in the Yukon to Nova Scotia's Cape Breton Highlands, the natural wonders never cease. When you're ready for civilisation you'll find cities that are among the world's most genteel and pleasurable. Although most people live within 100km of the US border, Canada boasts a multicultural society that combines elements of Britain, France, Asia and almost every other world region. It's an intoxicating melange found no place else. The nation's indigenous peoples have robust cultures that enrich the nation, while First Nations art honours both the glories of nature and aeons-old traditions.

1. The world-class waves
   of Cape Verde are
   popular with kitesurfers

2. Sitting amid the
   mountains of Santa
   Antão is the precipitous
   settlement of
   Fontainhas

3. Commerce and colour:
   a vegetable market in
   Praia, Santiago

C | **CAPITAL** PRAIA // **POPULATION** 531,046 // **AREA** 4033 SQ KM // **OFFICIAL LANGUAGES** PORTUGUESE & CRIOULO

Cape Verde

Rising up from the Atlantic depths some 500km off the coast of West Africa, the islands of Cape Verde are at once unmistakeably African and a world away from the continent. Wherever you are in the archipelago it's easy to be overwhelmed by the raw power of nature – active volcanoes, canyons, desert plains and beaches all vie for space in this astonishing place that is brushed with Atlantic breezes and Saharan trade winds. With these winds has come a complicated cultural mix that blends Portuguese and African influences in the islands' food, architecture and world-famous music, which is in turns melancholy and uplifting. The overall effect is like nowhere else on earth.

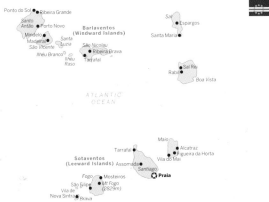

Best time to visit
October to August

Top things to see
- Mindelo, the prettiest city with a moon-shaped bay, stark mountains and a lovely old quarter
- São Filipe, a gorgeous town of colonial architecture, set high on the cliffs
- Ponta Do Sol, one of the wildest and most beautiful coastlines in Africa
- The Unesco-listed remnants of West Africa's first European settlement, Cidade Velha
- The sandy beaches, desert plains and verdant, mountainous interior of Santiago

Top things to do
- Windsurf off the islands of Sal and Boa Vista
- Trek alongside the precipitous cliffs and green valleys of Santa Antão
- Join the famous Mardi Gras festivities in Mindelo
- Climb to Cape Verde's highest point, the active volcano of Mt Fogo (2829m)
- Take up residence in a smoky bar to hear Cape Verde's unmistakeable *mornas* (mournful music)

Getting under the skin
Read: poet Jorge Barbosa's *Arquipélago*, which is laden with melancholic reflections on the sea
Listen: barefoot diva Cesária Évora's heartbreaking *mornas* and *coladeiras* (sentimental love songs)
Watch: *Fintar o Destino* (Dribbling Fate) by Fernando Vendrell, a very African tale of a young footballer
Eat: the national dish *cachupa* (a tasty stew of beans, corn and meat or fish)
Drink: Ceris (the local beer); *grogue* (sugar-cane spirit); and white or rosé wines from Fogo

In a word
Ta bon (I'm fine)

Trademarks
Afro-Portuguese mix; successful economic development; Cesária Évora; wild volcanic beauty

Random fact
Benito Mussolini purchased rights to build an airport on the island of Sal in 1939

Best time to visit
Weather is beautifully balmy year-round except during the sticky months of July and August; hurricanes can hit between June and November

Top things to see
- Wedge-shaped Cayman Brac has sweeping views and enervating hikes from its namesake bluff
- Rare old-growth tropical trees on Grand Cayman's Mastic Trail
- Pedro St James, an 18th-century grand plantation house that cast off its slavery heritage by serving as the site of abolition in 1835
- Emerald green parrots at Cayman Brac's National Trust Parrot Preserve
- Red-footed boobies and imposing frigate birds at Booby Pond Nature Reserve on Little Cayman

Top things to do
- Take a tour of the blue iguana breeding centre at the lush Queen Elizabeth II Botanic Park
- Savour some of the world's best wall diving at Bloody Bay Wall, off Little Cayman
- Take several lazy days to explore the length of spectacular Seven-Mile Beach on Grand Cayman
- Search for undiscovered pirate booty in the labyrinth caves on Cayman Brac
- Feed the languid and mellow stingrays at Grand Cayman's Stingray City

Getting under the skin
Read: *Cayman Cowboys*, the first novel in the popular series of Cayman-based scuba thrillers by US journalist and author Eric Douglas
Listen: to West Indian soca, calypso and reggae
Watch: *The Firm* (from the John Grisham book); and *Into the Blue* (with Josh Brolin et al)
Eat: seafood, with most dishes featuring conch in one form or another
Drink: 'jelly ice' (chilled coconut juice sucked out of the shell)

In a word
Brac (actually a Gaelic word meaning bluff, refers to the most rural of the islands)

Trademarks
Shipwrecks; pirate history; condos; snorkelling and diving; tax haven

Random fact
The Caymans have close to 600 banks and trusts, although only a few are recognisable as such (with lobbies, tellers, ATMs etc); most are secretive institutions with little more than a brass plaque above an office building mail drop

1. A coconut vendor on Grand Cayman

2. Southern stringrays are found in abundance off Grand Cayman

3. Stingray City from the air; its waters are a paradise for divers and snorkellers

CAPITAL GEORGE TOWN // POPULATION 53,737 // AREA 264 SQ KM // OFFICIAL LANGUAGE ENGLISH

Cayman Islands

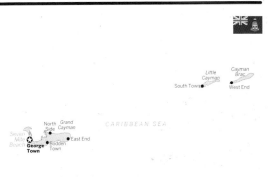

The three islands that comprise this British Overseas Territory couldn't have more different personalities. Grand Cayman lives up to its name; it is home to most of the population, development and resorts. Seven-Mile Beach is lazy holiday heaven, backed by a strip of resorts and condos where the well-heeled cash in on the good life. Just a 40-minute flight, but seemingly a world away, are Cayman Brac and neighbouring Little Cayman. The former is an untrammelled sliver of tropical charm, with large areas of preserved natural beauty on land and underwater, plus a smattering of slow-paced, pastel-painted villages. The latter is the ultimate castaway spot for honeymooners, low-key celebrities and divers; its 100-odd residents are vastly outnumbered by birds, huge iguanas and fish.

C **CAPITAL** BANGUI // **POPULATION** 5.2 MILLION // **AREA** 622,984 SQ KM // **OFFICIAL LANGUAGE** FRENCH

Central African Republic

The Central African Republic is sadly a study in creating chaos. First, the republic's sophisticated society, which had been several thousand years in the making, was shattered by the slave trade. The desperate remnants were then catapulted into the harsh yoke of French colonial rule, only to be subsequently subjected to agonisingly egocentric governments after independence. After a few years of stability between 2008 and 2012, the country was thrust back into civil war, and despite a UN-led peacekeeping mission, the Central African Republic is still too dangerous to visit. Beyond the conflict, wildlife still looms in its darkest jungles, and warmth, generosity and pride steadfastly survive in the hearts of its people. CAR is Africa at its most raw.

Best time
November to April, during the dry season

Places of interest
- The pristine rainforests of the Dzanga-Sangha Reserve, home to a few thousand western lowland gorillas
- Chutes de Boali, a 50m-high waterfall that bursts to life in the rainy season
- Dzanga-Sangha National Park, home to lowland gorillas and the Baka people (Pygmies)
- The ruined palace of former 'Emperor' Bokassa at Berengo
- Megalithic stone monuments that dot the landscape around Bouar

Local customs
- Baka summoning forest spirits as they hunt *mboloko* (blue duiker)
- Drinking palm wine and dancing the *gbadoumba* and *lououdou*
- Initiation rites and traditional religious practices occur in the dry season's grass-burning hunts
- Traditional storytelling, with the folklore being sung to the music of drums, *ngombi* (harp) and *sanza* (guitar)

Getting under the skin
Read: *The Central African Republic: The Continent's Hidden Heart* by Thomas E O'Toole, which delves into the nation's social history
Listen: to African Rhythms by Aka Pygmies and Pierre-Laurent Aimard
Watch: *Song From the Forest*, a documentary about an American who makes his home among the Baka in the Central African jungle
Eat: plenty of manioc – *ngunza* (manioc leaf salad) and *gozo* (manioc paste) are particular local favourites
Drink: locally brewed banana or palm wine

In a word
Bara ala kwe (Hello, in Sango)

Trademarks
Post-colonial chaos; western lowland gorillas; butterflies; forest elephants; Baka; big game trophy hunting by the French; corruption; uranium; diamonds; lush tropical rainforests

Random fact
Jean-Bédel Bokassa wasn't happy with just being president of the country, so in 1976 he converted the Central African Republic into the Central African Empire; most of the bill for the US$20 million coronation to make him emperor was footed by France

1. The solemn gaze of 'Makumba', a western lowland gorilla, Dzanga-Ndoki National Park

2. Three Bayaka boys pose for a portrait; the Bayaka are a nomadic Mbenga Pygmy people

3. A Bayaka honey gatherer climbs a 40m tree using an axe and a length of liana

Best time
December to mid-February

Places of interest
- Zakouma National Park, one of the last strongholds for wildlife in Central Africa
- The Sahara and its powdery sands, complete with elegant, perfectly preserved shells of aquatic molluscs
- The cooling waters of the dramatic Guelta d'Archei, which hundreds of camels (and a few crocodiles) share
- Emi Koussi and its cratered summit standing high above the desert it dominates
- The mud-brick houses of the Sao people in the village of Gaoui
- The transcendent Tibesti Mountains rising from the Saharan sea of sand
- The banks of the Chari River in N'Djaména, where hippos roam

Local customs
- Wives in the families of the Taubou or Daza peoples make most major decisions
- Life for nomads revolves around their livestock, which provides both sustenance and status
- The traditional Arab family unit is the *kashimbet*, a compact lineage made up of a few generations of men, their wives and children

Getting under the skin
Read: *Le Commandant Chaka*, a work denouncing military dictatorships, by Baba Moustapha; *Chad: A Nation in Search of its Future* by Mario J Azevedo and Emmanuel U Nnadozie for an indepth overview of the nation
Listen: to Tibesti, a group who popularised the rhythmic *sai* sound
Watch: *Abouna*, a gripping story following two boys' misguided search for their father
Eat: *nachif* (finely minced meat in sauce); *salanga* and *banda* (sun-dried/smoked fish)
Drink: a bottle of Gala beer, from the brewery in Moundou

In a word
Lale (A warm greeting in southern Chad)

Trademarks
Harmattan (the Saharan trade wind); coups; assassinations; conflicts with Libya and Sudan; surprising wildlife

Random fact
Chad may eventually be without its namesake, Lake Chad – desertification and human water use over the past 50 years have reduced its size from over 26,000 sq km to less than 1500

1. Sandstone sentinel: a dramatic stone arch in the Ennedi Region

2. Young Wodaabe men take part in an annual courtship ritual, the Guérewol

3. A farmer from N'Djaména herds his cattle

C // **CAPITAL** N'DJAMÉNA // **POPULATION** 11.2 MILLION // **AREA** 1,284,000 SQ KM // **OFFICIAL LANGUAGES** ARABIC & FRENCH

Chad

Bullet vs ballot. Christian vs Muslim. These battles define modern Chad. Tragically, the only thing uniting the north's Muslims with the south's Christians is abject poverty. Without obvious natural resources, Chad was virtually ignored during French colonial rule, leaving it teetering towards political turmoil upon independence. And what tragic turmoil it has been. Recent terrorism – most of it sponsored by Boko Haram – has put fuel to the flames, making travel here unsafe. Devoid of pity, the Sahara has continued its march south, leaving its beautiful but bleak calling cards – parched aquatic shells poking from the desert floor. Meanwhile, beyond the headlines and the desert's grip, life abounds. Chad, like its people, contains glimpses of surreal beauty with harsh doses of reality.

1. A shepherd guiding her flock through Guatin Gorge in the Atacama Desert; the Atacama is the world's driest non-polar desert

2. The perfectly circular crater of Rano Kau, an extinct volcano on Easter Island

3. Bred tough: farmers from the Atacama Desert

C CAPITAL SANTIAGO // POPULATION 17.2 MILLION // AREA 756,950 SQ KM // OFFICIAL LANGUAGE SPANISH

Chile & Easter Island

Long and slim, Chile spreads down a coastal strip of South America between the Pacific and the Andes, spanning half the length of the continent from the earth's driest desert to the largest glacial fields outside the poles. Capital Santiago is one of South America's most modern cities, but heading south, staggering nature soon sets in. First come the lush valleys of one of the New World's premium viticulture regions and then, in increasing splendour, craggy Andean summits, vast forests, cerulean lakes and the myriad mist-cloaked, mystery-soaked islands of the lonely, lacerated, seemingly endless southern coast – not to mention the mysteries of Easter Island. No surprises, with such scenery, that the country has inspired a glut of renowned writers, such as Pablo Neruda and Isabel Allende, as well as a regular influx of adventure-seekers.

Best time to visit
Year-round in the north, November to April in the south, June to August for skiing

Top things to see
- Pablo Neruda's poetically decorated homes in Santiago, Valaparaiso and Isla Negra
- The alerce, a tree native to temperate Valdivian rainforest with specimens over 3000 years old
- Santiago's glittering skyline from the powder-clad ski slopes above it
- The thousands of islands studding the end-of-the-earth Strait of Magellan
- Rano Raraku, the mountain quarry of the mammoth Easter Island statues

Top things to do
- Sip wines in the Central Valley's vineyards
- Trek under the sharp spires of Torres del Paine, South America's premier national park
- Feast on fresh oysters in the archipelago of Chiloé
- Mosey with pack horses through the lush river valleys of northern Patagonia

Getting under the skin
Read: Gabriel García Márquez's exposé on Chile under Pinochet's dictatorship, *Clandestine in Chile*
Listen: to groundbreaking '90s rock outfit La Ley
Watch: Pablo Larráin's Oscar-nominated *No*, about the momentous 1988 referendum
Eat: conger eel soup; crab casserole; a *completo*: hotdog with a hotchpotch of sauces and seasonings
Drink: a tart pisco sour (grape brandy shaken with fresh lime and powdered sugar)

In a word
Bacán! (Cool!)

Trademarks
Seismic shocks; cowboys; the great Andean condor; red wine; poets; Patagonia; the legacy of Pinochet

Random fact
The Atacama Desert has the planet's best star-gazing potential: the Alma Observatory here is the world's largest astronomic project

Best time to visit
March to May and September to November

Top things to see
- The Great Wall – you can't actually see it from space, but it's astonishing to see close-up
- The Forbidden City, China's historic imperial palace, and the surrounding courtyard homes in Běijīng's *hútòngs* (narrow alleyways)
- The 6000 sculpted faces of Xī'ān's Army of Terracotta Warriors
- Snow-capped peaks rising above the 2km-deep cliffs of Tiger Leaping Gorge
- The seemingly endless swirling green landscape of the Lóngjǐ Rice Terraces

Top things to do
- Take an overnight train journey across China to grasp the scale of this enormous country
- Ride a bamboo raft between spiking karst mountains near Yángshuò
- Sample China's vast culinary landscape, from fiery Chóngqìng hotpot to crispy Peking roast duck
- Stroll past the kite flyers and colonial office buildings on Shànghǎi's Bund

Getting under the skin
Read: *Country Driving: A Chinese Road Trip*, Peter Hessler's engaging travel memoir; and *Tiger Head, Snake Tails* by Jonathan Tenby for insights into China's recent political history
Listen: to the dissonant melodies of Chinese opera – skip the touristy shows in Běijīng for the real deal in Chéngdū
Watch: Zhang Zimou's *Raise the Red Lantern* or Fei Mu's *Spring in a Small Town* and marvel at the wistful beauty of Chinese film-making
Eat: the fiery cuisine of Sìchuān – flavoured with 'flower pepper', an incendiary spice unrelated to chillies or black pepper
Drink: *chá* (tea) at a traditional teahouse – leaves are rolled, brewed and roasted to create an astonishing variety of brews

In a word
Chīfàn le ma? (Have you eaten?)

Trademarks
Chopsticks; calligraphy; Mao-era nostalgia; taichi; green tea; rice terraces; kung fu; the Olympic Games; rapid development; high-speed trains; ancient pagodas

Random fact
Among other things, the Chinese invented paper, printing, gunpowder, the compass and the umbrella

1. Imperial shopfronts in one of Běijīng's traditional *hútòng* districts

2. Sìchuān's Lèshān Big Buddha is a 71m-high statue carved from a cliff face

3. A girl in traditional Miao dress; the Miao people are an ethnic minory from the mountains of southern China

4. A serpentine road winds its way up the flanks of Tianmen Mountain National Park, Zhāngjiājiè, Húnán

C | **CAPITAL** BĚIJĪNG // **POPULATION** 1.3 BILLION // **AREA** 9,596,961 SQ KM // **OFFICIAL LANGUAGE** MANDARIN

China

Having shed its 20th-century reclusiveness, China today ranks among the world's powerhouse economies, as you might expect from a nation that is home to one in seven human beings on the planet. The guiding light of modern China is not Chairman Mao but the yuan – consumerism is the new religion and vast swathes of the country are being concreted over to provide space for shopping centres and apartment buildings. Nevertheless, China's captivating culture and history shine through. For every newly built skyscraper there is a centuries-old pagoda, and for every fast-food franchise, there is a teahouse serving hand-pulled noodles and steamed buns.

Best time to visit
January to March (the dry season)

Top things to see
- The cobbled lanes of Cartagena, Colombia's most romantic colonial city
- Zona Cafetera, the coffee-growing region set against a backdrop of volcanoes
- The rebirth of Bogotá, a vibrant and style-conscious city with a burgeoning arts scene
- Laid-back Capurgana and Sapzurro, two blissfully old-fashioned settlements ringed by rainforest on the Caribbean coast
- The hauntingly beautiful subterranean salt cathedral in Zipaquirá

Top things to do
- Head to the adventure capital of San Gil, with incredible rafting, caving, horseback riding and mountain biking
- Journey to Colombia's Amazonian wilderness at the Reserva Natural Zacambú
- Trek through rainforest and mountains to the ruins of the Ciudad Perdida
- Explore the archaeological sites in the rolling hills around San Agustín
- Party till dawn in Medellin, Colombia's renaissance city

Getting under the skin
Read: *Love in the Time of Cholera*, the fantastical love story by Nobel Prize–winning Colombian author Gabriel García Márquez
Listen: to pop vocalists Carlos Vives and Shakira, or the Afro-Caribbean beats of *Toto La Momposina*
Watch: *Maria Full of Grace*, Joshua Marston's complex film about a pregnant drug mule seeking a new life in the US
Eat: satisfying *arepas* (corn cakes served with cheese, pork and many other toppings); *sancocho* (a hearty soup made with meat, yucca and other vegetables)
Drink: arguably the world's best coffee: order a *tinto* (black, espresso size), *pintado* (small milk coffee) or *cafe con leche* (standard size, with more milk than coffee)

In a word
Que hubo? (What's up?)

Trademarks
Coffee; Gabriel García Márquez; emeralds; lost cities; Shakira; drug wars; Pablo Escobar

Random fact
Avianca, Colombia's flagship airline, was the first commercial airline founded in the Americas

1. The colourful streets of the old colonial city of Cartagena

2. Start them young; salsa dancers practise at an academy

3. Beach goers frolic in the idyllic waters of Tayrona National Park

C CAPITAL BOGOTÁ // POPULATION 45.7 MILLION // AREA 1,138,914 SQ KM // OFFICIAL LANGUAGE SPANISH

Colombia

Once typecast as the bad boy of South America, Colombia is one of the continent's most remarkable success stories. A decades-long civil war has been largely relegated to the past, and Colombians and foreign travellers alike are rediscovering this captivating country. Colombia's trump card is its diverse geography, which includes Andean peaks, rainforests and savannahs, supporting an astounding 10% of the world's biodiversity. A flurry of urban renewal projects has breathed new life into Colombia's cities, and after being off-limits for years, its natural wonders are now more accessible than ever. Whether you seek jungle adventures or prefer to kick back in a colonial village with a cup of Colombian coffee, you can expect the famed hospitality of the nation's people – who share a heady mix of indigenous, African and European ancestry – at every turn.

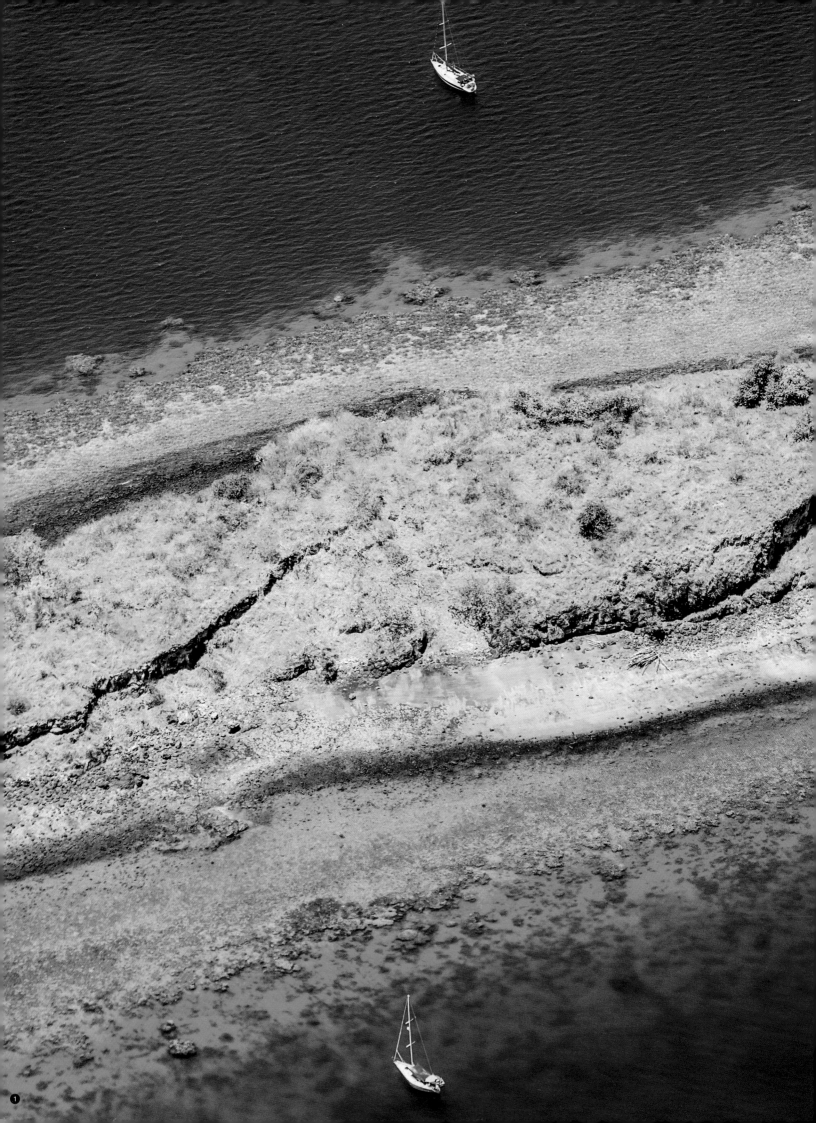

CAPITAL MORONI (C), MAMOUDZOU (M) // **POPULATION** 752,288 (C), 223,765 (M) // **AREA** 2235 SQ KM (C), 374 SQ KM (M) **OFFICIAL LANGUAGES** ARABIC & FRENCH (C), FRENCH (M)

Comoros & Mayotte

Born of fire, these Indian Ocean islands have seldom come off the boil. Discontent, intrigue and ambition, much like the omnipresent lava lurking beneath this archipelago, have all erupted habitually, resulting in numerous coups and civilian riots. However, for visitors, the melange of Polynesian, Swahili and Arabic cultures is as intoxicating as the fragrant fields of ylang-ylang, jasmine, cassis and orange flowers. Also rooted in the islands' fertile volcanic soils are virgin rainforests, which host everything from giant bats to rare lemurs. Surrounding it all is a coast blessed with turquoise waters, colourful sand beaches and ports laden with historical architecture.

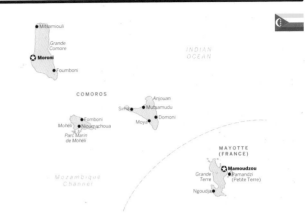

Best time to visit
May to October (the dry season)

Top things to see
- The entirety of this Indian Ocean archipelago spread out below you from the lofty summit of Mt Ntingui
- A mere fraction of the 600 colourful species of fish inhabiting the mammoth coral reef that surrounds the island of Mayotte
- The faultless sandy beaches fringing the islets of Parc Marin de Mohéli
- Locals transfixed by the ancient African game of bao
- Your sails filled while cruising one of the world's largest lagoons

Top things to do
- Trek up to Lac Dzialaoutsounga and Lac Dzialandzé, peaceful crater lakes on the flank of Mt Ntingui
- Swim with sea turtles off the Sazilé Peninsula
- Spend a few sweaty hours reeling in a marlin, then replenish your fluids chilling on a gloriously empty beach
- Meander through shadows and past intricately carved Swahili doors in the crooked alleys of Moroni's ancient medina
- Inhale the sweet fragrance wafting from the ylang-ylang distillery in Bamboa

Getting under the skin
Read: The Comoros Islands: Struggle Against Dependency in the Indian Ocean, Malyn Newitt's outline of the region's turbulent, coup-riddled modern history
Listen: to Mohammed Hassan singing twarab, a Comoran version of Swahili music accompanied by a gabusi (short-necked lute) and a ndzendze (box-shaped zither)
Watch: the films of Hachimiya Ahamada about the Comoran diaspora: La Résidence Ylang-Ylang (The Ylang-Ylang Residence) and Ivresse d'une Oasis (Ashes of Dreams)
Eat: your first ever inexpensive lobster, and you'll remember more than the petite price tag – langouste à la vanille is particularly divine

Drink: tea spiced with lemongrass and ginger

In a word
Salama (Hello, in Comoran)

Trademarks
Azure waters lapping on long beaches; plantations of ylang-ylang, jasmine and cassis; incredible seafood; volcanic eruptions; countless coups; poor aviation safety record

Random fact
A wedding, or grande marriage as it's known in the Comoros, can last up to nine days – the groom is expected to fund the toirab (celebration) that caters for the entire village

1. Yachts moored amidst the rainbow palette of a coral lagoon on Mayotte

2. Deft hands; a women weaves coconut fibre in a craft workshop in Sada, Mayotte

3. Fisherman return with the morning's catch to the small hamlet of Hamouro, Mayotte

Best time
December to February (north of equator), May to October (south of equator)

Places of interest
- Parc National de la Salonga, with bonobos and forest elephants running wild in the untouched jungle
- Wagenia Falls, where working fisherfolk balance deftly above the torrents on wobbly wooden platforms
- A flood in a 347m freefall from the top of Lofoi Falls, Parc National de Kundelungu
- Lava spewing skyward from the crater of Mt Nyiragongo, one of the world's most active volcanoes
- The legendary Congo River, which meanders through the wilderness and past remote villages
- Parc National des Virunga, one of a handful of parks worldwide to host wild mountain gorillas

Local customs
- Obeying the automated robots – complete with waving arms and tin voices – which now control traffic in the chaotic streets of Kinshasa
- Dressing to the nines as part of the Congolese Society of Ambience-makers and Elegant Persons (aka the *sapeurs*)
- Production of embroidered textiles, ornate cosmetics boxes and monumental masks by descendants of the Kuba Kingdom

Getting under the skin
Read: *King Leopold's Ghost* by Adam Hochschild; and *In the Footsteps of Mr Kurtz,* Michaela Wrong's compelling look into President Mobutu's regime
Listen: to the kings of *soukous* (African rumba), Franco Luambo and Papa Wemba, Africa's equiavalent of James Brown and Elvis Presley
Watch: *Lumumba,* a gripping story of the political upheaval surrounding Patrice Lumumba's life and death
Eat: *liboke* (fish stewed in manioc leaves) with the omnipresent *fufu* (manioc porridge)
Drink: a Primus beer, or Turbo King if you prefer darker brews

In a word
Sángo níni? (How are you? in Lingala)

Trademarks
Zaïre; The Rumble in the Jungle; *Heart of Darkness*; blood diamonds; kleptocracy; UN peacekeeping soldiers

Random fact
On the Congo River's southern bank, Kinshasa sits across from Brazzaville in the Republic of Congo; it's the only place in the world where two national capitals are situated on the opposite banks of a river within sight of each other

1. Wagenia fishermen, from the village of Kisangani, net fish from platforms built in the raging rapids of the Congo River

2. A woman carries her crop (cassava leaves) to a market in Shasha, eastern DRC

3. The steaming maw of Mt Nyiragongo (3470m), an active volcano in Parc National des Virunga

C   **CAPITAL** KINSHASA // **POPULATION** 75.5 MILLION // **AREA** 2,344,858 SQ KM // **OFFICIAL LANGUAGE** FRENCH

Congo, Democratic Republic of

When it comes to African treasures, the Democratic Republic of Congo has plenty – huge tracks of rainforest, smoking volcanoes, gushing rivers, mountain gorillas, mineral wealth and cultural riches. Yet, it also has more than its share of suffering. Generations of its people have had to witness successive kleptocrats sucking government coffers dry, and – worse still – endure violent conflict, including Africa's first 'world war', which left over five million dead. Intrepid travellers long for more peaceful encounters, such as compelling conversations with locals in cities and remote villages; exhilarating interactions with silverbacks and elephants in impenetrable forests; and beckoning rivers offering a serpentine path into the truly unknown. While continued insecurity and a lack of development puts the DRC out of reach, the country remains an adventurer's dream.

1. Hippopotamuses fight; war in the region has caused hippo numbers to crash in the last 40 years

2. Evangelical churchgoers in Brazzaville

3. Baka women carry cassava they've grown to a market in Brazzaville

❶

C CAPITAL BRAZZAVILLE // POPULATION 4.6 MILLION // AREA 342,000 SQ KM // OFFICIAL LANGUAGE FRENCH

Congo, Republic of

A place of legendary explorers, wildlife and tribes, the Congo's name alone stirs the adventurous spirit in every intrepid traveller. Travel north and the sultry air beneath the thick canopy of the Congo's dense jungles reverberates with the chest thumping of lowland gorillas, the pan hoots of chimpanzees, the sound of forest elephants and the hunting calls of the Mbenga people (formerly known as Pygmies). Not to be confused with the neighbouring, and far more unpredictable, Democratic Republic of Congo, this nation is finally safe and stable after years of turbulence. Visitors will welcome the fact that oil and timber revenues are being used to expand infrastructure and rehabilitate national parks – the rewards of travel here will continue to be intense, but they'll be more comfortable to attain in the years to come.

Best time to visit
December to February (north of equator), May to September (south of equator)

Top things to see
- Congolese navigating the shifting currents of the Congo River in their pirogues
- The inconceivable concentration of the nation's wealth in Pointe-Noir
- Herds of forest elephants congregating in Wali Bai, a natural clearing in Parc National Nouabalé-Ndoki
- The joyous celebrations when you've been narrowly beaten by a local youth in *babyfoot* (table football)
- Rusty, tendril-like ridges of rock snaking through the rainforest in Diosso Gorge

Top things to do
- Drift through Parc National d'Odzala's waters in search of gorillas and elephants
- Peruse Brazzaville's fragrant markets
- Explore the protected marine areas of Parc National Conkouati-Douli, home to sea turtles and rare West African manatees
- Sip a cappuccino on a terrace in Brazzaville and watch Africans, Arabs, Europeans and Asians peacefully going about their daily life

Getting under the skin
Read: *Congo Journey*, Redmond O'Hanlon's captivating travelogue
Listen: to Congo's jazz king, Jean Serge Essous
Watch: *Congo*, Frank Marshall's adaptation of the novel by Michael Crichton
Eat: fresh fish with fried bananas
Drink: the ubiquitous palm wine

In a word
Losáko (Hello, in Lingala)

Trademarks
Congo River; untamed rainforests; lowland gorillas; candlelit night markets; oil; Marxist revolution

Random fact
The Congo River is the ninth longest river on the planet (4700km), but it's easily the deepest

1. Aitutaki lagoon: home to green turtles and giant eagle rays

2. Young Cook Islanders pose on an outrigger canoe

3. The Cook Islands is a paradise for divers and snorkellers; coral reef off Aitutaki

C

Cook Islands

Smack in the centre of the Pacific, these 15 flecks of land are spread over an oceanic space about the size of Western Europe. Named after the great explorer Captain James Cook, these dazzling tropical morsels have long been a refuge for runaways, hermits and wannabe Robinson Crusoes. And who can blame them? Combining a heady mix of South Seas air, pristine beaches, cerulean lagoons, and fish and fruit aplenty, the Cook Islands are the definition of a remote island paradise. To get a fix of civilisation, head to the capital Avarua for a laid-back mix of cafes and restaurants, souvenir shopping and exuberant Polynesian culture.

Best time to visit
May to November is the driest season but any time of year is warm and sunny

Top things to see
- Ancient *marae* (temples) and gardens at the Highland Paradise Cultural Centre
- Humpback whales from June to October
- Green turtles and eagle rays gliding beneath a glass-bottomed boat on Aitutaki lagoon
- The view of Aitutaki lagoon from Maungapu peak

Top things to do
- Traverse Rarotonga on foot via the lush, tropical wonderland of the cross-island trail
- Snorkel the fish-filled *ra'ui* (traditional conservation areas) around Rarotonga
- *Motu*-hop (island-hop) throughout the impossibly blue Aitutaki lagoon
- Explore the jungle-clad burial caves on 'Atiu and Mangaia Islands
- Enjoy the dancing, singing and fire-juggling at an Island Nights extravaganza

Getting under the skin
Read: *An Island to Oneself*, the classic desert-island read by Tom Neale, who lived on Suwarrow Atoll
Listen: to anything on the Heimana Music label, promoting Cook Islands' music for over 30 years
Watch: *Merry Christmas Mr Lawrence*, the gritty prisoner-of-war movie filmed partly on Rarotonga
Eat: *ika mata* (raw fish marinated in lime and coconut milk), and *rukau* (steamed taro leaves)
Drink: at a *tumunu* (bush beer-drinking club) with an intoxicating orange homebrew

In a word
Kia orana! (May you live long!)

Trademarks
Traditional dancing and music *(karioi)*; pandanus-thatched roofs; black pearls; deserted atolls

Random fact
Residents of Palmerston can trace their lineage back to one man, William Masters, who arrived on the atoll with three Polynesian wives in 1863

CAPITAL SAN JOSÉ // **POPULATION** 4.7·MILLION // **AREA** 51,100 SQ KM // **OFFICIAL LANGUAGE** SPANISH

Costa Rica

A spot of calm in a region of strong political riptides, Costa Rica is a haven for beachcombers, nature lovers, wave riders and adventure seekers. The star attraction is the characterful cast of creatures roaming the rainforest who put on a fantastic show for visitors with keen eyes. Plus, the waves are prime, the beauty is staggering and the slow pace of life is seductive. Of course playing paradise to the world has its consequences. Now two-thirds of the coast is foreign-owned and development often outpaces sustainability. Luckily, the country's many fans include do-gooders, ecologists and proud Ticos (Costa Ricans) who are vocal and vigilant about protecting their natural heritage.

Best time to visit
December to April (the dry season)

Top things to see
- The fantastic biodiversity of Parque Nacional Corcovado
- The windswept wilderness beaches at the tip of the Nicoya Peninsula
- Misbehaving monkeys staging guerrilla raids on picnics in Parque Nacional Manuel Antonio
- Leatherback sea turtles making their epic migration to Playa Grande
- Masked devils schooling the colonial Spanish in the Fiesta de los Diablitos

Top things to do
- Whiz across the cloud forest canopy on a zip line in Monteverde
- Soak in the hot springs in the shadow of the smoking Arenal Volcano
- Ride the waves at Witch's Rock
- Dance to calypso beats in Cahuita, on the steamy Caribbean coast
- Paddle a maze of jungle canals thick with wildlife in Parque Nacional Tortuguero

Getting under the skin
Read: *Costa Rica: A Traveler's Literary Companion*, edited by Barbara Ras, 26 short stories that capture the soul of the county
Listen: to *Costa Rica: Calypso*, fun Caribbean sound from rootsy trad to pop
Watch: *El Regreso* (The Return) – Hernán Jímenez wrote, crowdfunded, directed and starred in this contemporary drama about a Tico émigré's difficult homecoming
Eat: *casado* (a plate of meat, beans, rice and fried plantain)
Drink: palm wine, the preferred firewater of rural farmers; coffee at any local lunch counter
In a word
Pura vida (Pure life) – for thumbs up or a salutation

Trademarks
Dripping rainforests; surf bums; active volcanoes; La Negrita (or the Black Madonna); soccer (football) fans; foaming waterfalls

Random fact
Since 1948, Costa Rica has had no armed forces

1. Celebrating Fiesta Dia del Boyero (Cow Herder's Day), San Antonio de Escazú
2. Catarata del Toro tumbles into the crater of an extinct volcano
3. A red-eyed tree frog – the eyes are an evolutionary adaption to startle predators
4. Costa Rica has superb surfing; Playa Guiones, Nosara

Best time to visit
November to March

Top things to see
- Abidjan's skyscrapers and roiling nightlife in the brash powerhouse of West Africa
- The languid coastal town of Grand Bassam with its decaying colonial buildings
- Yamoussoukro, the village-turned-capital with the tallest basilica in Christendom
- Hippos and other wildlife within the verdant Abokouamekro Game Reserve
- If the security situation improves, the stunning mountain region of Man, with mask ceremonies and stilt dancers

Top things to do
- Surf the Atlantic breakers at Assinie, arguably Côte d'Ivoire's loveliest beach
- Set off in search of chimpanzees in Parc National de Taï when security improves in the southwest
- Haggle for the famous Korhogo cloth in the rust-red city of the same name in northern Côte d'Ivoire
- Take a slow pirogue ride close to Assinie

Getting under the skin
Read: the magic-realist tale *Waiting for the Wild Beasts to Vote* by Ivoirean novelist Amadou Kourouma
Listen: to Alpha Blondy, the king of West African reggae, or the *coupé decalé* (cut and run) dance sensation
Watch: Henri Duparc's acclaimed *Bal Poussière* (Dancing in the Dust), which tackles traditional polygamy; or Désiré Ecaré's *Visages des Femmes* (Faces of Women)
Eat: *poisson braisé* (grilled fish) with *attiéké* (grated cassava); or *kedjenou* (chicken or guinea-fowl simmered with vegetables in a mild sauce)
Drink: Flag or Tuborg beers; or *bandji* (palm wine)

In a word
I-ni-cheh, I-kah-kéné (Hello, how are you? in Dioula, the market language)

Trademarks
Yamoussoukro basilica; Korhogo cloth and Dan masks; eating out in *maquis* (rustic open-air restaurants); reggae and *coupé decalé* music; former economic powerhouse; postponed elections

Random fact
Despite its name translating as 'Ivory Coast' (and its national football team being called Les Éléphants), fewer than 800 of the mighty pachyderms are estimated to live in the country

1. Atlantic Ocean breakers and the roaring metropolis of Abidjan

2. Ivoirian women wear brightly coloured *pagnes*

3. Traditional homes made of mud and straw in the village of Dioulatièdougou

C **CAPITAL** YAMOUSSOUKRO // **POPULATION** 22.4 MILLION // **AREA** 322,463 SQ KM // **OFFICIAL LANGUAGE** FRENCH

Côte d'Ivoire

Côte d'Ivoire has always been beautiful – its sweeping beaches, rainforests and mountains all have the power to charm. Unfortunately the nation, which was once lauded as West Africa's success story, was tragically thrust back into civil war in 2011. But with a fragile peace taking root in all but the southwest, a trickle of travellers is beginning to return. Aside from its many stand-out attractions, Côte d'Ivoire's appeal resides – as it always has – in its ability to project modern Africa in microcosm, from the confidence and sophistication of muscular Abidjan to the deeply traditional Dan and Baoulé peoples of the rural interior.

C // CAPITAL ZAGREB // POPULATION 4.4 MILLION // AREA 56,594 SQ KM // OFFICIAL LANGUAGE CROATIAN

Croatia

Croatia's idyllic stretch of Adriatic bays, beaches and rocky islets is well and truly buzzing with visitors, and with good reason. In many places the Mediterranean lifestyle of harbourside strolls, seafood and liberally poured wine continues. But Croatia's youthful energy means you'll find little time to siesta in between thought-provoking galleries and some of Europe's best music festivals. Croatian culture has manifold influences – Venetian merchants, Slavic folklore, rugged geography, devout Catholicism and maritime adventurism – all of which contribute to this sun-drenched country of warm stone architecture where oleanders seem to bloom year-round and the water is implausibly clear.

Best time to visit
April to June and September to October

Top things to see
- Dubrovnik, the 'pearl of the Adriatic', a limestone-walled city on the sea
- The sparkling lakes, waterfalls and walkways at Plitvice Lakes National Park
- Diocletian's Palace in Split, an enormous Roman complex now brimming with cafes, plazas and boutique shops
- Zagreb's galleries, churches, museums and kicking nightlife
- Untouched forests and hidden coves on Cres Island

Top things to do
- Sail, catch a ferry, or paddle a canoe along the sublime Adriatic coast
- Hunt truffles, sample the finest olive oil, or just enjoy a slow-food banquet in Istria, Croatia's ecotourism capital
- Get your gear off and plunge into the sea in your birthday suit on the islands off Hvar, and plenty of other spots besides
- Nod and smile at passers-by during the *corso*, the communal, early-evening promenade that happens in every Croatian town

Getting under the skin
Read: *Black Lamb and Grey Falcon* by Rebecca West, a classic Balkan travelogue; or noted journalist Slavenka Drakulić's *Cafe Europa*
Listen: to traditional *tamburica* (lute) music or hit cutting-edge festivals like Hideout and INmusic
Watch: *Armin,* directed by Ognjen Sviličić, a poignant observation of father-son relationships on the road to Zagreb; or *Libertas*, a biopic about a 16th-century poet from Dubrovnik, Marin Držić
Eat: *ćevapčići* (skinless sausages) with hot bread and raw onions; *pašticada* (beef stewed in wine and spices); *paški sir*, a distinctive sheep's cheese made on Pag Island
Drink: Ožujsko or Karlovačko, the two most popular beers; wine from Kvarner or Baranja

In a word
Zdravo (Hello)

Trademarks
Azure seas; Dubrovnik's city walls; baroque cathedrals; terracotta roofs; yachties; islands; music festivals

Random fact
The sea provides a soundtrack in the town of Zadar, where an open-air organ is powered by the movement of the waves

1. The ramparts of Dubrovnik's intimidating Old Town overlook the Adriatic Sea

2. Tourists pause in Dubrovnik's Old Town

3. Water cascades into one of the emerald pools of Plitvice Lakes National Park

C CAPITAL HAVANA // POPULATION 11.1 MILLION // AREA 110,860 SQ KM // OFFICIAL LANGUAGE SPANISH

Cuba

Cuba has been at the centre of intrigue for centuries, from the late 1800s when the US flexed its colonial muscles to its iconic revolution in 1959. Years of isolation have preserved colonial architecture from destruction even as it crumbles, but change is well and truly afoot. Creative entrepreneurs are revolutionising the food, accommodation and arts scene – things unheard of under former president Fidel Castro. Its raucous stew of African, Caribbean and Latin culture lures fans from around the globe as well as sunseekers. While no one can predict how the re-establishment of diplomatic relations between itself and the USA will affect the country, it's inevitable that such a monumental change will forever alter this bizarre, beautiful and beguiling nation.

Best time to visit
November to May, to avoid the heat and hurricanes

Top things to see
- Havana, the steaming, bubbling centre of the nation
- The quieter side of the country in rural Valle de Viñales, with its limestone cliffs, tobacco fields and primordial forest
- Santiago de Cuba, an often-overlooked city with rich traditions as old as colonialism and as recent as the revolution
- Las Parrandas de Remedios (Christmas festival), year-round street-party nights, and languid beach days
- Habana Vieja, Havana's Unesco-recognised ancient quarter, the largest and best-preserved in the Caribbean
- Classic American cars plying the streets and turning them into a '50s film set

Top things to do
- Spend the night in a *casa particular* (private homestay) in a colonial homestead filled with antiques
- Learn how to roll one of the country's fabled cigars at the tobacco plantations in Viñales
- Stroll the impromptu street festival that is Havana's waterfront Malecón
- Cheer on your team of choice at a baseball game rich with talent
- Experience some of the best diving in the world, spying giant lobsters and manatees, at Punta Frances on Isla de la Juventud, an unspoiled wonderland rich with life

Getting under the skin
Read: *Our Man in Havana* by Graham Greene, a classic Cuban spy story; or *Enduring Cuba* by Zoe Bran for an insight into the fascinating country
Listen: to Cuban *son* and Cuban takes on reggaeton, the combo of hip hop, dance-hall and reggae
Watch: everyone's favourite, the hit Havana comedy *Fresa y Chocolate*; or the music documentary *The Buena Vista Social Club*
Eat: homecooked *ajiaco* stew, featuring potatoes, meat, plantains, corn and old beer

Drink: a minty, sweet rum mojito

In a word
Queué bolá assure? (What's up, brother?)

Trademarks
Cigars; rum; salsa; Fidel Castro; communists; vintage American cars; Cuba libre cocktails

Random fact
Baseball was introduced by American dock workers in the late 1800s and remains the national sport; games at stadiums across the nation are, like the country itself, passionate, raucous affairs

1. Colonial architecture and classic American cars in Old Havana

2. Baseball is a national obsession; boys put bat to leather in the streets of Havana

3. Three icons of Cuba: music, cigars and the national flag

Best time to visit
April to May and September to October, avoiding the baking heat of mid-summer

Top things to see
- Frescoes of sword-wielding angels in the Byzantine churches at Pedoulas and Kakopetria
- Amazing mosaics in the Greco-Roman cities of Salamis, Kourion and Pafos
- Mile after mile of untouched golden sand in the remote Karpas (Kırpaşa) Peninsula
- Ten thousand years of treasures in the museums of Nicosia (Lefkosia)
- Echoes of 1975 in the maze-like backstreets of Nicosia, where roads end abruptly at UN sentry posts

Top things to do
- Sip mountain wine in the pine-scented Tröodos Mountains
- Feast on a Cypriot meze in the crescent-shaped harbour at Kyrenia (Girne)
- Gaze in awe at the Frankish churches, Ottoman mosques and Byzantine city walls of Nicosia
- Swim with turtles in the Karpas and Akamas Peninsulas
- Storm the Crusader castles at St Hilarion, Kolossi and Kantara

Getting under the skin
Read: *Journey Into Cyprus* by Colin Thubron or *Bitter Lemons of Cyprus* by Lawrence Durrell for evocative descriptions of pre-partition Cyprus
Listen: to Pelagia Kyriakou's *Paralimnitika* recordings, a superb collection of Cypriot demotic songs
Watch: *Attila 74*, directed by Michael Cacoyannis, or *The Slaughter of the Cock*, by Andreas Pantazis, for insights into the Turkish invasion of 1974
Eat: the classic Cypriot *mezedes* – a pick-and-mix of savoury bites, from fried halloumi cheese to *seftalia* (pork crepinettes)
Drink: the local firewater, distilled from fermented grape skins – Greek Cypriots call it *zivania*, Turkish Cypriots call it *rakı*

In a word
Avrio/yarhun (Tomorrow) – the best time to do anything on this laid-back island

Trademarks
Turkish coffee; fried halloumi; orange groves; Aphrodite; ancient ruins; financial crises; army bases; turtle beaches; the Green Line; DJ bars and hangovers in Agia Napa and Lemesos (Limassol)

Random fact
Around 3% of the island is officially part of Great Britain thanks to the sovereign army bases at Akrotiri and Dekelia

1. A young woman from Kyrenia in traditional Cypriot costume

2. Dramatic cliffs and colourful coral at Cape Greco

3. Agioi Anargyroi, an austere Greek Orthodox church in Paphos

C **CAPITAL** NICOSIA (LEFKOSIA/LEFKOŞA) // **POPULATION** 1.2 MILLION // **AREA** 9251 SQ KM // **OFFICIAL LANGUAGES** GREEK & TURKISH

Cyprus

Basking in balmy seas at the sunny end of the Mediterranean, Cyprus is an island with a split personality. After the Turkish invasion of 1974, this sleepy isle was split into two entities, and despite attempts at rapprochement, the two sides coexist like estranged siblings in different wings of the family home. The southern, Greek-speaking half is a vision of the package-holiday Mediterranean, while the politically isolated Turkish part to the north feels like the year 1975 just popped outside for a glass of raki and never came back. Yet the two sides of Cyprus have more in common than they care to admit: fine beaches and sea turtles, pine-forested mountains, terracotta-tiled villages and more historic ruins than you can shake an amphora at.

1. Connecting Prague Castle and the Old Town, Charles Bridge has spanned the Vltava since the 15th century

2. The sandstone towers of Adršpach-Teplice Rocks are popular with rockclimbers

3. Historic Český Krumlov on the Vltava is a Unesco World Heritage site

C CAPITAL PRAGUE // POPULATION 10.6 MILLION // AREA 78,867 SQ KM // OFFICIAL LANGUAGE CZECH

Czech Republic

There's more to the Czech Republic than Prague, but what a capital city! From the cobbled streets of Staré Město to the architectural majesty of the castle district, Prague could have been plucked from a medieval fairy tale, and even the constant tide of tourists doesn't diminish the magic. Get your Prague fix, then escape to the elegant Renaissance and baroque cities of Olomouc, Český Krumlov and Telč to marvel at the artistic and cultural heights achieved by the sophisticated Czech people. And be sure to make time for the spectacular local beer; the Republic was home to the original Bohemians, and even decades after the fall of communism, it feels like the victory party is still going on.

Best time to visit
April to June, or stunning Christmas time

Top things to see
- Centuries of history and legend in Prague Castle
- The Renaissance facades and Gothic arcades of the old town square in Telč
- Sedlec Ossuary's creepy 'bone chapel', assembled from thousands of human skeletons
- The charm of Olomouc, with its astronomical clock and religious architecture
- Elegant Český Krumlov on the serpentine bends of the Vltava River

Top things to do
- Stride out across Prague's iconic Charles Bridge
- Savour a hoppy ale in Plzeň, home of the original pilsner, and České Budějovice
- Ponder the sad fate of European Jewish communities in the cemetery of Josefov
- Explore the richly forested hills of Šumava on foot or mountain bike
- Take a treatment and mix with B-list celebrities in the elegant spas of Karlovy Vary

Getting under the skin
Read: *The Book of Laughter and Forgetting* by Milan Kundera on communist Czechoslovakia
Listen: to Antonín Dvořák's *Slavonic Dances*, or his religious masterpiece *Stabat Mater*
Watch: *Kolya*, an Academy Award–winning tale set during the Velvet Revolution
Eat: *knedlícky* (dumplings) and *svícková na smetaně* (roast beef with sour cream and cranberries)
Drink: *pivo* (beer) at countless breweries and raffish pubs throughout the county

In a word
Dobrý den (Good day)

Trademarks
Astronomical clocks; Good King Wenceslas; spa towns; the Velvet Revolution; Europe's best beer

Random fact
The sugar cube was invented in the former Czechoslovakia

D CAPITAL COPENHAGEN // POPULATION 5.6 MILLION // AREA 43,094 SQ KM // OFFICIAL LANGUAGE DANISH

Denmark

Neat, easily navigable and just plain nice, Denmark's big advantage is its user-friendliness. Its history is impeccably preserved, as numerous castles and medieval towns testify, but it's also state-of-the-art: a slick approach to design, forward-looking social developments, smooth-running public transport and chic restaurants. This blend fosters the nation's distinctive style and wins it a regular chart-topping place among the happiest nations on earth. You won't have to search hard to find some much-prized *hygge*: a sense of cosiness, camaraderie and contentment. But *hygge* comes with a dash of introspectiveness, and perhaps this has given rise to the country's colourful legacy of fairy tales: with all those fortresses about, you won't need to wander long to run into a scene straight out of Hans Christian Andersen.

Best time to visit
May to September

Top things to see
- Charming cobblestoned streets in Ribe, Denmark's oldest town
- Danish style personified in the streets, stores and eateries of Copenhagen
- Viking history up close and personal at Roskilde's Viking Ship Museum
- The gleaming white chalk cliffs of Møns Klint

Top things to do
- Escape to the beaches and bike trails of the island of Bornholm
- Stand with one foot in the Skagerrak (North Sea), the other in the Kattegat (Baltic Sea), at postcard-pretty Skagen
- Join 100,000 others at the Roskilde Festival, northern Europe's biggest music event
- Dine in one of Copenhagen's famous foodie hot spots – restaurants here match Madrid or Rome for Michelin stars
- Go kite-surfing at Denmark's 'Cold Hawaii', Klitmøller

Getting under the skin
Read: *Miss Smilla's Feeling for Snow* by Peter Hoeg or, for a change of pace, Hans Christian Andersen's fairy tales
Listen: to indie rockers Veto; or singer-songwriter Broken Twin
Watch: Academy Award winner *Babette's Feast*; *After the Wedding*; anything directed by Lars von Trier; or gritty detective drama series *Forbrydelsen* (The Killing)
Eat: *smørrebrød* (open-faced sandwich); *frikadeller* (Danish meatballs); *sild* (pickled herring); and of course Danish pastries, known locally as *wienerbrød* (Vienna bread)
Drink: *øl* (beer – the biggies are Carlsberg and Tuborg); or *akvavit* (schnapps)

In a word
Det var hyggeligt! (That was cosy!)

Trademarks
Akvavit; Danish pastries; furniture design from the likes of Arne Jacobsen and Hans Wegner; Hans Christian Andersen fairy tales; Lego; Vikings

Random fact
Denmark really does have an extraordinary inventive streak: many innovative creations including the loudspeaker, magnetic storage and Lego have Danish roots

1. The 17th- and 18th-century townhouses of Copenhagen's Nyhavn

2. ARoS Aarhus Kunstmuseum's translucent walkway

3. An abandoned lighthouse overlooking the North Sea

4. Danish literary icon, Hans Christian Andersen, surveying the streets of Odense

D CAPITAL DJIBOUTI CITY // POPULATION 792,198 // AREA 23,200 SQ KM // OFFICIAL LANGUAGES FRENCH & ARABIC

Djibouti

All good things come to an end – although few endings will be as epic a show as Djibouti's. Straddling the meeting point of three diverging tectonic plates, Djibouti is currently being ripped apart by Mother Nature: fumaroles spew steam from the earth's insides; magma seethes beneath ever-thinning crust; and its dramatic, lunar-like deserts are collapsing. In geological terms, it is occurring at breakneck pace. In human terms, it is in spectacularly slow motion – a reason to make travel plans, not to cancel them! The intoxicating culture, dominated by Somali and Afar peoples, is peppered with influences from Arabia, India and Europe. Meanwhile, setting the speed of life to 'unhurried' is *qat*, a mild narcotic herb that's a national obsession.

Best time to visit
November to mid-April, when temperatures are tolerable

Top things to see
- Afar tribesmen gathering gleaming salt crystals from the blinding floor of Lac Assal
- Whale sharks swimming silently past you in the Gulf of Tadjoura
- French legionnaires rubbing shoulders with traditionally robed tribesmen in the streets of Djibouti City
- The ancient juniper forests in the national park of Fôret du Day, one of Djibouti's rare spectacles of green

Top things to do
- Search for heaven-sent shadows in the otherworldly landscape that is Lac Abbé
- Absorb the Arabian atmosphere of Tadjoura, a coastal town fringed with palms
- Remember to breathe while floating among an armada of manta rays in the Ghoubbet al-Kharab
- Stand on the 'bridge of lava', perhaps the thinnest piece of the earth's crust
- Follow in the footsteps of Afar nomads along the ancient salt route

Getting under the skin
Read: *Le Pays Sans Ombre,* a series of short stories by Djiboutian Abdourahman Waberi – non-French speakers can pick up Jeanne Garane's English translation, *The Land Without Shadows*
Listen: to the solo guitar of Aïdarous, Djibouti's leader of modern music
Watch: *Total Eclipse,* a film – partly shot in Djibouti – that follows the tumultuous life of French poet Arthur Rimbaud
Eat: *cabri farci* (stuffed kid) roasted on a spit; or *poisson yéménite* (fish suppers served in newspaper)
Drink: black coffee; or tea with lemon

In a word
Tasharrafna (Pleased to meet you)

Trademarks
Salt lakes; fumaroles; *qat;* $5 cucumbers; whale sharks; French and American military presence

Random fact
It has been estimated that 40% of an average family's expenditure is spent on *qat,* and over two months of productivity is lost per worker per year due to its effects

1. An Afar camel caravan skirting the salt-encrusted edges of Lake Assal, before heading west towards Ethiopia

2. Volcanic cones rise above the cove of Ghoubbet el-Kharab (the Devil's Throat)

3. A mother and child from Balho, near the border with Ethiopia

1. The lush, vertiginous topography of Morne Trois Pitons National Park

2. Dominica's picturesque capital, Roseau, taken pre-Hurricane Maria

3. The perfect swimming hole? Emerald Pool, Morne Trois Pitons National Park

(D) CAPITAL ROSEAU // POPULATION 73,286 // AREA 754 SQ KM // OFFICIAL LANGUAGE ENGLISH

Dominica

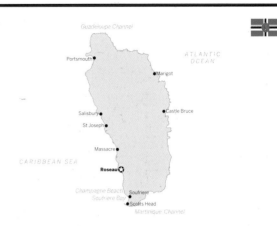

Wedged between the two modern, French-speaking and very heavily developed Caribbean islands of Martinique and Guadeloupe, Dominica is a different world: wild, poor and staggeringly beautiful, this former British colony still sees locals get dressed up in their Sunday best for the walk to church, while its harbours house far more fishing boats than yachts. The island is still recovering from a succession of devastating blows from hurricanes, and visits here require patience and a solid sense of adventure. The reward is a walker's paradise: mountainous and shrouded in lush jungle, Dominica overflows with waterfalls, lakes and rushing rivers, while twisting dirt roads and scattered villages create a mood of isolation that's an escapist's fantasy.

Best time to visit
Outside of hurricane season, mild trade winds keep Dominica beautifully pleasant

Top things to see
- Cabrits National Park, encompassing 18th-century British Fort Shirley, swamps and coral reefs
- Morne Trois Pitons National Park, famed for its incredible volcanic scenery
- Emerald Pool, a crystalline jungle pool at the base of a waterfall
- Scotts Head, a minnow-sized fishing village on dramatic Soufriere Bay
- The Macoucherie Distillery, the country's most famous rum producer

Top things to do
- Plunge into thick jungle alive with birdlife, rushing rivers and waterfalls
- Wonder at the natural fizz of the waters below the surface while diving at Champagne Beach
- Traverse deep canyons on a trek to Trafalgar Falls
- Percolate in the wonderfully named Boiling Lake, directly above a lava-filled crack in the earth's crust
- Serenely glide alongside whales on a sailing boat

Getting under the skin
Read: *Voyage in the Dark* by Jean Rhys; or Dominica's other noted novelist, Phyllis Shand Allfrey, who is best known for *The Orchid House*
Listen: to African *soukous*, Louisiana zydeco and a variety of local bands at the annual World Creole Music Festival in Roseau
Watch: the second and third *Pirates of the Caribbean* movies for scenes shot in Dominica
Eat: *callaloo* soup (a creamy concoction made with dasheen leaves)
Drink: fruit punch made with fresh fruit and rum

In a word
Irie (Hi, bye, cool)

Trademarks
Diving; bananas; rainforests; cricket; Creole culture; undiscovered areas, Sunday processions to church

Random fact
Dominica's national bird, the Sisserou parrot, is the largest of all the Amazon parrots and thrives in trees along the island's 200 rivers

Best time to visit
December to July (to avoid the hurricane season)

Top things to see
- Santo Domingo's Zona Colonial, Spain's original stepping stone into the New World
- Humpback whales, which gather every January to March to mate and give birth at Península de Samaná
- The white sand and turquoise waters of Playa Rincón, one of the Caribbean's finest beaches
- Carnival, celebrated most raucously in Santo Domingo, Santiago and La Vega
- Damajagua, a cascade of 27 waterfalls tumbling into glorious limestone pools

Top things to do
- Dive beneath the waves to explore the coast's myriad reefs and wrecks
- Pick up the Atlantic breeze at the kitesurfing heaven of Playa Cabarete
- Go for the home run at a baseball match, the DR's (other) national religion
- Put on your dancing shoes to the heady rhythms of the merengue clubs
- Buzz from the adrenaline rush of white-water rafting on the Río Yaque del Norte

Getting under the skin
Read: Junot Díaz's *The Brief and Wonderful Life of Oscar Wao*, about a Dominican-American family in New Jersey; or *In the Time of the Butterflies*, a novel by Julia Alvarez about life under the Trujillo regime
Listen: to merengue legends Johnny Venture and Coco Band; or *bachata* (popular guitar music based on bolero rhythms) stars Raulín Rodriguez and Juan Luís Guerra
Watch: *Sugar* by Anna Boden and Ryan Fleck, about a Dominican baseball player going to the USA to play in the minor leagues
Eat: *la bandera* ('the flag') – red beans, white rice and green plantain with meat stew
Drink: beer – a cold glass of Presidente at a sidewalk bar is a quintessentially Dominican experience

In a word
¡Que chulo! (Great!)

Trademarks
Palm-lined beaches; plantains; merengue; rum; cigars that are better than but not as famous as those from Cuba; Sammy Sosa

Random fact
The foundation stone of Santo Domingo's Catedral Primada de América was laid in 1514, making it the oldest cathedral in the Americas

1. In the far east of the island you will find the white-sand beaches of Playa Blanca

2. A folk dancer from the southern city of La Romana

3. The idyllic village of Mano Juan on Saona Island is the perfect place to escape

D   **CAPITAL** SANTO DOMINGO // **POPULATION** 10.3 MILLION // **AREA** 48,670 SQ KM // **OFFICIAL LANGUAGE** SPANISH

Dominican Republic

Dominicans will tell you that it's no accident their country is one of the most popular tourist destinations in the Caribbean. What's not to like? they'd ask, pulling you out for a night soaked in rum and merengue dancing. It's a hard argument to dispute. Santo Domingo boasts colonial architecture dating back to the time of Columbus, the coast is fringed with white beaches and scuba diving sites, while the more energetic can delve into the lush green interior to trek along mountain trails. In a country that lists baseball diamonds alongside churches as hallowed ground, you can expect fun to be taken seriously – why else insist on having not one but two annual carnival celebrations?

115

Best time to visit
May to December on the mainland, or January to April for the Galápagos

Top things to see
- The splendid colonial centres of Quito and Cuenca, Unesco World Heritage sites with foundations dating back to the 16th century
- Ecuador's Amazon rainforest, a vast region of unsurpassed biodiversity
- The 5897m-high Volcán Cotopaxi, best seen from atop a horse or from the windows of a colonial mountainside hacienda
- Cloud forest reserves like those around Mindo or Parque Nacional Sumaco-Galeras, in which hundreds of bird species have been recorded

Top things to do
- Go wildlife watching in the Galápagos Islands and see giant tortoises, water-loving iguanas and sea lions
- Hike the Andes amid the striking scenery of the Quilotoa Loop
- Browse for handicrafts in Otavalo, one of Latin America's largest craft markets
- Take to the rails on the impressively revamped train between Quito in the Andes and coastal Guayaquil

Getting under the skin
Read: *Selected Poems of Jorge Carrera Andrade*, profound verse from one of Latin America's most influential poets, now widely translated
Listen: to Morfeo, a Guayaquil-based band combining dreamy folk-rock with world music
Watch: Tania Hermida's *Que Tan Lejos?* (How Much Further?), a road movie about two young women on an unplanned journey of self-discovery in the highlands
Eat: *encocado* (Afro-Ecuadorian seafood stew cooked with coconut milk and spices)
Drink: *canelazo*, a warming drink of hot *aguardiente* (sugar-cane alcohol) served with cinnamon, sugar and citrus

In a word
Naturaleza (Nature)

Trademarks
The Galápagos Islands; Panama hats; pan pipes; chocolate

Random fact
Tiny Ecuador is home to some 300 mammal species and over 1600 bird species – more than Europe and North America combined

1. The striking Galápagos land iguana, endemic to the Galápagos Islands

2. Pinnacle Rock on Bartolomé Island, Galápagos Islands

3. If you're after a Panama hat, you've come to the right place: a shop in Cuenca

E CAPITAL QUITO // POPULATION 15.4 MILLION // AREA 283,561 SQ KM // OFFICIAL LANGUAGE SPANISH

Ecuador & The Galápagos Islands

This Andean nation appears diminutive beside its far larger neighbours, yet there are years' worth of diversions packed between its Amazonian rainforest, bird-rich cloud forests, 5000m-plus peaks sprinkled with volcanoes and awe-inspiring tropical coastline, including the nature lover's paradise of the Galápagos Islands. Ecuador's cultural diversity is equally varied. A dozen indigenous groups, a sizeable Afro-Ecuadorian population and more recent immigrants from Asia each offer their own take on the quintessential Ecuadorian experience. Add highland towns renowned for textiles, laid-back fishing villages thrumming with cumbia, rivers boasting South America's best white-water rafting and some stunningly situated jungle lodges, and you've got a very colourful travel experience.

Best time to visit
October to May to avoid the heat

Top things to see
- Pyramids of Giza, the last intact Ancient Wonder of the World, and don't forget the Sphinx
- Ancient Egypt's heartland, Luxor, from the Valley of the Kings to the sublime Karnak Temple
- Cairo, the clamorous 'Mother of the World', with mosques, mausoleums and the Egyptian Museum
- The Abu Simbel temple complex, arguably the single most beautiful landmark from Ancient Egypt
- Siwa, one of the Sahara's most beguiling oasis towns, rich in ancient myths

Top things to do
- Dive or snorkel in the Red Sea, in an unbelievable world beneath the water
- Climb to the summit and watch the sunrise from Mount Sinai
- Spend days drifting down the Nile aboard a felucca (traditional sailing boat)
- Drive out into the White Desert from the western oasis of Bahariya
- Go on a camel safari with the Bedouin in Sinai

Getting under the skin
Read: Naguib Mahfouz's *The Cairo Trilogy*; Bahaa Taher's Siwa-set novel *Sunset Oasis*; and Alaa Al Aswany's masterful *The Yacoubian Building*
Listen: to Umm Kolthum, forever Egypt's diva
Watch: Oscar-nominated documentary *The Square* by Jehane Noujaim, and the acclaimed *678* by Mohamed Diab, both windows into modern Egypt
Eat: *fuul* (salty fava bean paste); *taamia* (felafel); or *kushari* (noodles, rice, black lentils and dried onions, served with a fiery tomato sauce)
Drink: *karkadai* (hibiscus) juice, mint tea and *ahwa* (Arabic coffee)

In a word
Inshallah (God willing)

Trademarks
Pyramids and pharaohs; King Tut and Cleopatra; Nile journeys and camels into the desert; world-class diving; souq shopping; incessant honking

Random fact
Don't pack your brolly – Egypt is the driest country in Africa with average annual rainfall of less than 51mm

1. Traditional feluccas ply the Nile near Aswan

2. A mud-brick hotel in the delightful oasis of Siwa

3. Two gentlemen relax in a sheesha cafe

4. The Pyramids of Giza: a sight more than 5500 years old

E CAPITAL CAIRO // POPULATION 85.3 MILLION // AREA 1,001,450 SQ KM // OFFICIAL LANGUAGE ARABIC

Egypt

Egypt is a colossus and a crossroads of continents. Its history reads like a grand epic and the country is rich in signposts to this story, from the peerless glories of Ancient Egypt to the jewels of Islamic Cairo, where the call to prayer will transport you back centuries. Even Egypt's geography has the quality of a myth, from the Sahara and its mysterious Cave of Swimmers or the Nile, that great river of legend, to the rich marine life of the Red Sea coast. But Egypt is above all a place where many worlds – Middle Eastern, African and Mediterranean – collide, in an intoxicating and sometimes overwhelming full-tilt frenzy. Dive into its squiggling souqs, donkey-filled backroads and chaotic city streets, then come up for air atop a vast desert dune – you won't be disappointed.

Best time to visit
November to April (the dry season)

Top things to see
- Hot springs, highland coffee farms and artists' workshops on the Ruta de las Flores
- The hours' quiet passage in Alegría, the country's mountain-top flower capital
- Rugged ridges and mountain grandeur in Parque Nacional El Imposible
- The bucolic highland town of San Ignacio, in the shadow of the nation's highest peak.
- Dreamy white-sand beaches around La Libertad

Top things to do
- Conquer the longest break in Central America at surfing mecca Punta Roca
- Sample marinated rabbit or grilled frog at colonial Juayúa's popular weekend food festival
- Strike up a conversation with an ex-guerrilla guide at the Museo de la Revolución Salvadoreña in Perquín
- Shop for *sorpresas* (intricate folk scenes carved in ceramic shells)
- Hike up to the volcanic crater lake at Volcán Santa Ana

Getting under the skin
Read: the bold erotic poems of Claudia Lars; or *Salvador* by Joan Didion, about the early days of the civil war
Listen: to pre-Hispanic fusion, cumbia and new-wave ska in San Salvador's progressive music scene
Watch: *Salvador*, the story of a war correspondent directed by Oliver Stone, for Hollywood's insights into the civil war; *Romero*, with Raul Julia, a true story about the high price of opposing tyrannical leadership
Eat: *pupusas* (cornmeal pockets filled with farmer's cheese, refried beans or pork rinds)
Drink: *refrescos de ensalada* (juices with chunks of fresh fruit)

In a word
Que chivo (How cool)

Trademarks
Hot surf spots; *pupusas*; Ruta de las Flores; woodcrafts; volcanoes

Random fact
Over a third of El Salvadorans live and work abroad, sending US$3 billion home yearly in remittances to support their families

1. A *historiante* prepares for a traditional celebration of the co-patron saint of the town of Apastepeque

2. The radically beautiful stained-glass windows of Iglesia El Rosario, San Salvador

3. Plaza Libertad, the Monumento de los Heroes and the domed San Salvador Cathedral

E **CAPITAL** SAN SALVADOR // **POPULATION** 6.1 MILLION // **AREA** 21,041 SQ KM // **OFFICIAL LANGUAGE** SPANISH

El Salvador

Resilient, real and sometimes raw, El Salvador is strong coffee for the senses. Ambivalent about the country's hardships and the not-so-distant civil war, most travellers have kept their distance. But the frank talk of war survivors is juxtaposed with artists' whimsical folk carvings in the brightly-painted towns of the Ruta de las Flores (Route of the Flowers), or the recycled US school buses done up as psychedelic chariots. More than anywhere else in Central America, this is a chance to dismount from the beaten path and see the region for what it is – in all its grittiness, gaudiness and, sometimes, just plain gorgeousness. And El Salvador does stash some surprises up its sleeves: countless volcanic mountains, swimming holes, exquisite handicrafts and a wild Pacific coast.

E CAPITAL LONDON // POPULATION 53 MILLION // AREA 130,373 SQ KM // OFFICIAL LANGUAGE ENGLISH

England

The British Empire spread English culture around the globe, but this is where it all started, from the cricket bats to the bowler hats. The largest of the four nations that make up the United Kingdom, England is famous for football and fine art, film makers and fashionistas, real ale and roast beef, live bands and dead playwrights, a nice cup of tea and the BBC, the Ministry of Sound and the Ministry of Silly Walks, Queen, *the* Queen, pearly kings and queens, and 4000 years of history. And the jibes about stodgy food? They're a thing of the past too, thanks to a wave of celebrated chefs and a population that's starting to care about what's on its plate.

Best time to visit
May to September

Top things to see
- In London, make time for St Paul's, the Tate Modern, the British Museum and a bar crawl through Shoreditch
- A gig by the 'next big thing' at the Leadmill in Sheffield or the Kazimier in Liverpool
- Giddy views over the Lake District from the top of Scafell Pike
- A home game at Arsenal, Chelsea or Manchester United
- The gorgeous gothic cathedrals at York, Durham and Lincoln

Top things to do
- Relive Spinal Tap's finest hour at Stonehenge, England's most iconic prehistoric monument
- Laze away a sunny afternoon drinking bitter beer at an English country pub
- Soak up classical history in the Roman baths at Bath
- Go crazy for curry in Birmingham's 'Balti Triangle'
- Slurp on a stick of seaside rock on Brighton Pier

Getting under the skin
Read: Charles Dickens for historical context; and *The English* by Jeremy Paxman for a contemporary exploration of the English psyche
Listen: to the English take on England by adding the Kinks, Kate Bush, Pulp, Dizzee Rascal and the Arctic Monkeys to your playlist
Watch: *The Madness of King George*, directed by Nicholas Hytner, and *This is England*, directed by Shane Meadows, for contrasting explorations of English culture
Eat: a pickled egg, munch some dry-roasted peanuts and nibble on a bag of pork scratchings for the full English pub experience
Drink: a craft beer from a growing number of independent breweries – look for Kernel in London, Sharp's in Cornwall and local brews in every other English county

In a word
Cheers!

Trademarks
The weather; the white cliffs of Dover; ageing rockers; the Royal Family; fish and chips; Beefeaters; cool clubs; period dramas; binge-drinking; the full English breakfast; James Bond; Wimbledon, Wembley and cricket at Lord's

Random fact
The closest language to English is Frisian, spoken by 500,000 people in Germany, Denmark and the Netherlands

1. Walltown Crags has one of the finest sections of Hadrian's Wall

2. A pint and dominoes at the Tunnel House Inn, Cirencester

3. The rugged shoreline of Kynance Cove, Lizard peninsula, Cornwall

4. The Baroque Tower Ballroom, Blackpool Tower

Best time to visit
December to February for Bioko Island; May to September for Rio Muni

Top things to see
- Hâkâ, the lengthy sandbar that snakes into the dark depths of the Atlantic from Isla Corisco's palm-dotted southeastern shore
- The seemingly irrepressible wave of Westernisation rolling back each evening as the streets of Bata come alive with Equatoguineans
- The tug of war between natural beauty and the oil industry off Bioko's coast
- Plaza de España and the colonial cathedral in the heart of Malabo

Top things to do
- Push your way through the jungle's undergrowth in Monte Alen National Park while on a quest for gorillas, chimpanzees and forest elephants
- Step gently into a pirogue and explore the wild fringes of the Estuario del Muni near Gabon's frontier
- Settle into the bleached sands and soak up what the peaceful heavens have to offer on Isla Corisco's deserted beaches
- Trek through the fern-tree forests on the volcanic slopes near Moka

Getting under the skin
Read: *The Wonga Coup: Guns, Thugs and a Ruthless Determination to Create Mayhem in an Oil-Rich Corner of Africa* by Adam Roberts – the title says it all
Listen: to the lyrics of Eyi Moan Ndong and his chorus, accompanied by drums and the *mvet* (a cross between a zither and harp)
Watch: the first feature film made in the country, 2014's award-winning *Where the Road Runs Out*, about a scientist who decides to discover his roots in Equatorial Guinea
Eat: seafood plucked from the ocean that very day
Drink: *osang* (local tea); or *malamba*, brewed from sugar cane

In a word
Mbôlo (Hello, in Fang)

Trademarks
An unbridled oil industry; corrupt officials; attempted coups; continental rainforests; gorillas; Eric Moussambani (aka 'Eric the Eel', for his heroically slow 100m freestyle at the Sydney 2000 Olympic Games)

Random fact
The decision to disqualify the national football team from the 2015 African Cup of Nations for fielding an ineligible player was reversed when Equatorial Guinea took over as host from Morocco (which had withdrawn over Ebola fears) – the Nzalang Nacional (National Thunder) ended up reaching the semi-finals

1. De Brazza's monkeys can be found throughout the country

2. A young girl from the port city of Bata; 60% of Equatorial Guineans are under the age of 24

3. Lush jungle on the south coast of the oil-rich Bioko Island

E CAPITAL MALABO // POPULATION 722,254 // AREA 28,051 SQ KM // OFFICIAL LANGUAGES SPANISH & FRENCH

Equatorial Guinea

A country of two worlds, Equatorial Guinea is divided not only by sea but also by oil. Large reserves of black gold were discovered beneath the ocean's floor off the coast of Bioko Island in the mid-1990s, and the subsequent industrial development forever changed the island's landscape, economy and culture. The country's mainland (Rio Muni), however, is much the same as it has been for centuries. For those who don't mind being treated like they're a potential foreign mercenary, Rio Muni's wild jungles, remote villages and pristine beaches are an authentic adventure into the Africa of old.

1. Two young girls from the Rashaida tribe of northern Eritrea

2. Camels transport wood to market in the central city of Keren

3. Women celebrate the Christian Festival of Timkat in Assab

E // **CAPITAL** ASMARA // **POPULATION** 6.2 MILLION // **AREA** 117,600 SQ KM // **OFFICIAL LANGUAGES** TIGRINYA, ARABIC & ENGLISH

Eritrea

Now one of the world's most secretive countries, Eritrea seems locked in a time capsule. But behind the repressive political climate and tricky travel restrictions (you need a permit just to leave the capital), it still offers travellers some hard-earned rewards. The art deco architecture in Asmara from the 1930s is nothing short of dazzling, as are the vestiges of truly ancient times – numerous archaeological sites are found in the quintessentially Abyssinian landscape of escarpments, peaks and plateaus. Although the nine ethnic groups that make up the nation's diverse cultural fabric all face economic hardships, they are always welcoming and a highlight for those who make the effort to visit.

Best time to visit
October to May, when temperatures have cooled

Top things to see
- Inspired examples of art deco, expressionist, cubist and neoclassical Italian architecture in Asmara, the 'Piccolo Roma'
- The Temple of Mariam Wakiro, one of the ancient archaeological ruins in Qohaito
- Debre Libanos, an extraordinary 6th-century monastery embedded into a lofty cliff face
- *Passeggiata*, an evening ritual when the people of Asmara take to the streets to stroll

Top things to do
- Get cosy with corals while diving the depths of the Dahlak Archipelago
- Imagine you have departed earth among the stark, otherwordly wonders of Dankalia
- Inhale the aromas (and a macchiato or two) in the art deco cafes on Asmara's Harnet Ave
- Wend through the whitewashed buildings, porticoes and arcades of the island of Massawa

Getting under the skin
Read: *I Didn't Do it for You: How the World Used and Abused a Small African Nation* by Michela Wrong, an entertaining and angering portrayal of Eritrea
Listen: to *Greatest Hits* by Atewebrhan Segid, Eritrea's leading traditional musician and singer
Watch: *Heart of Fire*, a film based on the real life of a young female soldier in Eritrea's civil war
Eat: *legamat*, deep-fried dough balls sold hot in newspaper cones
Drink: a piping-hot macchiato

In a word
Selam (Hello, in Tigrinya)

Trademarks
Infallible politeness; classic art deco architecture; marvellous macchiatos; conflict with Ethiopia; Africa's North Korea; mass emigration

Random fact
Having fought together as friends to finally defeat

the Derg in 1991, Eritrea's President Isaias and Ethiopia's Prime Minister Zenawi soon waged war against each other – the trigger was Eritrea's decision to introduce its own currency

Ⓔ CAPITAL TALLINN // POPULATION 1.2 MILLION // AREA 45,228 SQ KM // OFFICIAL LANGUAGE ESTONIAN

Estonia

Gutsy Estonia has long stood apart from its neighbours, with its unique language and culture having survived all that history has thrown at it, whether it be occupation by Sweden, the Nazis or the Soviet Union. Now in its third decade of independence, this nation on the edge of the EU is at once fantastically modern and charmingly old fashioned. Soaking up Tallinn's long white nights and medieval history, or exploring the country's coastline, are joys to be savoured. Superb national parks get you back to paganistic nature, quaint villages evoke a timeless sense of history, and uplifting song festivals celebrate age-old traditions.

Best time to visit
May to September

Top things to see
- The chocolate-box confection of Tallinn's medieval Old Town
- The bucolic splendour of Lahemaa National Park, with its manor houses and slices of deserted coastline
- Live music at the hugely popular midsummer Viljandi Folk Music Festival
- The futuristic, award-winning KUMU art museum in Tallinn's Kadriorg Park

Top things to do
- Island-hop along the west coast, ensuring a visit to both Saaremaa and Hiiumaa
- Go bog-shoe-walking and canoeing in the wetlands of Soomaa National Park
- Do a spot of cross-country skiing in the picturesque countryside around Otepää
- Get sand in your shorts at Pärnu, the country's summertime mecca
- Down a beer among students in the university town of Tartu

Getting under the skin
Read: *The Czar's Madman* by Jaan Kross, Estonia's most internationally acclaimed author; *Between Each Breath* by Adam Thorpe, in which Tallinn and the Estonian islands provide the setting for an Englishman's midlife crisis
Listen: to the austere but stunning music of contemporary composer Arvo Pärt
Watch: *Sügisball* (Autumn Ball), based on a 1979 novel portraying six residents of a drab high-rise apartment in Soviet-era Tallinn
Eat: *verivorst* (blood sausages) if you're feeling bloodthirsty; pork and potatoes (it's on every menu); smoked fish; fresh summer berries
Drink: Vana Tallinn – few know what this syrupy liqueur is made from, but it's sweet and strong and best served in coffee, or over ice with milk

In a word
Terviseks! (Cheers!)

Trademarks
A fiendishly difficult language; folk tales; the sport of *kiiking*; Skype (it was invented here); saunas; song festivals; Vana Tallinn

Random fact
Estonians invented the weird and wonderful sport of *kiiking*, whereby competitors stand on a swing and attempt to complete a 360-degree loop around the top bar

1. Snow dusts the rooftops of Tallinn's Old Town

2. Song and dance celebrations are old and important traditions for Estoni; a gathering in Harju County

3. Rich farming country in Seidla, Järva County

Best time to visit
October to January, when the watered highlands are blooming marvellous

Top things to see
- Endemic walia ibex butting heads on a dramatic Abyssinian precipice in the Simien Mountains
- The vibrant tribes of the Omo Valley
- Africa's Camelot and its emperors' 17th-century castles in Gonder
- Hyenas being fed outside the fabled gates of the walled city of Harar
- Lake Chamo's crocodile market – be careful, the reptiles are the ones shopping

Top things to do
- Flirt with gravity when climbing to reach Tigray's most precariously positioned church, Abuna Yemata Guh
- Island hop across Lake Tana to visit remote, centuries-old monastic churches
- Step into the medieval shadows to see Lalibela's light, its 11 rock-hewn churches
- Soak up the ambience during a traditional coffee ceremony
- Emerge from Aksumite tombs and stare skyward at the ancient civilisation's stelae

Getting under the skin
Read: *Wax and Gold* by Donald N Levine, which offers an insightful look into Amharic culture
Listen: to *The Very Best of the Éthiopiques*, a compilation of evocative Ethiopian jazz
Watch: Mary Olive Smith's documentary *A Walk to Beautiful*, the telling journey of five outcast women rebuilding their lives
Eat: *injera* (rubbery, sponge-like flatbread of national importance) laden with *berbere*-spiced beef and *gomen* (minced spinach)
Drink: superb coffee (the bean is thought to have originated here)

In a word
Ishee (OK, hello, goodbye) – or with a smile it's a gesture of friendliness and goodwill

Trademarks
Ethiopian Orthodox Church; rock-hewn churches; African castles; stelae; the coffee ceremony; 'bleeding heart' baboons; Abyssinia; middle- and long-distance runners

Random facts
When the Ethiopian People's Revolutionary Democratic Front tanks rolled into Addis Ababa in 1991, they were navigating with the map in Lonely Planet's *Africa on a Shoestring*

1. Ground-dwelling gelada baboons are only found in the Ethiopian Highlands

2. The colourful Procession of Timkat, a Christian Orthodox tradition in Addis Ababa

3. Pilgrims circle the remarkable rock-hewn Church of St George, Lalibela

E   **CAPITAL** ADDIS ABABA // **POPULATION** 93.9 MILLION // **AREA** 1,104,300 SQ KM // **OFFICIAL LANGUAGES** AMHARIC

Ethiopia

Ethiopia proudly blurs the line between present and past. As the oldest sovereign state in Africa, and having successfully routed Italian armies seeking colonisation, it is understandable that Ethiopians embrace their ancient rituals and all the relics associated with their 2000-year-old civilisation. Ornate, rock-hewn churches dating back to the first millennium AD are not simply showpieces of past grandeur – they are active places of daily worship, hosting age-old ceremonies for locals. The historical treasures pepper a dramatic, mountainous landscape where dozens of animal species seen nowhere else on earth play. For the traveller, entering this unique world, with its own culture, language, script, calendar, timekeeping and wildlife, is as exciting as it is enlightening.

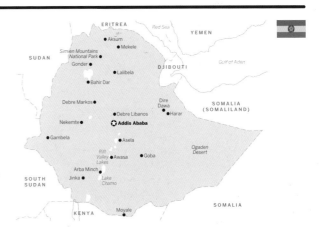

F CAPITAL STANLEY // POPULATION 3140 // AREA 12,173 SQ KM // OFFICIAL LANGUAGE ENGLISH

Falkland Islands

Rising bleakly from the South Atlantic, 490km east of Patagonia, the Falklands are one of the remotest vestiges of the former British Empire. First-timers to the 700-odd islands the Argentinians call the Islas Malvinas can be taken aback by the explicit touchstones of English culture to be found in the capital, Stanley – cosy pubs, a reverence for tea, and the unmistakable scarlet silos of the Royal Mail. Beyond this enclave, however, they're more likely to encounter damp, stoical sheep, and colonies of seals, albatrosses and penguins, all staying warm as best they can in this land of harsh and unforgettable beauty.

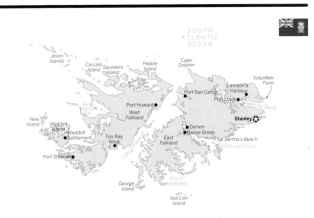

Best time to visit
October to March

Top things to see
- Stanley's ramshackle assemblage of buildings and distinctly English pubs
- Saunders Island, a birdwatching wonderland, home to five species of penguin, plus black-browed albatross and cormorants
- The white sands of Bertha's Beach, to spot dolphins and gentoo penguins
- Goose Green and nearby Darwin, where some of the fiercest fighting occurred in the Falklands War

Top things to do
- Hike to the summit of Mt Usborne, offering expansive views over Cape Dolphin and the Berkeley Sound
- Photograph sea lions and elephant seals on the aptly named Sea Lion Island
- Get to know the penguins of Carcass Island which, hosting no predators, is a haven for flightless birds
- Take a scenic stroll around Gypsy Cove, taking in views over Yorke Bay and Mt Lowe

Getting under the skin
Read: *A Falkland Islander Till I Die* by Terrence Severine Betts, a fascinating portrait of life on the islands from the 1950s to the 1982 invasion and up to the present
Listen: to Ian Strange's evocative collection of animal calls on *South Atlantic Islands: A Portrait of Falkland Islands Wildlife*
Watch: *An Ungentlemanly Act*, an eye-opening film describing behind-the-scenes events leading up to the Falklands War
Eat: deep-sea delights such as squid and Patagonian toothfish; and local, organic lamb and beef
Drink: a cup of tea during a regular smoko (traditional tea break)

In a word
All right, *che*? (How are you, friend?)

Trademarks
Sea lion colonies; penguin mating grounds; snow-covered islands; near-dark winters; sheep; rain; snow and plenty of it

Random fact
Anywhere outside of Stanley is known as 'camp', from the Spanish word *campo* (countryside): with over 500,000 sheep scattered across camp, ovines outnumber humans by around 200 to one

1. A raucous colony of black-browed albatrosses

2. Rambling Government House in Stanley, home to many English governors and one Argentine commander

3. A remote settlement on tiny New Island

3. Gentoo penguins march in single file

3

4

Best time to visit
May to October, when rainfall and humidity are lower

Top things to see
- Navala, Fiji's most picturesque traditional village
- Indo-Fijians walking across glowing coals at the South Indian fire-walking festival
- Taveuni's lush tropical flora and beautifully weathered mountains
- The immense windswept Sigatoka Sand Dunes on Viti Levu
- Orchids, walking tracks and lily ponds at the Garden of the Sleeping Giant

Top things to do
- Dive or snorkel with manta rays at Kadavu's Great Astrolabe Reef
- Island-hop through the Mamanuca and Yasawa islands, bask on beaches, snorkel and lap up local culture
- Swim through the ethereal Sawa-i-Lau caves made famous by Brooke Shields in *The Blue Lagoon*
- Birdwatch and trek through prehistoric rainforest to lofty Des Voeux Peak
- Surf the world-class breaks, Cloudbreak, Wilkes Passage and Namotu Lefts off the southern Mamanuca islands

Getting under the skin
Read: *Kava in the Blood* by Peter Thompson, an autobiography of a white Fijian imprisoned during the 1987 coup
Listen: to the harmonies of choral music at Sunday service – a major part of Fiji life
Watch: *Pear Ta Ma'on Maf* (The Land Has Eyes), the tale of a girl's struggle with poverty and the strength she finds in her traditional mythology
Eat: a Fijian pit-cooked *lovo* (traditional feast) one day, Indian thali and roti the next, and Chinese specialities the day after
Drink: a bowl of traditional *yaqona* (kava) to numb your mind and your lips

In a word
Bula (Health, happiness, cheers, and 'bless you' if you sneeze)

Trademarks
Kava; *The Blue Lagoon; Cast Away;* surfing; coral reefs; Melanesian smiles; white-sand beaches; Indo-Fijian culture

Random fact
Europeans adopted the name 'Fiji', which is actually the Tongan name of these islands; the inhabitants formerly called their home Viti

1. The riot of colour that is Sri Siva Subramaniya Swami Temple, a Hindu temple in Nadi, Viti Levu

2. Colours most vivid: a cyclist traverses lush Taveuni Island above turquoise seas

3. A game of rugby (a national obsession) is played outside the Parliament of Fiji in Suva

F **CAPITAL** SUVA (VITI LEVU) // **POPULATION** 903,207 // **AREA** 18,300 SQ KM // **OFFICIAL LANGUAGES** ENGLISH & FIJIAN

Fiji

Fiji is the embodiment of the South Pacific dream. Fall into a sun-induced coma on the beach, listen to palms in the trade winds and dive into electric-blue seas. Inland there's a wonderland of traditional villages where, with your *sevu-sevu* (gift) of kava and the word *'bula!'*, you'll be greeted warmly. And how about some chai to wash down your taro? Indo-Fijians have introduced Hindu temples and curries, the Chinese community has made fried noodles omnipresent and Europeans have left their mark with colonial architecture and pizza. Decades of coups and Fiji's tentative democracy have slightly tainted the allure, but visitors tend to ignore politics as they sizzle on the beach.

1. Bengtskar Lighthouse and its service huts in Dragsfjard glow in the afternoon light

2. The northern lights dance over the Pyhä-Luosto National Park

3. The brown bear is the national animal of Finland and there are excellent opportunities to see one in the wild

(F) **CAPITAL** HELSINKI // **POPULATION** 5.3 MILLION // **AREA** 338,145 SQ KM // **OFFICIAL LANGUAGES** FINNISH & SWEDISH

Finland

Traditionally thrown in with Nordic neighbours Sweden, Norway and Denmark, Finland is Scandinavia's eccentric cousin from out-of-town: quirky, enigmatic and a little strange, but with a contagious and captivating self-confidence. So while you get the Nordic staples of cinnamon buns, hand-knit sweaters, cross-country skiing and ice-cool interior design, you also get Sami reindeer herders with hand-embroidered slippers listening to ear-splitting death metal and goth rock. This is, don't forget, the land that invented the sauna and the sport of wife-carrying. For both visitors and locals, the real appeal is the landscape – a vast, sparsely populated natural adventure playground, cloaked with silent forests and tranquil lakes. The trade-off is the cost of living, particularly when it comes to alcohol; it's easy to see why the Finns are the largest per capita consumers of milk and coffee.

Best time to visit
May to September to avoid the cold, or December to February for snow, Santa and the northern lights

Top things to see
- Beer terraces sprouting all over Helsinki at the first hint of summer
- Relics of Finland's tumultuous history at the fault-line between Russia and Sweden on the fortress island of Suomenlinna
- The mesmerising aurora borealis (northern lights)
- Opera performances at Olavinlinna Castle during the Savonlinna Opera Festival in July

Top things to do
- Join in one of the offbeat festivals like the wife-carrying or air-guitar world championships
- Sweat it out in the world's largest smoke sauna in Kuopio, interspersed with dips in the lake
- Get pulled through the snow by a team of huskies (or reindeer) in Lapland

Getting under the skin
Read: the Moomin children's books by Tove Jansson – stories of a family of lovable Nordic trolls
Listen: to the classical music of Jean Sibelius; or the deafening hard rock of Lordi and Children of Bodom
Watch: Aki Kaurismäki's *Man Without a Past* or *Leningrad Cowboys Go America!*
Eat: fish (herring, whitefish); reindeer stew; Lapland cloudberries and lingonberries
Drink: coffee, or *salmiakkikossu* – a handmade spirit made from salt liquorice dissolved in vodka

In a word
Onko sauna lämmin? (Is your sauna warm?)

Trademarks
Architect and designer Alvar Aalto; Formula One racing drivers; Marimekko designs; Moomintrolls; Nokia; Sami reindeer herders; Santa Claus village;

Random fact
Finns are renowned for being quiet – there's an old joke that they invented text messaging so they wouldn't have to speak to each other

1

2

F CAPITAL PARIS // POPULATION 66 MILLION // AREA 551,500 SQ KM // OFFICIAL LANGUAGE FRENCH

France

A stubborn conviction that they live in the best place on the planet is what makes most French tick – which accounts for an awful lot of those zesty stereotypes showered on this Gallic goliath: arrogant, snooty, officious, opinionated, sexy and super-stylish are insults and accolades bestowed upon this cultured set who have some of the world's greatest philosophers, artists, musicians and literati in their gene pool. It is no surprise then to find France is a timeless land of deep-rooted tradition and modern innovation, a fabled feast of fine food and wine, a place which has unfaltering romance woven into every second footstep, a cinematic trip from opulent Renaissance chateau to Parisian jazz bar to electric-blue seascape.

Best time to visit
April to June, September and October

Top things to see
- The signature spire of Paris' Eiffel Tower: scale the art nouveau tower for unbeatable views of the capital
- The mindblowing glacial panorama atop Aiguille du Midi (3842m), a cable-car ride from the mountaineering resort of Chamonix in the French Alps
- Capital art in Paris: *Mona Lisa* at the Louvre, *The Kiss* at Musée du Rodin and cutting-edge contemporary at the Centre Pompidou
- The garden Monet painted at his home in Giverny
- Europe's highest sand dune (Dune du Pilat) overlooking views of amazing surf

Top things to do
- Taste Champagne in ancient cellars at Reims and Épernay in this Unesco World Heritage region
- Walk barefoot across kilometres of wave-rippled sand to Mont St-Michel
- Pedal through vineyards, cherry orchards and lavender fields in rural Provence
- Tuck into French gastronomic *art de vivre* in gourmet Bordeaux
- Motor the mythical corniches (coast roads) on the French Riviera

Getting under the skin
Read: Victor Hugo's phenomenal *Les Misérables*; *A Moveable Feast* by Hemingway on 1920s Paris; and Françoise Sagan's *Bonjour Tristesse* (Hello Sadness), published when she was just 18
Listen: to Serge Gainsbourg's breathless *Je T'Aime… Moi Non Plus* and feel your soul turn Francophile
Watch: *La Fabuleux Destin d'Amélie Poulain* and imagine yourself a Parisian in Montmartre
Eat: Breton crêpes in a traditional long house encircled by a *cromlech* (prehistoric megalith) in Brittany
Drink: cider in Normandy, pastis in Provence and well-aged red in Burgundy

In a word
Salut! (Hi!)

Trademarks
Baguettes; cheese; cafe society; wine; designer fashion; cabaret; Tour de France

Random fact
Among other things, the French invented the first digital calculator, the hot-air balloon, Braille and margarine

1. Val d'Isère, in the upper Tarentaise Valley, is the centre of a popular skiing area

2. Classic Provence: the lavender fields of Abbaye Notre-Dame de Sénanque in Gordes

3. Mont St-Michel in Normandy will transport you back to the Middle Ages

4. Paris's Moulin Rouge, immortalised by Toulouse-Lautrec and later by Baz Luhrmann

Best time to visit
July to December, or during carnaval (February or March)

Top things to see
- Îles du Salut, peaceful tropical islands with the ruins of South America's most notorious penal colony
- The Centre Spatial Guyanais (Guianese Space Center), one of the world's busiest satellite launchers (about nine per year)
- The village of Cacao, with its sparkling rivers, Hmong residents and colourful market days: a surreal piece of Laos in South America
- Jaw-dropping numbers of giant leatherback turtles swimming ashore to lay their eggs (April to July) at Awala-Yalimopo

Top things to do
- Journey into the rainforest on a two-day trek along the Sentier Molokoi de Cacao
- Stroll the colourful streets of Cayenne, taking in the vibrant markets, ethnic diversity, colonial architecture and tasty Creole fare
- Photograph nature's finery in the virgin rainforest of the Trésor Nature Reserve
- Travel by boat up the Maroni River en route to Amerindian settlements

Getting under the skin
Read: *Papillon*, by Henri Charrière, the remarkable first-person account of the infamous penal colony on Devil's Island
Listen: to the Caribbean-style dance grooves of *bigi pokoe*, a rhythmic style common in western French Guiana
Watch: the legendary film version of *Papillon* starring Steve McQueen and Dustin Hoffman
Eat: the so-called *jamais goute* (never eaten), a delicious fish native to the country
Drink: *ti' punch*, a rum-based drink with lime and sugar that's served as an aperitif

In a word
Bonjour (Good day)

Trademarks
Penal settlements (particularly Devil's Island); French colonial architecture; European space rockets; Francophiles; sea turtles

Random fact
Plage les Hattes contains the highest density of leatherback-turtle nesting sites found anywhere in the world

1. The toothy grin of a caiman

2. Musicians set up their instruments on the streets of Cayenne

3. Unspoilt rainforest blankets much of French Guiana

F **CAPITAL** CAYENNE // **POPULATION** 221,500 // **AREA** 91,000 SQ KM // **OFFICIAL LANGUAGE** FRENCH

French Guiana

Technically not a country at all (but rather an Overseas Department of France), French Guiana, with its impenetrable rainforests, Caribbean rhythms and unique pre- and post-colonial history, could never be confused with Old Europe. South America's smallest and least populous 'nation' is a surprising melange of Europeans, Creole-speaking Haitians, Buddhist Hmong refugees from Laos, Maroons (descendants of escaped African slaves) and Amerindian tribes. Funds pouring in from France keep Europe's premier space centre in operation, while also providing one of South America's highest standards of living. With over 90% of its rainforests intact and incredible biodiversity, French Guiana is one of the region's least discovered ecotourism destinations.

G CAPITAL LIBREVILLE // POPULATION 1.6 MILLION // AREA 267,667 SQ KM // OFFICIAL LANGUAGE FRENCH

Gabon

Gabon is Africa's last Eden – it is where hippos surf, buffaloes bask on the beach and elephants roam vast slabs of equatorial rainforest. Find your way into some of the 13 national parks, which together protect 10% of the entire country's landmass, and you may also swap glances with chimpanzees, gorillas, mandrills and more. When the parks were all created in 2002, many envisaged Gabon's new-born ecotourism industry would blossom quickly. However, despite the continued peace and stability this country is known for, tourism is still trying to find its feet. Outside the capital it is truly a wild, wild world, with thick jungles, otherworldly landscapes and little, if any, reliable infrastructure – for the adventurous, this may be travel heaven.

Best time to visit
May to August (the dry season)

Top things to see
- Hippos surfing in the Atlantic swells breaking onto Loango National Park's shores
- Cirque de Léconi, the Bateke Plateau's spectacular red-rock abyss
- Turtles nesting on the beaches of Mayumba National Park while humpback whales breach in the distance
- Fire dancers lighting up the night in a traditional Bwiti initiation ceremony
- A bird's-eye view of gorillas and forest elephants from Langoué Bai's observation platform in Ivindo National Park

Top things to do
- Shake your bootie on a dance floor in Libreville's Quartier Louis
- Learn how to track chimpanzees in the jungle of Réserve de la Lopé
- Stroll along Mayumba's gloriously deserted beach
- Roll through dense jungles and dramatic landscapes on the Transgabonais railway
- Meander along the scenic Rive Droite (Right Bank) in Lambaréné to Albert Schweitzer's landmark hospital

Getting under the skin
Read: Michael Fay's Megatransect expedition reports from his 3000km, 15-month walk across Gabon and other parts of Central Africa
Listen: to the *Best of Oliver N'Goma*, the greatest hits of Gabon's most popular singer

Watch: *The Great White Man of Lambaréné,* a docudrama revealing the disturbing cultural chasm between Albert Schweitzer and the Gabonese he was there to help
Eat: smoked fish with rice and *nyembwe* (a sauce of pulped palm nuts)
Drink: a Régab – beer from the Sobraga brewery in Libreville

In a word
Mbôlo (Hello, in Fang)

Trademarks
Presidents Bongo (there have been two of them); surfing hippos and beach-bathing elephants; national parks; ecotourism; oil; Africa's last Eden

Random fact
High on nature – Gabon's forest elephants are particularly fond of *iboga*, a shrub known for its strong hallucinogenic properties

1. Brightly coloured mandrills may be glimpsed in the Réserve de la Lopé

2. These curious chimpanzees are delighted by a mirror

3. Surfing the green room in Mayumba National Park

(G) CAPITAL BANJUL // POPULATION 1.9 MILLION // AREA 11,295 SQ KM SQ KM // OFFICIAL LANGUAGE ENGLISH

Gambia

This tiny sliver of land – Gambia is the smallest country in mainland Africa – packs a lot into a small space. Its beaches and the adjacent resorts long ago became famous among sun-starved Europeans. Among birdwatchers, Gambia is revered as one of Africa's best and most accessible birding destinations – it lies on the main migratory path between Europe and Africa and more than 560 bird species have been sighted here. Beyond these two big-ticket reasons to visit, however, you'll find a host of smaller-scale attractions, including thriving traditional music and ecotourism scenes, landmarks to the country's slaving past and the chance to take a slow wooden pirogue up the river that gives Gambia its name.

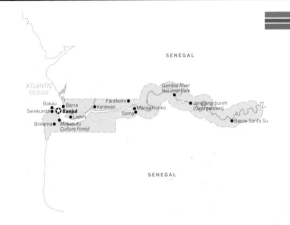

Best time to visit
November to April (dry season)

Top things to see
- The Atlantic Coast resorts, where lovely beaches are lined with party resorts and fishing villages
- Kartong, the pretty town that has become the centre of Gambia's ecotourism projects
- James Island, the focal point for treading gently through Africa's slaving past
- Georgetown (Janjang-bureh), the historic inland Gambian town with islands and a bird-call soundtrack
- Banjul, one of the quietest capital cities in Africa, with a fine market

Top things to do
- Learn to play the traditional *kora* (21-stringed harp-like musical instrument) from a famous *griot* family in Brikama
- Take a pirogue ride through the mangroves or walk through the sacred jungle of Makasutu Culture Forest
- Go birdwatching and spot Nile crocodiles and monkeys in Abuko Nature Reserve
- Track down chimpanzees reintroduced into the wild in the Gambia River National Park
- Learn African dance, drumming, batik or yoga in Serekunda

Getting under the skin
Read: *Chaff on the Wind* by Gambian author Ebou Dibba, which follows two rural boys seeking a new life in the city
Listen: to Jali Nyama Suso, Tata Dindin, Pa Jobarteh and Jaliba Kuyateh, *kora* masters from the birthplace of the instrument
Watch: *Roots* by Alex Haley, who traced his origins to Jufureh, a village on the lower Gambia River
Eat: *domodah* (peanut stew) or *benechin* (rice baked in a sauce of fish and vegetables)
Drink: *bissap* (hibiscus juice), *bouyi* (baobab juice) or JulBrew, the refreshing local beer

In a word
I be ñaading (Hello, in Mandinka)

Trademarks
Birdwatching and beaches; a tiny Anglophone island in an ocean of French

Random fact
Gambia may be famous for its beaches, but it has the second-shortest coastline in Africa (80km), after Democratic Republic of Congo (37km)

1. A city street in peaceful Banjul

2. Fishing boats line the beach at Bakau on the Atlantic Coast

3. A local woman wears finery for a wedding

Best time to visit
April to October

Top things to see
- Tbilisi, a city of ramshackle elegance, balconied mansions, markets, a gallery-filled old town and thumping nightlife
- The hilltop silhouette of Tsminda Sameba Church in front of Mt Kazbek
- The wild and spectacular mountain provinces of Svaneti, Tusheti and Khevsureti, so remote that there are often no roads
- The imposing churches of Mtskheta, Georgia's spiritual heart since Christianity was introduced in AD 327
- The wine region of Kakheti, including Italianate hilltop Sighnaghi

Top things to do
- Raise your glass with the locals for an alcohol-laden dinner and some polyphonic singing
- Head north to the mountains and take advantage of almost limitless opportunities for trekking between remote mountain hamlets
- Ponder the ascetic life in the extraordinary monastery complex of Davit Gareja, located in the semi-desert near the border with Azerbaijan
- Sweat it up amid belle époque architecture and subtropical greenery in Batumi, Georgia's 'summer capital' on the steamy Black Sea coast

Getting under the skin
Read: *Bread and Ashes*, Tony Anderson's wonderful account of walks in the Caucasus; and *Georgia: in the Mountains of Poetry* by Peter Nasmyth
Listen: to extraordinary Georgian polyphonic singing whenever you have the chance – groups of singers often perform in restaurants for visitors, but you may also see a totally authentic and ad hoc performance in any mountain village
Watch: Julie Bertucelli's wonderful *Since Otar Left*, a deeply moving tale about life in post-Soviet Georgia
Eat: *khachapuri* (cheese pie), a national institution; delicious meats and stews always cleverly spiced and flavoured with walnut paste
Drink: sublime Saperavi and Tsinandali wines, or, if you dare, *chacha*, the local firewater

In a word
Gaumarjos (Cheers)

Trademarks
Snow-topped mountains; Joseph Stalin; lofty churches; fabulous trekking; *chacha*; polyphonic singing

Random fact
Joseph Stalin was Georgian, hailing from the small town of Gori in Central Georgia, and he remains a popular figure in the country among older people

1. Eclectic Tbilisi architecture: the president's residence, Concert Hall and Peace Bridge

2. A Kakheti vineyard

3. Iconic Tsminda Sameba Church in Kazbegi (Stepantsminda)

G **CAPITAL** TBILISI // **POPULATION** 4.9 MILLION // **AREA** 69,700 SQ KM // **OFFICIAL LANGUAGE** GEORGIAN

Georgia

At the heart of the mountainous Caucasus, Georgia is a unique and fascinating land of ancient tradition, deep spirituality and legendary hospitality. Here dramatic mountains rise, wolves, bears and hyenas lurk, rivers race through steep gorges, and devout locals still cross themselves three times when they pass a church. Centred on its accessible and lively capital Tbilisi, full of excellent restaurants and cultural goings on and with a gorgeous old town at its heart, Georgia is nevertheless best appreciated by getting out to the mountains. Amid the soaring snow-capped peaks of the Caucasus visitors will experience the warmest welcome imaginable, complete with food and wine that will make you understand why many Georgians truly believe their land to have been blessed by God.

Ⓖ CAPITAL BERLIN // POPULATION 81.2 MILLION // AREA 357,672 SQ KM // OFFICIAL LANGUAGE GERMAN

Germany

A powerhouse of Europe's economy, industry and innovation, Germany has given the world the printing press, the automobile, aspirin and audio digital technology, as well as seminal works by luminaries like Martin Luther, Albert Einstein, Karl Marx, Bach, Beethoven and the Brothers Grimm. At the continent's geographic heart, Germany's fairy-tale scenery spans the windswept maritime north, where white-sand-fringed islands scatter offshore, to dark, wooded forests, vineyard-ribboned river banks and the towering, snow-capped Alps in the south. These diverse landscapes are sprinkled with half-timbered villages and towns, chess-piece castles, Roman relics, centuries-old breweries, and mighty cities home to palaces, museums, and traditional and cutting-edge drinking, dining and nightlife venues – along with a palpable sense of ancient and recent history.

Best time to visit

June to August (summer) for beer gardens at their best; September for beer festivals including Oktoberfest; late November to late December for magical *Weihnachtsmärkte* (Christmas markets)

Top things to see

- Berlin, which continues to reinvent itself a quarter-century after the fall of the wall
- The soaring Gothic spires of Cologne's Unesco World Heritage–listed cathedral
- The inhuman horrors of Holocaust sites, such as Dachau and Buchenwald
- Dresden's baroque Grünes Gewölbe, one of the world's richest treasure chests
- Munich with its Alpine accents, gregarious locals and fully realised good life

Top things to do

- Get lost in perfectly preserved small cities, such as Bamberg or Weimar
- Float past vineyards and castles on a river cruise along the picturesque romantic Rhine
- Drink your way to nirvana finding your favourite Bavarian beer hall or garden
- Hike the meadows and forests of the Alps
- Explore the tiny hamlets nestled amid the Harz Mountains

Getting under the skin

Read: Goethe's *Faust*, which tells of the classic deal with the devil
Listen: to classics by Bach or Beethoven, Berlin-style punk symbol Nina Hagen, Kraftwerk's '80s techno, contemporary electro punk rocker Jennifer Rostock, and alternative pop-rock band Tokio Hotel
Watch: cult classic *Run Lola Run*, an inventive, breathlessly paced thriller with vivid backdrops of Berlin's post-reunification city streets
Eat: *Wurst* (sausages) such as *Bratwurst* and *Leberwurst*
Drink: Beers including *Dunkel* (dark), *Hell* (light), and *Weissbier* (wheat beer); Moselle and Rhine Rieslings

In a word

Wie gehts? (How's it going?)

Trademarks

Cuckoo clocks; speed-limitless Autobahns; Oktoberfest; the Berlin Wall; fast trains; high-performance cars (BMW, Mercedes, Audi and Porsche); black eagle; Black Forest cake

Random fact

Some 5000 varieties of beer are produced by Germany's 1300 breweries, including many small, local brewers; annual consumption averages 107 litres per person (the second-highest worldwide after the Czech Republic)

1. Glorious Schloss Neuschwanstein, near Füssen in Bavaria

2. Munich's legendary celebration of beer, Oktoberfest

3. Berlin and its tallest structure, the Fernsehturm TV tower

4. The Black Forest region is the spiritual home of the cuckoo clock

1. Bongo drums are played during an Asante funeral, Kumasi

2. Seagoing fishing canoes hauled up on the beach

3. A local woman outside St George's Castle in Elmina

G   CAPITAL ACCRA // POPULATION 25.7 MILLION // AREA 238,533 SQ KM // OFFICIAL LANGUAGE ENGLISH

Ghana

Ghana has always been West Africa's golden child. It was from here that the pre-colonial Asante (Ashanti) Empire ruled the region and gave birth to legends of fabulous wealth; Asante artefacts remain as prized by collectors of African art as Asante history is beloved by historians. Centuries later, Ghana shrugged off the shackles of colonialism long before other West African countries dared and has since become a poster child for stability and democracy. But this is only half the story. For travellers Ghana has signature African attractions like beautiful beaches, poignant slaving castles and large herds of elephants in its fine national parks, as well as easy transport and affable English-speaking citizens.

Best time to visit
November to March, for cooler and drier weather

Top things to see
- Cape Coast and Elmina, two of many former colonial (and slaving) forts overlooking the Atlantic
- Kejetia Market (West Africa's largest) in Kumasi, the ancient Asante capital
- Accra's busy markets, restaurants and sprinkling of historic buildings
- The mud-brick mosques of Wa and a nearby hippo sanctuary in the far northwest

Top things to do
- Set off on Africa's cheapest safaris in search of elephants in Mole National Park
- Learn how to play the balafon (West African xylophone) by the beach at Kokrobite
- Go surfing at Busua or laze on the beach at nearby Akwidaa, Ghana's most beautiful beach

Getting under the skin
Read: *The Beautiful Ones Are Not Yet Born* by Ghanaian novelist Ayi Kwei Armah
Listen: to guitar-heavy highlife music, or the edgier sounds of its heir, hip-life
Watch: *Heritage Africa* by Ghanaian director Kwaw P Ansah, an exploration of colonialism in Ghana
Eat: *fufu* (pounded cassava or plantain) with a fiery sauce; *omo tuo* (rice balls in fish or meat soup)
Drink: *pito* (millet beer) in the north, palm wine in the south

In a word
Hani wodzo (Let's dance)

Trademarks
Highlife and hip-life, the soundtrack of a nation; formidable coastal forts with a slaving past; beautiful beaches; a rich Asante past

Random fact
The Ga people of southern Ghana are often buried in elaborate 'proverbial coffins', which are carved and painted in incredible detail to resemble fish, aeroplanes, cars, pianos and more

G **CAPITAL** ATHENS // **POPULATION** 10.8 MILLION // **AREA** 131,957 SQ KM // **OFFICIAL LANGUAGE** GREEK

Greece

Ulysses lingered 10 years before coming home; Byron fell in love with the land and people; Lawrence Durrell wrote lyrically of island life: Greece seems to inspire all who come here. While it is commonly associated with blue seascapes and white-washed villages, Greece, with a rugged Balkan hinterland, architecture from classical to modern periods and islands dotted across three seas, exhibits stunning diversity. There are olive groves in flower, Chios' mastic villages, sprawling Athens, crimson poppies every April, hirsute priests, old men sitting for hours over a single coffee, and ferries nudging into rickety piers. Many visitors come seeking sun and sea, but are smitten by the hospitality of the Greeks and find they are as captivated as all who went before.

Best time to visit
Easter until June

Top things to see
- The imposing white columns of the Parthenon, on a hill lording it over Athens
- Spectacular sunsets from Oia village at the northern tip of Santorini (Thira)
- The monasteries of Meteora astride rocky pillars on the plain of Thessaly
- Greek Easter in Corfu: priests in glorious vestments, candlelit midnight church services, sweet breads, coloured eggs
- The Knights Quarter and Turkish relics of Rhodes' walled old town
- The underground museum in Vergina, burial place of Alexander the Great's son, where you can embrace your inner Tomb Raider

Top things to do
- Hop on a ferry in Piraeus and cruise between countless Greek islands, each with their own distinctive character and attractions
- Keep an eye out for centaurs, satyrs or stray Greek gods as you trek up Mt Olympus
- Discover an undersea wonderland on a diving course in Ios
- Wander the mountain hamlets of the Zagorohoria, and trek the Vikos Gorge
- Mountain bike the gleaming coast of Halkidiki, mainland Greece's triple-pronged peninsula

Getting under the skin
Read: *The Hill of Kronos* by Peter Levi, a record of a lifetime exploring Greece; and *The Little Infamies* by Panos Karnezis, tales from the backwoods
Listen: to melancholy and passionate *rembetika*, sometimes called the Greek blues
Watch: the films of Theodoros Angelopoulos, including *Ulysses' Gaze* and *Eternity and a Day*
Eat: *saganaki* (fried cheese); *yemista* (stuffed peppers); *spanakopita* (spinach pastry); *soutzoukakia* (meatballs); grilled octopus; roast lamb; sticky *soutzouk loukoum* (sausage-shaped candy rolled in nuts)
Drink: *ouzo* (grape brandy with anise); *retsina* (wine with resin); Greek coffee

In a word
Yamas (Cheers)

Trademarks
The Acropolis; Kalamata olives; old women in black; *Zorba the Greek*; white-washed villages; Homer; myths and fables of classical antiquity

Random fact
Around 500 BC the poet Thespis is said to have improvised during a religious choral performance, thus becoming the first 'thespian', ie theatre performer

1. Ethereal sunbeams enveloping the eyrie-like Holy Monastery of Rousanou

2. Patmos, the island where St John wrote the Book of Revelations

3. Guards goose-step at the Tomb of the Unknown Soldier, Athens

4. An opera is performed in the Odeon of Herodes Atticus, Athens

1. An Inuit hunter walks his dog team across sea ice during a snow storm

2. Qeqertarsuaq (Godhavn), a small town on Disko Island far off the west coast

3. The national costume of Greenland is decorated with hundreds of glass beads, originally signifying wealth

G CAPITAL NUUK // POPULATION 57,714 // AREA 2,166,086 SQ KM // OFFICIAL LANGUAGES GREENLANDIC & DANISH

Greenland

The best known fact about Greenland? It isn't green, well not for most of the year anyway. What Greenland is, however, is vast, frozen and mysterious. The world's largest non-continental island is actually more than 80% ice, with just a few scattered areas of solid bedrock that provide a precarious foothold for the sparse population. Getting here at all is hard enough; getting around Greenland is even harder. With virtually no roads, most people get from A to B by kayak, on skis or by dog-sled, but you can shave off a few hundred frozen miles by chartering a boat, plane or helicopter (expensive, yes, but worth every penny). En route, you can bask in views of awe-inspiring mountainscapes and glaciers and spectacular, iceberg-littered fjords, perhaps with an orca, musk ox or polar bear for company. It's an adventurer's playground, so pack your snowshoes and seal-skin gloves and head north into the frozen wastes.

Best time to visit
April for dog-sledding and skiing tours, or July to mid-September during the thaw

Top things to see
- The gloriously scenic island of Uummannaq
- The awesome force of the Sermeq Kujalleq glacier at Ilulissat, one of the planet's most active glaciers
- Norse ruins around Qassiarsuk, and a reconstructed longhouse built and furnished to a 10th-century Viking design
- The picture-perfect old town of Nanortalik, with its pantomime mountain backdrop

Top things to do
- Dog-sled under the midnight sun on the fabulously named Disko Island
- Kayak the ice-choked fjords around Tasiilaq village, to the eerie creak of grinding icebergs
- Sail through south Greenland's magnificent fjordland scenery from Aappilattoq

Getting under the skin
Read: *Last Places – A Journey in the North* by Lawrence Millman
Listen: to the beloved 'old man' of Greenlandic pop, Rasmus Lyberth; rock band Chilly Friday
Watch: the Oscar-nominated 1950s classic *Qivitoq*
Eat: preserved Greenland shark; caribou; fish
Drink: the symbolic cocktail *Kalaallit Kaffiat* (Greenland Coffee): Kahlua, whisky and fresh coffee, with whipped cream as metaphorical ice, and flaming Grand Marnier, representing the northern lights

In a word
*Ha*luu (Hello)

Trademarks
Dog sleds; glaciers; icebergs; Inuit people; igloos; kayaks (the word comes from the Inuit *qajaq*)

Random fact
Numbers in Greenlandic only go up to 12 – after 12 there is only *amerlasoorpassuit* (many); otherwise you have to use Danish numbers

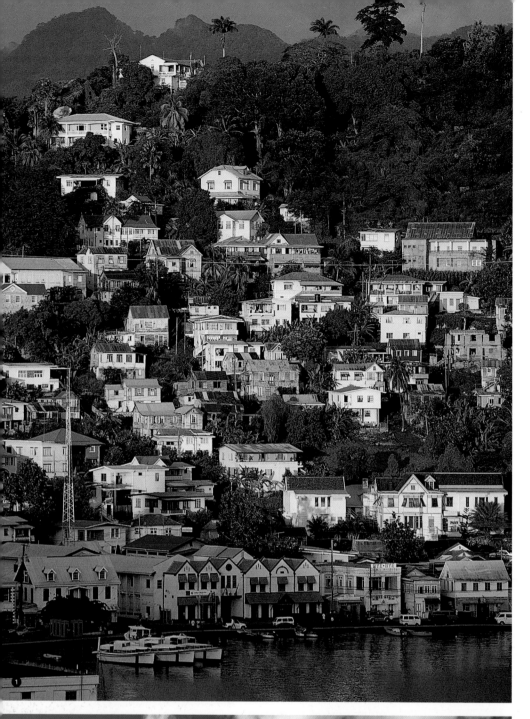

Best time to visit
The weather is warm throughout the year; January to April are the driest months

Top things to see
- St George's: a rainbow of Caribbean colours, ranged up the hillsides around the horseshoe-shaped Carenage Bay and topped by a historic fort
- Carriacou: the pint-sized sibling of the big island, with all the charms distilled down to a rich essence
- Petit Martinique: the smallest of the Grenada trio, this seafarer's paradise is the ultimate hideaway
- La Sagesse Nature Centre, which preserves and promotes the local fauna and sits on a splendid beach
- Antique River Antoine Distillery, brewing up eye-watering Rivers Rum, Grenada's strongest tipple

Top things to do
- Pound the crystalline sands at Grand Anse beach, Grenada's trademark beauty
- Dive into the underwater art gallery at Moliniere Bay, where coral and statues combine to create masterpieces
- Join the sea turtles at Anse La Roche, a hidden beach on isolated Carriacou
- Hike amid mahogany trees and dew-dropping ferns in the Grand Etang rainforest, and spot some birds at the tranquil crater lake
- Build a sandcastle on Bathways Beach or soak up the secluded charms of next-door Levera

Getting under the skin
Read: native Grenadian Jean Buffong's *Under the Silk Cotton Tree*
Listen: to reggae master David Emmanuel and Mighty Sparrow, the 'Calypso King of the World'
Watch: *Nothing Like Chocolate* – Grenada's brown-gold renaissance, as narrated by Susan Sarandon
Eat: the national dish, 'oil down', which is spicy vegetables and meat cooked up in coconut milk
Drink: the nonalcoholic *mauby* (a bittersweet drink made from the bark of the rhamnaceous tree)

In a word
Sa ki fé'w? (What's happening? in Grenadian Creole)

Trademarks
'The Spice Islands'; Grand Anse beach; the *Bianca C* shipwreck

Random fact
Grenada produces one third of the world's nutmeg; the kernel is the odd-looking yellow blob on the left side of the Grenada flag

1. Carenage, a quaint and bustling harbour in St George's

2. Tiny Sandy island, off Carriacou, is a favourite with snorkellers and sailors

3. Lowering the Flag ceremony at Fort George, St George's

G CAPITAL ST GEORGE'S // POPULATION 109,590 // AREA 344 SQ KM // OFFICIAL LANGUAGE ENGLISH

Grenada

In an ocean of beautiful islands ringed by dazzling white-sand beaches, Grenada is an underrated star. Tipping toes in powdery sand and enjoying the turquoise waters is appropriately sublime, but away from the developed southwest you'll likely have only your partner and some sea turtles for company. The rural towns are like visions from Gauguin, with their bright tropical colours accenting lush, green hillsides. Besides the country's main namesake island, there are two tiny charmers: Carriacou and Petit Martinique, which are idyllic, isolated and intoxicating.

Best time to visit
December to May are the driest and busiest months

Top things to see
- Remote beaches that reward after pushing through the cane fields of northern Grand-Terre
- Deshaies, a luxe port stop for yachties sailing the globe
- The tiny island of Terre-de-Haut and its 19th-century Fort Napoleon
- Guadeloupe National Park, the orchid-studded, Unesco-protected wilderness that covers the high interior of Basse-Terre
- Terre-de-Bas, the Caribbean at its untouristed best – a tiny island of coffee plantations and traditional villages

Top things to do
- Get stuck into a *bokit* – a deep-fried bread pocket stuffed with saltfish, salad and creole sauce
- Abandon yourself to the hedonism of *jou gra* – the 'greasy days' that mark the culmination of the annual Carnival
- Stroke Jacques Cousteau underwater at the aquatic preserve that bears his name (and memorial statue)
- Scour the teeming outdoor markets of Pointe-à-Pitre for clothes, spices and trinkets
- Do nothing at all on La Désirade, the archipelago's least-visited island (but still one with silky sands and alluring waters)

Getting under the skin
Read: *Oiseaux*, the poem by Nobel laureate Alexis Léger that inspired Georges Braques' *L'Ordre des Oiseaux*
Listen: to the often-explicit songs of musician, painter and independence campaigner Francky Vincent, Guadeloupe's most prominent musical export
Watch: *Sucre Amer* (Bitter Sugar), Christian Lara's much-lauded story of a freed slave-turned-general in the Napoleonic wars
Eat: *crabes farcis* (spicy stuffed land crabs) or *colombo de cabri* (curried goat)
Drink: *ti-punch* (white rum, cane sugar and fresh lime)

In a word
Bonjour (Hello) – used at every interaction

Trademarks
Stunning coral; exuberant festivals; fishing villages; Creole food

Random fact
Under the terms of the Anglo-Swedish treaty of 1813, Guadeloupe became part of Scandinavia – Sweden generously ceded it back to France, after an imperium of just 15 months

1. A fisherman's haul on Grande Terre

2. Costumed for carnival

3. The charming view of Bourg des Saintes from the summit of Le Chameau

G CAPITAL BASSE-TERRE // POPULATION 458,000 // AREA 1780 SQ KM // OFFICIAL LANGUAGE FRENCH

Guadeloupe

Historically stained with sugar, slavery and rebellion, the insular region of Guadeloupe has blossomed into one of the most intriguing of France's overseas territories. Its recognisably French culture (baguettes and bitter coffee are ubiquitous) has been thoroughly creolised by African, Indian and wider Caribbean influences. Dominated by the 'mainland' (the butterfly-shaped islands of Basse-Terre – rough, rocky, and crowned by the active volcano La Soufrière, the highest peak in the Lesser Antilles – and Grand-Terre – gentler, and ringed with quiet beaches) Guadeloupe also encompasses a smattering of pristine, smaller islands, such as La Désirade and Marie-Galante.

1. Paddle boarding into a gorgeous Guam sunset

2. The water playground of Tumon Bay

3. Looking towards Tumon from the sheer cliffs of Puntan Dos Amantes (Two Lover's Point)

G

CAPITAL AGANA (HAGATNA, G); SAIPAN (GARAPAN, NM) // POPULATION 180,000 (G); 51,483 (NM) // AREA 549 SQ KM (G), 477 SQ KM (NM) SQ KM OFFICIAL LANGUAGES ENGLISH & CHAMORRO

Guam & Northern Marianas

Thick with American accents, Japanese tourists and convenience stores, Guam and Saipan, the Northern Marianas capital, are package-tour favourites. Get beyond the two main islands and you'll find a less-cluttered version of paradise where turquoise waters and white beaches are livened up by an exuberant Chamorro culture. When caught at the right angle, all the islands offer poignant experiences: flame trees in bloom, melancholy historical sights, outrageous diving and tiered waterfalls. Watch out for typhoons (this area is called 'Typhoon Alley'), put on your WWII history caps and plunge into deep thought about the Mariana Trench; then head to the two capitals for poker and duty-free shopping.

Best time to visit
January to June (the dry season), October and November are the worst months for typhoons

Top things to see
- Towering latte stones thought to be ancient house pillars on Guam
- Boiling pools of sulphur, Micronesian megapodes (birds that use volcanic heat to incubate their eggs) and rare beaked whales at the Mariana Trench Marine National Monument
- Sublime, lofty views from Puntan Dos Amantes (Two Lover's Point) atop a 125m limestone cliff

Top things to do
- Feast and party local-style at Chamorro and Mangilao night markets
- Escape to the pristine beaches and azure waters of Ritidian Point
- Dive at Southern Guam or the underwater passageways of the Grotto in Saipan

Getting under the skin
Read: *Captured: The Forgotten Men of Guam* by Roger Mansell, harrowing WWII tales of POWs on Guam
Listen: to the melancholy Chamorro tones of Jesse Bais and Ruby Santos singing 'Guam Take Me Back'
Watch: *Under the American Sun* about Filipino-American immigrants on Guam post-WWII
Eat: *finadene*, a fiery sauce that turns a dish into a real Chamorro meal
Drink: *tuba*, made from the fermented sap of a young coconut tree

In a word
Inafa'maolek (Interdependence, a key value in Chamorro culture)

Trademarks
Chamorro culture; Mariana Trench; WWII history; Japanese tourists; Spanish colonial influences; latte stones; Battle of Guam

Random fact
Enola Gay, the B-29 that dropped the atomic bomb on Hiroshima in WWII, flew from the island of Tinian

Best time to visit
November through to May (the dry season)

Top things to see
- Lost temples climbing above the jungle canopy at Tikal, the country's foremost Mayan ruin
- The almost impossibly nostalgic city of Antigua, with its Spanish-era convents, colonial ruins and backpacker bars
- Sunrise from atop Volcán Tajumulco, the highest point in Central America
- The tradition of Quema del Diablo, where lapping bonfires and fireworks psychically purge the year's trash
- The rugged route from Huehuetenango to Cobán, which teeters through highland coffee plantations

Top things to do
- Barter for rainbow-coloured Mayan textiles at the Chichicastenango market
- Paddle the placid waters of Lake Atitlán, ringed by an honour guard of active volcanoes
- Finesse your bar talk by studying at a Spanish language school in Antigua
- Soak in the cool emerald pools of Semuc Champey
- Board the breaks at Sipacate, the country's largely undiscovered surf capita

Getting under the skin
Read: *Hombres De Maíz* by Miguel Ángel Asturias, the Nobel Prize–winning author and long-time exile who combines Mayan mysticism and social consciousness to deliver an indictment of dictatorial rule
Listen: to *Guatemala: Celebrated Marimbas*; Paco Pérez's 'Luna de Xelaju' is the best-known composition for marimbas
Watch: *Ixcanul* (Volcano): the debut of Guatemalan writer/director Jayro Bustamente, this 2015 feature about an arranged marriage within the indigenous Kaqchikel has won numerous international awards
Eat: a hearty Chapín breakfast of eggs, corn tortillas, beans, fried plantain and coffee
Drink: the velvety hot chocolate and Zacapa rum

In a word
De huevos (Cool)

Trademarks
Ancient gods; the Maya; ruined pyramids in the jungle; astonishing textiles; toucans; mesmerising masks; brooding volcanoes; the quetzal; Spanish colonial gems; Mayan trouble dolls

Random fact
Based on measurements of the passage of the stars, the ancient Maya were able to calculate the length of the solar year to within a few minutes

1. Temple V, the second-tallest structure at Tikal and in pre-Columbian America

2. Pretty Antigua has many photogenic facades

3. A cheerful 'chicken bus' in Panajachel (Pana)

4. Placid and atmospheric Lake Atitlán

G   **CAPITAL** GUATEMALA CITY // **POPULATION** 14.4 MILLION // **AREA** 108,889 SQ KM // **OFFICIAL LANGUAGE** SPANISH

Guatemala

Mexico's exotic cousin from the south, Guatemala is the heartland of the Maya people, whose rhythms flow seamlessly from the ancient world to the modern day. Like its neighbours, Guatemala carries the scars of tinpot dictatorships and socialist uprisings, but somehow, these contemporary trials and tribulations have had only a passing effect on the lifestyle of Guatemala's Maya inhabitants, who still adhere to ancient customs and dress in vividly colourful tribal costume. A visit to Guatemala is a journey into an *Indiana Jones* fantasy, where colonial towns and coffee plantations cling precariously to the slopes of active volcanoes and where the ruins of vanished civilisations wait to be revealed by the next slash of your machete. Factor in a lively backpacker scene and some of the most colourful markets in the Americas and it's easy to see the appeal.

Best time to visit
November to February (the dry season – otherwise, Guinea is one of the wettest countries in the world)

Top things to see
- Îles de Los' palm beaches that are a world (or pirogue-ride) away from the capital
- Conakry, with its clamour and chaos, and a world-class live music scene
- Bel Air's lovely golden stretch of sand
- The source of the Niger – the trickle that becomes one of Africa's greatest rivers
- The fascinating Sahelian town of Kankan, spiritual home of the Malinké people

Top things to do
- Hike from Mali-Yemberem up La Dame de Mali with its womanly shape and sweeping views
- Learn the *kora* (21-stringed instrument) or acrobatics from the Conakry experts
- Trek through the beautiful and historic highlands of the Fouta Djalon
- Chase some of West Africa's last chimps through the forest in remote Bossou
- Look for forest elephants in the Tabala Conservation Zone

Getting under the skin
Read: Camara Laye's *The African Child* (also called *The Dark Child*), first published in 1954 and one of the most widely printed works by an African
Listen: to Sekouba Bambino Diabaté and Ba Cissoko as a primer for seeing them live in the clubs of Conakry, or the big-band sound of Bembeya Jazz National
Watch: the ground-breaking *Dakan*, by Mohamed Camara, one of the first African movies to address homosexuality
Eat: *kulikuli* (peanut balls cooked with onion and cayenne pepper); grilled fish
Drink: *cafe noir*; or the beers Skol, Guiluxe and Flag

In a word
Bonne soirée (Have a good evening)

Trademarks
Traditional music and dance; Fouta Djalon highlands; political instability; Ebola

Random fact
At least 22 West African rivers begin in the Guinean highlands, including the Niger, Senegal and Gambia Rivers

1. Guinea's people and architecture bloom with colour

2. Cathédrale Sainte-Marie is the centre of Catholic life in Conakry

3. Artisanal gold mining near Kouremale

G CAPITAL CONAKRY // POPULATION 11.2 MILLION // AREA 247,857 SQ KM // OFFICIAL LANGUAGE FRENCH

Guinea

Guinea could be a West African paradise. With a strong self-reliant streak that saw it defy France to claim independence, and with almost half of the world's bauxite reserves, post-colonial Guinea had all the ingredients for success. As a traveller destination, its future looked similarly assured with a vibrant capital, world-class musical scene and stunningly beautiful scenery in the interior. Sadly it hasn't quite worked out that way. Decades of dictatorial rule, followed by a seemingly perpetual stand-off between the army and restless population, ensured the long-suffering Guinea people's dreams of a prosperous future remained just that, dreams. The devastating West Africa Ebola outbreak that started here in 2013 only set the country further behind. Neglected infrastructure makes travelling here a challenge, but for all the country's travails, it's almost always worth it.

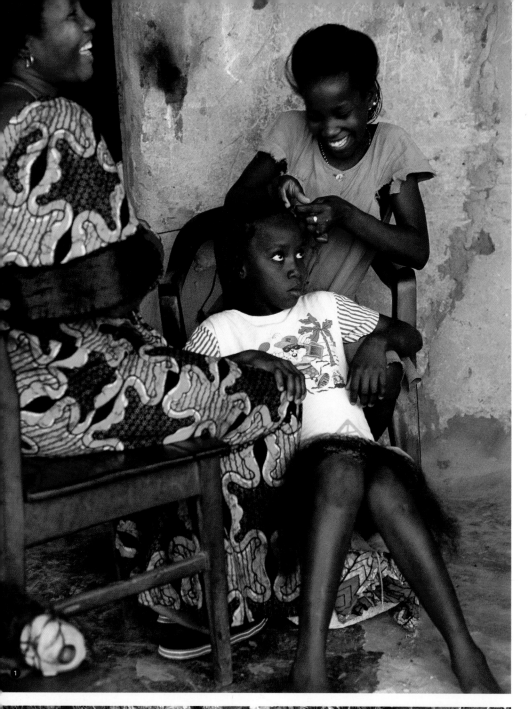

Best time to visit
Late November to February, when it's dry and relatively cool

Top things to see
- The capital's decadent old colonial quarter, Bissau Velho
- Ilha de Bolama, an island charmingly frozen in time from its days as the colonial capital
- Ilha de Bubaque, the most accessible of the islands with luxury accommodation
- Kere, the most beautiful island in the Arquipélago dos Bijagós
- Bafatá, a lovely riverside town with the eerie tranquillity of a ghost town

Top things to do
- Take a week-long minicruise around the Arquipélago dos Bijagós
- Search for rare saltwater hippos and crocodiles in Orango Islands National Park
- Commune with endangered sea turtles on the near-perfect beaches of the João Vieira Poilão National Marine Park
- Laze on the gorgeous beaches of mainland Varela
- Discover elephants and Africa's westernmost chimps in the Parque National de Cantanhez

Getting under the skin
Read: Susan Lowerre's *Under the Neem Tree*, which recounts a Peace Corps volunteer's experiences
Listen: to the classic band Super Mama Djombo; and modern singers Dulce Maria Neves of Manecas Costa (*Paraiso di Gumbe*)
Watch: *The Blue Eyes of Yonta*, by Flora Gomes, about dreams and revolution
Eat: *chabeu* (deep-fried fish served in a thick, palm-oil sauce with rice)
Drink: *cajeu* (a sickly sweet and dangerously strong cashew liquor)

In a word
Pode mostrar-me (no mapa)? – Can you show me (on the map)?

Trademarks
Arquipélago dos Bijagós; Portuguese colonialism; saltwater hippos; forest elephants

Random fact
At independence from Portugal, Guinea-Bissau and Cape Verde were ruled as one nation, with a dream of permanent unification – however, following the 1980 coup in Guinea-Bissau the two separated permanently

1. Plaiting takes patience in Bissau

2. An absorbing game of checkers on a village street

3. The Fortress of Cacheu, a former Portuguese colonial trading post and slaving centre

G CAPITAL BISSAU // POPULATION 1.7 MILLION // AREA 36,125 SQ KM // OFFICIAL LANGUAGE PORTUGUESE

Guinea-Bissau

One of Africa's most forgotten corners, Guinea-Bissau is also one of its most beautiful and diverse. Wildlife-rich rainforests and decaying colonial-era towns dominate the mainland, and there are 23 different ethnic groups. But it's the offshore Arquipélago dos Bijagós, among the world's prettiest (and least-visited) island chains, that will really take your breath away. The peace and tranquillity of the archipelago's secluded coves stands in stark contrast to the turmoil that has blighted the country for decades. A brutal war of liberation was the precursor to Guinea-Bissau's extremely late independence from Portugal in 1974, and peace and prosperity have proved just as elusive ever since. Not that you'd know it, however, as Guinea-Bissau's people are some of Africa's friendliest.

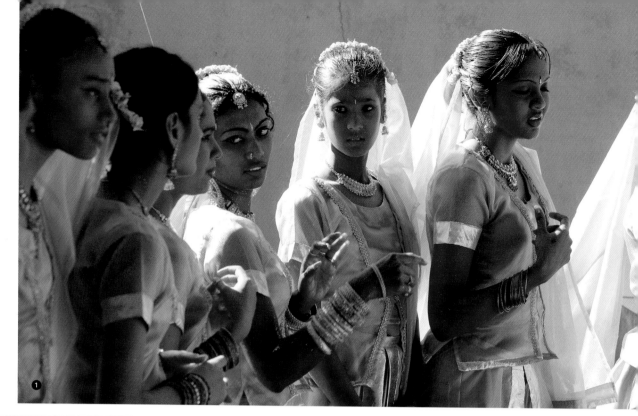

1. Celebrating a Hindu Festival in Georgetown

2. Thunderous Kaieteur Falls

3. The waxy monkey tree frog is one of the many inhabitants of Guyana's rainforests

G CAPITAL GEORGETOWN // POPULATION 739,903 // AREA 214,969 SQ KM // OFFICIAL LANGUAGE ENGLISH

Guyana

Guyana has an eclectic cultural heritage owing to its colonial past, which becomes even more interesting when paired with its wild rainforest-to-Caribbean-coast geography. The present population is descended largely from African slaves and indentured immigrants brought from East India, while scattered Amerindian settlements dot the interior. Guyana's rough-and-tumble capital, Georgetown, has a frontier aspect to it, though tensions tend to dissolve when the national cricket team takes the field. Beneath the headlines of corruption, power outages and economic trouble, is a joyful mix of people who are turning Guyana into a top wildlife-watching and adventure destination. The pristine forests and incredible biodiversity within them are increasingly seen as Guyana's greatest assets.

Best time to visit
Mid-October to mid-May

Top things to see
- Kaieteur Falls, one of the highest single drop falls in the world, located deep in the jungle and only accessible by small plane or three days' trek
- Wildlife, including giant anteaters, rare birds, jaguars and giant river otters, in the country's central virgin rainforests
- The Rupununi savannahs, African-like plains sprinkled with indigenous villages, pockets of jungle and exceptional wildlife

Top things to do
- Search for endangered black caimans on the Rupununi River by night in a dugout canoe as part of a long-term scientific study
- Join *vaqueros* (cowboys) on a cattle drive in the remote Kanuku Mountains
- Travel by boat from Charity to Shell Beach, a pristine stretch of coastline

Getting under the skin
Read: *Buxton Spice* by Guyanese writer Oonya Kempadoo, an enthralling coming-of-age story set in 1970s Guyana
Listen: to hits such as 'Electric Avenue' by Eddy Grant, Guyana's most famous son
Watch: *Guiana 1838*, Rohit Jagessar's riveting story about the struggles against empire following the abolition of slavery and the ensuing arrival of labourers from East India
Eat: pepperpot (a spicy stew cooked with different meats and a fermented juice made from cassava)
Drink: refreshing Banks beer

In a word
Howdy (How are you?)

Trademarks
Sugar cane; the Jim Jones tragedy; cricketer Clive Lloyd

Random fact
An astounding 500,000 Guyanese are estimated to live abroad – almost as many as in the country itself

H CAPITAL PORT-AU-PRINCE // POPULATION 9.9 MILLION // AREA 27,750 SQ KM // OFFICIAL LANGUAGES HAITIAN CREOLE & FRENCH

Haiti

Haiti's birth two centuries ago out of the only successful slave revolution in history has bequeathed it a proudly singular indentity. Of all Caribbean countries, it is the closest to its African roots, and has the richest tradition of visual arts, literature and music, as well as a deep spirituality that draws on its mixed Vodou and Christian heritage. Yet its recent history has been a difficult one, fraught with political instability and the 2010 earthquake that the country is still rebuilding from. Haiti was at the forefront of kickstarting Caribbean tourism in the 20th century, and the country is putting tourism front and centre of its economic recovery. While the path of reconstruction remains rocky, Haitians welcome visitors and the opportunity to show them a country removed from the media headlines.

Best time to visit
December to July (to avoid hurricane season)

Top things to see
- The Citadelle fortress built to defend Haiti against Napoleonic invasion
- The fancy 'gingerbread' houses of Victorian-era Port-au-Prince
- Haiti's Museé du Panthéon National, housing King Christophe's suicide pistol and the anchor salvaged from Columbus' *Santa Maria*
- Congregations of the Vodou faithful at the great celebrations at Saut d'Eau, Souvenance and Soukri
- The scrap metal turned cyberpunk Vodou sculpture of Port-au-Prince's Grand Rue artists' collective

Top things to do
- Catch a brightly painted *tap tap* (local bus) across Port-au-Prince
- Party at Jacmel Carnival, one of the Caribbean's liveliest carnivals
- Pay your respects at a Vodou ceremony to get a new insight into this unfairly maligned religion
- Hike through the mountainous pine forests of Parc National La Visite
- Trek to the cobalt-blue waterfalls and pools of Bassins Bleu

Getting under the skin
Read: Post earthquake reportage *The Big Truck That Went By: How the World Came to Save Haiti and Left Behind a Disaster* by Jonathan Katz; or Edwidge Danticat's short story cycle *The Dew Breakers*
Listen: Vodou rock 'n' roots band RAM; Freshla, the king of *rabòday* (Haitian electronic dance music)

Watch: Jonathan Demme's *The Agronomist*, about the life of Haitian journalist and activist Jean Dominque
Eat: *griyo* and *bannan peze* (fried pork and plantain) with *pikliz* (pickled slaw with chilli)
Drink: rum (preferably Barbancourt), the only drink that matters

In a word
M pa pli mal (No worse than before) – the standard answer to 'How are you?'

Trademarks
Vodou; Wyclef Jean; rum; Toussaint Louverture and slave revolutionary history

Random fact
Vodou is a blend of West African and Catholic beliefs – the spelling 'voodoo' is avoided due to lurid associations with Western popular culture

1. Worshippers at a vodou ceremony in Port-au-Prince

2. Farmland in Kenscoff, which at 1980m above sea level is refreshingly cool

3. A drinks vendor can be a welcome sight in Port-au-Prince

Best time to visit
May to June for the festivals

Top things to see
- The extraordinary and intricate temples of Copán Ruinas
- Rare whale sharks trolling the Caribbean coast from May to September
- The dozy cloud forest hamlet of Gracias, which once served as the capital of Spanish Central America
- Muddy jaguar prints in the wilderness in Río Plátano Biosphere Reserve
- Neighbourly goodwill at Guancasco, an annual Lenca ceremony promoting peace and friendship

Top things to do
- Get scuba certified, affordably, in the gemstone waters around Roatán
- Spot some of the 400 bird species that teem Lago de Yojoa
- Pay your respects at a shrine to the Virgen de Suyapa in the former men's room of a Tegucigalpa restaurant
- Set out in the spectacular cloud forest of Parque Nacional Celaque
- Glide down jungle rivers to find guzzling tapirs along the banks in La Moskitia

Getting under the skin
Read: *El Gran Hotel* by Guillermo Yuscarán, one of Honduras' most celebrated writers; or *The Soccer War* by Ryszard Kapuscinski, about the 100-hour war between Honduras and El Salvador
Listen: to Garífuna band Los Menudos
Watch: *Sin Nombre* (The Nameless), directed by Cary Fukunaga, about gangs and US migration; and *El Espiritu de mi Mama* (Spirit of my Mother), directed by Ali Allie, about a young Garífuna woman
Eat: fresh-from-the-sea *sopa de caracol* (conch soup) or *baleada* – Honduran flour tortillas stuffed with mashed beans
Drink: ice-cold Port Royal or Salva Vida beer

In a word
Todo cheque (It's all cool)

Trademarks
The Mosquito Coast; the Mayan ruins of Copán; jaguars and howler monkeys; cloud forests; bananas; lush tropical islands with cheap diving; record-breaking murder rates

Random fact
Honduras was the original banana republic – the American writer O Henry coined the phrase in the 1890s to describe the influence American banana companies wielded over the Honduran government

1. Keel-billed toucans are best spotted in Parque Nacional Pico Bonito

2. Parque Central, the main square of pretty Copán Ruinas

3. Plaiting palms for the country's biggest Easter procession in Comayagua

H CAPITAL TEGUCIGALPA // POPULATION 8.4 MILLION // AREA 112,090 SQ KM // OFFICIAL LANGUAGE SPANISH

Honduras

Columbus may have discovered Honduras on his final voyage, but many would struggle to mark it on a map today. Honduras is the quiet child of Central America, blessed with abundant natural and historical riches, but not really known beyond its borders for anything in particular. Dotted around this tropical nation are extravagant Mayan ruins, atmospheric colonial cities, lush rainforests, reef-circled islands and the blissfully isolated inlets of the Mosquito Coast (La Moskitia), but Honduras has never attracted floods of tourists, and with the current surge in violent crime, tourism has slowed to a trickle. Since San Pedro Sula was declared the world's murder capital, most visitors skip the cities in favour of the national parks, the Mayan relics close to the Guatemalan border, and the languorous Bay Islands, where diving with whale sharks provides a welcome distraction from the troubles on the mainland.

H **POPULATION** 7.1 MILLION // **AREA** 1104 SQ KM // **OFFICIAL LANGUAGES** CANTONESE & ENGLISH

Hong Kong

The world's most densely populated city is a throbbing, neon-lit extravaganza. A Special Administrative Region of China and former British colony, much of the city still retains an East-meets-West feel – dried seafood stalls vie for space with global clothing chains, locals tuck into both fish ball soup and fish and chips, expat bankers park their Maseratis in front of ancient temples to the Goddess of the Sea. The action is centred on Kowloon and Hong Kong Island, with their bustling shopping streets and sky-piercing towers, but peaceful beaches and jungle trails await in the outlying islands of the New Territories.

Best time to visit
October to December (to avoid the rains)

Top things to see
- Narrow streets lined with dried mushroom and bird's nest shops in old Sheung Wan
- The curious, quad-sparing street escalators of the Mid-Levels
- Delightfully frenetic race nights at the Happy Valley Racecourse
- Otherworldly, incense-cloaked Man Mo Temple
- Kowloon's Symphony of Light show, with disco-style light effects dancing on the skyscrapers across the harbour

Top things to do
- Rumble up to Victoria Peak on the Peak Tram
- Tuck into a dim sum feast at a traditional teahouse in Kowloon
- Take in the city's stunning skyline on the cheap and cheerful Star Ferry across Victoria Harbour
- Escape the bustle on a jungle hike across Lantau Island or Sai Kung Country Park
- Ride the cable car across the mountains to visit the house-sized Tian Tan Buddha statue

Getting under the skin
Read: James Clavell's unashamedly populist *Tai-Pan*; or *The Piano Teacher* by Janice YK Lee
Listen: to the Canto-pop beats of the Four Heavenly Kings (Jacky Cheung, Andy Lau, Aaron Kwok and Leon Lai)
Watch: John Woo's *A Better Tomorrow*; Andrew Lau and Alan Mak's *Infernal Affairs*; or Wong Kar-Wai's *In the Mood for Love* – essential Hong Kong viewing
Eat: dim sum, char siu (roasted pork), egg tarts, pork chop buns, congee, beef brisket noodles, fish balls on a stick
Drink: sugar cane juice, milk tea, or *yuanyang* (half tea, half coffee)

In a word
Yum cha (Drinking tea – and the act of feasting on dim sum)

Trademarks
Skyscrapers; double-decker buses; shopping sprees; that skyline; the Peak Tram; Jackie Chan; Chinese New Year; dim sum

Random fact
Hong Kong has more skyscrapers than any other city, with more than 300 buildings higher than 150m

1. The skyscraper jungle viewed from Victoria Peak

2. A woman wearing traditional Chinese headwear on Kat O island

3. A junk cruises past the lights of Victoria Harbour

4. Elaborate lanterns displayed in Victoria Park for the Mid-Autumn Festival

Best time to visit
April to June and September to October

Top things to see
- Fabulous views of Budapest's Parliament building and Danube River frontage from the Fisherman's Bastion on Castle Hill
- The whip-cracking performances of *csikós* (cowboys) astride bareback horses in Hortobágy National Park
- Almond trees in blossom and ceramics, embroidery and other folk arts in Tihany
- The galleries, museums, mosques, beautifully preserved synagogue and Ottoman-era baths of Pécs
- The week-long Sziget music festival, one of Europe's biggest, on a leafy island in the middle of the Danube

Top things to do
- Plunge in for a hot soak and rub down with the locals in the steamy surrounds of Budapest's elegant thermal baths
- Wet your whistle sampling feisty local wines in Eger's Valley of Beautiful Women
- Cruise the Danube on a ferry from Budapest to Szentendre, a former artists' colony
- Dip your toes in the northern shore of Lake Balaton, Hungary's freshwater 'riviera'
- Raise a glass in ruin bars, abandoned buildings given a decadent nightlife makeover, across Budapest and in second city Debrecen

Getting under the skin
Read: Nobel Prize–winner Imre Kertész' semiautobiographical novel *Fateless*, about a teenage Jewish boy sent to the Nazi death camps
Listen: to the *Hungarian Rhapsodies* of Franz Liszt or the haunting Hungarian folk music of Márta Sebestyén, as heard in the soundtrack to *The English Patient*
Watch: *Kontroll*, a comedy-thriller involving ticket inspectors and an elusive killer on the Budapest metro
Eat: *paprikás csirke* (paprika chicken); or *gulyás* (goulash), full of beefy goodness
Drink: Tokaji Azsú, a sweeter-than-sweet dessert wine; Egri Bikavér, a full-bodied red known as 'bull's blood'; or local firewater *pálinka*, fruit brandy often made at home

In a word
Egészségére (Cheers!)

Trademarks
Paprika; Tokaji Azsú; goulash; Rubik's Cube; thermal baths; home-grown cowboys

Random fact
The ballpoint pen was invented by Hungarian László Bíró

1. The Széchenyi Chain Bridge and Parliament grace the Danube

2. A spot of chess at the Széchenyi Baths, Budapest

3. Fisherman's Bastion and the neo-Gothic Matthias Church in Budapest

H | CAPITAL BUDAPEST // POPULATION 9.9 MILLION // AREA 93,028 SQ KM // OFFICIAL LANGUAGE HUNGARIAN

Hungary

Hungary lies in the Carpathian basin, slap-bang in the middle of Europe, and the Hungarians themselves will tell you that theirs is a Central (not Eastern) European nation – even though they trace their ancestry to beyond the Ural Mountains. A flat land dominated by the *puszta* (great plain), Hungary's culture is anything but featureless. With a predilection for zesty paprika-infused cuisine and thermal baths (even during chilly winter days), traditions of horseback cowboy acrobatics and heel-clicking folk songs, and an inscrutable language, the Hungarians remain entirely distinct from any of their neighbours. Hungary still pays homage to homegrown greats like Franz Liszt and painter Mihály Munkácsy, but today trendy coffee shops and ruin bars flourish alongside monuments and period architecture.

Best time to visit
May to September to avoid the dark and cold, or December to February to see Iceland at its iciest

Top things to see
- The mighty spurt of water from Geysir, the original hot-water spout after which all other geysers are named
- A breaching whale and curious dolphins on a whale-watching cruise from Húsavík
- The smouldering volcanic wastelands of Krafla
- The peaks and glaciers (and waterfalls and twisted birch woods) of Skaftafell
- Thousands of puffin chicks taking flight every August from Vestmannaeyjar

Top things to do
- Cavort with crowds of partygoers on the drunken Reykjavík *runtur*
- Breathe cool, pure Icelandic air while bathing alfresco in volcano-heated water at the Blue Lagoon
- Explore the fjords on a kayaking trip under the midnight sun
- Stake out a light-pollution-free vantage point for a horizon-to-horizon view of the northern lights

Getting under the skin
Read: *Independent People* and other novels by Nobel Prize–winner Halldór Laxness; crime fiction from Arnaldur Indriðason; the sagas of the late 12th and 13th centuries
Listen: to the genre-defying works of Björk; pop/folk singer-songwriter Emilíana Torrini; the ethereal sounds of Sigur Rós
Watch: *101 Reykjavík*, based on Hallgrímur Helgason's book of the same name – a painful, funny tale of a Reykjavík dropout's fling with his mother's lesbian lover
Eat: some challenging local dishes: *hakarl* (putrefied shark meat), or singed sheep's head complete with eyeballs
Drink: *brennivín* ('burnt wine'); schnapps made from potatoes and caraway seeds with the foreboding nickname *svarti dauði* (black death)

In a word
Skál! (Cheers!)

Trademarks
Björk; the Blue Lagoon; geysers, glaciers and volcanoes; tiny Icelandic horses; puffins; Viking sagas; whale-watching and the whaling controversy; trolls and elves

Random fact
Due to the unique way in which surnames are formed (girls add the suffix -dóttir, 'daughter', to their father's first name; boys add the suffix -son), telephone directories in Iceland are alphabetised by first name

1. The Blue Lagoon geothermal spa, Grindavík

2. Hardy and docile, Icelandic horses hold a special place in the island's culture

3. Reykjavík's immense white-concrete church, Hallgrímskirkja

4. Behind the falls at Seljalandsfoss

CAPITAL REYKJAVÍK // POPULATION 315,281 // AREA 103,000 SQ KM // OFFICIAL LANGUAGE ICELANDIC

Iceland

Iceland is a country in the making, a vast volcanic laboratory where mighty forces shape the land and shrink human onlookers to insignificant specks. See it in the gushing geysers, glooping mud pools, lava-spurting volcanoes and slow, grinding glaciers. Experience it first hand, bathing in turquoise-coloured hot springs, kayaking through a fjord, scanning the horizon for breaching whales, or crunching across a dazzling-white icecap. Once a benchmark for prosperity, this land of former Vikings tanked briefly during the global financial crisis, but some painful belt-tightening has restored the economy to an even keel. Most visitors welcome the lower prices, which make Icelandic rituals such as the *runtur*, a weekend-long pub crawl with the party people of Reykjavík, a bit less taxing on the pocket.

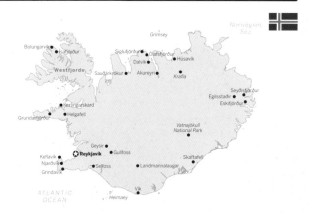

CAPITAL NEW DELHI // **POPULATION** 1.2 BILLION // **AREA** 3,287,263 SQ KM // **OFFICIAL LANGUAGES** HINDI, ENGLISH, BENGALI, TELUGU, MARATHI, TAMIL, URDU, GUJARATI, MALAYALAM, KANNADA, ORIYA, PUNJABI, ASSAMESE, KASHMIRI, SINDHI & SANSKRIT

India

Crowned by the Himalaya, crossed by sacred rivers, coveted by empires from the Persians to the British Raj, India is vast and unfathomable, a kaleidoscope of cultures and the birthplace of at least two of the world's great religions. Countless civilisations have risen and fallen among the paddy fields, deserts and jungles, but India still endures. Asia's most colourful country has its problems – overcrowding, poverty, religious tensions and grinding bureaucracy are daily challenges, but locals take it all as part of the tapestry of life in this chaotic, colourful and unbelievably complex country. Besides, for every rush-hour crush there is a moment of utter serenity – dawn breaking over a sacred pool, a tiger breaking cover in a sultry jungle clearing, or a monk chanting to the music of the spheres.

Best time to visit
November to March in the plains; July to September for the Himalaya

Top things to see
- The white marble magnificence of the Taj Mahal
- Pilgrims crowding the banks of the Ganges River in the sacred city of Varanasi
- The astounding crush of humanity in Mumbai and Kolkata
- Mountain views and relics of the Raj in Shimla and Darjeeling, the quintessential Indian hill stations
- The toppled temples of a vanished civilisation, scattered across the boulder-strewn badlands of Hampi

Top things to do
- Embark on a camel safari through the desert dunes of Rajasthan
- Scan the jungle for tigers in one of India's glorious national parks
- Kick back on the palm-brushed beaches of Goa
- Bend your body into shapes you never thought possible in Rishikesh, India's yoga capital
- Strap on your hiking boots and find mystic monasteries and mountain majesty in the high passes of the Indian Himalaya

Getting under the skin
Read: Salman Rushdie's *Midnight's Children*; Vikram Seth's *A Suitable Boy*; or Kiran Desai's *The Inheritance of Loss*
Listen: to the *myriad filmi* (movie soundtracks) recordings of Allah Rakha Rahman
Watch: Ramesh Sippy's Bollywood classic *Sholay*; or Satyajit Ray's haunting *Pather Panchali*

Eat: delicious *thalis* (rice, curries, chapatis, pappadams and condiments, served on a metal platter or banana leaf)
Drink: *lassi* (sweet or salty yoghurt shakes); *chai* (sweet Indian tea) or Kingfisher beer

In a word
Jai hind! (Long live India!)

Trademarks
Hindu gods; Maharajas; holy cows; Gandhi; the Taj Mahal; hill stations; the Himalaya; towering temples; bottomless slums; Bollywood; curry; chillum-smoking Sadhus; religious tussles

Random fact
There is no such thing as curry in India – the Southern Indian word *kari* simply means 'fried' or 'sauce'

1. Kites above the rooftops during Uttarayan, Ahmedabad's kite festival
2. Celebrations during Holi, the festival of colour
3. Mumbai by night
4. Military ceremony at Wagah, the border with Pakistan

Best time to visit
May to September, for dry skies (in most places)

Top things to see
- The geometric perfection of the Buddhist stupa at Borobudur
- Shadow puppetry, batik dyeing and other ancient arts in Yogyakarta
- Death rituals straight out of *Indiana Jones* in other-worldly Tana Toraja
- Rice terraces and tiered temples on touristy but sublime Bali
- Views over a primordial landscape of steaming volcanoes from the top of Gunung Bromo

Top things to do
- Soak up the tropical vibe on the gorgeous Gili Islands
- Catch the perfect wave at Uluwatu, the Holy Grail of Bali surfing
- Descend into a kaleidoscope of colour at dive sites scattered throughout the islands
- Come face-to-face with the world's largest lizard in Komodo National Park
- Trek to timeless Dani villages in Papua's Baliem Valley

Getting under the skin
Read: Ayu Utami's *Saman*, a novel of gender taboos, political repression and religious intolerance
Listen: to the unmistakable sound of gamelan – the traditional orchestra of Java, Bali and Lombok
Watch: arthouse cinema, Indonesian-style, in the layered films of Garin Nugroho
Eat: the ubiquitous *nasi goreng* (fried rice); or rich and spicy *rendang* (beef cooked slowly with roasted coconut and lemongrass)
Drink: Bintang beer; *kopi* (coffee)

In a word
Tidak apa-apa (No problem)

Trademarks
Rumbling volcanoes, coffee; oil-palm plantations; blissful island beaches; legendary surf breaks; gamelan orchestras; Komodo dragons; shadow puppets; no tolerance for drugs

Random fact
On Bali's annual Nyepi 'Day of Silence', the whole island – even the international airport – shuts down for 24 hours

1. Gunung Agung watching over the rice fields of Rendang

2. A member of the Dani tribe of the Baliem Valley, Papua

3. Small stupas at the top of magnificent Borobodur

4. A schooner negotiates the Wayag islands in marine-life-rich Raja Ampat

CAPITAL JAKARTA // POPULATION 251 MILLION // AREA 1,904,569 SQ KM // OFFICIAL LANGUAGE BAHASA INDONESIA

Indonesia

The world's largest archipelago stretches from the southern fringe of the Malay Peninsula to the western half of New Guinea, taking in chunks of the islands of Borneo and Timor along the way. Earthquakes and volcanoes are constantly changing the landscape – at the latest count, Indonesia boasts more than 17,000 islands, home to a staggering variety of peoples and cultures, from Muslim-heavy Java and the Hindus of Bali to the animist tribes of Papua. Factor in spectacular temples and a stunning natural environment, characterised by glorious beaches, dazzling reefs, lush jungles and animals found nowhere else in the world, and it's easy to see the appeal.

Best time to visit
April to June and September to November

Top things to see
- The arched market arcades and beautiful mosques of Imam Square in Esfahan
- Winding lanes and wind towers in the mud-brick old town of Yazd
- The tea terraces and hills surrounding Masuleh on the Caspian Sea littoral
- Magnificent Persepolis, now in ruins, but an awe-inspiring reminder of the might of the ancient Persian Empire
- The domes and minarets of the Holy Shrine of Imam Reza in Mashhad

Top things to do
- Settle in for an afternoon of banter, bluffing and tea while haggling for a carpet
- Listen to the silence amid the date palms of Garmeh oasis
- Accept an invitation to someone's home for dinner – you are sure to receive one – to experience first-hand Iranian hospitality
- Escape the smog and rumble of Tehran on the walking trails of Darband in the foothills of the Alborz Mountains

Getting under the skin
Read: *The Way of the World* by Nicolas Bouvier, a rollicking tale of a 1950s road trip; and *Mirrors of the Unseen* by Jason Elliot, an observation of modern Iran
Listen: to the sombre melodies of Persian epic poetry sung to traditional accompaniment
Watch: *Gabbeh*, directed by Mohsen Makhmalbaf, a colourful evocation of nomadic life; or *The Lizard*, by Kamal Tabrizi, a comedy box-office smash
Eat: mouthwatering *mirza ghasemi* (mashed aubergine with garlic, egg and tomato); or *kababs* in all sorts of varieties
Drink: *chay* (tea) at a *chaykhane* (traditional teahouse)

In a word
Khosh amadin (Welcome)

Trademarks
Carpets; bazaars; desert citadels; oil refineries; poetry; the Islamic revolution; the Persian Empire

Random fact
Iranians use Arabic script, but their language, Farsi, is related to European languages

1. Driving with the top down in modern Iran

2. A landmark of Tehran, the Azadi Tower

3. Mt Damavand, northeast of Tehran, the highest mountain in the Middle East

CAPITAL TEHRAN // POPULATION 79.9 MILLION // AREA 1,648,195 SQ KM // OFFICIAL LANGUAGE FARSI (PERSIAN)

Iran

With its fabulously tiled mosques and palaces, a rich history of poetry and storytelling, and fabled lakes and mountains to explore, Iran is an adventurer's dream. Long-awaited political changes means the country is slowly becoming more accessible for travellers, who are hungry to experience its famed hospitality and fragrant cuisine. Iran's history, both recent and distant, is nothing if not dramatic; stories of heroes and villains past seem to tell themselves everywhere, through the Persian Empire's incredible ruins to the beautifully curated exhibits in Tehran's museums. Iran is no stranger to modernity either – snowboarding in the Alborz Mountains, hitting the capital's contemporary art galleries and enjoying an afternoon of cafe culture are all part of the lifestyle here.

CAPITAL BAGHDAD // POPULATION 31.9 MILLION // AREA 438,317 SQ KM // OFFICIAL LANGUAGES ARABIC & KURDISH

Iraq

Iraq, or Mesopotamia as it was known, once played host to many of the great civilisations of the ancient world, with Baghdad as the Middle East's cultural powerhouse. Many monuments of this golden age, such as the Lion of Babylon and the Great Ziggurat of Ur, remain standing today, scattered throughout a country which has otherwise been largely ravaged by war. While peace remains a distant dream for most Iraqis, life is more promising in the more stable north of the country, Iraqi Kurdistan. The remarkably resilient Kurds of this semi-autonomous region have a distinct and vibrant culture, some of the loveliest, greenest mountain scenery in the Middle East and an unquenchable thirst for tea and conversation.

Best time
April to September

Places of interest
- The citadel of Erbil, one of the oldest continuously inhabited cities on earth
- The breathtaking village of Amadiya, perched in the mountains
- The hillside town of Akre and the former Jewish signposts in the country's north
- Ur, with one of the world's best-preserved ziggurats and the possible birthplace of Abraham
- Lalish's intriguing Yazidi temples

Local customs
- Finding a perfect spot in the hills for a long and raucous family picnic
- Pushing the boundaries in Sulaymaniyah's infectiously optimistic cultural scene
- Driving the unrelentingly scenic Hamilton Road in northeastern Iraqi Kurdistan
- Sipping a beer in Ainkawa, Erbil's Christian quarter
- Hiking the high country around Ahmadawa

Getting under the skin
Read: the fantastical tales of *A Thousand and One Nights* to see what Baghdad once was; or *The Occupation of Iraq* by Ali A Allawi to see what it has become
Listen: to Kazem (Kadim) al-Saher, an Iraqi musical megastar; or the more sedate, haunting oud (lute) of Naseer Sharma on *Le Luth de Baghdad*
Watch: *My Sweet Pepper Land*, directed by Hiner Saleem – a moving and often funny story of tensions playing out in Iraqi Kurdistan

Eat: *masgouf* (skewered Tigris River fish barbecued on an outdoor grill)
Drink: thick black coffee and dark sweet tea

In a word
Salaam aleikum (Peace be with you)

Trademarks
One of the world's flashpoints; long-suffering people; the cradle of civilisation

Random fact
The Bible's Garden of Eden is believed by some archaeologists and amateur historians to have been in Iraq

1. Jalil Khayat Mosque, in Erbil, Kurdistan
2. Martyr's Monument in Baghdad commemorates the victims of the Iran-Iraq war (1980-1988)
3. Showing off his wares in a souk

Best time to visit
May to September, when the weather is warmer and the days are longer

Top things to see
- The Dingle Peninsula combines classic craggy Irish coastal scenery with beautiful villages
- Impossibly quaint and photogenic lanes through green fields freshened by bracing ocean winds in Donegal
- The Rock of Cashel's ancient fortifications soaring above Tipperary's plains
- Bobbing boats, narrow lanes and seaside walks in the precincts of Kinsale
- Dark tunnels and ancient wonders at Neolithic Brú na Bóinne

Top things to do
- Shed your preconceptions and misconceptions in the Irish metropolis of Dublin
- Traverse the dramatic surf-sprayed western coastline along the Wild Atlantic Way, linking iconic Irish sights
- Bounce from one venue to the next in rollicking Galway
- Find your own authentic musical moment in a hidden County Clare pub
- Get lost and hope not to be found on confounding and enchanting rural backroads

Getting under the skin
Read: *Angela's Ashes* to understand why Ireland's biggest export for centuries was people; plough through James Joyce to understand the Irish gift for words
Listen: to U2 for sounds bigger than the land; or the Chieftains for sounds of the land
Watch: Roddy Doyle's words come to life in *The Commitments*, a melodic lark, and *The Snapper*, about the comedic travails of modern life
Eat: hearty bacon and cabbage; seafood chowder; or smoked salmon and soda bread
Drink: Guinness, possibly chased by a shot of boggy, smoky whiskey

In a word
What's the *craic?* (What's happening?)

Trademarks
Potatoes; harps; shamrocks; Guinness; leprechauns; tech companies; infinite shades of green; greetings that turn into 20-minute conversations

Random fact
Ireland is the only country with a musical instrument as its national symbol (until the 19th century, the flag featured a gold harp on a blue background)

1. The Long Room in the library of Trinity College, Dublin, contains 200,000 books

2. A classic pub in Ballyshannon: pub culture is deeply ingrained in Irish life

3. The staggering vertical drop of the Cliffs of Moher

4. Ha'penny Bridge (named for the original toll to cross it) stretches across Dublin's River Liffey

CAPITAL DUBLIN // **POPULATION** 4.8 MILLION // **AREA** 70,273 SQ KM // **OFFICIAL LANGUAGES** ENGLISH & IRISH (GAEILGE)

Ireland

Like a properly poured Guinness (or a simple exchange of pleasantries), this diminutive country flung out in the Atlantic at Europe's far western edge is best enjoyed slowly. That's how to really appreciate the haunting Celtic notes of its traditional music, the lilt to everyday discourse and the intricacies of the minutely featured countryside – undulating bogs and sheep-flecked green fields criss-crossed by uneven stone walls, silent slate-toned lakes framed by steep-sided valleys, mist-shrouded mountain peaks and filigreed coastline concealing scalloped bays and sandy strands. Even in its lively cities, towns and brightly painted villages, Ireland encourages you to stop altogether, soak up your surroundings and become part of the merriment (or *craic*), beguiled by seemingly nothing at all.

Best time to visit

Year-round, although travelling here can be difficult during major religious holidays, when transport and accommodation are overbooked

Top things to see

- Jerusalem's shimmering gold Dome of the Rock
- The West Bank's ancient, cliffside Mar Saba Monastery
- Tel Aviv, the beachy, on-trend city that never sleeps
- Caesarea's Roman ruins and a Crusader castle
- The Church of the Nativity in atmospheric Bethlehem

Top things to do

- Float atop the waters of the Dead Sea
- Devour warm bread and hummus in a Ramallah cafe
- Visit Palestinian brewery Taybeh to sample local beer
- Explore the desert wilderness of the Negev and climb Maktesh Ramon Crater
- Climb Mt Tsfahot for sunrise views of the Red Sea, Jordan, Egypt and Saudi Arabia

Getting under the skin

Read: *My Promised Land: The Triumph and Tragedy of Israel* by Ari Shavit; *The Iron Cage: The Story of the Palestinian Struggle for Statehood* by Rashid Khalidi
Listen: to *The Idan Raichel Project*, a blend of Israeli love songs, Ethiopian instruments, Jamaican rhythms and Yemeni vocals
Watch: Oscar-nominated *Omar*, directed by Hany Abu-Assad, a love story set against the backdrop of the Israel-Palestine conflict
Eat: hummus, a national obsession
Drink: award-winning Israeli wines from boutique wineries

In a word

Shalom (Hello; peace)

Trademarks

The Dome of the Rock; political debate; international kids on kibbutzim; biblical landscapes

Random fact

The shore of the Dead Sea is the lowest place on earth, and water levels are dropping at the rate of about a metre a year, reportedly due to water being diverted from the inflowing Jordan River

1. Jerusalem's golden domes – the Dome of the Rock and the Church of Mary Magdalene

2. Backgammon is a favourite pastime

3. Tel Aviv's Jerusalem Beach becomes party central on a Friday night

CAPITAL JERUSALEM (DISPUTED; I); RAMALLAH (P) // **POPULATION** 12.1 MILLION //
AREA 26,770 SQ KM // **OFFICIAL LANGUAGES** HEBREW & ARABIC

Israel & Palestinian Territories

Israel and the Palestinian Territories are rich with the most poignant
of holy sites, archaeological treasures, buzzing cities and exhilarating
natural beauty. The region is also one of the most bitterly contested
on earth, fought over for decades between Israelis and Palestinians.
With a backdrop like this, it's almost inevitable that politics ends up
colouring many experiences here – not least a visit to Jerusalem's
magnificent and contentious Old City. But there's plenty more to this
place than news headlines. Artsy, liberal hubs, gorgeous beaches and
scenes of sincere spirituality are just some of the highlights of a visit
here, topped only by discovering the many unexpected areas where
Arab and Jewish cultures overlap.

CAPITAL ROME // POPULATION 61.5 MILLION // AREA 301,340 SQ KM // OFFICIAL LANGUAGE ITALIAN

Italy

As elegant as a finely staged opera, as exuberant as a street carnival, as earthy as a white truffle snouted fresh from the ground – Italy manages to be all things to all people. It's almost a cliche to list Italy's abundant assets, so well-known are they on the world stage. Almost any kind of holiday you could imagine is possible in this boot-shaped nation, from ski-trips through the icy Alps to cultured city breaks or beach escapes on the shores of Sicily. Whether your tastes run to Roman ruins and Renaissance sculpture or catwalk fashion and Europe's most passionate cuisine, Italy always delivers. The only challenge is how to fit in all the architectural tours, gourmet tastings and languorous, two-hour long lunches.

Best time to visit
April, June, September

Top things to see
- Ancient Rome – all of it, but particularly the Colosseum, Forum, Palatine Hill and Pantheon
- Priceless masterpieces in Florence's Uffizi and *David* at the Galleria dell'Accademia
- Baroque Sicily, a treasure-house of masonry flourishes and curling architectural motifs
- Venice's Piazza di San Marco, bewitched by the spangled spires of Basilica di San Marco
- The romantic remnants of Pompeii, a thriving commercial town until Mt Vesuvius erupted in AD 79

Top things to do
- Seek Italy's finest pizza in the backstreets of Rome or the cobbled lanes of Naples
- Have the drive of your life on the cliff roads of the Amalfi Coast
- Be an adrenalin junkie: ski the Alps, hike the Dolomites, climb the cliffs of Sardinia or mountain bike through the hills around Lake Garda
- Savour a night at the opera at Milan's La Scala
- Make a gourmet pilgrimage through the foodie towns of Piedmont or Emilia Romagna, sampling legendary cheeses, wines, cold meats and truffles

Getting under the skin
Read: Peter Moore's *Vroom by The Sea: The Sunny Parts of Italy on a Bright Orange Vespa*, a brilliantly written Italy travelogue
Listen: to Andrea Bocelli's uplifting renditions of popular opera classics

Watch: Fellini's classic, *La Dolce Vita*, or *Il Postino*, *Cinema Paradiso* and *Roman Holiday* to get you in the travel mood
Eat: *trippa alla Romana* (tripe with potatoes, tomato and pecorino cheese) in Rome; *bistecca alla fiorentina* (T-bone steak) in Florence; and pizza in Naples
Drink: a fine red Brunello di Montalcino in Tuscany; or Barolo in Piedmont

In a word
Ciao bella! (Hi/Bye beautiful!)

Trademarks
Roman ruins; Renaissance art; pizza, pasta and olive oil; famous fashion; espresso; Pavarotti; mad drivers; Vespas; world's best ice cream

Random fact
On average €3000 a day is tossed into the Fontana di Trevi, Rome's lucky fountain that promises another visit to the capital in exchange for a coin

1. No visit to Venice is complete without a gondola ride

2. Rome's ancient Forum, an impressive sprawl of ruins

3. Manarola, one of the five villages of the dramatic coastal route Cinque Terre

1. The Blue Mountains, named for the azure haze that settles lazily around their peaks

2. Bamboo raft is a great way to view Somerset Falls, near Hope Bay

3. A local craftsman in Negril

J | CAPITAL KINGSTON // POPULATION 2.9 MILLION // AREA 10,991 SQ KM // OFFICIAL LANGUAGE ENGLISH

Jamaica

From the 16th century, Jamaica was the nexus of the brutal Caribbean economy whereby slaves from Africa produced sugar and rum for Europe and America. First a colony of Spain and later Britain, today's Jamaica is the result of this grim past. The country still retains strong links to Africa, through food, culture and politics. The ubiquitous sound of the island, reggae, is drawn from African folk music and is the nation's greatest export (the studios of Kingston churn out 500 tunes a month). And tunes blasting are just one of the cacophonous features of this heavily populated island where wildly popular, and often hedonistic, resorts mix with urban life in all its raucous glory.

Best time to visit
The weather is beautiful year-round but high season is December to April

Top things to see
- Sunset from the 11km stretch of beach bars and fun at Long Bay on Negril
- The museum dedicated to Bob Marley – see his home and studio, and learn about his life
- One of the coffee plantations clinging to cool green mountainsides
- Port Royal, the collapsing former pirate capital of the Caribbean

Top things to do
- Climb 2256m Blue Mountain Peak, part of a lushly forested Unesco World Heritage Site
- Raft the foamy green waters of the Rio Bueno
- Balance on limestone ledges at Dunn's River Falls, which cascade down to a beach
- Get jammin' to the trademark beat of Jamaica: reggae

Getting under the skin
Read: Jean Rhys' *Wide Sargasso Sea*, a tale of post-emancipation Jamaica
Listen: to Bob Marley in his homeland
Watch: 1972's *The Harder They Come*, a cult hit crime flick starring reggae legend Jimmy Cliff, credited with bringing reggae to the masses
Eat: *jerk* (tongue-searing spice-rubbed barbecued meat)
Drink: the famous Blue Mountain coffee; or the region's greatest variety of rums

In a word
Evert'ing cool, mon? (A common greeting much like 'how are you?')

Trademarks
Reggae; rum; Bob Marley; Rastafarianism; Kingston; palm-fringed beaches; anything-goes couples resorts

Random fact
Once the major celebration on the slave calendar, Jonkanoo is a Christmas party in which masked revellers parade through the streets

J CAPITAL TOKYO // POPULATION 127.3 MILLION // AREA 377,915 KM // OFFICIAL LANGUAGE JAPANESE

Japan

Japan is one of those places that both conforms to and confounds your expectations. All the cliches – Zen gardens, sumo wrestlers, bullet trains, geisha – are easy to find, but what blows travellers away is how Japan consistently delivers the unexpected. For every Shinto shrine and futuristic city, there is a beach-fringed tropical island or a forest trail climbing the slopes of a snowcapped mountain. Then there's the famous Japanese quirkiness – this is a nation where street vending machines sell beer and neckties, and where dressing up as a manga character is as commonplace as checking the news update each day in spring to track the arrival of the cherry blossom moving through the country.

Best time to visit
March to May, to avoid winter snow and summer rain

Top things to see
- The staggering constant surge of humanity making its way across Tokyo's iconic Shibuya Crossing
- Zen gardens, temples, Shinto shrines and geisha in historic Kyoto
- Sculptures and contemporary work scattered around the dedicated art island of Naoshima in the Inland Sea
- World Heritage–listed wonders in Nara, the ancient capital of Japan
- Mt Fuji: whether you're speeding past on the bullet train, hiking up it or admiring it reflecting off the waters of the nearby Fuji Five Lakes

Top things to do
- Witness another side to the Japanese as they let their hair down at a festival such as Gion in Kyoto
- Soak away your worries in one an onsen (hot springs) such as historic Dogo Onsen in Matsuyama or tranquil riverside Takawagara in Gunma
- Be humbled by the lessons of history at Hiroshima and Nagasaki
- Treat yourself to an unforgettable stay in a ryokan (traditional inn) such as Tawaraya in Kyoto
- Strap on some skis and pound the perfect powder on the slopes of Niseko or the Japan Alps

Getting under the skin
Read: Natsume Sōseki's satirical I am a Cat; Shikibu Murasaki's The Tale of Genji, claimed to be the world's oldest novel; or Norwegian Wood by Nobel laureate Haruki Murakami
Listen: to the sentimental sounds of the enka genre, Japanese Pop (J-pop) chart-toppers Mr.Children, punk rock legends Guitar Wolf and the all-female punk pop group Shonen Knife, around since the '80s
Watch: Akira Kurosawa's epic Seven Samurai; master animator Hayao Miyazaki's fantasy tale Spirited Away; or Hideo Nakata's chilling Ringu

Eat: raw fish, preferably as sashimi – slices served with soy, wasabi and preserved daikon radish
Drink: shochu, the national spirit of Japan; or sake, Japanese rice wine – served hot it infuses the senses

In a word
Sugoi (The universal exclamation, used whenever something is terrific, or terrible or just worth shouting about)

Trademarks
Mt Fuji; ninjas; sumo; sushi; kimonos; shinkansen (bullet trains); paper walls; bowing; cosplay; anime and manga; cherry blossoms

Random fact
It's common for Japanese to give gifts of fruit as it can be considered a luxury product; one of the most expensive is the rare black-rind Densuke watermelon, which can cost thousands of dollars

1. Young sumo wrestlers training at a sumo stable
2. Cherry blossoms in all their glory along the Path of Philosophy, Kyoto
3. A neon-lit alley in Shinjuku, Tokyo
4. Tokyo's frenetic and fascinating Tsukiji fish market

1. A Bedouin man leads his two dromedaries through Wadi Rum

2. The carved facade of Petra's Treasury (Al-Khazneh) glows by candlelight

3. A young Bedouin guide: there are many opportunities to experience Bedouin culture in Jordan

J CAPITAL AMMAN // POPULATION 6.5 MILLION // AREA 89,342 SQ KM // OFFICIAL LANGUAGE ARABIC

Jordan

Buffeted on all sides by conflicts in the Middle East, Jordan could be forgiven for cursing its luck. And yet, this remarkable country remains an oasis of stability in the toughest of neighbourhoods. Biblical stories, mysterious lost cities and Lawrence of Arabia – all these and so much more have always placed Jordan at the centre of great historical events, and signposts to an epic past still provide the focus for Jordan's many attractions, including Petra, Wadi Rum and the Dead Sea. But it's the warmth and gracious hospitality of ordinary Jordanians – perfected through centuries of watching the world pass through – that you'll remember most from a visit here.

Best time to visit
April to May or September to October

Top things to see
- Petra's rose-red, rock-hewn Nabataean city
- Jerash's stunning Roman ruins that would be the star of the show were it not for Petra
- Crusader castles, the formidable, evocative bastions in Karak and Shobak
- Madaba's Byzantine-era mosaics, and Mt Nebo, where Moses looked out upon the Promised Land
- Remote desert castles dating back to Umayyad times

Top things to do
- Listen for the echo of Lawrence of Arabia while camping with the Bedouin in Wadi Rum
- Dive or snorkel through some of the Red Sea's most beautiful underwater scenery
- Float effortlessly in the salty waters of the Dead Sea
- Hike the stunning Dana Nature Reserve, the Middle East's most impressive ecotourism project
- Dive into Amman, one of the Arab world's most hip and sophisticated cities

Getting under the skin
Read: *Seven Pillars of Wisdom* by TE Lawrence; or *Petra: Lost City of the Ancient World* by Christian Augé and Jean-Marie Dentzer
Listen: to Sakher Hattar, revered as the Arab world's finest oud (lute) player
Watch: *Lawrence of Arabia*
Eat: *mensaf* (a Bedouin speciality of spit-roasted spiced lamb served on a platter of rice and pine nuts)
Drink: tea, that symbol of Jordanian hospitality

In a word
Ahlan wa sahlan (Welcome)

Trademarks
Petra and Wadi Rum; Bedouins and Palestinians in *keffiyah* (head robes); hospitality

Random fact
Bethany Beyond the Jordan is where Jesus is believed to have been baptised – it was authenticated by the Pope in 2000

Best time to visit
May to September

Top things to see
- The glittering blue domes and 15th-century Timurid tilework of the Yasaui Mausoleum in Turkistan
- Kazakhstan's futuristic capital city, Astana, which boasts an indoor tropical beach resort within the world's largest tent
- Cosmopolitan Almaty, with Orthodox cathedrals and leafy sidewalk cafes
- Fishing boats marooned in the desert seabed of Aralsk, miles from the nearest waters of the Aral Sea

Top things to do
- Take a horse trek to the base of Mt Belukha in the magnificent Altay Mountains
- Hike to the three Kolsay Lakes in the southeastern Zailiysky Alatau range
- Glide around Medeu's giant ice rink or snowboard at nearby Shymbulak ski resort
- Spot flamingos in their most northerly habitat at Korgalzhyn Nature Reserve
- Buy some birch twigs and give yourself a good lashing at Almaty's Arasan Baths

Getting under the skin
Read: *Apples are from Kazakhstan: The Land that Disappeared* by Christopher Robbins, a witty and engaging travelogue that blends history with modern insight
Listen: to *The Silk Road: A Musical Caravan*, a collection of traditional music from across Central Asia, including several tracks from Kazakhstan
Watch: Kazakh hordes battle the Dzungarian armies in Sergei Bodrov's *Nomad*, Kazakhstan's US$40-million blockbuster
Eat: *kazy* (smoked horsemeat sausage) – the ultimate nomad snack
Drink: *shubat* (fermented camel's milk); *kymyz* (fermented mare's milk); or play it safe with a local Derbes beer

In a word
Salametsyz be? (Hello/How are you?)

Trademarks
Steppe; wacky architecture; Aral Sea; oil; Tian Shan mountains; Baikonur Cosmodrome; Semipalatinsk nuclear site; horses; Borat

Random fact
Kazakhstan sits atop an estimated 100 billion barrels of oil, most of it along the shores of the Caspian Sea

1. Eagle hunters in traditional dress with their trained golden eagles

2. Song Fountain and Bayterek Tower, part of Astana's surreal cityscape

3. The haunting and hostile Ustyurt Plateau

K CAPITAL ASTANA // POPULATION 17.7 MILLION // AREA 2,724,900 SQ KM // OFFICIAL LANGUAGES KAZAKH & RUSSIAN

Kazakhstan

Kazakhstan is the world's ninth-largest country, but it remains a mystery to many travellers. Its big draws are definitely the superb Altay and Tian Shan mountains bordering China, but the bleak, bewildering steppe also beckons with surreal, surprising secrets ranging from Soviet-era cosmodromes and underground mosques to the rusting ruins of the Aral Sea. After years of collectivisation, the former horsemen of the Golden Horde are now getting rich on petro-dollars, while trying to deal with the legacy of serving as the Soviet Union's favourite dumping ground. Today the Kazakh steppe offers one of the last great undiscovered frontiers of travel.

(K) CAPITAL NAIROBI // POPULATION 44 MILLION // AREA 580,367 SQ KM // OFFICIAL LANGUAGES ENGLISH & KISWAHILI

Kenya

The earth moved when Kenya was created. And the evidence is thankfully clear for all to see, with the Great Rift Valley cutting dramatically across the country's length – its escarpments, lakes, savannahs and volcanoes are some of the continent's most beautiful landforms. They also form habitats for an astounding diversity of iconic African wildlife and enigmatic peoples, such as the Maasai, Samburu, Turkana, Kikuyu and Luhya. Ecotourism and community conservancies in the Masai Mara and Laikipia are protecting more ecosystems than ever before, as well as helping to ease modern pressures on traditional cultures. The stunning Swahili coast remains a bonus to the many safari destinations, though northern sections are now off limits due to their proximity to Somalia.

Best time to visit
January to February, June to October

Top things to see
- Hundreds of thousands of wildebeest and zebras dodging crocs while crossing the Mara River during the great migration
- Huge herds of elephants within Amboseli National Park walking in the impressive shadow of Kilimanjaro
- Black rhinos and rare Grevy's zebras in the outstanding Lewa Wildlife Conservancy
- The sunrise from Point Lenana (4979m) on Mt Kenya – a just reward for five gruelling days of trekking
- A bird's-eye view of the beautiful Laikipia Plateau from the window of the original *Out of Africa* G-AAMY biplane at Segera

Top things to do
- Rent a bicycle and pedal through the wilds and wildlife of Hell's Gate National Park
- Follow a Maasai guide on a walking safari through one of the Masai Mara's private conservancies
- Meet the Turkana people in Loyangalani and explore their traditional lands on the shore of the legendary Jade Sea
- Walk the serrated crater rim of Mt Longonot and look down into a forgotten world
- Learn how to kite surf on beautiful Diani Beach, south of the historic city of Mombasa

Getting under the skin
Read: *The Man-Eaters of Tsavo* by John Henry Patterson; or *The Lunatic Express* by Charles Miller for the tragic, gripping story of the Mombasa–Uganda railway
Listen: to *benga*, the upbeat, popular dance music of the nation – best exemplified by the songs of Extra Golden, Okatch Biggy and Dola Kabarry
Watch: Robert Redford and Meryl Streep earning their Oscars in Sydney Pollack's *Out of Africa*, based on the famous memoir by Isak Dinesen
Eat: *nyama choma* (Kenyan-style roasted meat), a perfect accompaniment to cold beer
Drink: milk mixed with cow's blood at a Maasai celebration – if you dare!

In a word
Hakuna matata (No worries)

Trademarks
Safaris; the Big Five (lions, elephants, rhinos, buffaloes and leopards); the Rift Valley; leaping Maasai warriors; shoes made from tyres; tribal beads; marathon runners; gin and tonics; Nairobbery

Random fact
Nairobi National Park is the only national park in the world to be in a capital city – on its savannah plains it is possible to view rhinos, lions, giraffes and other safari species with the city's skyline as a backdrop

1. Maasai men perform the *adumu*, or jumping dance

2. Rare reticulated giraffes on the Laikipia Plateau

3. A dhow negotiates the Lamu archipelago

K

1. A canoe sails past a pristine atoll

2. Millennium Atoll, one of the most remote coral atolls on earth

3. Locals of Kiritimati (Christmas) Island

(K) CAPITAL TARAWA // POPULATION 103,248 // AREA 811 SQ KM // OFFICIAL LANGUAGES ENGLISH & GILBERTESE

Kiribati

Kiribati (pronounced 'Kiribas'), with its aqua lagoons and sensational sunsets, is as alluring for its real-world simplicity. Isolated by the vast Pacific Ocean and untainted by tourism, the country is made up of 33 low-lying islands and atolls flung across the equator. The sound and sight of the sea dominates here, fish are the staple and boats are the major form of transport. Locals might wonder why you've come to visit, but with a friendly attitude you'll be greeted with sunny smiles and invited in. Explore densely populated and increasingly modern Tarawa, or get completely back to Kiribati roots on the outer islands. Wherever you go, don't expect schedules or luxury, just go with the warm and easy Gilbertese flow.

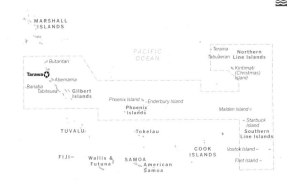

Best time to visit
March to October, the dry season, when it's marginally less like living in a sauna

Top things to see
- Traditional dances that emulate the movements of the frigate bird
- An abundance of seabirds, crabs and turtles at the isolated Phoenix Islands Protected Area, the largest marine protected area in the Pacific Ocean
- Rusted tanks, ships and aeroplanes on the reef, all remains from the WWII Battle of Tarawa
- Kiribati crafts from the outer islands including *te wii ni bakua* (hand-smocked tops) and conical woven pandanus fishermen's hats

Top things to do
- Saltwater fly-fish for famously feisty bonefish
- Surf the lonely reef breaks English Harbour and Whaler's Anchorage off Fanning Island
- Dive or snorkel the sublimely clear waters off Christmas Island
- Salt or smoke your catch and learn to be self-sufficient in the outer islands

Getting under the skin
Read: *A Pattern of Islands* by Sir Arthur Grimble, who loved the islands
Listen: to beautiful singing emanating from *maneaba* (traditional meeting houses) across the country
Watch: *Tinau* (My Mother), a documentary by Victoria Burns on the threat of rising rising sea levels
Eat: fresh fish, breadfruit and rice
Drink: *kaokioki*, also called sour toddy, a local brew made from fermented coconut palm sap

In a word
Mauri-i-Matang! (Hello stranger!)

Trademarks
Far-flung coral atolls; deep-blue ocean; bonefish; frigate birds; WWII Battle of Tarawa; Kiritimati (Christmas) Island; hydrogen-bomb testing

Random fact
Kiribati is spread over 3.55 million sq km of ocean, giving it the largest ocean-to-land ratio in the world

Best time to visit
May to September

Top things to see
- Old Prizren, with its cobbled lanes, arched Ottoman bridge, Sinan Pasha Mosque and hammam (Turkish bath)
- The serenity of Dečani Monastery, complete with friendly monks who make cheese and honey
- Otherworldly stalagmites in Gadime Cave
- Slivers of sunlight carving through the atmospheric gloom in Gračanica Monastery

Top things to do
- Talk up a storm with the philosophical crowd in the lively bars of Pristina
- Visit the rescued bears of Kosovo at the excellent Bear Sanctuary Pristina, where formerly caged bears are kept in wonderful conditions
- Enjoy the view of Prizren from Kalaja Fortress
- Pull on your walking shoes in the wild mountain scenery of the Balkans Peace Park straddling the borders of Kosovo, Albania and Montenegro
- Hit the slopes skiing at Brezovica, Kosovo's premier destination for winter sports

Getting under the skin
Read: *Kosovo: What Everyone Needs to Know* by Tim Judah, a brief and admirably impartial overview of the very complex issue of Kosovo
Listen: to traditional folk music featuring skirling flutes and goat-skin drums
Watch: Isa Qosja's *The Kukum*, a lyrical tale of three escapees from an asylum and a poignant observation on the meaning of freedom
Eat: a variety of Balkan staples including Turkish baklava, Serbian *ćevapčići* (grilled kebab) or fabulously creamy yoghurt or goat's cheese
Drink: tea by the glassful at a traditional teahouse; a fine selection of macchiatos in cafe-packed Pristina; or locally brewed Peja beer almost anywhere

In a word
Tungjajeta/Zdravo (Hello in Albanian/Serbian)

Trademarks
Peacekeeping forces; Orthodox churches; mosques; war damage and new construction; NGO 4WDs; ethnic tension; barbed-wire-protected monasteries

Random fact
Tony Blair became so popular in Kosovo in the late 1990s that there are now numerous young adults coming of age with the former British Prime Minister's name

1. Kosovars celebrate their cultural heritage at a festival in Pristina

2. The city of Mitrovica seen from a neighbouring hillside

3. A church choir rehearses in Prizren, Kosovo's cultural capital

K CAPITAL PRISTINA // POPULATION 1.8 MILLION // AREA 10,887 SQ KM // OFFICIAL LANGUAGES ALBANIAN & SERBIAN

Kosovo

Synonymous still with the brutal ethnic war that happened here in the late '90s, Kosovo was one of the last pieces of the former-Yugoslav puzzle to secede, and is now Europe's newest country, having declared independence in 2008. While Kosovo's status remains contested by many, most particularly by next-door Serbia, for whom the area is considered holy ground, it's a functional and safe place to visit these days, largely administered by EU and UN agencies. For travellers Kosovo offers superb mountain scenery and hiking, the charming old quarters of Prizren and Peja (Peć), several ancient NATO-protected Orthodox monasteries and a charming and friendly (if rather slapdash) capital in Pristina.

1. Students confer at Kuwait University, Kuwait City

2. The Grand Mosque, Kuwait City, can accommodate 5000 worshippers in the main hall

3. The Al Hamra Tower dwarfs the skyscrapers of Kuwait City

K CAPITAL KUWAIT CITY // POPULATION 2.7 MILLION // AREA 17,818 SQ KM // OFFICIAL LANGUAGE ARABIC

Kuwait

A tiny oil-rich city state surrounded by three Middle Eastern giants, Kuwait occupies one of history's most contested regions. Iraq's 1990 invasion of Kuwait may be what most people know about the country, but civilisation here dates back millennia to the fabled Dilmun Empire. Fast forward to the present and Kuwait is one of the most intriguing corners of the Gulf. Fascinating old-style markets and dhow harbours sit alongside eye-catching feats of contemporary architecture and some of the best museums in the Middle East. Home to traditional Bedouin tribesmen and thoroughly modern oil-rich sheikhs, a bastion of Gulf tradition and an emerging battleground for women's rights and liberalising trends, Kuwait is the Gulf's past, present and future in one small space.

Best time to visit
February to April

Top things to see
- The stunning modern architecture of the Kuwait Towers
- An extraordinary collection of Islamic art at Tareq Rajab Museum
- Giant spider crabs and crocodiles at the Middle East's largest aquarium, Scientific Center
- Failaka Island, holding some of the richest archaeological sites in the Gulf

Top things to do
- Learn about the Kuwaiti past in Kuwait City's fabulous National Museum
- Bargain for kitsch and search for treasure in Kuwait City's sprawling souq
- Dine on Persian Gulf fish in Al-Boom Restaurant, housed in the hull of an ancient dhow

Getting under the skin
Read: *Days of Fear* is a definitive, first-hand account of the Iraqi invasion and occupation by John Levin
Listen: to Abdullah al-Rowaishid, who blends traditional music with Arabic pop
Watch: *Fires of Kuwait* by David Douglas, which follows the teams cleaning up burning oil wells after the Iraq war
Eat: Gulf fish baked or stewed with coriander, turmeric, red pepper and cardamom
Drink: coffee served Arabic-style

In a word
Gowwa (Hello)

Trademarks
Iraq's 1990 invasion of Kuwait and its 1991 liberation; Kuwait Towers; blend of strong tradition and creeping liberalisation

Random fact
During the Iraqi invasion and occupation, the custodians of the Tareq Rajab Museum bricked up the doorway at the bottom of the entry steps and littered the steps with rubbish, thereby fooling would-be looters into going no further

LOOK-DIE BILDAGENTUR DER FOTOGRAFEN | ALAMY // WAEL HAMDAN | GETTY IMAGES // GAVIN HELLIER | GETTY

K · CAPITAL BISHKEK // POPULATION 5.5 MILLION // AREA 199,951 SQ KM // OFFICIAL LANGUAGES KYRGYZ & RUSSIAN

Kyrgyzstan

A land of mountain valleys, glittering lakes and felt yurts, Kyrgyzstan is a dream for DIY adventurers, responsible tourists and apiring nomads (visit immediately if you are all three). After the collapse of the USSR, tiny Kyrgyzstan turned to tourism, creating a cutting-edge network of community-based ecotourism ventures and homestays. Dozens of adventures await the intrepid, from horse treks and yurt stays to heli-skiing and felt-making, safe in the knowledge that your tourist dollars are going to local families. Throw in some Silk Road bazaars, two spectacular mountain passes to China, a tradition of open hospitality and most who have visited agree that Kyrgyzstan is Central Asia's don't-miss destination.

Best time to visit
June to September

Top things to see
- Issyk-Köl, a huge inland sea fringed with beaches and framed by snowy peaks
- Tash Rabat, Central Asia's most evocative *caravanserai* (historic inn for Silk Road merchants)
- Kyrgyzstan's second city of Osh; an ancient Silk Road bazaar town on the edge of the Fergana Valley
- The national sport of *Ulak tartysh*, colloquially known among travellers as 'goat polo'
- The production process for *shyrdak* (felt carpets), Kyrgyzstan's most iconic souvenir

Top things to do
- Live like a nomad on a two-day horse trek to remote Song-Köl lake
- Overnight in a yurt or community-tourism homestay to gain an insight into traditional local life
- Hike through the pristine alpine valleys of the Tian Shan range near the city of Karakol
- Go heli-skiing in the Tian Shan mountains, just an hour from the capital Bishkek
- Cross into China over the Irkeshtam or Torugart passes, Asia's most scenic border crossings

Getting under the skin
Read: the Kyrgyz novel *Jamilla* by Chingiz Aitmatov, Central Asia's best known novelist
Listen: to *Music of Central Asia Vol 1: Mountain Music of Kyrgyzstan*, (Smithsonian Folkways), a playlist of Kyrgyz music from traditional ensemble Tengir-Too

Watch: Aktan Abdykalykov's *Beshkempir* (Five Old Women)
Eat: *beshbarmak* ('five fingers'), a traditional dish of flat noodles and mutton, cooked in broth and eaten by hand
Drink: *kumys* (fermented mare's milk), sold along country roads in spring and summer

In a word
Ishter kanday? (How are things?)

Trademarks
Horses; eagle hunters; Tian Shan mountains; yurts; community-based tourism; *kalpak* hats; mountain peaks, felt rugs

Random fact
The Kyrgyz oral poem, the *Epic of Manas*, is the world's longest poem, 20 times longer than the *Odyssey*, and has been recognised by Unesco as intangible cultural heritage

1. A Kyrgyz cemetery protected by mountains in Naryn province

2. In a family yurt, a girl wears the six braids of an unmarried female

3. A local of Jaman Echki Jailoo wears a *kalpak* hat and traditional silks

L | CAPITAL VIENTIANE // POPULATION 6.7 MILLION // AREA 236,800 SQ KM // OFFICIAL LANGUAGE LAO

Laos

Like neighbouring Vietnam and Cambodia, Laos dropped off the overland trail during the Vietnam War, and it took a generation for this fascinating Buddhist backwater to be fully rehabilitated into the backpacker fold. Today, Laos is the country that everyone falls in loves with in Southeast Asia, partly for its laid-back way of life and rich culture, but mostly for its famously friendly people. Escaping the hubbub is the most popular thing to do, whether that means sipping a Beer Lao in the sleepy colonial city of Luang Prabang, trekking to remote tribal villages in the mountainous north, drifting around the pocket-sized capital, Vientiane, or literally drifting on the surging waters of the Mekong at Si Phan Don.

Best time to visit
November to February, to avoid the worst of the humidity

Top things to see
- A forest of golden spires at the Pha That Luang stupa in Vientiane
- One monk's vision of heaven and hell in the sculpture garden at Xieng Khuan
- Irrawaddy dolphins splashing around the 4000 river islands at Si Phan Don
- Royal relics and ancient monasteries in World Heritage–listed Luang Prabang
- Rafting, caving and climbing around the dramatic karst outcrops at Vieng Xai and Vang Vieng

Top things to do
- Drop into a Lao *wat* (Buddhist temple-monastery) for a chat with the novices
- Trek to tribal villages in the Nam Ha National Protected Area
- Take a slow boat along the Mekong from Luang Prabang to Nong Khiaw
- Eat a Lao lunch of barbecued pork and sticky rice overlooking the Mekong River
- Stay in tree houses that are only accessible by zip line in the forest home of the black gibbon

Getting under the skin
Read: Brett Dakin's *Another Quiet American* or Dervla Murphy's *One Foot in Laos* for a personal take on the Lao PDR (People's Democratic Republic)
Listen: to the undulating melodies of the *khene* (the traditional reed pipe of the Lao tribes)
Watch: *Good Morning, Luang Prabang*, the first ever privately funded Lao movie
Eat: *laap* (spicy, marinated meat); or *tam maak hung* (green papaya salad)
Drink: *lao-lao* (rice liquor); or Beer Lao, the nation's favourite brew

In a word
Su kwan (The calling of the soul)

Trademarks
Angular stupas; monks with umbrellas; monsoon rains and rice paddy fields; dragon boat races along the Mekong; unexploded ordnance (UXO)

Random fact
Laos has the unenviable status of being the most bombed nation in the world – the estimated 80 million unexploded bombs left at the end of the Vietnam War continue to be a threat to the populace

1. Buddhist monks circumnambulate Pha That Luang in Vientiane
2. Jagged karst peaks surrounding Vang Vieng
3. Street markets offer a variety of handicrafts
4. Traditional paper umbrellas for sale in Luang Prabang

Best time to visit
May to September

Top things to see
- The medieval castle complex in Cēsis and its elegant 18th-century manor
- Enchantingly desolate and hauntingly beautiful Cape Kolka
- Rūndale Palace, Latvia's miniature version of Versailles (but without the crowds)
- Hilltop Turaida Museum Reserve with its medieval ramparts and verdant walking trails
- Liepāja's windswept shores and art nouveau buildings
- Rīga's Museum of Occupation and the imposing Freedom Monument

Top things to do
- Uncover emerald lakes and wispy blueberry fields in the Latgale Lakelands
- Bobsled down a 16-bend track at 80km/h in high-adrenaline Sigulda
- Hobnob with Russian jetsetters in the heart of Jūrmala's swanky spa scene
- Snack your way around the zeppelin hangars of Rīga's bounteous Central Market
- Stumble upon yawning caves, nature trails and Soviet bunkers in Gauja National Park

Getting under the skin
Read: *The Merry Baker of Riga* by Boris Zemtzov, an amusing tale of an American entrepreneur setting up shop as a baker in Rīga in the early 1990s
Listen: to Prāta Vētra (aka Brainstorm) for popular pop/rock; synth-heavy rock from the reborn Otra Puse, a band originally formed in the 1990s
Watch: Jānis Streičs' *The Child of Man*, about a boy growing up and falling in love in Soviet-occupied Latvia; and *The Mystery of the Old Parish Church*, tackling the prickly issue of locals collaborating with Nazi and Soviet occupiers during WWII
Eat: the almighty pig and ubiquitous potato; sausages; smoked fish; soups of beets, nettles and sorrel with dark rye bread; freshly picked berries in summer, mushrooms in autumn
Drink: Latvia's famous Black Balzām, a jet-black, 45 proof concoction that Goethe called 'the elixir of life'

In a word
Labdien (Hello)

Trademarks
Amber; art nouveau; Black Balzām; ballet dancer Mikhail Baryshnikov; artist Mark Rothko; explorer Aleksandrs Laime, who discovered Venezuela's Angel Falls; song and dance festivals

Random fact
Held every five years, Latvia's Song and Dance Festival unites close to 40,000 participants in a jaw-dropping (and sweet-sounding) display of patriotism

1. Rīga's hippest club, Piens, even has a mini velodrome

2. Retro trams traverse Rīga's art nouveau district

3. Rīga's vibrant Old Town

L CAPITAL RIGA // POPULATION 2.2 MILLION // AREA 64,589 SQ KM // OFFICIAL LANGUAGE LATVIAN

Latvia

If you've an appetite for Europe's lesser-known lights, a taste of Latvian life should stimulate the senses. Tucked between Estonia to the north and Lithuania to the south, Latvia is the meat of the Baltic sandwich, the savoury middle, loaded with colourful fillings. Thick greens take the form of Gauja Valley pine forests peppered with castle ruins – though these days as many people visit for adventure sports as medieval treasures. Onion-domed orthodox cathedrals cross the land from salty Liepāja to gritty Daugavpils. Cheesy Russian pop blares along the beach in Jūrmala. And spicy Rīga adds an extra zing as the country's cosmopolitan nexus. Finish with a serving of Rīga's rich eye candy: Europe's largest and loveliest collection of art nouveau architecture, and cobbled lanes hidden behind gingerbread trim.

Best time to visit
Year-round – summer for beaches, winter for skiing and spring or autumn for hiking

Top things to see
- Pigeon Rocks, huge, natural offshore rock arches in Beirut
- The capital's collection of art museums and galleries, including the reopened Sursock Museum
- Byblos, a gorgeous fishing port and one of the oldest continuously inhabited settlements on earth
- Qadisha Valley, the Unesco World Heritage–listed site with rock-hewn monasteries
- The pretty mountain village of Bcharre, birthplace of artist and poet Khalil Gibran

Top things to do
- Take the Jounieh Teleferique for dizzying mountaintop views
- Trek 6km through the extraordinary stalactites and stalagmites of Jeita Grotto
- Hike through the Chouf Mountains, arguably Lebanon's most spectacular scenery
- Party like there's no tomorrow in the wild, all-night clubs of Beirut

Getting under the skin
Read: Robert Fisk's *Pity the Nation*, the best account of Lebanon's civil war; or Amin Maalouf's novel *The Rock of Tanios*
Listen: to Fairuz, an enduring icon of Middle Eastern music
Watch: *West Beirut*, a classic tale of civil war by Ziad Duweyri; or *Caramel* by Nadine Labaki, the story of five Lebanese women
Eat: *mezze* (small dishes served as starters); *kibbeh* (spiced minced lamb in a fried bulgur-wheat shell)
Drink: Lebanese wines; arak mixed with water and ice; Almaza (the local beer)

In a word
Ahlan wa sahlan (Welcome)

Trademarks
Destination for the Middle East's jetset; Roman ruins; sectarian melting pot

Random fact
Although little remains, the southern Lebanese coast around Tyre and Sidon is where the ancient Phoenician Empire was born

1. Qadisha Valley, home to isolated monasteries, wildflowers and wildlife

2. Beirut's Corniche is a popular place for an afternoon stroll

3. Le Gray hotel bar overlooks Mohammad al-Amin Mosque, Beirut

4. The Temple of Bacchus is a highlight of the stupendous Roman ruins of Baalbek

L | **CAPITAL** BEIRUT // **POPULATION** 4.1 MILLION // **AREA** 10,400 SQ KM // **OFFICIAL LANGUAGE** ARABIC

Lebanon

With its gorgeously green valleys, Mediterranean coastline, wine regions and 1500-year-old cedar trees, Lebanon is one of the Middle East's most beautiful destinations. It's home to a mosaic of peoples who have coexisted here for centuries, both at peace and at war, frequently caught up in the region's wider troubles. Yet the Lebanese are famously resilient and in the cocktail bars, restaurants and hedonistic nightclubs of Beirut's most fashionable districts, you'd never guess there had been even a hint of conflict. The one-time 'Paris of the Middle East' remains as fun-loving and sophisticated as it's ever been. Elsewhere in the country, ancient cities and Roman ruins still stand and no matter where your travels take you, you'll never be in want of a good meal – the *mezze*, grilled meats and fresh salads of Lebanese cuisine are unforgettable.

Best time to visit

May to October, to avoid the rains and mist

Top things to see

- The rolling grasslands and wildflowers in Sehlabathebe National Park
- Vistas from the top of Thaba-Bosiu (Mountain at Night) – the old stronghold of King Moshoeshoe the Great and the birthplace of the Basotho nation
- Tapestry makers at work in Teyateyaneng (Place of Quick Sands), the craft centre of Lesotho
- Lovely mountain panoramas around the Moteng Pass and Oxbow
- San rock paintings around Malealea and the aptly named Gates of Paradise Pass

Top things to do

- Ride Basotho ponies through Lesotho's rugged interior
- Make your way up Sani Pass and take in the views from Sani Top
- Sleep in a traditional trading post for the views and a glimpse of authentic village life
- Hike in wild and beautiful Ts'ehlanyane National Park or Bokong Nature Reserve
- Hunt for fossilised dinosaur footprints around Quthing, Leribe and Morija

Getting under the skin

Read: *Basali! Stories by and about Women in Lesotho* edited by K Limakatso Kendall, or *Singing Away the Hunger* by Mpho 'M'atsepo Nthunya, for insights into the lives of women in Lesotho
Listen: to the *lekolulo*, a flute-like instrument played by herd boys
Watch: the artists at the Morija Arts & Cultural Festival
Eat: *papa* (maize meal) and *moroho* (greens)
Drink: *joala* (traditional sorghum beer) – a white flag flying in a village means that it's available

In a word

Khotso (Peace)

Trademarks

Basotho ponies; snow-dusted mountains; Basotho hats and blankets; highest lowest point of any country in the world (1400m); the world's only country entirely above 1000m; Prince Harry volunteer visits

Random fact

The Basotho are traditionally buried in a sitting position, facing the rising sun and ready to leap up when called

1. Cattle are herded past village rondavels

2. In Basotho culture, the blanket is an indispensable item of clothing and symbol of status

3. The breathtaking Maletsunyane Falls are almost twice the height of Victoria Falls

L CAPITAL MASERU // POPULATION 1.9 MILLION // AREA 30,355 SQ KM // OFFICIAL LANGUAGES SESOTHO & ENGLISH

Lesotho

In tiny Lesotho – the 'Kingdom in the Sky' – the thin urban veneer of Maseru, the capital, quickly gives way to traditional Basotho culture and customs. Herd-boys tend their sheep on steep hillsides, horsemen wrapped in *kobo* (Basotho blankets) ride their sure-footed ponies over high mountain passes and village festivals are a focal point of local life. South Africa is just a mountain pass or two away, but Lesotho's towering peaks and isolated valleys, and the pride of the Basotho in their identity, have served to insulate Lesotho's culture from that of its larger neighbour. For anyone seeking adventure, wilderness, a laid-back pace and the chance to get acquainted with people living traditional lifestyles, Lesotho is a magical destination.

L CAPITAL MONROVIA // POPULATION 3.99 MILLION // AREA 111,369 SQ KM // OFFICIAL LANGUAGE ENGLISH

Liberia

Long regarded as a byword for child soldiers and one of Africa's most brutal civil wars, Liberia was emerging from the ashes when it was caught up in the world's worst ever Ebola outbreak. Hopefully the country can soon get back on its feet. Tourism can undoubtedly play a huge role in its economic recovery, because despite all the ravages, one thing hasn't changed: Liberia is blessed with extraordinary natural beauty, its coastline lined with splendid beaches and its interior awash in barely penetrable rainforest. Founded by freed American slaves in the 19th century and inhabited for far longer by traditional groups famous for their artistic traditions and secret societies, Liberia's complicated cultural mix hasn't always worked. Travelling here is rarely easy, but it has the potential to be one of West Africa's most fascinating countries.

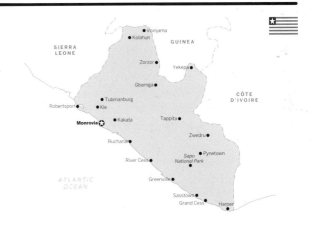

Best time to visit
November to April (the dry season)

Top things to see
- The village-turned-city, Monrovia, with the ruins of war and the frenetic activity of peace
- The much-damaged, but somehow surviving Sapo National Park, with forest elephants, pygmy hippos and chimps
- Buchanan, the vibrant yet tranquil port city and home to the Fanti people
- Harper, with its charming small-town feel and a fascinating history close to Côte d'Ivoire
- Firestone Plantation, where you can learn about rubber-tapping, one of Liberia's few industries

Top things to do
- Join local families on the beaches southeast of the capital
- Enjoy the perfect breaks while surfing off Robertsport
- Picnic at the pretty semicrater lake of Bomi, near Tubmanburg
- Enjoy the scenery around Yekepa and climb Goodhouse Hill, Liberia's highest point
- Dive into the clamour of Monrovia's Waterside Market

Getting under the skin
Read: Graham Greene's *Journey Without Maps*, describing his 1930s trek through Liberia and Sierra Leone; for something more recent, try *The Mask of Anarchy*
Listen: to *We Want Peace* by Gebah and Maudeline (The Swa-Ray Band)
Watch: *Johnny Mad Dog*, a 2008 Franco-Belgo-Liberian co-production filmed in Liberia and starring former child combatants
Eat: goat soup and traditional rice bread made with mashed bananas
Drink: ginger beer; *poyo* (palm wine); and strong coffee

In a word
Peace, man

Trademarks
Diamond smugglers; rubber plantations; one of the wettest and most humid places on earth; Ebola

Random fact
In 2005, former World Bank economist Ellen Johnson-Sirleaf defeated international soccer star George Weah to become Africa's first woman president

1. A man reads the Quran; Liberia is predominantly Christian, but Muslims form a significant minority

2. A woman lays out fish to smoke in West Point, a Monrovian slum

3. Liberian children gather outside a mosque near Bolahun; more than half of Liberia's population is under the age of 24

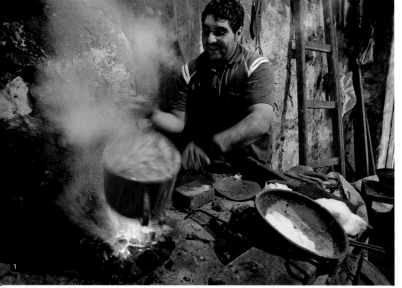

Best time
October to March, for cooler temperatures

Places of interest
- The pretty Roman city of Leptis Magna strung out along the Mediterranean
- Cyrene, the sophistication of Ancient Greece and Rome grafted onto African soil
- Ghadames, the Sahara's most captivating oasis and caravan town
- Cosmopolitan capital city, Tripoli, with a wonderfully preserved Ottoman-era medina and world-class museum
- Jebel Acacus, the haunting desert massif in the Sahara's heart with 12,000-year-old rock art

Local customs
- Packing a picnic and head for a beach along the country's unspoiled Mediterranean coastline
- Floating in the salty waters of the Sahara's Ubari Lakes, surrounded by towering sand dunes
- Joining friends at an outdoor restaurant for a *shay* (tea) and a meal in the streets surrounding Martyrs Square in Tripoli
- Escaping the heat of the coast and climbing up into the hills of the Jebel Nafusah (in the west) or Jebel al-Akhdar (east)

Getting under the skin
Read: *In the Country of Men* by Hisham Matar, a searing novel about modern Libya; or *Libya: Continuity and Change* by Ronald Bruce St John, the dry but definitive account of modern Libyan history
Listen: to *malouf*, a traditional musical form from Andalucía that's the accompaniment to most celebrations
Watch: *The English Patient*: it may not have been filmed in Libya, but this Oscar-winning epic captures the essence of old Libya from Tobruk to the Sahara
Eat: home-made bread, cooked beneath the sand and enjoyed under Saharan stars
Drink: three glasses of strong, sweet tea with the Tuareg around a campfire in the Sahara

In a word
Bari kelorfik (Thank you) – a blessing

Trademarks
Unesco World Heritage–listed ancient cities and rock art; vast seas of sand; lakes in the heart of the desert

Random fact
For 90 years Libya was famed for holding the world record for the highest air temperature recorded (57.8°C), until the claim was rejected by the World Meteorological Organisation as spurious in 2012

1. A coppersmith at work in a medina

2. A Tuareg man gazes out over Ubari Lakes; Tuaregs are Berber peoples and traditionally nomadic pastoralists

3. Magnificent Roman ruins at Leptis Magna

4. The oasis of Ubari Lakes, with an ocean of sand dunes beyond

L CAPITAL TRIPOLI // POPULATION 6 MILLION // AREA 1,759,540 SQ KM // OFFICIAL LANGUAGE ARABIC

Libya

Libya is at war with itself. In the post-Gaddafi era, militias, many openly hostile to Westerners, have divided the country into a series of mini-states, and it will be some years before Libya is safe to visit. When that changes, Libya will once again welcome travellers with a stunning coastline studded with ruined Roman and Greek cities, poignant WWII sites and some of the most beautiful stretches of the Sahara Desert, where the shifting sands serve as a reminder that nothing stays the same forever.

Best time to visit
December to March for winter sports; May to late September for summer hikes

Top things to see
- Schloss Vaduz, the turreted fairy-tale castle looming over the town
- Postage stamps issued in the principality since 1912 at the Post Museum in Vaduz
- The snowy slopes of Malbun where British royal Prince Charles learnt to ski
- Austria, Switzerland and most of little Liechtenstein from the lofty crests of Malbun's circular Fürstin-Gina hiking trail

Top things to do
- Toast His Majesty on 15 August – the only day when he opens the grounds of his castle in Vaduz for all and sundry to visit (and watch a magnificent firework display)
- Lunch amid royal vines at Torkel, the ivy-clad royal restaurant in the capital
- Enjoy a concert in style at Balzers's fairy-tale 13th-century castle, Burg Gutenberg
- Hike the Fürstensteig, a rite of passage for every Liechtensteiner
- Skate along the Väluna Valley on cross-country skis

Getting under the skin
Read: David Beattle's *Liechtenstein: A Modern History* for the complete story on how this tiny country almost got wiped off the world map
Listen: to Vaduz-born classical composer Joseph Gabriel Rheinberger (1831–1901)
Watch: movies beneath the stars during July's atmospheric Vaduz film festival
Eat: traditional local dishes like savoury *Käsknöpfle* (tiny cheese-flavoured flour dumplings) and sweet *Ribel* (a semolina dish served with sugar and fruit compote or jam)
Drink: local, rarely exported, wine

In a word
Guten Tag (Hello, good day)

Trademarks
Quality living; downhill skiing; fairy-tale castles; story-book panoramas; constitutional monarchy; tax haven; exporter of false teeth and sausage skins

Random fact
Liechtenstein is the only country in the world named after the people who purchased it

1. The low-rise capital of Liechtenstein, Vaduz

2. Traditional dress on National Day (15 August)

3. Vaduz Castle: palace and official residence of the Prince of Liechtenstein

L // CAPITAL VADUZ // POPULATION 37,009 // AREA 160 SQ KM // OFFICIAL LANGUAGE GERMAN

Liechtenstein

With a history and monarchy as storybook as its melodious mountain scenery speckled with tiled-roof stone castles and wintery snow scenes, rich old Liechtenstein puts a whole new perspective on the European tour guide's 'doing a country'. Indeed, this tiny, wealthy nation landlocked between Alpine greats Austria and Switzerland can be 'done' in a day…or three at most. And what a sweet, toy-like experience it is. Its capital city, crowned with the king's castle and his vineyards, is of miniature proportions; mountains envelop two-thirds of the country, and a 25km stroll takes you from Liechtenstein's northern to southern tip.

L CAPITAL VILNIUS // POPULATION 3.5 MILLION // AREA 65,300 SQ KM // OFFICIAL LANGUAGE LITHUANIAN

Lithuania

Mother Nature has sprinkled a decent dose of fairy dust over Lithuania, but you'll find that humans have left their stamp too, in undeniably weird and wonderful ways. White sandy beaches edge the Curonian Spit, an enchanting pig-tail of land dangling off the country's western rump, and deep magical forests guard twinkling lakes. The capital, Vilnius, is a beguiling artists' enclave, with mysterious courtyards, worn cobbled streets and crumbling corners overshadowed by baroque beauty beyond belief. The country's oddities – among them a hill covered in crosses, a forest peopled with carvings of witches, and a sculpture park littered with Lenins – bring a flavour found nowhere else. Add a colourful history, and raw pagan roots fused with Catholic fervour, and you've got a country full of surprises.

Best time to visit
May to September

Top things to see
- Vilnius, the baroque bombshell of the Baltics
- Thousands of crosses – some tiny, others gigantic – at the Hill of Crosses near northern town Šiauliai
- The slither of shifting sands that constitutes the remarkable Curonian Spit, with its mysterious Witches' Hill
- The red-brick gothic castle of Trakai, in a fairy-tale lakeside locale
- Hip second-city Kaunas with its art deco and street art, thumping nightlife and Museum of Devils

Top things to do
- Go fishing, boating, bathing and berry-collecting in the country's beloved Lakeland
- Brave the winter and go ice fishing on the Curonian Spit
- Dunk yourself in the silky spa waters of Druskininkai
- Ponder the past at Grūtas Park, dubbed Stalin World
- Grab a beer with a sea view at port city Klaipėda

Getting under the skin
Read: *The Last Girl* by Stephan Collishaw, bringing Vilnius to life in a brilliant historical novel covering WWII to the 1990s
Listen: to avant-garde jazz from the Ganelin Trio; rock from Andrius Mamontovas, a household name in Lithuania for more than two decades; Skamp, for hip hop and R&B
Watch: *Dievų Miškas* (Forest of the Gods), about a man imprisoned by both the Nazis and the Soviets
Eat: the formidable national dish of *cepelinai* (zeppelins), airship-shaped parcels of potato dough stuffed with cheese, meat and mushrooms, topped with a creamy sauce; save room (if you can) for *šimtalapis*, poppy seed cake
Drink: *midus* (mead: honey boiled with water, berries and spices, then fermented with hops); *stakliskes* (a honey liqueur); local beers Utenos and Švyturys; artisan coffee in Vilnius

In a word
Labas (Hello)

Trademarks
Baroque architecture; Catholicism; *cepelinai*; folk festivals; Stalin World; spa waters and amber beauty treatments

Random fact
Basketball is akin to religion in Lithuania, with Joniškis' Museum of Basketball as its temple – the worshipped national team enjoyed a victorious run, finishing in the top four for five successive Olympic Games

1. The Hill of Crosses, a place of pilgrimage a short distance north of the city of Šiauliai

2. Kaunas, Lithuania's second-largest city, is a centre of industry, culture and academia

3. The Church of St Michael in Vilnius now houses a religious museum

L CAPITAL LUXEMBOURG CITY // POPULATION 514,862 // AREA 2586 SQ KM // OFFICIAL LANGUAGES FRENCH, GERMAN & LËTZEBUERGESCH

Luxembourg

The Grand Duchy of Luxembourg is a throwback to the days when Europe was a constantly evolving patchwork of tiny states. Sitting in the heart of Western Europe, its own heart is Luxembourg City, a Unesco-listed stunner commanding the confluence of the Alzette and Pétrusse rivers. To the north lies Gutland – the 'Goodland' of villages, pasture and the Moselle vineyards – and, beyond that, the Luxembourgish portion of the Ardennes, watered by numerous rivers and studded with perfect towns such as Esch-sur-Sûre and Vianden. Throughout this tiny country, ruled by Grand Duke Henri and his Cuban-born queen, you'll find a people as proud and cosmopolitan as they are friendly.

Best time to visit
May to August, the sunniest months

Top things to see
- Modern art in a building designed by IM Pei of Paris Louvre fame at Luxembourg City's Musée d'Art Moderne Grand-Duc Jean
- Superb views of the Old Town and river valleys from the Passerelle, Luxembourg City's dramatic 19th-century viaduct
- Primeval rock formations in the Müllerthal region, also known as Luxembourg's 'Little Switzerland'
- Echternach, a town steeped in Christian history and ensnared by forest
- The white walls of Vianden's castle, rising imperiously above the town's cobbled streets and the surrounding forest

Top things to do
- Delve into the honeycomb innards of Luxembourg City's fortress casements, dating back to 1744
- Stroll Luxembourg City's Old Town, then lunch alfresco on tree-lined Place d'Armes
- Mosey from one winery to another along the Route du Vin in the Moselle Valley
- Wander the five-tiered remains of the shattered Château Beaufort
- Visit the Unesco World Heritage–listed permanent exhibition by Luxembourg photographer Edward Steichen inside a castle in Clervaux

Getting under the skin
Read: *How to Remain What You Are*, a humorous look at Luxembourg ways by writer and psychologist George Müller

Listen: to the Luxembourg Philharmonic Orchestra
Watch: *Lèif Lëtzebuerger* (Charlotte: A Royal at War) to catch Luxembourg's WWII history through the eyes of exiled grand duchess Charlotte
Eat: *quetschentaart,* an open tart, traditionally made with damson plums in autumn, now also made with other fruit and more widely available
Drink: a bubbly or fruity white Moselle wine

bearing the quality label *'Marque Nationale du Vin Luxembourgeois'*

In a word
Moien (Hello, in Lëtzebuergesch)

Trademarks
Banking; fairy-tale castles; beautiful china; traditional woollen clothes; trilingual citizens; winning Eurovision (five times)

Random fact
Luxembourg's commitment to the pan-European ideal was confirmed in 1985, when the Schengen Agreement was concluded in the southern Luxembourgish village of that name

1. The European Court of Justice (on left) and the Philharmonie Luxembourg (right), Luxembourg City

2. A small stone footbridge over the Alzette River, Luxembourg City

3. The historic Grund, home to the ancient Abbey of Neumünster, Luxembourg City

Best time to visit
October to December, to avoid the muggy summer weather

Top things to see
- The free-standing facade of the vanished Church of St Paul
- Winding lanes and grand colonial mansions on Ilha de Coloane
- Incense smoke drifting around the A-Ma Temple
- Swirls of black and yellow sand at Hac Sa Beach
- Giant statues of Matsu, Goddess of the Sea, and Kun Iam, Goddess of Mercy

Top things to do
- Admire the views from the top of the Macau Tower – or, if you feel brave, bungee-jump off the top
- Feast on Macanese delicacies like Portuguese egg tarts, African chicken and *minchi* (stir-fried soy sauce pork and beef mince with potatoes)
- Enjoy the roar of engines at the Macau Grand Prix
- Try to spot Hong Kong's Lantau Island from the top of Guia Fort
- Win or lose a few hundred pataca (the Macau currency) at the Venetian Macao casino

Getting under the skin
Read: Austin Coates' *City of Broken Promises,* a fictionalised account of the life of Martha Merop, Macau's most famous *taipan* (trader)
Listen: to the captivating melodies of Cantonese opera, performed at religious and cultural festivals throughout the year
Watch: Cai Yuan-yuan's *The Bewitching Braid*, the first-ever Macanese feature film
Eat: *galinha à Portuguesa* ('Portuguese chicken' cooked in a coconut sauce)
Drink: Portuguese *vinho verde* wine

In a word
Dou bok (To gamble)

Trademarks
Casinos and high-rollers; Portuguese architecture; boisterous festivals; fusion cuisine; almond cakes

Random fact
With more than half a million people crammed into 28.2 sq km, Macau is the most densely populated region on earth

1. Senado Square, the heart of the old city

2. The petitle Na Tcha Temple, set in the shadow of the Ruins of St Paul's church

3. Macau Tower and the city skyline

M POPULATION 583,003 // AREA 28.2 SQ KM // OFFICIAL LANGUAGES CANTONESE & PORTUGUESE

Macau

The last outpost of the Portuguese empire, Macau only became part of China in 1999, two years after the British withdrawal from Hong Kong. Even today, the city-state at the mouth of the Pearl River has a tangible Iberian feel, with baroque basilicas, cobblestone lanes, colonial mansions and grand civic squares. Nevertheless, Chinese culture shines through in the form of clicking chopsticks, Buddhist statues, incense-filled temples and signs illuminated with neon *hanzi* characters. For tourists from the mainland, the main attraction is the chance to gamble in Macau's glittering casinos; international visitors come for the Portuguese relics, the shopping and the beaches of Coloane, the former island at the tip of the Macau peninsula.

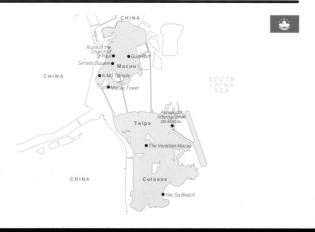

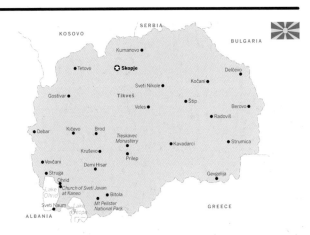

M CAPITAL SKOPJE // POPULATION 2.1 MILLION // AREA 27,713 SQ KM // OFFICIAL LANGUAGES MACEDONIAN & ALBANIAN

Macedonia

Macedonia is a fascinating combination of ethnicities, history and cultures that coalesce in a small, land-locked but immensely picturesque nation at the heart of the Balkans. With a staunchly Slavic Orthodox majority and thriving Albanian, Serbian, Turkish and Jewish minorities, not to mention tiny pockets of Vlachs and Roma, this multicultural republic has seen harmony prevail in a way that many of its neighbours have been unable to. The government has been hard at work creating what they see as a much-needed national consciousness, largely by peppering the charming capital city, Skopje, with monuments to historic Macedonians. Outside the capital mountain peaks soar, wonderful Lake Ohrid glistens and meadows full of flame-red poppies are the order of the day.

Best time to visit
April to September

Top things to see
- Ohrid's graceful domes and the diminutive 13th-century Church of Sveti Jovan at Kaneo
- Skopje's frankly bizarre collection of quirky statues, bridges and neoclassical-style buildings that have sprung up as part of the city's controversial makeover
- Undulating vine-covered hillsides and placid lakes in the Tikveš wine region
- Vivid frescoes alongside Roman remains and tombs at Treskavec Monastery
- The sublime Ottoman floral motifs of the Painted Mosque at Tetovo, and the nearby Arabati Baba Tekke dervish lodge

Top things to do
- Haggle for traditional crafts, carpets and dolls in Skopje's Čaršija, the Turkish bazaar at the heart of the city
- Kneel down to hear Sveti Naum's heartbeat at his tomb next to magnificent Lake Ohrid
- Enjoy great local hospitality and home cooking at Villa Dihovo, a guesthouse in the village of the same name outside Bitola
- Hike into Mt Pelister National Park, passing through the Vlach village of Malovište

Getting under the skin
Read: *Black Lamb and Grey Falcon*, Rebecca West's Balkan travel masterpiece; or Hidden Macedonia by Christopher Deliso
Listen: to anything by Toše Proeski, a Macedonian singer beloved across the Balkans who died in a car accident in 2007 aged just 26
Watch: *Before the Rain*, a cycle of three linked stories directed by Milcho Manchevski
Eat: *skara* (grilled meat), the national favourite, accompanied by *nafora* (crusty bread sprinkled with white cheese and baked) and *ajvar* (red-pepper relish)
Drink: *rakija* (grape brandy) or hearty red wines from the Kavadarci region

In a word
Haydemo (Let's go)

Trademarks
Lake Ohrid; untouched countryside; Skopje bazaar; Orthodox monasteries; Roman ruins; the endangered Ohrid trout; naming controversy

Random fact
In 2008, 200,000 Macedonians (10% of the entire population) planted two million trees in the first Macedonian Tree Day, which has since become a semi-annual event

1. The Church of Saint Clement of Ohrid in Skopje has a Macedonian Orthodox congregation

2. Traditional Macedonian folk costumes feature elaborate embroidery

3. Samuel's Fortress sits above the old town of Ohrid and is a Unesco World Heritage site

M CAPITAL ANTANANARIVO // POPULATION 22.6 MILLION // AREA 587,041 SQ KM // OFFICIAL LANGUAGES MALAGASY & FRENCH

Madagascar

Who says science isn't fun? The great Madagascar experiment began some 165 million years ago when it was ripped from Africa and sent floating off into the newly formed Indian Ocean. Isolated, the island's plants and animals evolved, creating thousands of dumbfounding species that Madagascar could call its very own. The remaining forests still teem with this outlandish life, and encounters with it can't help but make you giggle with delight. The Malagasy, who are relatively recent arrivals, are equally captivating. Fiercely patriotic, they believe family is central to life, and their startling exhumation ceremonies prove the dead are just as important to them as the living. Pure fantasy? No. Unforgettable? Yes.

Best time to visit
April to October (the dry season)

Top things to see
- *Tsingy*, surreal limestone pinnacles that would make Antoni Gaudí proud
- Remote Madagascar from a pirogue floating down the Manambolo River
- Drive down Allée des Baobabs, a wild dirt road lined by giant, ancient trees
- Famadihana, or 'turning of the bones', a sacred ceremony of exhumation
- Malagasy life in fast forward on the colourful streets of Antananarivo

Top things to do
- Try not to get caught up in it all when walking through the remarkable 'spiny forest' in Parc National d'Andohahela
- Trek deep into the lush cloud forests of Parc National de Ranomafana to swap looks with lemurs
- Step into an envy-evoking postcard at Andilana's beach on the island of Nosy Be
- Experience the geological and biological wonders of Parc National de l'Isalo while hiking, cycling or swimming
- Find your own personal treasure when diving the reef off Nosy Ve, a former haunt of Malagasy pirates

Getting under the skin
Read: *A History of Madagascar* by Mervyn Brown, an eminently readable, authoritative description of the island's history
Listen: to *hira gasy*, live storytelling spectacles in Madagascar's central highlands
Watch: Raymond Rajaonarivelo's *Quand les Étoiles Rencontrent la Mer* (When the Stars Meet the Sea), the story of a boy born during a solar eclipse; Rajaonarivelo's *Tabataba*, a film about the bloody rebellion against the French in 1947
Eat: *vary hen'omby* (rice served with stewed or boiled zebu)
Drink: *rano vola* (rice water), a brown, smoky-tasting concoction – it's an acquired taste!

In a word
Manao ahoana ianao (How do you do?)

Trademarks
Lemurs; *tsingy*; chameleons; Allée des Baobabs; zebu-drawn carts; aggressive forestry; economic stagnation

Random fact
Rice is so significant in Malagasy culture that words used to explain the growth of it are the same as those used to describe a woman becoming pregnant and giving birth

1. Verreaux's sifaka with baby, Réserve Privée de Berenty

2. Locals pass between giants on the Allée des Baobabs

3. *Tsingy*, eroded limestone pinnacles, in Parc National des Tsingy de Bemaraha

M

M CAPITAL LILONGWE // POPULATION 17.3 MILLION // AREA 118,484 SQ KM // OFFICIAL LANGUAGES ENGLISH & CHICHEWA

Malawi

Malawi is dominated by its lake – known as Lake Malawi, Lake Nyasa or 'Lake of Stars' – and by its reputation for friendly people and easy travel. But away from the stereotypes you'll find much more. The country has beautiful, diverse landscapes, ranging from dramatic peaks to rolling grasslands, from hills and waterfalls to a tropical shoreline. Its national parks have slowly been restocked and the nation is once again home to the Big Five (lion, leopard, rhino, buffalo and elephant), along with other enigmatic creatures such as zebras, impalas, crocodiles, hippos and birds galore. Traditional culture thrives in villages and on the lake's islands. Stay for a week or three, relax on the lake, hike in the hills, explore the Nyika Plateau, and – best of all – get to know Malawians. You'll be hooked.

Best time to visit
April/May to September

Top things to see
- A wealth of birds in the swamplands of Elephant Marsh, an ornithologist's paradise
- More than a thousand colourful cichlid fish species in the clear waters of Lake Malawi
- The beaches, the cathedral, the baobabs and the mango trees on lovely Likoma Island
- Elephants, impalas and buffaloes at Vwaza Marsh Wildlife Reserve
- The annual Lake of Stars Festival, perhaps Africa's greatest music celebration

Top things to do
- Hike or ride a horse past zebras and antelopes in magnificent Nyika National Park
- Scale majestic Mt Mulanje
- Meander down Lake Malawi on the *MV Ilala* ferry, Malawi's grande dame of water-going vessels
- Paddle a dugout canoe along the Lake Malawi shoreline, listening to the calls of fish eagles circling above
- Spot hippos and crocs in the Shire River in Liwonde National Park

Getting under the skin
Read: *The Rainmaker*, a poetic drama by Steve Chimombo; or Legson Kayira's *The Looming Shadow*, an exploration of conflicts between traditional and modern beliefs
Listen: to Lucius Banda's 'Malawian-style' reggae
Watch: *Up in Smoke*, a documentary exploring the effects of the tobacco industry in Malawi

Eat: *nsima* (maize meal) and *chambo* (a fish from Lake Malawi)
Drink: *chibuku* (shake-shake beer), a commercially produced local brew

In a word
Zikomo (Thank you)

Trademarks
Lake Malawi; carved wooden chief's chair; laid-back beach resorts; friendly locals; tobacco; *MV Ilala* ferry; wildlife

Random fact
Malawi is home to over 600 species of bird, and there are more fish species (over 1000) in Lake Malawi than in any other inland body of water in the world

1. Otter Point, Lake Malawi; the lake has been a major source of food for millennia
2. A cyclist rides past the lush tea plantation of Satemwa Tea Estate
3. Elephants used to be common in Malawi, but illegal poaching has seen their numbers plummet
4. A woman carries her child on her back; close to half of Malawi's population is under the age of 14

Best time to visit
May to September, for the least chance of rain (though it can be hazy)

Top things to see
- Kuala's Petronas Towers illuminated at night
- Tea plantations sprawling across the Cameron Highlands
- The dawn view from the summit of Mt Kinabalu, Malaysia's highest peak
- Colonial grandeur and dragon-tiled temples in George Town (Penang)
- Surreal acts of self-mortification during the Thaipusam festival at Batu Caves

Top things to do
- Get up close to the 'old man of the forest' at Sepilok Orangutan Rehabilitation Centre
- Stay in an Iban longhouse on Sarawak's mighty Batang Rejang river
- Dive with sharks and turtles on the awesome reefs of Sipadan
- Enjoy the full tropical island experience at Pulau Perhentian or Pulau Langkawi
- Munch on *nasi lemak* (coconut rice steamed in banana leaves) in a traditional Melaka coffeeshop

Getting under the skin
Read: Tash Aw's *The Harmony Silk Factory* and Rani Manicka's *The Rice Mother* for two different takes on Malaysian multiculturalism
Listen: to *dondang sayang* (Chinese-influenced love ballads); or the wholesome Malay pop of Siti Nurhaliza and Mawi
Watch: Yasmin Ahmad's award-winning *Sepet*, which challenges taboos about cross-cultural relationships in Malaysia
Eat: *roti canai* (fried, flat bread with a rich curry dipping sauce) at one of Malaysia's 24-hour *mamak* (halal south Indian-Malay) canteens
Drink: *teh tarik* ('pulled' tea with condensed milk); or *tuak* (rice wine from Borneo)

In a word
Malaysia boleh! (Malaysia can do it!)

Trademarks
The Petronas Towers; orangutans; dense jungles; logging; Michelle Yeoh; tribal longhouses; colonial relics; hawker food; Mt Kinabalu, the Malaysian F1 Grand Prix

Random fact
Malaysia is home to the largest flower in the world, the foul-smelling rafflesia, which can grow to more than a metre in diameter

1. An Iban tribesman paddles down the Jelia River in Sarawak

2. Kuala Lumpur's vertiginous skyline, the Petronas Towers brightly lit

3. Orangutans swinging from branches at Semenggoh Wildlife Centre

4. Tea picker at work in the Cameron Highlands

M | CAPITAL KUALA LUMPUR // POPULATION 29.6 MILLION // AREA 329,847 SQ KM // OFFICIAL LANGUAGE BAHASA MALAYSIA

Malaysia

Malaysia offers two vastly different territories for the price of one – Peninsular Malaysia, with its sprawling cities, forested highlands and fringing islands, and Malaysian Borneo, whose lush jungles provide a haven for orangutans and indigenous tribes. 'Unity in diversity' is the national motto of this famous melting pot, a heady blend of Malay, Indian and Chinese culture (among others), with a garnish of animist traditions, courtesy of the Orang Asli – literally 'original people' – of Sabah and Sarawak. A steamy colonial air hangs over the mainland cities of George Town (Penang), Melaka and Kuala Lumpur, while Malaysian Borneo is a playground for divers, trekkers and modern-day explorers.

Best time to visit
December to April for fine weather, manta rays and whale sharks; or May to December for schooling hammerheads

Top things to see
- Sunrise over the surf from a palm-draped coral-sand beach
- The mesmerising underwater world just metres from your beach towel
- The mosques and bustling fish market in Male', the pocket-sized Maldivian capital
- Laid-back villages and the ruins of the British WWII air base on Gan island
- Whale sharks, manta rays and hammerheads performing a natural ballet beneath the surface of the Indian Ocean

Top things to do
- Dive or snorkel on spectacular *thilas* and *giris* (isolated reefs) and *kandus* (deepwater channels)
- See the Maldives from above on a scenic seaplane flight between the atolls
- Take a cruise to an outlying island on a *dhoni* (traditional Maldivian boat)
- Drop into a local cafe in Male' for a snack-sized feast of *hedika* (short eats)

Getting under the skin
Read: Imogen Edward-Jones' *Beach Babylon*, allegedly based on true events at a luxury Maldives resort
Listen: to *bodu beru* (big drum), the traditional folk music of the islands
Watch: *The Island President*, an award-winning documentary following the efforts of then-President Mohamed Nasheed to tackle rising sea levels caused by climate change
Eat: *garudia* (smoked-fish soup); or *hedika* – delicious, spicy fish-based snacks
Drink: *raa* (a sweet and tasty toddy tapped from the coconut palm)

In a word
Mabuti naman (I'm fine)

Trademarks
Coral atolls; white sand; swaying palms; coconuts; honeymoons; Condé Nast–friendly resorts; world-class diving; politically motivated arrests; the ever-present threat of climate change

Random fact
The highest point in the Maldives is just 2.4m above sea level – if sea levels continue to rise, plans are afoot to move the entire population to a new homeland overseas

1. Somewhere to get stranded for a week; a sliver of an island off North Male' Atoll

2. Boys at play in the capital, Male'

3. A traditional *dhoni* sails the cerulean waters off North Male' Atoll

M CAPITAL MALE' // POPULATION 393,988 // AREA 298 SQ KM // OFFICIAL LANGUAGE DIVEHI

Maldives

Floating just above the surface of the Indian Ocean, the islands of the Maldives are the world's most glamorous playground for sun-seekers. This is where tourist brochure pictures come to life, and the scattered atolls are home to some of the most exclusive resorts on earth, each on its own idyllic tropical island. The islands where ordinary Maldivians live were once off-limits, but the Muslim communities of the so-called 'inhabited islands' are increasingly opening up to visitors, and the postcard perfection of the islands is matched only by the staggering richness of the coral reefs that lie between the atolls. Above the water though, there is sometimes trouble in paradise, thanks to the heavy-handed rule of the islands' autocratic government and the growing effects of climate change.

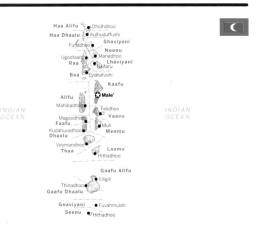

Best time to visit
October to February

Places of interest
- Djenné's Grande Mosquée, the largest (and most breathtaking) mud structure on the planet
- The legendary (yet humble) city of Timbuktu, with its historic manuscripts and mosques
- Bamako's live music venues where Mali's master musicians play
- The sleepy riverside town of Ségou with its *bogolan* (mud cloth) workshops
- The bustling port and salt trading centre of Mopti, which rests at the confluence of the Niger and Bani Rivers
- Timeless Dogon villages at the foot of the dramatic Bandiagara Escarpment

Local customs
- Sharing and gift-giving are key elements of Malian society
- When nomadic Fulani women are not travelling by donkey caravans, they make handicrafts such as engraved gourds
- Tea, which forms a key part of the Tuareg culture's daily rhythm, is considered a friend of conversation
- The five-day Dogon Fête des Masques sees men wearing masks representing buffaloes, hyenas and Amma, the Dogon goddess of creation

Getting under the skin
Read: *Ségu* by Maryse Condé, a sweeping generational tale that captures the essence of Malian history and its ethnic groups
Listen: to Tinariwen, Toumani Diabaté, Amadou and Mariam, the late Ali Farka Touré, Salif Keita, Oumou Sangaré…the list is endless
Watch: *Yeleen* by Souleymane Cissé, which won the Special Jury Prize at Cannes in 1987
Eat: *capitaine* (Nile perch)
Drink: *bissap* or *djablani* juice (brewed from hibiscus petals); Castel (Malian beer)

In a word
Bonjour, ça va? (Hello, how are you?)

Trademarks
Mud architecture; the Mali and Songhaï Empires of the Middle Ages; Timbuktu; Bambara woodcarvings and *bogolan* cloth; Tuareg nomads; UN peacekeepers

Random fact
King Kankan Musa of the Mali Empire distributed so much gold en route to Mecca in the 14th century that it was a generation before the world gold price recovered

1. Dogon men perform a traditional masked dance to honour their ancestors

2. Djenné's Grande Mosquée is considered to be the pinnacle of Sudano-Sahelian architecture

3. Mudbrick granaries and houses in the Dogon village of Banani, Bandiagara Escarpment, Dogon Country

(M) CAPITAL BAMAKO // POPULATION 16.4 MILLION // AREA 1,240,192 SQ KM // OFFICIAL LANGUAGE FRENCH

Mali

More than a thousand years before Mali was Mali, it was at the heart of West Africa – and the now fabled city of Timbuktu, located on the southern edge of the Sahara, was one of the world's greatest centres of learning and a key trading post for its gold- and salt-rich empire. The city's legend and other compelling cultural attractions – Dogon Country, the mammoth mud-built Grande Mosquée of Djenné, the river port of Mopti, and the modern nation's enthralling music scene – later ensured the nation became the darling of West African tourism in the 20th century. However, an armed rebellion by Tuareg nomads and subsequent Islamic militant incursions due to the collapse of Libya in 2011 have sadly made Mali off-limits to travellers.

(M) CAPITAL VALLETTA // POPULATION 411,277 // AREA 316 SQ KM // OFFICIAL LANGUAGES MALTESE & ENGLISH

Malta

Guarding the entrance to the eastern Mediterranean, miniscule Malta has a strategic significance that dwarfs its tiny size. Over the centuries, a succession of empires have squabbled over this rocky outpost to protect their fleets from rival empires across the water. Today, the Maltese islands – there are actually three – are best known for beaches, nightlife, scorching summer sun and, increasingly, for scuba diving. But scratch beneath the holiday-brochure gloss and you'll find tantalising glimpses of Europe's earliest civilisation, with rock-hewn temples carved centuries before the Egyptians even thought of their pyramids. Then there's the culture: a little bit British, a little bit Italian and a tiny bit Middle Eastern, tinged by memories of pirates, knights and sultans.

Best time to visit
February to June

Top things to see
- The fortified capital of Valletta built by the crusading Knights of St John, with its new City Gate, Parliament Building and Opera House designed by Renzo Piano
- The view from the elegant 'silent city' citadel of Mdina
- The eerie Hal Saflieni Hypogeum, a mysterious subterranean necropolis
- Malta's magnificent megalithic temples: Ġgantija, Ħaġar Qim and Mnajdra
- Marsaxlokk, a picture-postcard fishing village with fresh seafood to die for

Top things to do
- Get lost in Roman, Maltese and British history at Vittoriosa's dazzling Maritime Museum – or in the town's cinematic web of stone-lined alleyways
- Watch the curtain rise at Valletta's sumptuous Manoel Theatre, one of Europe's oldest, dating to 1731
- Splash, swim and frolic like a fish in the turquoise waters of the Blue Lagoon
- Don scuba tanks and duck beneath the waves to sea caves, reefs and a legion of shipwrecks
- Party like a Maltese during a *festa* – an infectious mix of music, food and fireworks

Getting under the skin
Read: British historian Ernle Bradford's *The Great Siege*, a gripping account of the epic 1565 battle between Ottoman Turks and the Knights of St John
Listen: to *għana*, Maltese folk music that mixes the Sicilian ballad and the wail of an Arabic tune, telling stories of village life and local history
Watch: *Simshar*, directed by Rebecca Cremona, based on a tragic true story; Angelina Jolie's *By the Sea*, in which Malta stands in for the French Riviera in the 1970s
Eat: a ricotta-stuffed *pastizza* (puff-pastry parcel); *aljotta* (garlic-spiked fish and tomato broth with rice); and *fenek* (rabbit) with spaghetti or baked in a pie
Drink: a thirst-quenching rum and Kinnie (bitter orange and herb-flavoured soft drink); or a fridge-cold bottle of local Cisk lager or Hopleaf ale

In a word
Kif inti (How are you?)

Trademarks
Crusading knights; falcons; the Maltese Cross; ancient ruins; wartime forts; sun and sand; British tourists; brightly painted fishing boats

Random fact
Malta's stunning and undeveloped landscapes have seen it feature as a location in many film and television productions, including *Gladiator*, *Troy*, *Captain Phillips* and *Game of Thrones*

1. The old fortified city of Birgu and its Grand Harbour

2. Built by the Knights of Malta, St John's Co-Cathedral in Valletta is a masterpiece of Baroque architecture

Best time to visit

The dry season from December to August in the south; the northern Marshalls are dry year-round and during September to November rains can be a blessing

Top things to see

- A red-hot sunset from the Delap-Uliga-Darrit (DUD) lagoon
- Navigational stick charts, model *korkor* canoes and shell tools at the Alele Museum and Library
- The twisted wreckages of Japanese WWII Zeros, Betty Bombers and more in the jungle foliage on Maloelap Atoll
- Beautiful, intricately woven mats, fans, baskets and 'kili bags' (once a favourite of Jackie Onassis) on sale

Top things to do

- Dive the WWII shipwrecks off Bikini Atoll
- Sail the waters of the Majuro lagoon in a *walap*, a traditional ocean-going canoe
- Catch a *boom-boom* (motorboat) for a *jambo* (trip) to one of the deserted outer islands
- Deep-sea fish off Longar Point on Arno Atoll
- Conquer your galeophobia and dive in the world's largest shark sanctuary

Getting under the skin

Read: *Stories from the Marshall Islands*, an anthology of traditional tales translated into English by Jack A Tobin
Listen: to the beat of *beet,* traditional Marshallese dance, influenced by Spanish folk music
Watch: 2015's *Jilel: The Calling of the Shell*, a Marshall Islands' global-warming fairy tale
Eat: a snack of boiled, sweet pandanus fruit (just watch out for the hairy insides!)
Drink: ice-cold coconut water

In a word

Yokwe yuk (Love to you)

Trademarks

Canoes; stick charts; sport fishing; diving; nuclear testing; US military; sharks

Random fact

In 1946, Bikini Atoll was the site for the first peacetime detonation of an atomic bomb; subsequently, the two-piece swimming costume (thought to be as awe-inspiring as the blasts) was named after the explosion site

1. Locals sail a traditional boat; the Marshallese have always been master navigators famed for their use of stick charts

2. A boy from Majuro Atoll; half of the Marshall Islands' population is under the age of 24

3. The tropical paradise you always dreamed of

Ⓜ CAPITAL MAJURO // POPULATION 70,983 // AREA 181 SQ KM // OFFICIAL LANGUAGES MARSHALLESE & ENGLISH

Marshall Islands

It's a neon-blue water world out in the Marshall Islands. This expanse of slender, flat coral atolls is so enveloped by tropical seas that anywhere at any time you can see, hear, smell and feel salt air and water. The people have embraced their remote, oceanic environment to become some of the world's finest fishermen, navigators and canoe builders. Throughout history, the British, Spanish, Germans, Japanese and Americans have all claimed these strategically located atolls. Today, the US military presence remains huge and the traumatic effects of bomb testing still linger. The charm, however, lies in the country's outer islands, which retain the pristine feel of a Pacific paradise.

Best time to visit
December to May when rains are moderate and hurricanes are few

Top things to see
- Ste-Luce, a charmer of a fishing village where a profusion of underwater life now lures divers
- The ruins of St-Pierre, the former capital destroyed by the eruption of Mt Pelée in 1902
- Presqu'île de Caravelle, a romantic mix of natural tropical beauty and tiny timeless villages
- The lonely black sand beaches dotting the north coast
- Fort-de-France's crumbling Creole charm and spectacular water views

Top things to do
- Pop a champagne bottle in the *très chic* yacht harbour, Pointe du Bout
- Stretch out on the sands of Les Salines, perhaps the most beautiful of this island's peerless beaches
- Surf the uncrowded breaks at Anse l'Etang, which is fronted by a palm-ringed beach
- Traverse the rainforest-clad interior on the mountainous Route de la Trace
- Try to speak some French with the locals, even if it is just a *'Bonjour'*

Getting under the skin
Read: *The Collected Poetry of Aimé Césaire*, the poet and politician behind the Black Pride phenomenon Negritude; *Texaco* by Patrick Chamoiseau and *Malemort* by Edouard Glissant are also excellent reads
Listen: to Dédé Saint-Prix, one of the leading exponents of Martiniquan styles such as *chouval bwa* and *zouk*
Watch: *Sugar Cane Alley* by Euzhan Palcy, documenting the love and sacrifice of a poor black family living on a sugar plantation in Martinique in the 1930s
Eat: *daube de lambis* (conch stewed with tomatoes, lime and chilli)
Drink: Fleur de Canne St James rum, redolent with the flowery essence of cane

In a word
Bonjou (Hello, in Créole Martiniquais)

Trademarks
Creole cuisine; lush mountains; banana plantations; *zouk* music; frangipani and hibiscus

Random fact
While French remains the official language of this offshore region of the mother country, most also speak Créole Martiniquais, the local variant of Antillean Creole

1. Sugar cane being harvested to produce the iconic AOC Martinique rum

2. The charming Church Les Anses-d'Arlet

3. Martinique is famed for its rich marine life; a young man finds a starfish at Anse Mitan

(M) CAPITAL FORT-DE-FRANCE // POPULATION 405,000 // AREA 1128 SQ KM // OFFICIAL LANGUAGE FRENCH

Martinique

A smouldering, coral-fringed tranche of France in the eastern Caribbean, Martinique parades its rich and varied history within a stunning natural setting. Dominated by Mont Pelée, the still-active volcano that took out the former capital Saint Pierre in 1902, its modern urban heart is the sprawling, sometimes raucous Fort-de-France. Beyond the capital's markets and museums can be found drowsy fishing villages, diving meccas such as Rocher du Dimant (Diamond Rock), beaches that practically command recumbency and a thickly rainforested interior. And, throughout this colourful 'Isle of Flowers', there's the food, music and conviviality of Creole culture to envelop the visitor.

Best time to visit
November to March

Places of interest
- Ben Amira: at 633m-high, it's one of the world's largest natural rock monoliths
- Terjît, one of the most verdant oases in the Sahara
- The dramatic old town of Ouadâne, built of brown stone
- Matmata's Saharan rock pools inhabited by Africa's unlikeliest crocodiles
- The nomad-built capital city of Nouakchott, facing the desert
- The charming vestiges of Chinguetti, an ancient Saharan city of Islamic learning
- Parc National du Banc d'Arguin and its prolific birdlife on the Atlantic coast

Local customs
- Extended family is the cornerstone of society, especially for the Moors
- There is a strong tradition of arts and craftwork, particularly silverwork
- Continued drought and desertification has pushed many nomads into the capital, Nouakchott
- Islamic tradition in Mauritania includes a belief in a variety of supernatural spirits, while still recognising the only God is Allah

Getting under the skin
Read: Peter Hudson's *Travels in Mauritania*, which follows the author's early 1990s exploration of the country on foot, donkey and camel
Listen: to Malouma, who has modernised traditional Moorish music
Watch: *Heremakono* (Waiting for Happiness) by Mauritanian director Abderrahmane Sissako, set in Nouâdhibou
Eat: at a *méchui* (traditional nomads' feast), where an entire lamb is roasted over a fire and stuffed with cooked rice
Drink: strong sweet tea; or the nomads' staple, *zrig* (curdled goat or camel milk)

In a word
Salaam aleikum (Hello, or Peace be with you)

Trademarks
The Sahara's beauty; desertification; priceless manuscripts in the desert; some of the longest and heaviest trains in the world

Random fact
Mauritania did not declare slavery a crime until 2007, making it the last country in the world to do so; however, tens of thousands of people are still thought to be enslaved here

1. The distinctive Fort Saganne Hotel, Chinguetti

2. November to February produces premium surf conditions off Cap Blanc, a headland jutting far out into the Atlantic Ocean

3. Cap Blanc is also known as the shipwreck capital of the world; the *United Malika* at rest

M CAPITAL NOUAKCHOTT // POPULATION 3.4 MILLION // AREA 1,030,700 SQ KM // OFFICIAL LANGUAGE ARABIC (HASSANIYA)

Mauritania

Although flanked by the might of the cold Atlantic Ocean, Mauritania's greatest sea is the one made of sand. The Sahara's shifting dunes dominate the country, flowing west from Algeria and Mali to the coast. The only interruptions are towering rock monoliths and remote oases, and some ancient Moorish towns like Chinguetti, which was a centre of Islamic learning from the 13th century. More than anything else, Mauritania is just unlike any other country in Africa – it's a deeply traditional Islamic republic that is part Arab and part African, but with an identity all its own. Before recent security issues made Mauritania out of bounds to travellers, it was traditionally the safest trans-Saharan route for overlanders and therefore an essential way station en route from Europe to West Africa.

1. Music is a big part of everyday Mauritian life

2. In the southwest of the island, Le Morne Brabant (556m) looms over the Indian Ocean

3. The lush Sir Seewoosagur Ramgoolam Botanical Garden, Pamplemousses

M CAPITAL PORT LOUIS // POPULATION 1.3 MILLION // AREA 2040 SQ KM // OFFICIAL LANGUAGE ENGLISH

Mauritius

Adrift in the Indian Ocean, this island paradise has collected many hangers-on since its fiery volcanic beginnings. One of the latest arrivals to wash up on its tropical shores was the human species. Today, Mauritius' social, gastronomic and architectural melange of Asian, African and European elements provides visitors with plenty to experience when not floating in azure seas, lounging on white-sand beaches or trekking through virgin rainforests. Minor tensions do exist between the Hindu majority, Muslims and Creoles, but respect and tolerance are intrinsic to Mauritian society. The cultural melting pot has been too hot for some to handle, however, with the island's most famous endemic species going the way of the dodo.

Best time to visit
May to November, for pleasant temperatures and the driest skies

Top things to see
- Lily pad power at Sir Seewoosagur Ramgoolam Botanical Gardens in Pamplemousses
- Rempart Serpent, La Passe St François and Colorado, three of Mauritius' best dive sites
- Virgin tropical rainforest in La Vanille Réserve des Mascareignes
- Trou d'Argent, an altogether staggering beach on the remote island of Rodrigues

Top things to do
- Surround yourself with casuarina trees and trek past waterfalls in Black River Gorges National Park
- Join local Mauritians on Belle Mare beach for a traditional Sunday picnic
- Soar over Rivière des Galets, past waterfalls and through lush forest on 13 zip lines that make up the 2km-route at St Felix

Getting under the skin
Read: Bernardin de St-Pierre's 18th-century classic *Paul et Virginie*, a romantic, moralistic tragedy inspired by real life events
Listen: to 'Anita' by the late Ti-Frère, a Mauritian singer who led the *séga* renaissance
Watch: *Lonbraz Kann* (Sugarcane Shadows)about the closing down of the island's sugar-cane factories
Eat: *rougaille* (a sauce of tomatoes, garlic and chilli with Creole-flavoured meat or fish)
Drink: *alouda* (an almond-based concoction best topped with ice cream)

In a word
Tapeta! (Cheers! in Mauritian Creole)

Trademarks
Land of the lost dodo; sugar-cane plantations; fusion cuisine; honeymooners; bleached beach sands

Random fact
A significant proportion of the country's electricity is produced from sugar cane, with condensing extraction steam turbines running in sugar mills

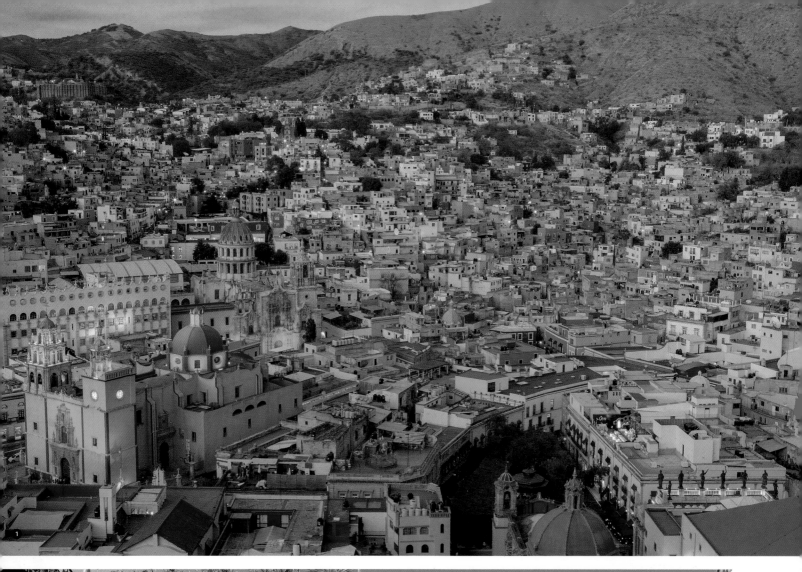

(M) **CAPITAL** MEXICO CITY // **POPULATION** 118.8 MILLION // **AREA** 1.9 MILLION SQ KM // **OFFICIAL LANGUAGE** MEXICAN SPANISH

Mexico

Mexico is a lot like its famous cuisine – spicy, full flavoured and exotic, but also rather familiar. Mexico's roll call of famous sights reads like a list of old friends: Mexico City; scuba diving around Cancún and Playa del Carmen; surfing and whale-watching in Baha; Chichén Itzá and the Riviera Maya; boisterous celebrations for the Day of the Dead. But there are plenty of surprises once you get past the touristy top drawer – lush jungles, silent deserts, snow-capped mountains, colonial cities and tribal culture. In recent years, Mexico's reputation as America's favourite escape has taken a knock from murderous rampages by Mexico's drug cartels, but travel patterns have flexed to avoid the hotspots, and the old charm still endures. Forget what you think you know, and you'll find more than you expected in Mexico.

Best time to visit
October to May, to avoid extreme temperatures

Top things to see
- Mexico's megacity capital: vast and chaotic but also cultured and cool
- Mayan temples rising above the dense jungle at Palenque
- Stately old-world charms in colonial Oaxaca and blissful beaches on the Pacific coast
- The vast abyss of the Copper Canyon, snaking through the Sierra Madre
- Classy beach life in Playa del Carmen, just miles from the tacky package-holiday version in Cancún

Top things to do
- Surf the waves washing the seemingly endless white beaches of mellow Puerto Escondido
- Go on the ultimate Mexican road trip through Baja's wild and desolate interior
- Sample real Mexican cuisine – not the sanitised Tex-Mex version – at a local *cantina*
- Admire Mexico's colonial legacy in Unesco-listed Guanajuato
- Feel the breeze of a billion butterfly wings at the winter refuge of Reserva Mariposa Monarca

Getting under the skin
Read: *The Air is Clear* by the great Carlos Fuentes; *Frida Kahlo and Diego Rivera* by Isabel Alcantara and Sandra Egnolff, the story of two pop culture icons
Listen: to Los Tigres del Norte and Cafe Tacuba – pioneers of *rock en español*
Watch: the landmark 1970s guerrilla struggles in the countryside in *The Violin*; a taste of near-hallucinatory romance in *Like Water for Chocolate*
Eat: the ubiquitous tortilla: soft and stuffed as burritos, enchiladas and quesadillas, or crisp and filled as tacos, taquitos and tostadas
Drink: *jugos naturales*, especially the bloodlike vampiro fruit juice (beet and carrot); the three spirits distilled from the maguey plant: tequila, mezcal and pulque

In a word
Mañana (Tomorrow) – the time to get everything done, but relax today

Trademarks
Tacos; mariachis; machismo; margaritas; moustaches; towering pyramids; *telenovelas*; fiestas; lawless border towns; mass migration to America

Random fact
Mexico City is sinking by up to 28cm per year as its burgeoning population drains water from the aquifer on which the city is built

1. Guanajuato, a former mining town, is famed for its colonial architecture

2. San Miguel de Allende is a beautiful city, with enchanting cobblestone streets and striking light

3. Buskers entertain diners at Mercado Juárez, Oaxaca City

Best time to visit
October to March, when the trade winds provide relief from FSM's energy-sapping humidity

Top things to see
- Yap's enormous stone money doughnuts, an ancient form of currency
- The ramshackle, pulsing hub of Kolonia, FSM's biggest town
- Hard working artisans and local dance performances at Yap's Ethnic Art Institute of Micronesia
- The 'Venice of Micronesia', Pohnpei's ancient stone city Nan Madol

Top things to do
- Dive Chuuk's veritable museum of Japanese WWII wrecks and spot Yap's graceful manta rays
- Imagine ancient life in the Lelu Ruins secreted in dense tropical vegetation on Kosrae
- Hike Pohnpei's and Kosrae's lush, rugged volcanic terrain
- Kayak through Kosrae's magical mangroves
- Watch the brilliant sun set behind the Faichuk Islands from Weno on Chuuk

Getting under the skin
Read: *His Majesty O'Keefe* by Lawrence Klingman, the true story of David O'Keefe, who landed on Yap in the late 1800s and became a very successful entrepreneur
Listen: to the compilation *Spirit of Micronesia*, recordings of traditional songs from around the region
Watch: *Globe Trekker's* Megan McCormick island-hop through Pohnpei, Yap and Chuuk
Eat: or rather chew *buw* (betel nut) with the locals and stain your mouth red
Drink: *sakau* (the local numbingly narcotic kava drink made from the roots of pepper shrubs)

In a word
Fager (Yapese), *Kompoakepai* (Pohnpeian), *Pwipwi* (Chuukese), *Kawuk* (Kosraean) – the word 'friend' from the respective islands

Trademarks
Giant stone money; traditional magic; betel nut; wreck diving; ancient stone cities; preserved cultures; seafood

Random fact
It's rumoured that the notorious American-born swindler Bully Hayes buried loot from the brigantine *Leonora* somewhere on Kosrae in 1874; many treasure hunts have ensued but nothing has been found

1. Losiep Atoll, a tiny coral islet in Yap State

2. Basket weaving is a traditional island craft handed down from one generation to the next

3. Micronesia has incredible marine life; swimming with a reef manta ray off Yap

Ⓜ CAPITAL PALIKIR (POHNPEI) // POPULATION 106,104 // AREA 702 SQ KM // OFFICIAL LANGUAGE ENGLISH

Micronesia, Federated States of

And now for somewhere completely different. The Federated States of Micronesia (FSM) is made up of four unique and otherwise unrelated island states: Kosrae, Pohnpei, Chuuk and Yap. Each region has cultures and traditions as colourful, distinct and diverse as the fish and coral formations that paint the fringing reefs. Kosrae is a Pacific paradise and arguably FSM's most beautiful island; Pohnpei is home to mysterious ancient ruins and a plethora of lush landforms; Chuuk is renowned for its wreck diving; and Yap is a fiercely traditional state retaining a true island spirit. If you can't find something in the diversity of FSM to expand your view of the world, check your pulse.

1. Closed by the Soviets in 1962, the Noul Neamț Monastery in Chițcani was reopened in 1989

2. Transnistria Parliament building in Tiraspol, with a statue of Vladimir Lenin in front

3. Lavender harvesters at work; there is a long tradition of growing lavender in Moldova

M CAPITAL CHIŞINĂU // POPULATION 3.6 MILLION // AREA 33,851 SQ KM // OFFICIAL LANGUAGE MOLDOVAN

Moldova

Buried deep inside the former Eastern Bloc, corralled from the sea by neighbouring countries, and strewn with rippling hills, Moldova remains out of sight and mind for most travellers. Sharing much, linguistically and culturally, with its northern neighbour Romania, it also contains two semi-autonomous regions: the largely Slavic Transdniestr, bordering Ukraine, and Gagauzia, the southern home of the Turkic Gagauz. While it's most famous for the precious output of its extensive vineyards, there's much more to Moldova than quality plonk, from the ebullient nightlife of the capital, Chişinău, to the 13th-century monastic complex dug into the caves of Orheiul Vechi.

M

Best time to visit
May to September

Top things to see
- Sprawling, lush Cathedral Park, framed by Chişinău's own Arc de Triomphe, flower market and Orthodox Cathedral
- Caves dug by 13th-century monks at Orheiul Vechi Monastery Complex
- The Kvint factory, distilling Transdniestr's finest brandy since 1897
- The Pushkin Museum, in Chişinău, where the great writer was exiled and wrote some of his classic novels

Top things to do
- Browse the world's largest wine collection in over 200km of subterranean cellars at Mileştii Mici
- Kick back over a bottle of wine with the locals in Chişinău's buzzing clubs and bars
- Travel back in time to Tiraspol, capital of breakaway Transdniestr and a lonely vestige of communism

Getting under the skin
Read: *The Moldovans: Romania, Russia and the Politics of Culture* by Charles King
Listen: to the unique 'bang and boom' sound of folk/hip hop/punk innovators Zdob şi Zdub
Watch: The films of Moldovan-born Emil Loteanu, including *Lautarii* and *Red Meadows*
Eat: *pelmeni* (Russian-style ravioli); or *sorpa* (a spicy mutton soup made by the Turkic Gagauz)
Drink: Local wine varietals including Fetească and Rara Neagra; or traditionally distilled vodka

In a word
Buna (Hello)

Trademarks
Wineries and vineyards in rolling countryside; horse-drawn carts and labourers swinging scythes in meadows; communist throwbacks

Random fact
While football is the pre-eminent sport in Moldova, the national sport remains *trânta*, upright wrestling in which contestants grip each other's cloth belts

Ⓜ POPULATION 30,500 // AREA 2 SQ KM // OFFICIAL LANGUAGE FRENCH

Monaco

Prince Albert II is king of this dynastic fairy tale, roughly wedged between France and Italy on Europe's most mythical, celebrity-studded coastline – the Côte d'Azur, or French Riviera. Glitzy, glam and bubbling over with self-assurance, this teensy-tiny seaside state sizzles with resident millionaires, luxury yachts and day trippers by the millions who traipse up to 'the Rock' to see the palace, sip Champagne at Café de Paris and have a flutter at the casino. Monégasque life is the high life, all-embracing the second you step off the train into Monaco's swanky, subterranean, marble-clad station. Above ground, Hong Kong–style skyscrapers jostle for sunlight as billion-dollar plans to expand Dubai-style out to sea hover on this unusual country's glittering-blue horizon.

Best time to visit
April to June, September, October

Top things to see
- The changing of the guard at the Palais du Prince
- Sharks above your head at the Musée Océanographique
- The graves of Grace Kelly and her Monégasque Prince Charming, Rainier III, in the cathedral
- Billionaire yachts moored at the port
- World-class racing drivers tearing around during the Formula 1 Grand Prix in May

Top things to do
- Risk a lot (or a little) amid belle époque opulence at Monte Carlo Casino
- Spoil yourself rotten with a caviar body treatment at the Thermes Marin de Monte Carlo
- Lunch at Le Louis XIV, Monaco's most prestigious dining address
- Hike between century-old cacti in the Jardin Éxotique
- Motor into France between sea and cliff along the hair-raising Grande Corniche

Getting under the skin
Read: Graham Greene's *Loser Takes All*, about a couple honeymooning in 1950s Monte Carlo
Listen: to 1930s music-hall singer Charles Colbert sing 'The Man Who Broke the Bank at Monte Carlo'
Watch: a VW Beetle speed through the Formula 1 Grand Prix tunnel in the Walt Disney classic *Herbie Goes to Monte Carlo*
Eat: Monégasque specialities *barbajuan* (spinach and cheese pasty) and *stockfish* (dried cod flavoured with aniseed)
Drink: Champagne aperitifs at celebrity-cool nightclubs on the waterfront

In a word
Bon giurnu (Hello, in Monégasque)

Trademarks
Millionaire lifestyle; banking; tax-free haven; Formula 1 Grand Prix; Grace Kelly; Monte Carlo Casino; the Grimaldi dynasty

Random fact
Although famous for its casino, Monaco forbids its citizens from even entering the gambling rooms

1. Little and large, yachts at rest in Port Hercules

2. 'The Rock', home to Monaco's historic Old Town and the Palais du Prince

3. The changing of the guard at the Palais du Prince

M

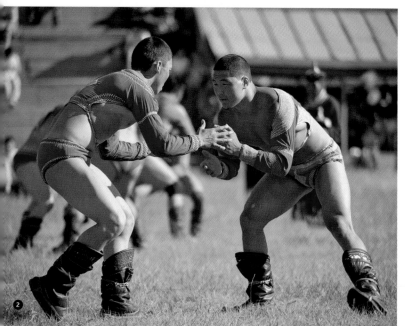

Best time to visit
June to September

Top things to see
- The Naadam festival, a traditional annual sporting contest featuring horse races, archery competitions and traditional wrestling
- Khövsgöl Nuur, a spectacular and pristine sub-Siberian lake
- Altai Tavan Bogd National Park, home to snowcapped peaks, sparkling blue lakes and Kazakh eagle hunters
- The ruined ancient Mongol capital of Karakorum and the nearby Tibetan Buddhist monastery of Erdene Zuu Khiid
- Ulaanbaatar, one of the world's strangest capital cities, where modern and nomadic lifestyles collide

Top things to do
- Conjure the spirit of Genghis Khan by galloping on horseback across open grasslands
- Spot gazelles, argali sheep, ibex and even reindeer in the country's epic and endless wildernesses
- Dig for dinosaurs or trek with Bactrian camels in the southern Gobi
- Overnight in a *ger,* where your Mongolian hosts will make you feel warmly welcomed with a feast and plenty of vodka

- Gaze up at the incredible ceiling of stars almost anywhere in the country

Getting under the skin
Read: *Moron to Moron: Two Men, Two Bikes, One Mongolian Misadventure* by Tom Doig
Listen: to the otherworldly sound of *khöömii* (Mongolian or Tuvan throat singing)
Watch: Sergei Bodrov's *Mongol,* the first in a planned trilogy depicting the life of Genghis Khan; or *The Weeping Camel,* a documentary about a camel-herding family in the Gobi
Eat: *boodog* (barbecued roast marmot, cooked from the inside with hot stones and crisped to perfection with a blow torch)
Drink: *airag* (fermented mare's milk); or *suutei tsai* (salty milk tea)

In a word
Sain baina uu (Hello)

Trademarks
Grasslands; endless steppe; horses; Gobi desert; Altai Mountains; eagle hunters; Genghis Khan; big blue skies; wrestlers; sub-Arctic winters; throat-singing

Random fact
Mongolia is the least densely populated of any country on earth

1. Traditional Mongolian *gers* on the steppe; the *ger* has been used in Central Asia for at least 3000 years

2. Wrestling is one of the main attractions at the annual Nadaam festival in Ulaanbaatar

3. Musicians play the *morin khuur* (horse-head fiddle) at a Nadaam festival in Arkhangai Province

4. A woman gallops her horse through a stream in Inner Mongolia

M | **CAPITAL** ULAANBAATAR // **POPULATION** 2.9 MILLION // **AREA** 1,564,116 SQ KM // **OFFICIAL LANGUAGE** MONGOLIAN

Mongolia

Blessed with huge horizons from the Gobi Desert to the Altai Mountains, Mongolia is the place for anyone who values a bit of personal space. Almost devoid of fences, roads or even towns, the best thing to do here is to hire a horse (or its modern equivalent, the 4WD) and set off on an epic trip across the grasslands. And just when you think you have reached the middle of nowhere, a herder will appear on horseback looking like a lost foot soldier from the time of Genghis Khan, to greet you like a long-lost friend and invite you to back to his *ger* (yurt). For anyone seeking untouched, vast landscapes, Mongolia rewards with a timeless sense of space and freedom that's simply intoxicating.

(M) CAPITAL PODGORICA // POPULATION 653,474 // AREA 13,812 SQ KM // OFFICIAL LANGUAGE MONTENEGRIN

Montenegro

Montenegro (Crna Gora) may have remained unknown to the West for centuries, but it was certainly well known to Adriatic pirates, Venetian plunderers, Ottoman pashas and Yugoslav technocrats. The unforgiving landscape and dogged people resisted all comers, emerging as an independent nation in 2006. It is a country that prides itself on 'humanity and bravery' – we'd add hospitality – and one that comfortably accommodates Orthodox monasteries, Albanian mosques and communal promenading every evening. As suggested by its brooding name (Crna Gora means 'Black Mountain'), Montenegro is a high, rugged place. The scree-covered mountains plummet to the coast, where flaming pomegranate trees and the impossibly blue waters of the Adriatic have an equally fierce beauty.

Best time to visit
April to September

Top things to see
- Almighty panoramas over Kotor and the cyan sea, from St John's Hill
- The historic capital of Cetinje, an idiosyncratic mix of grand city and cosy village
- Ostrog Monastery, dramatically carved into a vertical cliff and the spiritual heart of Montenegro
- Durmitor National Park, home to eagles, bears, wolves and hospitable highlanders
- The tiny, yet tremendously photogenic island of Sveti Stefan

Top things to do
- Hang on for the white-knuckle ascent from Kotor to Cetinje
- Feel the rush on a rafting trip down the Tara River
- Cool off in the limpid waters of the Adriatic at the beaches around Budva
- Peer through your binoculars at Lake Skadar, one of Europe's most important wetlands
- Pay your respects to national hero, Petar II Petrović-Njegoš, on a hike to his mausoleum in Mount Lovćen National Park

Getting under the skin
Read: *Realm of the Black Mountain* by Elizabeth Roberts, a lively history
Listen: to epic poetry sung to the accompaniment of the *gusle* (vaguely akin to a single-stringed sitar)
Watch: *Ljepota Poroka,* about old-school highlanders confronting modern life in a nudist colony

Eat: grilled squid on the coast; or, in the mountains, *jagnjetina ispod sača* (lamb baked in a metal pot under hot embers) and *kajmak* (mildly fermented heavy cream)
Drink: *loza* (grape brandy); or Nikšićko, the fabulous local beer

In a word
Dobro došli (Welcome)

Trademarks
Dreamy Adriatic coastline; Orthodox monasteries; resistance and resilience; wild mountains; stone architecture

Random fact
During the Romantic age, Western European observers developed a rose-tinted view of the Montenegrins, describing them as a 'race of heroes' and 'born warriors'

1. Sunrise over the glacier-carved peaks of Durmitor National Park
2. Our Lady of the Rocks, a Roman Catholic church on an artificial islet in the Bay of Kotor
3. The historical town of Kotor was first settled more than 2000 years ago by the Romans
4. The island of Sveti Stefan on the Bay of Budva, once a fishing village and now a luxury hotel

Best time to visit
October to April

Top things to see
- Marrakesh's Djemaa el-Fna square, a joyful riot of music, food, storytellers and snake charmers
- The ancient medina in Fez, the most intact medieval Arab city in the world
- Sunset over the Sahara Desert, where an ocean of sand dunes washes up at Erg Chigaga
- The quiet mountain town of Chefchaouen, where every house is painted cornflower blue
- The palm oases and rocky red cliffs of the central Dadès Gorge

Top things to do
- Trek deep into the Atlas Mountains with mules, sleeping at local Berber homestays
- Haggle for souvenirs in the souqs until you're knee-deep in carpets
- Lounge in a trendy *riad* (townhouse-cum-boutique hotel)
- Soak your cares away in a *hammam* (bath house) – go traditional or for the full spa experience
- Indulge your sweet tooth with a pot of scalding mint tea and a plate of pastries

Getting under the skin
Read: *The Caliph's House* by Tahir Shah, an account of restoring a *djinn*-haunted house in Casablanca
Listen: to the hypnotically bluesy grooves of *gnawa* (the Sufi- and slave-inspired music of Marrakesh and Essaouira)
Watch: *Hideous Kinky*, an odyssey of 1960s hippie dreams, with Kate Winslet and Morocco itself competing for top billing
Eat: *seksu* (couscous) – steamed for hours and heaped with meat or vegetables, the highpoint of any feast
Drink: local wine – red or white, Morocco has some surprisingly good wineries

In a word
Lebas? (How are you?)

Trademarks
Mint tea; Berbers; Marrakesh riads; couscous; quality rugs; Bogart and Bergman in *Casablanca*

Random fact
Casablanca's Hassan II Mosque accommodates 25,000 worshippers at prayer, and its minaret is 210m high – the tallest in the world

1. The chaotic cascades of Ouzoud Waterfalls, Atlas Mountains

2. Berber horsemen recreate a *razzia* (raid) during a *fantasia* (traditional display of horsemanship)

3. Chefchaouen in the Rif Mountains is famed for its houses painted in shades of blue

4. A red mosque stands out in the village of Adai in central Morocco

M **CAPITAL** RABAT // **POPULATION** 32.6 MILLION // **AREA** 446,550 SQ KM // **OFFICIAL LANGUAGES** ARABIC & BERBER

Morocco

Morocco is a cultural melange of Africa and the Middle East, with a few European colonial influences thrown in the mix, all of which are reflected in the brightly coloured handicrafts, fascinating architecture and bold flavours of the food. A casual visitor to Morocco might wonder if they hadn't been whisked there by magic carpet, as the cities of Marrakesh, Tangier and Fez fulfil every *Arabian Nights*–style fantasy of exotic souqs and kasbahs, spices and date palms. Away from the invigorating hustle and bustle the medinas, Morocco also offers solitude along wild coastlines, high mountain passes and an endless sea of sand dunes.

Best time to visit
May to November, during the cooler, drier season

Top things to see
- The Quirimbas Archipelago – just as stunning whether seen from above in a flyover or from the prow of a dhow
- Dugongs, corals and colourful fish in the waters of the Bazaruto Archipelago
- The lions and elephants that are now back at home in Gorongosa National Park
- Cahora Bassa Dam and the mighty Zambezi River
- Living history in the narrow, atmospheric lanes of Mozambique Island (Ilha de Moçambique)

Top things to do
- Sail on a dhow past deserted white sandbanks and beautiful beaches in remote island archipelagos
- Wind your way through the heart of rural Africa on the Nampula–Cuamba train
- Explore Lake Niassa (aka Lake Malawi), with its clear waters, secluded coves and star-filled skies
- Hike over precipitous log bridges and through rushing mountain streams in the cool Chimanimani Mountains
- Dance until dawn at Maputo's lively nightclubs

Getting under the skin
Read: *The Last Flight of the Flamingo* or any other work by Mia Couto for lyrical insights into Mozambique's soul
Listen: to the upbeat rhythms of *marrabenta*, Mozambique's national music
Watch: an explosive, rhythmic, colour-filled performance of the Mozambican National Company of Song and Dance
Eat: *matapa* (cassava leaves with peanut sauce)
Drink: a 2M (Dois M) beer – cold, if you can find it

In a word
Paciência (Patience)

Trademarks
Marrabenta music; Makonde woodcarvings; giant prawns; *mapiko* dancing; dhows; idyllic beaches; successful demining campaigns

Random fact
Mozambique's national flag is the only one in the world to feature a modern weapon, an AK-47 to be exact

1. Big air and the Catholic Nossa Senhora da Conceição, Maputo

2. While away a week or two on Ilha das Mogundula, Quirimbas Archipelago

3. Traditional rondavels with stick-and-mud walls and palm-thatched roofs

M | **CAPITAL** MAPUTO // **POPULATION** 24.1 MILLION // **AREA** 799,380 SQ KM // **OFFICIAL LANGUAGE** PORTUGUESE

Mozambique

If it were not for a world's worth of misconceptions, Mozambique would be one of Africa's most popular destinations. The dune-backed beaches on the mainland and lining the remote archipelagos are resplendent, and the azure waters lapping them are alive with a multitude of aquatic species. Away from the coast, national parks such as Gorongosa are having success with wildlife conservation efforts. And culturally visitors will find an enigmatic fusion of African, Arabic, Indian and Portuguese influences. Although the civil war ended in 1992 Mozambique continues to celebrate peacetime milestones: a new peace deal was signed in 2014 with the former rebel group Renamo, and a year later the country was declared free of landmines.

(M) CAPITAL NAY PYI TAW // POPULATION 55.7 MILLION // AREA 676,578 SQ KM // OFFICIAL LANGUAGE BURMESE

Myanmar

Long treated as a pariah state because of its repressive military government, the nation formerly known as Burma is becoming an increasingly popular stop on the traveller trail. After 60 years of self-imposed isolation, Myanmar is decades behind most of its neighbours in terms of modern amenities and tourism, and that's part of the appeal. In place of chain stores and backpacker bars, you'll find monks and monasteries, hill tribes and towering golden stupas, and a pace of life dictated by the steady flow of the Ayeyarwady River. Myanmar is not without its problems, however. Despite the return of civilian government in 2015, the oppression of minority Rohingya people has tarnished the reputation of national leader Aung San Suu Kyi, keeping Myanmar in the news for all the wrong reasons.

Best time to visit
November to February (the cool season)

Top things to see
- The breathtaking plain of temples at Bagan, ransacked to ruin by Kublai Khan
- Jewel-encrusted Shwedagon Paya, perhaps the grandest Buddhist monument in the world
- Wonky bridges and hilltop stupas in the serene villages around Mandalay
- Foot-rowers swirling through the morning mist on Inle Lake
- The timeless pace of village life in sleepy Hsipaw

Top things to do
- Cruise along the Ayeyarwady on a charmingly decrepit passenger boat
- Trek to fascinating tribal villages around Kalaw or Kengtung
- Run through the surf on idyllic Ngapali Beach
- Climb Mt Popa to commune with the *nats* (animist spirits)
- Shop for Buddhist trinkets at Yangon's Bogyoke Aung San Market

Getting under the skin
Read: Pascal Khoo Thwe's moving memoir *From the Land of Green Ghosts;* or George Orwell's classic *Burmese Days*
Listen: to the Maha Gita (the traditional classical music of the Burmese court); or the rousing rock of Lay Phyu and Iron Cross
Watch: the satirical comedy performances of the two surviving Moustache Brothers in Mandalay
Eat: at a traditional Burmese canteen – a typical meal includes *htamin* (rice), *hin* (curries), *peh-hin-ye* (lentil soup) and *balachaung* (fiery shrimp and chilli paste)
Drink: Dagon Beer, Myanmar Beer or Spirulina Beer, which claims to have anti-ageing properties

In a word
Mingalaba (We are blessed)

Trademarks
Golden stupas; teak bridges; school-aged monks; jade mines; the Ayeyarwady River; *cheroots* (cigars);

opium and the Golden Triangle; Aung San Suu Kyi; military crackdowns; persecuted Rohingya

Random fact
Myanmar is one of only three nations to hold out against the metric system; locally, weights are measured in *viss* (equivalent to 1.6kg) and a series of smaller divisions

1. The gilded dome of Myanmar's most sacred temple, Shwedagon Paya
2. Dawn breaks over the ancient temples of Bagan, Mandalay Region
3. Trainee Buddhist monks light candles
4. A fishermen practises the (men-only) leg-rowing technique unique to Inle Lake

(N) CAPITAL WINDHOEK // POPULATION 2.2 MILLION // AREA 824,292 SQ KM // OFFICIAL LANGUAGE ENGLISH

Namibia

It's life and death. And never has the battle been so beautifully fought. One look at the Namibian landscape and you will understand. Nowhere in the world is such visual splendour matched with such unmerciful harshness – if anything is to survive here, in the sea of dunes, within the rocky canyons or along the Skeleton Coast, it has to be equally extraordinary. Thankfully, nature has provided just such a cast. Its members include desert-adapted elephants, rhinos and lions, fog-basking beetles, great white sharks, rare mountain zebra, cartwheeling spiders and some of the most intriguing people you'll meet on the planet.

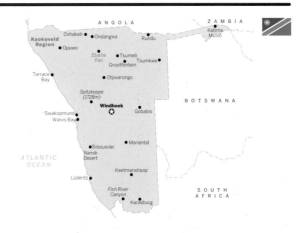

Best time to visit
May to September (the dry season)

Top things to see
- Classic safari wildlife emerging from the heat haze on Etosha Pan
- The hungry sands of the Skeleton Coast consuming the massive rusty relics that ran aground on this mist-shrouded shore
- The earth opening up before you as you approach the edge of the gaping Fish River Canyon
- Spitzkoppe, the 'Matterhorn of Africa', rising boldly from the Damaraland plains
- The wild horses of the Namib

Top things to do
- Cruise the Caprivi Strip and embrace the wet and wild life on the banks of the Chobe River
- Skydive over the extraordinary meeting place of two great seas, the Namib Desert and the Atlantic Ocean
- Hike along the serpentine spine of a dune at Sossusvlei during sunrise
- Track endangered black rhinos through the parched landscape of the Kaokoveld
- Slide down the garnet-laced dunes near Terrace Bay to hear (and feel!) them roar

Getting under the skin
Read: *Born of the Sun*, which follows the coming of age and political awakening of author Joseph Diescho
Listen: to Damara Punch (aka *ma /gaisa*), a dance music style that evolved from traditional Damara music

Watch: *Namibia: The Struggle for Liberation*, a story about the nation's first president and his fight for independence
Eat: *oshiwambo* (a memorable mixture of spinach and beef)
Drink: prickly-pear-cactus schnapps

In a word
Goegaandit?/Matisa?/Kora? (How are you?) in Afrikaans/Damara/Herero

Trademarks
Mountainous parabolic dunes; shipwrecks; Sperrgebiet, or 'Forbidden Zone' (aka Diamond Area 1); the Skeleton Coast; sandboarding

Random fact
The *Welwitschia mirabilis* plant that grows in the Namib Desert has a lifespan that can reach 2000 years – it's justifiably called a living fossil

1. Desert-adapted gemsboks traverse a dune in the Namib Desert
2. Portuguese sailors used to refer to the Skeleton Coast as 'the Gates of Hell'
3. The distinctive hairstyles of Himba women are made with goat hair, butter and ochre
4. Namibia is famous for its wildlife: lions relax in the sun near Okonjima

Best time to visit
Hot and humid year-round, it's best to visit from March to October when it's driest

Top things to see
- The eerie rusted cantilever cranes used to load phosphate for export
- WWII relics scattered around the island, including a Japanese jail block on Command Ridge
- A game of Australian Rules football or locals weightlifting – Nauru's two national sports
- *Ekawada,* string figures stretched across the hands like 'cat's cradle' to tell traditional stories
- The ruins of the once-splendid presidential palace, burned down by a local mob in 2001

Top things to do
- Walk the pinnacled remnants of the now defunct phosphate mines
- Catch, tag and release marlin, yellow-fin tuna, barracuda and more with the island's fishermen
- Quaff a cold beer while watching a fiery South Seas sun set over coconut palms
- Swim and snorkel off the beach by the Menen Hotel

Getting under the skin
Read: *Nauru: Australia's Stressed Client State,* a 2015 state-of-affairs article by investigative journalist Michael J Field
Listen: to the strange *kik-kirrik* cry of the noddy bird
Watch: *Nauru – Paradise Ruined,* the 2011 documentary about Nauru's rise and fall
Eat: a fresh seafood barbecue
Drink: *demangi,* the island's take on fermented toddy made from coconut palm sap

In a word
Kewen (Gone, dead)

Trademarks
Phosphate; camps of Australia-bound asylum seekers; weightlifting; noddy birds; limestone pinnacles; 1878–88 tribal war; Nauruan high-rollers in the 1970s and '80s

Random fact
During the phosphate boom in the 1980s, Nauru was the second-richest country in the world in terms of per-capita income; 35 years later the estimated average yearly income is around US$2000

1. Food choice is limited in the world's smallest republic

2. Nearly half Nauru's population is under the age of 24

3. Children escape Nauru's notorious heat in the ocean

N **POPULATION** 9434 // **AREA** 21 SQ KM // **OFFICIAL LANGUAGE** NAURUAN

Nauru

Nauru's limited beauty can be glimpsed along its coast: seabirds swoop over green cliffs beside wild seas and sunsets are nothing short of spectacular. Head to the tiny island's interior however, and you'll find deforestation from phosphate mining and an eerie landscape of limestone pinnacles. The exposed rock reflects the sun's rays and chases away the clouds so there's lots of sunshine but frequent drought. Meanwhile, the wealth accrued and squandered from mining, followed by poverty and rampant unemployment, have brought the country to near collapse. Nauru's isolation and a lack of attractions have also kept the tourists away. In fact, the island's most prominent imports are the hundreds of asylum seekers transported here by the Australian government in exchange for financial aid.

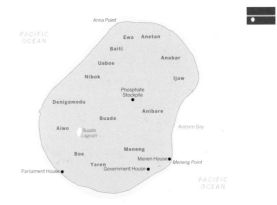

N

N CAPITAL KATHMANDU // POPULATION 30.4 MILLION // AREA 147,181 SQ KM // OFFICIAL LANGUAGE NEPALI

Nepal

One of the world's most epic travel destinations, the former Himalayan kingdom of Nepal has faced its share of troubles in recent times, from a decade-long Maoist uprising to a series of massive earthquakes that destroyed landmark monuments and entire villages along some of the country's top trekking trails. But somehow, Nepal always bounces back. We credit the natural resilience of the people who inhabit this rugged land of monasteries, mountains and mystery. As Nepal rebuilds after the 2015 earthquakes, travellers are starting to return, lured – as always – by the chiming of temple bells, the chanting of Buddhist monks, the medieval majesty of the Kathmandu Valley, and the timeless appeal of trekking over snow-cloaked passes in the high Himalaya.

Best time to visit
September to November and March to May, to avoid summer rains and icy winters

Top things to see
- The winding, temple-strewn backstreets of Kathmandu
- Stupendous stupas at Bodhnath and Swayambhunath
- The royal squares in Patan and Bhaktapur, earthquake scarred, but still magnificent
- Chariot parades and rainbow-coloured festivals in the Kathmandu Valley
- Views of the highest mountains in the world on treks through the Annapurnas and Solukhumbu

Top things to do
- Test muscle against mountain on the trek to Everest Base Camp
- Take a row boat across the placid waters of Phewa Tal in Pokhara
- Haggle for singing bowls and Tibetan rugs in the bazaars of Thamel in Kathmandu
- Raft or kayak on the wild white waters of the Bhote Kosi or Sun Kosi
- Track rhinos and tigers in the elephant grass at Chitwan National Park

Getting under the skin
Read: *Arresting God in Kathmandu* by Samrat Upadhyay; or WE Bowman's mountaineering spoof *The Ascent of Rum Doodle*
Listen: to the evocative Nepali folk music of Sur Sudha

Watch: Eric Valli's classic *Himalaya,* with all characters played by Dolpo villagers; or Stephanie Spray and Pacho Velez's *Manakamana,* a cultural snapshot of Nepal told through interviews with temple pilgrims
Eat: *dal bhat* (lentils, vegetables and rice) – it's what you'll be eating twice a day, every day if you go trekking
Drink: salted butter tea; *chang* (milky beer made from rice or barley); or hot *tongba* (millet beer)

In a word
Ke garne? (What to do?)

Trademarks
High altitude thrills; the Himalaya; towering temples; Buddhist lamas; Maoists; mountaineers with icicles in their beards; prayer flags; mandalas; yaks and yetis; buffalo steaks; perilous nature

Random fact
Sagarmatha (Mt Everest) moved three centimetres southwest during the April 2015 earthquake

1. A yak train passes beneath Nupste (7861m)
2. Traditional boats and the little isle of Taal Barahi Temple on Phewa Lake, Pokhara
3. The fierce gaze of a Hindu deity
4. The colourful visage of a sadhu – a Hindu holy man – from Kathmandu

N

277

1. Meervogel windmill in Groningen overlooks unbroken flat-lands and big horizons

2. The colours of industrial farming; tulips are big business in the Netherlands

3. A crowd gathers for Rembrandt's *The Night Watch,* Rijksmuseum

N CAPITAL AMSTERDAM (GOVERNMENT SEAT IS THE HAGUE) // POPULATION 16.8 MILLION // AREA 41,526 SQ KM // OFFICIAL LANGUAGE DUTCH

Netherlands

The Netherlands is one country in Europe where modernism and tradition fuse seamlessly. It's a nation where creativity flourishes: from innovative start-ups and cutting-edge architectural statements to eco-initiatives and a burgeoning food scene. This goes hand-in-hand with 17th-century canals, tulip fields, windmills, ancient churches, candlelit brown cafes and the masterpieces of Van Gogh and Rembrandt. Beautiful old cities such as Amsterdam, Haarlem, Leiden, Delft, Utrecht and many more attest to the wealth that fuelled the growth of the Netherlands – the ever-tolerant Dutch have always excelled at making the most of what they have. From the swamps and shallows of their land (that mostly sits below sea level) they've created a modern, comfortable country and one of the world's best places for cycling.

Best time to visit
April for tulips, May to October for cafe-friendly weather

Top things to see
- Amsterdam, one of Europe's best-preserved great cities with canals, 17th-century vistas and an incongruous mix of neighbourhoods
- The striking, cutting-edge architectural landmarks of one of Europe's most innovative cities, Rotterdam
- Dutch masterpieces by the likes of Rembrandt, Vermeer, Van Gogh and Mondrian at Amsterdam's Rijksmuseum and Stedelijk Museum
- Millions of tulips posing every spring at Keukenhof

Top things to do
- Bicycle along the flattest and best-maintained cycle paths in the world, such as the North Sea Cycle Route between The Hague and Zandvoort
- Retrace the life of Vermeer in tidy old Delft
- While away an afternoon tucked cosily into one of the country's historic brown cafes

Getting under the skin
Read: the classic *Diary of Anne Frank*, which never loses its impact
Listen: to Tiësto, the face of the killer Dutch club scene
Watch: Paul Verhoeven's *Turks Fruit*, made before he found vast fame in Hollywood
Eat: crispy *frites* (hot chips) doused with mayonnaise or any of dozens of other sauces
Drink: rich ales like Palm

In a word
Dag (Hello/goodbye)

Trademarks
Bikes; dykes; windmills; tulips; red-light district; pot smoking; Van Gogh; canals; Rembrandt; tall people

Random fact
Of the area claimed as the Netherlands, 20% is underwater (canals, lakes, marshes etc) while another 20% is below sea level and protected by 2400km of dykes

1. Amédée lighthouse, constructed in Paris and assembled on its eponymous island

2. Nouméa's Jean-Marie Tjibaou Cultural Centre celebrates indigenous Kanak culture

3. Preparing for a traditional dance ceremony on Île des Pins

N CAPITAL NOUMÉA // POPULATION 264,000 // AREA 18,575 SQ KM // OFFICIAL LANGUAGE FRENCH

New Caledonia

Très français yet warmly Melanesian, New Caledonia is a place of gourmet cuisine savoured beneath palm trees and flip-flops worn with designer clothing. A massive World Heritage–listed lagoon encircles the main island of Grande Terre, embuing the coasts with light in every shade of blue. From cosmopolitan Nouméa down through the south's iron-rich red soils to Île des Pins' lofty pines and the depths of the indigo lagoons, New Caledonia feels much bigger than most island nations. And it's no wonder: Grande Terre is the third-largest island in the Pacific, with the largest enclosed lagoon on the planet.

Best time to visit
September to December, when it's not too hot or cold and there's the least chance of rain

Top things to see
- Three highlights of Nouméa: the magnificent Jean-Marie Tjibaou Cultural Centre, the green turtles of Aquarium des Lagons and the colonial Musée de la Ville de Nouméa
- Fishermen unloading their catch, and the band singing by the water, at Nouméa's Le Marché
- Panoramic views over sea-turtle territory and the unusual rock formations at La Roche Percée

Top things to do
- Swim in a 'natural swimming pool' after a lobster lunch on Île des Pins
- Lounge on a gorgeous Loyalty Island beach keeping an eye out for humpback whales
- Kayak under a full moon, abseil down waterfalls and hike the landscapes of the Far South
- Experience Kanak life at a homestay in Hienghène

Getting under the skin
Read: *Nights of Storytelling*, a fascinating insight into the islands' indigenous and Euro-influenced culture
Listen: to laid-back OK! Ryos who fuse traditional Melanesian sounds with pop
Watch: *Rebellion*, a riveting true story set in modern-day New Caledonia
Eat: *bougna* – yam, sweet potato, taro and meat, fish or seafood covered in coconut milk, wrapped in banana leaves and cooked in an earthen oven
Drink: good coffee, an enduring French influence

In a word
Ti-Va-Ouere (Brothers of the Earth) – the Kanaks' name for themselves

Trademarks
Kanak communities; French tourists; grass beach huts; colonial strife; immense lagoons; clan societies

Random fact
The rare kagu bird (*cagou* in French), endemic to New Caledonia, is nearly flightless and has a call that sounds like a dog bark or a rooster crowing

CAPITAL WELLINGTON // POPULATION 4.4 MILLION // AREA 267,710 SQ KM //
OFFICIAL LANGUAGES ENGLISH, MĀORI & NEW ZEALAND SIGN LANGUAGE

New Zealand

As the planet heats up environmentally and politically, it's good to know that
New Zealand exists. This uncrowded, green, peaceful and accepting country is the
ultimate escape. Mother Nature decided to take her best features and condense
them all in this South Pacific gem, from sublime forests, pristine beaches and
snowcapped mountains to winding fjords and active volcanoes. The decadent
scenery is not just there for admiring – it's for trekking through, paragliding over,
hiking up or skiing down. Once you've exhausted yourself, take sleepy inland
roads to find superb wineries and a thriving Māori culture before discovering the
nation's cosmopolitan cities. With all this at their feet Kiwis have a distinct lust for
life, and it's easy to understand why all who visit fall in love with their country.

Best time to visit
November to April for fun in the sun, June to
August for fun in the snow

Top things to see
- Volcanic mud bubbles, spurting geysers and neon
  geothermal pools at Rotorua
- Rare kiwi birds in the wild on Stewart Island
- The icy grandeur of the Franz and Fox Glaciers
  from the ground or the air
- The astonishing maze of subterranean caves,
  canyons and rivers at Waitomo
- The world-beating collage of waterfalls, verdant
  cliffs and towering peaks that is Milford Sound

Top things to do
- Kayak or trek the golden-sand beaches and
  turquoise inlets of Abel Tasman National Park
- Sip world-famous sauvignon blanc at gorgeous
  wineries and gourmet restaurants throughout
  the Marlborough wine region
- Jump off a bridge or out of a plane in
  Queenstown
- Experience New Zealand's best nightlife and
  caffeine-scene in Wellington
- Catch a glimpse of orcas and explore the 150-odd
  islands and that dot the beautiful Bay of Islands

Getting under the skin
Read: *The Bone People* by Keri Hulme, a Booker
Prize–winning magic realist novel exploring New
Zealand identity
Listen: to anything on the *Great New Zealand
Songbook*, a compilation of the greatest Kiwi tunes
from the last two centuries
Watch: *Whale Rider,* a mystical glimpse into
modern Māori life
Eat: grass-fed lamb off the grill followed by
pavlova, an addictive meringue cake topped with
fruit and cream
Drink: craft beer from any of the country's growing
selection of microbreweries

In a word
Sweet as, bro

Trademarks
Sheep; Māori; the All Blacks rugby team; nuclear-
free; bungee jumping; *The Lord of the Rings*; Kiwi
birds and fruit; *Flight of the Conchords*

Random fact
No matter where you are in New Zealand you are
never more than 120km from the sea

1. At the very northern
   tip of the South Island,
   you will find Wharariki
   Beach, Cape Farewell

2. Adventure central:
   Queenstown, Lake
   Wakatipu and the
   Remarkables range

3. All roads lead to
   Aoraki-Mt Cook
   (3724m), New
   Zealand's highest peak

4. Marlborough, at the top
   of the South Island, is
   New Zealand's premier
   wine-growing region

Best time to visit
June to March, to avoid the dusty end of the dry season

Top things to see
- Moonrise over the cathedral in colonial Granada
- One island, two volcanoes on the biggest lake in Central America: Isla de Ometepe
- Jungle-covered Spanish fortresses along the Río San Juan
- Bright handicrafts piled high at Masaya's Mercado Viejo
- The sapphire waters of Laguna de Apoyo

Top things to do
- Ride the waves in the laid-back surfer's haven of San Juan del Sur
- Climb up Cerro Negro then sandboard down its soft steeps
- Dive with hammerheads and eagle rays off Little Corn Island
- Sip coffee and talk politics with the intelligentsia in the charming university town of León
- Play castaway on the white sand of the Pearl Keys

Getting under the skin
Read: *Stories and Poems* by Rubén Darío, the founder of Spanish modernism; Salman Rushdie's *The Jaguar Smile: A Nicaraguan Journey;* and Gioconda Belli's *The Country Under My Skin: A Memoir of Love and War*

Listen: to electro-pop goddess Clara Grun; the Bossa-pop of Belén; the Manu Chau–influenced Perrozompopo; and legendary marimba-folk artists Los Mejía Godoy

Watch: *Nicaragua Was Our Home* – a documentary about Miskito Indian repression; or the Oscar-nominated *Alsino and the Condor,* about a boy in war-torn Nicaragua

Eat: *nacatamales* (a mixture of cornmeal, potato, pork, tomato, onion and sweet chillies packed into a banana leaf and steamed to perfection)

Drink: Flor de Caña rum; *pinol,* toasted corn powder sweetened with sugar or taken with *cacao* (chocolate)

In a word
¡Va pue'! (All right!)

Trademarks
Contras and Sandinistas; rice and beans; volcanoes; coffee; remote white sand beaches; baseball

Random fact
Nicaragua is the least densely populated country in Central America but that's child's play: 72% of the population is under 30 years old

1. Geoffroy's spider monkey is critically endangered in Nicaragua

2. Cathedral de Granada looms over the colourful streets of Granada

3. The smoking maw of Volcán Telica, one of the country's most active volcanoes

N | CAPITAL MANAGUA // POPULATION 5.8 MILLION // AREA 130,370 SQ KM // OFFICIAL LANGUAGE SPANISH

Nicaragua

Poet Rubén Darío called it 'Our America, trembling with hurricanes, trembling with love'. Recent history roller-coastered residents through dictatorships, revolution, civil war and economic collapse, but Nicas, as they're known, are persistent and proud. Fast forward and today's Nicaragua is considered among the safest countries in Central America. The politics are still far from settled or straightforward. Yet travellers are starting to come in large numbers. With its seductive colonial settings, big beach breaks and a passion for poetry, Nicaragua has become a regional hot spot. Dollars stretch far here, and a warm tropical welcome eases the transition. Just don't offend your hosts by calling it 'the next Costa Rica'.

1

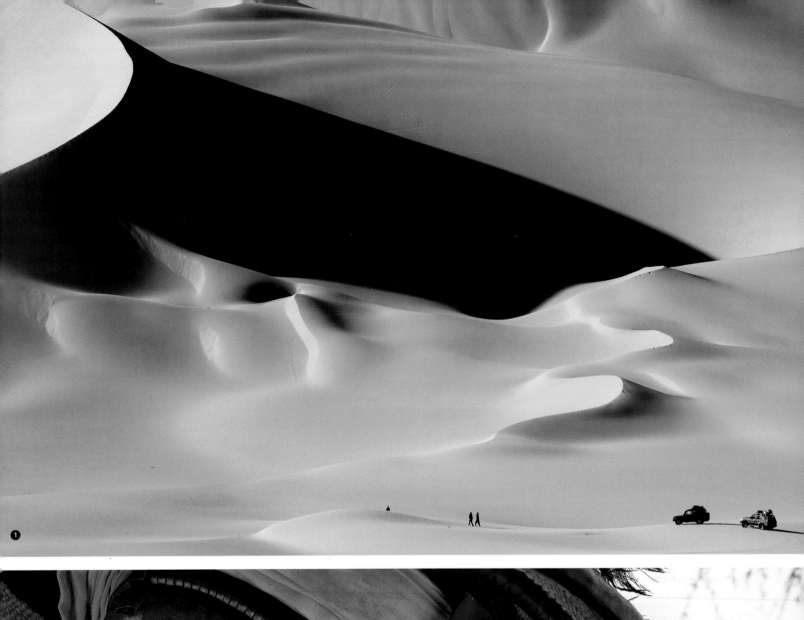

2

(N) CAPITAL NIAMEY // POPULATION 16.9 MILLION // AREA 1,267,000 SQ KM // OFFICIAL LANGUAGE FRENCH

Niger

The Sahara may be unbelievably hostile to life, but it also holds untold beauty. And Niger's remote north contains two of the desert's most truly astounding sights: the Aïr Mountains and the great dunes of the Ténéré. Eeking out life in this incredible environment is one of the Sahara's most enigmatic groups, the Tuareg. Economic realities elsewhere in the country make life unrelentingly tough on the country's diverse population, even for those living on the banks of the Niger River in the southwest, but they all bear these difficult times with remarkable dignity. With Niger's participation in both the French-led intervention in Mali and regional fight against Boko Haram, the security situation has unfortunately deteriorated to a point where travel is not currently possible.

Best time to visit
October to February, when it's dry and relatively cool

Places of interest
• Agadez, one of the Sahara's most romantic caravan towns, with an iconic pyramid-shaped mud mosque
• The languid riverside capital of Niamey, which has a terrific museum and traditional pirogue trips
• Zinder's ancient Hausa sultanate with a palace, weekly market and fine old quarter
• The Niger River town of Ayorou, which has a wonderful Sunday market, pirogue trips and hippos
• Kouré, home to the Sahel's last, highly endangered giraffe herd
• The remarkable Aïr Mountains, a barren and beautiful desert massif
• Parc Regional du W, where elephants and lions still roam

Local customs
• During La Cure Salée festival, Wodaabé men don elaborate make-up and dance in the hopes of being proposed to by a woman
• Buses, bush taxis and the country in general grind to a halt at *salat* (Muslim prayer)
• Traditional wrestling is wildly popular, and incorporates prayer, poetry and the wearing of *grigri* (charms)
• Due to the harsh dictates of the Sahara, some Tuareg forgo fasting during Ramadan

Getting under the skin
Read: *Riding the Demon: On the Road in West Africa* by Peter Chilson, which sees Niger through its bush taxis

Listen: to Mamar Kassey (*Alatouni*), or to Etran Finatawa (*Desert Crossroads*), Tuareg and Wodaabé bands famous for their desert blues
Watch: *The Sheltering Sky,* directed by Bernardo Bertolucci and filmed partly in Agadez
Eat: dates, yoghurt, rice, mutton, rice with sauce and couscous
Drink: Bière Niger, a local lager

In a word
Bonjour (Hello)

Trademarks
Tuareg nomads and salt caravans; dinosaur bones and ancient rock art in the desert; a difficult life; uranium mines

Random fact
The Arbre du Ténéré was lucky enough to be the last remaining acacia in the heart of Sahara, standing alone in the sand some 400km from any other tree – its luck ran out in 1973 when it was knocked down by a truck

1. Vast dunes near Agadez, Aïr Mountains
2. A young Wodaabe-Fulani man takes part in Guérewol, an annual courtship ceremony
3. Young boys playing pipes in Agadez
4. The vivid colours of a salt mine in the Sahara Desert

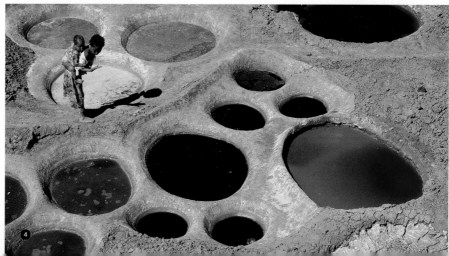

(N) CAPITAL ABUJA // POPULATION 174.5 MILLION // AREA 923,768 SQ KM // OFFICIAL LANGUAGE ENGLISH

Nigeria

Nigeria can be an overwhelming experience. Indeed, such is its reputation that few travellers dare to venture into the continent's most populous country. But this is also West Africa's most exciting country, a place where the sensory overload of Lagos yields to the wilds of the Gashaka-Gumti National Park, where tranquil forests protect creatures of every size and shape: buffaloes, chimpanzees, elephants and around one million birds. The riches of the Muslim north, with its ancient trading towns, have sadly been overshadowed by the tension and violence associated with the unfortunate growth of Boko Haram. But for the most part, ordinary Nigerians of all faiths, when faced with an uncertain future, throw themselves wholeheartedly into celebrating the present. Join them and you'll really 'get' Nigeria.

Best time to visit
November to February

Top things to see
- Intimidating and exciting in equal measure, Lagos, the capital in all but name
- Benin City, the rich legacy of ancient Benin with bronze casting, museum and the Oba's Palace
- The modern, made-to-measure Nigerian capital of Abuja, where amenities abound
- The historic old river port and primate conservation centres in the capital of Cross River state, Calabar
- Zuma Rock, a mammoth granodiorite monolith whose rounded shoulders tower 750m above the plains outside Abuja

Top things to do
- Spot elephants, lions and hippos in the terrific Gashaka-Gumti National Park
- Wander through the World Heritage–listed Sacred Forest in Yoruba Oshogbo
- Walk through the rainforest canopy at the Afi Mountain Drill Ranch, home to rehabilitated drills
- Climb Olumo Rock in Abeokuta to take in shrines, sacred trees, war-time hideouts and an incredible vista over the city
- Make a musical pilgrimage to the New Afrika Shrine, the enduring epicentre of Afrobeat in Lagos

Getting under the skin
Read: anything by Chinua Achebe, Ben Okri, Chimamanda Ngozi Adichie or Nobel Prize–winner Wole Soyinka

Listen: to Afrobeat, that unmistakeably Nigerian musical style mastered by the late Fela Kuti and his son and heir-apparent Femi Kuti
Watch: any film from 'Nollywood', the world's third-largest film industry
Eat: 'chop' (food), such as pepper soup and *suya* (spiced kebabs)
Drink: Star beer or Guinness

In a word
Dash (Bribe or tip)

Trademarks
The cultural powerhouse of Anglophone Africa for music, literature and artistic traditions; squandered oil wealth; Boko Haram; #bringbackourgirls

Random fact
By some estimates, one out of every five Africans is a Nigerian

1. Buses and taxis gather outside Lagos' Cathedral Church of Christ

2. Desert-adapted red Fulani cattle drink at a well near Yusufari

3. Celebrating the Durbar festival in Maiduguri

4. Abuja National Mosque; roughly half of the population is Muslim

Best time to visit
April, for the national day celebrations, and September to October when humidity lessens and the weather is good for sightseeing

Top things to see
- Four kilometres of landmines and warning signs in the Demilitarized Zone (DMZ), one of the world's most militarised spaces
- Blissful mountain scenery at the hill resort of Kumgangsan
- Talented young North Koreans performing martial arts, music and gymnastics at Mangyongdae Children's Palace
- Sacred Paekdusan – the mountain birthplace of Hwanung, the founder of the first Korean kingdom
- Pyongyang's Juche Tower, a three-dimensional embodiment of the Korean principle of self-reliance

Top things to do
- See locals with their guard down at the popular picnic spot of Moran Hill
- Step back into Korea's history at Kaesong, the ancient capital of the Koryo kings
- Pay your respects by bowing and presenting flowers at the Mansudae Grand Monument (but then, you have to)
- View Supreme Leaders Kim Il-sung and Kim Jong-il lying in state at the Kumsusan Memorial Palace of the Sun
- Soak up the surreal spectacle of the Arirang Mass Games, or see synchronised acrobatics on a smaller scale at the Pyongyang Circus

Getting under the skin
Read: *Nothing to Envy: Ordinary Lives in North Korea* by Barbara Demick; *The Impossible State: North Korea, Past and Future* by Victor Cha
Listen: to the rousing patriotic anthems played continuously on the Pyongyang metro
Watch: Daniel Gordon's *A State of Mind*, a surprising documentary about the lives of two young North Korean gymnasts
Eat: *naengmyeon* (cold kudzu-flour or buckwheat noodles)
Drink: *soju* (local vodka); or Taedonggang, the national beer of North Korea

In a word
Juche (The national policy of 'Self Reliance')

Trademarks
The revered Kim family, including Supreme Leader Kim Jong-un; vast military parades; the Mass Games; the 38th parallel; 1.2 million landmines in the DMZ

Random fact
Now-deceased former Supreme Leader, Kim Jong-il, uttered only six words in public: 'Glory to the heroic soldiers of the People's Army!'

1. A salute to Kim Il Sung and Kim Jong-il at the Grand Monument on Mansu Hill, Pyongyang

2. Autumn colours around the mountain of Kumgagnsan, a popular holiday retreat

3. Dancers in the Arirang Mass Games, May Day Stadium, Pyongyang

CAPITAL PYONGYANG // **POPULATION** 24.7 MILLION // **AREA** 120,538 SQ KM // **OFFICIAL LANGUAGE** KOREAN

North Korea

Secretive only just describes North Korea, the insular northern half of the Korean peninsula, which closed its doors to the world at the end of the Korean War and now leaves them open just a crack, to visitors on strictly regimented tours. When not rattling sabres at South Korea, the nation condemned as the eastern end of the Axis of Evil spends much of its time on extravagant propaganda exercises, making for some spectacular, if surreal, tourist experiences. With an official escort, you can visit pristine, empty state institutions, roam to mountain resorts and ancient capitals, and pay your respects to a massive statue of the supreme leader (just so you know, this is not optional). Only 1500 tourists peer over the wall ever year, and even fewer roam beyond the capital, Pyongyang, into Asia's least-explored frontier.

Best time to visit
April is typically the driest month; May to September promise the warmest temperatures

Top things to see
- Titanic Belfast, a superb multimedia visitor attraction situated where the famous liner was built
- The 40,000 hexagonal basalt columns of the Giant's Causeway, a Unesco-listed wonder
- Downpatrick, where St Patrick's mission began and ended, and home to a mighty cathedral
- The ancient walls encircling the history-steeped city of Derry
- Strangford Lough's Castle Ward Estate, an iconic *Game of Thrones* filming location

Top things to do
- Wander among reconstructed farmhouses, forges and mills at the Ulster Folk Museum near Belfast
- Wobble across the narrow, swaying Carrick-a-Rede Rope Bridge on the Causeway Coast
- Surf the Atlantic breakers at the sweeping beaches around Portrush
- Learn the secrets of whiskey making on a behind-the-scenes tour of Bushmills' Old Bushmills Distillery
- Tee off at revered Royal County Down Golf Course in Newcastle

Getting under the skin
Read: *Eureka Street* by Robert McLiam Wilson, set before and after the 1994 ceasefires; *The Eggman's Apprentice* by Maurice Leitch, depicting contemporary rural life
Listen: to Van Morrison's wonderfully evocative renditions of his formative childhood haunts in and around Belfast
Watch: *Good Vibrations,* about record-shop owner Terri Hooley who was instrumental in Belfast's punk-rock scene, and the Oscar-winning short, *The Shore,* for insights into the Troubles
Eat: bountiful Ulster fry breakfasts incorporating crispy golden-brown soda bread and potato farls
Drink: Bushmills whiskey or flavour-packed craft beers from 1981-established Hilden Brewery

In a word
Bout ye? (How are you?)

Trademarks
The *Titanic;* the Troubles; *Game of Thrones;* political murals; the Causeway Coast; Bushmills whiskey; the linen industry

Random fact
At 392 sq km, Lough Neagh is Britain and Ireland's largest freshwater lake, big enough to swallow the city of Birmingham (UK or USA – either would fit)

1. A monument to Belfast's maritime heritage: Titanic Belfast, Ulster

2. Tangled beech trees rise above the road at Dark Hedges, Ballymoney

3. In legend the Giant's Causeway in County Antrim was built by Irish giant Fionn mac Cumhaill

N CAPITAL BELFAST // POPULATION 1.8 MILLION // AREA 14,130 SQ KM // OFFICIAL LANGUAGE ENGLISH

Northern Ireland

Otherworldly geological formations, spectacular surf coast, magical glens and mystical standing stones make the northeastern corner of the Emerald Isle a fascinating place to explore, as does its complex history. Northern Ireland has been a separate country since the partition of Ireland in 1921, under the Government of Ireland Act 1920, and these six Ulster counties opted out of the Irish Free State in 1922 to remain within the United Kingdom. The arising conflicts infamously peaked during the Troubles, but in recent decades Northern Ireland has forged an inspiring path to peace. It has also reinvented itself as a thriving visitor destination, not only for its history but also its burgeoning drinking, dining and nightlife scenes and photogenic landscapes.

N CAPITAL OSLO // POPULATION 5.1 MILLION // AREA 323,802 SQ·KM // OFFICIAL LANGUAGE NORWEGIAN

Norway

Norway is the supermodel of Scandinavia, a peak- and fjord-blessed country that gives its neighbours a serious case of mountain envy. There's a reason why artists, photographers and outdoor enthusiasts rave over this country: at almost every corner stunning wilderness lurks to overwhelm the senses. Much of Norway lies above the Arctic Circle, home to the midnight sun's ceaseless light, the polar night's gloomy darkness, or the ghost-like, swirling northern lights. Set amid these natural phenomena is some of the world's most scenic hiking and skiing. There's a rugged frontier feel to much of the country, but this is still Scandinavia – design-driven bars and hotels are never too far away.

Best time to visit
May to September for sunshine, or December to February for skiing and the northern lights

Top things to see
- The perfectly preserved mining cottages of Unesco World Heritage–listed Røros
- Lofoten Islands – mountain-islands littered with fishing villages so postcard-perfect they look fake
- The jawdropping beauty of the Geirangerfjord, by boat or on foot
- Bryggen, the old medieval quarter of Bergen, with its long timber buildings housing museums, restaurants and shops
- Oslo's Vigeland Park, with its walkway lined with photogenic statues of screaming babies and entwined lovers

Top things to do
- Take a trip on a Hurtigruten coastal steamer, heading north from Bergen
- Stare spellbound out the windows on the spectacular, seven-hour Oslo–Bergen train route
- Spot polar bears in the Arctic archipelago of Svalbard, the definitive polar-adventure destination
- Take the ultimate selfie without falling off Preikestolen (Pulpit Rock), high above Lysefjord
- Hike among the high peaks and glaciers of the sublime Jotunheimen National Park

Getting under the skin
Read: *My Struggle* by Karl Ove Knausgaard, a six-volume series of controversial autobiographical novels and Norway's unrivalled publishing phenomenon
Listen: to the synthtastic '80s sounds of A-ha; the dark and controversial tones of black metal; the cool electro stylings of Röyksopp
Watch: *Max Manus* (Man of War), Norway's biggest budget blockbuster, recounting the true story of a resistance fighter during WWII
Eat: *laks* (smoked salmon); warm *moltebær syltetøy* (cloudberry jam) with ice cream
Drink: coffee; *aquavit* (or *akevitt;* a potent liquor distilled from potato)

In a word
Skal vi gå på ski? (Shall we go skiing?)

Trademarks
Fjords; glaciers; playwright Henrik Ibsen; midnight sun; artist Edvard Munch; high taxes, high prices; oil tycoons; polar explorers and polar bears; skiing; stave churches; trolls; Vikings

Random fact
'Ski' is a Norwegian word, and thanks to aeons-old rock carvings depicting hunters travelling on skis, Norwegians make a credible claim to having invented the sport

1. Svalbard, an island north of mainland Norway, is the best place to see polar bears

2. Glacier-carved Geirangerfjord and Seven Sisters Waterfall

3. Norway's fjords are beautiful but chilly places to swim

4. Northern lights over the tiny island of Hamnøy and its fishing village, Lofoten Islands

Best time to visit
October to April has comfortable weather throughout the country, or catch Dhofar's *khareef* (monsoon) season between June and September to see this region at its lushest

Top things to see
- Muscat, the lovely port city with a beautiful bay, atmospheric souq and Portuguese forts
- Yitti's gloriously unspoiled beach with craggy mountains
- Masirah's palm-strewn oases, postcard-perfect beaches and flamingos
- Nizwa, the beguiling inland town with a 17th-century fort and expansive souq
- Mughsail's jaw-dropping bay with sheer cliffs and frankincense trees close to Yemen

Top things to do
- Walk in wonder though Wadi Shab, the verdant gorge that feels like paradise
- Explore the copper-coloured dunes of the Wahiba Sands by camel or 4WD
- Drive over the Hajar Mountains from Al-Hamra to Wadi Bani Awf, Oman's most spectacular road
- Ponder the mysteries of Ubar, Arabia's fabled 'Atlantis of the Sands'
- Get away from it all on the Musandam Peninsula, a dramatic Omani outpost guarding the gates of the Gulf

Getting under the skin
Read: *Sultan in Oman* by renowned travel writer Jan Morris; or *Atlantis of the Sands* by Ranulph Fiennes
Listen: to Salid Rashid Suri, a 20th-century *sawt* singer and oud player known as the Singing Sailor
Watch: *Al-Boom,* directed by Khaled Abdul Raheem Al-Zadjali and set in a small coastal fishing town: it was the first ever Omani feature film – the country's cinematic history is almost non-existent
Eat: *harees* – steamed wheat, boiled meat, lime, chilli and onions garnished with *ma owaal* (dried shark); *shuwa* (marinated meat cooked in an earth oven)
Drink: camel's milk

In a word
Tasharrafna (Nice to meet you)

Trademarks
Frankincense; ancient forts; Bedouin and the sands of the Empty Quarter

Random fact
The coastal oasis of Sohar will forever be remembered from the *Arabian Nights* as the starting point for Sinbad's epic journeys

1. Camping under the stars in the Rub' al Khali (Empty Quarter)

2. The Empty Quarter: endless dunes and world's largest deposits of oil

3. The impressive 17th-century fortifications of Nizwa Fort, Nizwa

CAPITAL MUSCAT // POPULATION 3.2 MILLION // AREA 309,500 SQ KM // OFFICIAL LANGUAGE ARABIC

Oman

The sultanate of Oman could be the Arabian Peninsula's most rewarding destination. More accessible than Saudi Arabia, certainly safer than Yemen and in many ways more traditional than the Gulf emirates, Oman has plenty to rival these countries' attractions and more. It has a stirring history that combines the great sweep of Bedouin tradition with some extraordinary forts and other traditional architecture. And Mutrah Souq in Muscat is a fantasy of an Arabian bazaar come to life, with glittering gold and clouds of incense. But it's Oman's diverse natural beauty that is the main drawcard. Here you'll find wildly beautiful beaches, the jagged ramparts of mountain ranges and the perfectly sculpted sands of the fabled Empty Quarter.

P CAPITAL ISLAMABAD // POPULATION 193.2 MILLION // AREA 796,095 SQ KM // OFFICIAL LANGUAGES URDU & ENGLISH

Pakistan

Always off the beaten track, Pakistan is one of the last great frontiers for travellers seeking white-knuckled adventure. However, with political instability and a seemingly endless insurgency, this is not a destination for the faint-hearted. Indeed, the Pakistan government mandates that tourists travel with an armed guard in many parts of the country. Which is all a great shame as there is an incredible amount to see here: ruined cities, mesmerising mosques, fascinating tribal culture, crumbling Raj-era relics and stunning Himalayan scenery, plus one of the world's great road journeys over the Karakoram Hwy. Nevertheless, with some strategic planning, it is perfectly possible to travel to Pakistan and discover a captivating Islamic civilisation that has changed only superficially since the time of the Mughals.

Best time to visit
November to April in the south, May to October in the north

Top things to see
- The Mughal brilliance of Lahore Fort and the Badshahi Masjid
- A courtyard with room for 300,000 of the faithful at the Faisal Masjid in Islamabad
- The ruins of one of Asia's earliest civilisations at Moenjodaro
- Sufi shrines and spectacular Mughal monuments in historic Multan
- Pantomime sabre-rattling at the Wagah–Attari border crossing between Pakistan and India

Top things to do
- Eat mutton biryani – the perfect quick lunch – in the bazaars of Hyderabad
- Sway along with the singers of *qawwali* (Sufi devotional music) at the Data Darbar in Lahore
- Rattle along the bone-shaking Karakoram Hwy to Kashgar in China
- Marvel at the outrageous ornamentation of Pakistan's lavishly decorated trucks and buses
- Trek through elemental landscapes in the Pakistan Himalaya and the Karakoram, Pamir and Hindu Kush mountain ranges

Getting under the skin
Read: Kamila Shamsie's *Burnt Shadows* or Mohsin Hamid's *The Reluctant Fundamentalist,* to see the world from a Pakistani perspective
Listen: to the ballads of Nusrat Fateh Ali Khan, the most famous performer of *qawwali*
Watch: Shoaib Mansoor's *Khuda Kay Liye* (In the Name of God), a thought-provoking exploration of some of the key issues facing Pakistan today
Eat: chicken *karahi*, the national curry of Pakistan and the forerunner to the British balti
Drink: fresh mango juice; *chai* (tea); or *badam* milk, flavoured with almonds

In a word
Insha'Allah (If God wills it)

Trademarks
Mangos, mosques and mountains; the Karakoram

Hwy; climbing K2; cricket; militants and despot generals; nuclear stand-offs with India

Random fact
The Sufi mystics of southern Pakistan follow an esoteric interpretation of Islam with a focus on music, dancing and smoking marijuana

1. Baltit Fort has protected Karimabad in the Hunza Valley for more than 700 years

2. Young boys in colourful traditional turbans

3. Pakistani truck drivers decorate their vehicles to attract attention

P

P CAPITAL NGERULMUD // POPULATION 21,186 // AREA 458 SQ KM // OFFICIAL LANGUAGES PALAUAN & ENGLISH

Palau

Above and below water, Palau showcases the best of Micronesia. The diving here is world renowned for its vivid reefs, deep-blue holes, WWII wrecks, caves, tunnels, giant clams and more than 60 vertical drop-offs. Without gills (or breathing apparatus) you can spot exotic birds, crocodiles slipping into the mangroves and orchids flourishing in shady corners. The archipelago is incredibly diverse, from coral atolls and tranquil specks with haunting WWII pasts, to Babeldoab, Micronesia's second largest island. With signs everywhere promoting feel-good vibes (such as WAVE: Welcome All Visitors Enthusiastically!), it's just as easy to fall in love with the people here as it is with their particularly blessed geography.

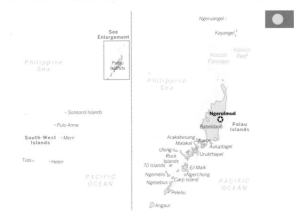

Best time to visit
It's driest from February to April, although it's warm year-round and can rain anytime

Top things to see
- The mushroom-shaped limestone islets of the Rock Islands on a scenic flight
- The abundance of marine life at Blue Corner, one of Palau's most magical dive sites
- The history and art of Palau on display at the Belau National Museum
- Ngardmau Waterfall, the highest falls in Micronesia
- Eerie Japanese WWII ruins on the tiny island of Peleliu

Top things to do
- Dive by trees of black coral, mammoth gorgonian fans, sharks and sea turtles around Peleliu
- Snorkel the alien-like, stingless-jellyfish world of Jellyfish Lake
- Take it really, really easy on the charming island of Angaur
- Get off-road on an all-wheel driving tour of Koror or Babeldaob
- Wend your way along the majestic Ngerdorch River on a boat cruise

Getting under the skin
Read: *Words of the Lagoon: Fishing and Marine Lore in the Palau District of Micronesia,* marine biologist RE Johannes' account of the knowledge of Palau's fishermen
Listen: to *Natural...*, the first album by the popular Palauan band, InXes
Watch: *The Last Reef: Cities Beneath the Sea,* the 3D cinematic spectacular that explores Palau's underwater world

Eat: Palau specialities like taro-leaf soup
Drink: an ice-cold amber ale from Red Rooster, Palau's only craft beer brewery

In a word
Omelengmes (The concept of politeness and respect)

Trademarks
Giant clams; storyboard art; Jellyfish Lake; wall diving; WWII relics; welcoming people; social responsibility

Random fact
Although peaceful now, Palau still has a scattering of live WWII ammunition in the bush; there's a US$15,000 fine for the removal of war relics for those caught without getting blown up

1. Palau: somewhere to lose yourself for a week or three

2. Aside from wonderful limestone formations, the Rock Islands have rich marine life

3. Traditional stories are often carved into 'storyboards' on Palau

P CAPITAL PANAMA CITY // POPULATION 3.6 MILLION // AREA 75,420 SQ KM // OFFICIAL LANGUAGE SPANISH

Panama

The waistline of the Americas, Panama is also the crucial connection. Its 80km belt of locks brings the Atlantic to the Pacific, wedding east to west in global commerce in the famous canal that has defined Panama in the last century. What lies just beyond could define the next. Pristine beaches, lush rainforest and big-city nightlife give a taste of the country's outstanding assets. Panama City is a major financial hub with a monumental Manhattan-esque skyline, yet one hour outside the city, indigenous Embera paddle dugout canoes and a couple of hours further, the roadless rainforests of the Darién harbour one of the world's greatest wildernesses. The Panama Canal expansion might signify increased business, but numerous isolated islands around the coastline will still mean a stint playing at *Survivor* is a possibility.

Best time to visit
Mid-December to mid-April (the dry season)

Top things to see
- Monster freighters and capuchin monkeys sharing the Panama Canal
- The hip, regal and ruinous intersecting in the 17th-century Panama City neighbourhood of Casco Viejo
- Perfect beaches and poisonous dart frogs in the Bocas del Toro Archipelago
- The great no-man's-land of jungle known as the Darién Gap, un-crossed by any road
- The serene 13km arc of sand at Playa las Lajas along the in-the-know surfers' paradise of the Gulf of Chiriqui

Top things to do
- Snorkel with sea turtles and sharks in Parque Nacional Coiba
- Trek through Parque Nacional Volcán Barú in search of the elusive quetzal
- Water-sopping and rum-soaked, revel on the crowded streets at Carnavales de Azuero
- Barter with Kunas, an autonomous indigenous group on the sun-soaked islands of San Blas
- Sip award-winning local java in the cool mountain town of Boquete

Getting under the skin
Read: *The Path Between the Seas* by David McCollough, on the elephantine undertaking of the Panama Canal
Listen: to the salsa of Rubén Blades or the Panamanian folk of Samy and Sandra Sandoval

Watch: the Academy Award–winning documentary *The Panama Deception,* by Barbara Trent, which investigates the US invasion of Panama
Eat: sancocho (chicken, *ñame* and cilantro soup); or *carimañolas* (meat-filled *yucca* puffs)
Drink: *chicheme* (sweet corn, cinnamon and vanilla in milk); or *seco* (sugar-cane liquor served with milk and ice)

In a word
¡Chuleta! (Wow!)

Trademarks
The world's most famous shortcut; Manuel Noriega; Panama hats; baseball; Darién Gap

Random fact
Panama hats actually originated in Ecuador – they acquired their name as they were shipped to Panama from Ecuador before being distributed worldwide

1. The towering skyscrapers of Panama City

2. Public transport art in Panama City

3. Hoffman's two-toed sloth is largely arboreal, Parque Nacional Soberanía

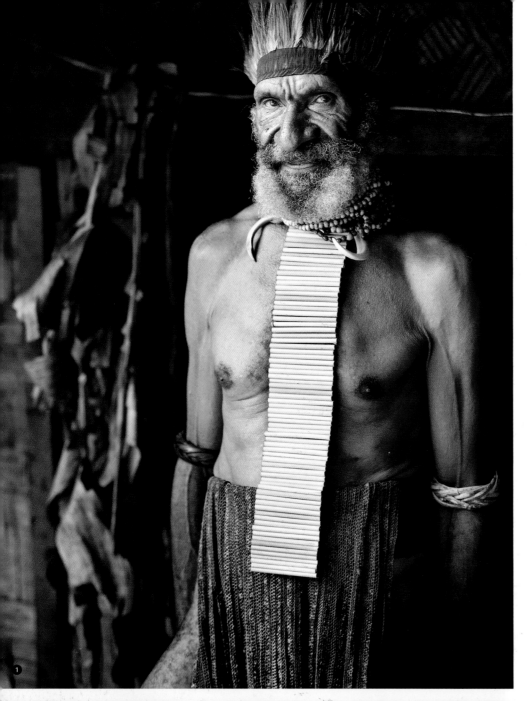

Best time to visit
June to September is cooler, drier and takes in the majority of the provincial celebrations and Highlands *sing sings* (festivals or dances)

Top things to see
- The dancing, singing, whistle blowing and sometimes magic involved in a crowded game of Trobriand cricket
- A traditional *sing sing* celebrating the ascension of a chief, initiation rites and more
- The rumbling, billowing string of volcanoes in New Britain, which often put on spectacular lava displays
- Astonishing biodiversity, including 35 species of birds of paradise, who put on fabulous displays in Varirata National Park and other forest areas

Top things to do
- Travel up the quintessentially primitive Sepik River into a treasure trove of Pacific art
- Trek into PNG's wild Highlands, for glimpses of astonishing indigenous culture and views from the lofty summit of Mt Wilhelm
- Dive shipwrecks, lost planes from WWII and reefs teeming with macro and megafauna, including whale sharks and mantas
- Follow in the muddy footsteps of WWII soldiers on the challenging, leech-infested Kokoda Track

Getting under the skin
Read: Tim Flannery's *Throwim Way Leg,* describing the author's trips in search of tree kangaroos; or Kira Salak's travelogue *Four Corners: A Journey into the Heart of Papua New Guinea*
Listen: to Telek's *Serious Tam*, showcasing the extraordinary voice of this native Papuan singer
Watch: Robin Anderson and Bob Connelly's triptych *First Contact,* Joe Leahy's *Neighbours* and *Black Harvest,* an outstanding exposition of Highlanders' first encounters with the outside world
Eat: *sasak* (sago), the staple in the swampy Sepik; *kaukau* (sweet potatoes) in the Highlands; fresh fish and lobsters on the coasts
Drink: PNG Highland-grown Arabica coffee

In a word
Em nau! (Fantastic! Right on!)

Trademarks
Penis-gourds; betel nut; *sing sings;* bilum bags; tribal art; spectacular reefs and beaches; the Kokoda Track; Asaro mud men; yam worship; *The Phantom; raskols*

Random fact
Over 820 languages are spoken in PNG with adults speaking an average of three languages each

1. A tribesman from Mt Hagen dressed for a spirit dance in the Western Highlands Province

2. Parliament Haus in Port Moresby was inspired by traditional ancestral worship houses from the Sepik region

3. Boys leap from a rusty wreck, the active volcano Tavurvur glowering beyond, in Rabaul, New Britain

P

CAPITAL PORT MORESBY // POPULATION 6.4 MILLION // AREA 462,840 SQ KM // OFFICIAL LANGUAGES ENGLISH, TOK PISIN & HIRI MOTU

Papua New Guinea

Just 3.7km separate Papua New Guinea from the nearest point in Australia, but the differences could not be more pronounced. Where Australia is parched and dry, mountainous PNG is draped in a steamy cloak of tropical rainforest. Where Australia tops global rankings for quality of life, PNG languishes at the bottom of the list of impoverished Asian nations. But there are more similarities than you might expect. The fascinating tribes of PNG share a rich history with Australia's aboriginal people, and the exotic birds and beasts that inhabit the dense jungles form a bridge between Australia and Asia. Most visitors skip the grubby capital for the coast's pristine coral reefs or the fascinating tribal culture of the interior. However, you'll have to dodge *raskols* (criminal gangs) to experience these cultural and natural riches.

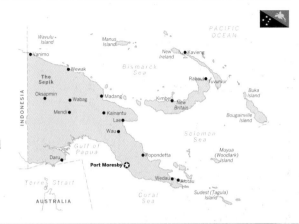

Best time to visit
May to September (winter)

Top things to see
- The engineering behemoth of Itaipu, one of the world's largest hydroelectric dams and supplier of 90% of Paraguay's energy
- The haunting 18th-century colonial remnants of the Jesuit Missions of Trinidad and Jesús, both Unesco World Heritage sites
- Parque Nacional Cerro Corá, with its forest and savannah, caves and petroglyphs
- The colourful Carnaval of Encarnación, smaller but no less wild than Rio's big fest

Top things to do
- Go wildlife watching in the Mbaracayú Biosphere Reserve, one of the most bio-diverse places on the planet
- Take off horseback riding, camping or simply admiring the beauty of Laguna Blanca
- Spot monkeys, macaws and other wildlife on a slow boat ride up the Río Paraguay
- Visit the intriguing Mennonite colonies in the Chaco

Getting under the skin
Read: *I the Supreme* by Augusto Roa Bastos, a fascinatingly complex novel delving into the mind of a dictator

Listen: to the song 'Pajaro Campana', which uses the bizarre call of the bellbird (Paraguay's national bird) as the main rhythm

Watch: Roland Joffe's epic film *The Mission* for depictions of Guaraní and Jesuit settlements in colonial days

Eat: succulent cuts of *tapa de cuadril* (similar to rump steak) and *chipas* (manioc, cheese and cornmeal rolls)

Drink: *terere* (iced herbal tea); and *mosto* (sugar-cane juice)

In a word
Mba'eichapa? (How are you? in Guaraní)

Trademarks
Football (soccer); jaguars; contraband; Jesuit missions; impassable jungle roads

Random fact
The War of the Triple Alliance (1864–70) devastated Paraguay with a loss of over 50% of its population and 25% of its territory in the conflict against Argentina, Brazil and Uruguay

1. The massive spillway of Itaipu Dam, the source of nearly all Paraguay's electricity

2. The 17th-century Jesuit Mission of La Santísima Trinidad de Paraná

3. Feral criollo horses; the breed is known for its stamina

P CAPITAL ASUNCIÓN // POPULATION 6.6 MILLION // AREA 406,752 SQ KM // OFFICIAL LANGUAGES SPANISH & GUARANÍ

Paraguay

Dwarfed by Brazil and Argentina, small, landlocked Paraguay is sometimes described as South America's 'forgotten country'. Like its better-known neighbours, football madness and a burgeoning beef industry are national hallmarks. Paraguayans, however, have followed a far different course through history. Most citizens, proudly touting their Guaraní heritage, scratch out a living at small-scale microenterprises or subsistence farming. The country is a remarkable study in contrasts, with horse-drawn carts sidling up to luxury automobiles, while huge Mennonite farms and rustic *campesino* (peasant farmer) settlements share space on the hard-scrabble Chaco. Paraguayans are famously laid-back, quick to share a *terrere* (iced herbal tea) with a visitor over long siestas in the sticky tropical heat.

P

Best time to visit
June to August (the dry season)

Top things to see
- Machu Picchu, the great Inca ruins hidden deep in mist-covered cloud forest
- Cuzco, a beautiful Andean town with Inca-made walls, cobblestone streets and gilded colonial churches
- The enchanting islands on Lake Titicaca, one of the world's highest navigable lakes
- Arequipa, a charming colonial city near smouldering volcanoes and the world's deepest canyons
- Parque Nacional Manu, home to cloud- and rainforest and astounding biodiversity

Top things to do
- Listen to live *trova* (folk music) at an atmospheric nightspot in Lima
- Hike the Santa Cruz trail through the towering peaks of the Cordillera Blanca
- Charter a flight over the Nazca Lines, the mystical drawings in the earth left by a past civilisation over 1000 years ago
- Visit the ruins of Chan Chan, once the largest pre-Columbian city in the Americas

Getting under the skin
Read: Mario Vargas Llosa's famed *Conversations in the Cathedral* about power and politics in 1950s Peru, but with universal repercussions
Listen: to Susana Baca's Afro-Peruvian rhythms
Watch: Claudia Llosa's award-winning fable *MadeinUSA* about the clash between old and new in a somewhat surreal Andean town
Eat: *ceviche* (fresh seafood marinated in lime juice and chilli peppers)
Drink: Inka Kola, bubble-gum flavoured soda; *pisco* (a white grape brandy)

In a word
Buenos dias (Good day)

Trademarks
Pan pipes; Andean peaks; llamas; Incan ruins; colourful textiles; indigenous villages; 16th-century Spanish architecture and artefacts

Random fact
Peru's pre-Columbian civilisations left such a mine of archaeological riches that treasures are still being unearthed, like the recently discovered 'lost city of the cloud people', a cliff-top citadel with rock paintings and 1000-year-old stone houses

1. Colonial period colour: Trujillo Cathedral and Plaza Mayor, Trujillo

2. Marinera is a Peruvian dance style using handkerchiefs as props

3. A traditionally dressed woman, with child in tow, at a market in Cuzco

4. The intricate terraces of the 15th-century Machu Picchu, Huayna Picchu towering above in the background

P CAPITAL LIMA // POPULATION 29.9 MILLION // AREA 1,285,216 SQ KM // OFFICIAL LANGUAGES SPANISH, QUECHUA & AYMARA

Peru

Birthplace of the great Inca civilisation, Peru remains deeply connected to its storied ancestral heritage. Nearly half the population is purely indigenous, inhabiting some of the most fantastical settings on earth. Quechua-speaking highlanders mingle in colourful markets in the shadow of towering Andean peaks, while Uros peoples eke out a living on the surreal floating islands in Lake Titicaca. A world away, remote tribes (some uncontacted) maintain ancient traditions deep in the Amazon. Peruvian cities provide a vivid contrast, a blend of frenetic and cosmopolitan neighbourhoods, scenic Spanish-colonial centres and folk-music clubs. Innovative ideas – like sustainable tourism projects run by indigenous groups – are helping to ensure Peru's treasures will be around for generations to come.

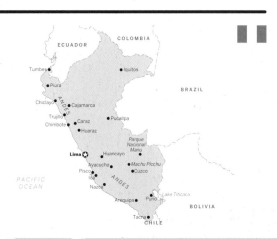

P | CAPITAL MANILA // POPULATION 105.7 MILLION // AREA 300,000 SQ KM // OFFICIAL LANGUAGE FILIPINO

Philippines

Scattered like jewels across the Pacific Ocean, the 7000-plus islands of the Philippines are dotted with palm trees, circled by coral reefs, and overlooked by the vast majority of travellers. However, things are changing; more and more people are discovering the enigmatic charms of Asia's largest Catholic country. Culturally, the islands are a surreal melting pot of American bravado, Chinese entrepreneurialism, tribal flamboyance and Spanish mysticism, set in a classic Southeast Asian landscape of coral beaches, volcanoes and rainforests. Sex tourism – a legacy of the Vietnam War – still casts a long shadow over these eclectic isles, but increasingly the focus has shifted to white-sand beaches, island-hopping by outrigger boat and the spectacular dive sites and surf breaks that dot a staggering 36,000km of coastline.

Best time to visit
October to May, to avoid the worst of the typhoon season

Top things to see
- The almost-too-perfect sands of Boracay Island
- Rice terraces on an epic scale at Banaue
- *Butanding* (whale sharks) on their annual migration past Luzon Island
- At least one fiesta; Filipino festivals are as flamboyant, energetic and eccentric as the Filipino people
- The spooky hanging coffins of Sagada, a flashback to pre-Christian tribal death rites

Top things to do
- Ride in a jeepney – the wildly decorated stretched jeeps that serve as buses across the Philippines
- Dive into an eerie graveyard of WWII shipwrecks at Coron on Busuanga
- Survive a night out in Manila – Asia's most notorious metropolis
- Meet the wildlife, whether that means graceful thresher sharks or tiny tarsiers, one of the world's teeniest primates
- Ride a dirt bike across rugged Palawan

Getting under the skin
Read: *In Our Image* by Stanley Karnow, a harrowing exposé of the American colonial period in the Philippines; or F Sionil José's Spanish-era epic *Dusk*
Listen: to the sentimental croonings of karaoke favourite Jose Mari Chan; or the agreeable Pinoy-rock of Eraserheads
Watch: Ishmael Bernal's emotional classic *Himala*; or Chito Rono's crowd-pleasing blockbuster *Sukob*, starring Kris Aquino, daughter of former president Corazon Aquino
Eat: *adobo* (pork or chicken stewed in vinegar and soy sauce); or *pasit canton* (fried noodles) for a taste of the islands' distinctive China-collides-with-Europe cuisine
Drink: Tanduay rum, typically served Cuba libre–style with Coke and a twist of lime

In a word
Mabuti naman (I'm fine)

Trademarks
Jeepneys; San Miguel beer; cock-fighting; Catholicism; coral reefs; US airbases; popular revolutions; more beaches than you can count; Imelda Marcos' shoes

Random fact
Every Easter dozens of devout Filipino Catholics offer themselves up to be crucified with real nails at San Fernando de Pampagna

1. Kadayawan sa Dabaw Festival in Davao is a celebration of tribal culture
2. Kayaking between the spectacular limestone formations of Palawan
3. The unusual Chocolate Hills of Bohol
4. Jeepneys are the ubiquitous means of public transport in the Philippines

P

LAST RESTING PLACE OF
H.M.S. BOUNTY
← 50 M

Welcome to
PITCAIRN ISLAND

MOSS

P CAPITAL ADAMSTOWN // POPULATION 65 // AREA 47 SQ KM // OFFICIAL LANGUAGE ENGLISH

Pitcairn Islands

As the smallest dependent territory in the world and one of the most remote destinations on earth, Pitcairn Island feels both claustrophobic and wildly exhilarating. The island's 4.5 sq km surface is almost entirely sloped and has landscapes that vary from desolate rock cliffs to lush tropical hillsides. Yet it's the island's tiny population, descended from the *Bounty* mutineers, who make the place famous. If you can find a way to get here, spend time hiking and meeting the locals – you'll quickly understand why these Anglo-Polynesians are proud to call Pitcairn home and preserve their unique heritage. The archipelago also consists of two atolls plus Henderson Island – a raised coral island with a virtually untouched environment and endemic birdlife.

Best time to visit
July and August are the driest months

Top things to see
- All the *Bounty* leftovers, from the rusty cannon and anchor, to the faded old bible on display at the island's museum
- The flightless and fearless Henderson crake foraging on the mosquito-free shores of Henderson Island
- Mysterious Polynesian petroglyphs at Down Rope, the island's only beach
- The island's resident Galápagos tortoise, Mrs Turpin, over on Tedside
- The grave of John Adams, the last of the surviving mutineers

Top things to do
- Take a dip in the neon-blue waters of cathedral-like St Paul's Pool
- Hike down the steep cliffs to Down Rope to go fishing
- Whiz around on the back of a quad bike up and down red-dirt slopes
- Follow Fletcher Christian's footsteps by gazing over Adamstown from high up in Christian's Cave
- Eat, drink and get to know the locals at Christian's Cafe

Getting under the skin
Read: *Serpent In Paradise* by Dea Birkett, a no-holds barred account of a journalist's time spent on the island
Listen: to locals speaking Pitkern, a strange mix of old English sailor slang and Tahitian
Watch: *The Bounty* (1984) starring Anthony Hopkins and Mel Gibson, the best re-enactment of the mutineers' tale
Eat: deep-fried seafood such as *nanwi* (bluefish), a Pitcairn staple
Drink: a tipple with the locals at Christian's Cafe on Friday nights

In a word
Whutta-waye? (How are you? in Pitkern)

Trademarks
Mutiny on the *Bounty*; Fletcher Christian; pirates; precipitous slopes; Seventh Day Adventists; honey; isolation; birdlife

Random fact
The islanders are Seventh Day Adventists, but few attend church and almost everyone drinks alcohol

1. Pitcairn's proud claim to fame
2. A white tern comes to rest on Ducie Atoll
3. Pitcairn's tiny and difficult-to-navigate harbour

Best time to visit
May to September

Top things to see
- The architectural treasures of the Old Town and Wawel Hill in the former capital of Kraków
- The Warsaw Rising Museum, testament to the bravery and determination of local Poles
- Malbork Castle, the largest Gothic castle in Europe and once headquarters of the Teutonic Knights
- Port city Gdańsk with its monuments to Poland's Solidarity movement, charming old town and surrounding white-sand beaches
- The countless lakes and canals of the Great Masurian Lake system

Top things to do
- Pay your respects at the infamous Nazi death camps of Auschwitz and Birkenau
- Spot a European bison emerging out of the undergrowth at Białowieża National Park
- Go gnome-spotting in the sculpture-rich city of Wrocław or admire its Panorama Racławicka painting, a whopping 114m long
- Join the pilgrims trekking to see the Black Madonna at the Jasna Góra monastery
- Hike into the Tatra Mountains, the highest range within the Carpathians, or catch the cable car to Mt Kasprowy Wierch
- Ski between snow-covered pine trees in pretty Zakopane

Getting under the skin
Read: *Heart of Europe* and *God's Playground* by revered historian Norman Davies
Listen: to the works of Frederic Chopin; or to Henryk Gorecki's *Symphony No 3*
Watch: the films of Krzysztof Kieslowski, such as *Three Colours: White,* a black comedy; or the Academy Award–winning *Ida,* directed by Paweł Pawlikowski
Eat: *pierogi* (dumplings stuffed with minced meat); *oscypek,* salty sheep's cheese served with berry relish; *borscht,* either hot or cold, depending on the season; and *bigos,* a hearty hunter's stew of cabbage, sausage meat and juniper
Drink: vodka, especially flavoured varieties like cranberry and bisongrass; or Polish beers like Tyskie and Okocim

In a word
Dzien dobry (Good day)

Trademarks
Chopin; *pierogi;* Baltic Sea amber; Solidarity; vodka shots; astrologer Nicolaus Copernicus; author Joseph Conrad; Pope John Paul II

Random facts
Nobel Prize–winning physicist Marie Curie completed her studies in Paris because, as a woman, she was denied a place at Kraków University

1. Museum of the History of Polish Jews (Polin), designed by Finnish architect Rainer Mahlamäki

2. Historical Old Town Square, Warsaw

3. An Eurasian elk in the Red Marsh Nature Reserve

P CAPITAL WARSAW // POPULATION 38.4 MILLION // AREA 312,685 SQ KM // OFFICIAL LANGUAGE POLISH

Poland

Stretching from the Baltic Sea to the Carpathian Mountains, Poland's fortunes have waxed and waned over centuries. Having shrugged off the Soviet mantle, Poland is embracing modernity with characteristic energy and passion. With its upbeat capital, Warsaw, and the timeless elegance of Kraków, industrial heartland cities and Unesco Biosphere Reserves, Poland is nothing if not diverse. Many locals remain family-oriented church-goers. But tastes are diversifying among the young, who increasingly choose travel, rock music, vegetarian food and artisan coffee over plates of dumplings and Sundays spent at Mass. Visitors can expect a warm welcome comprised of a raised glass of vodka, always drunk neat, accompanied by a hearty handshake. A second glass usually follows; then a third, and so on...

P CAPITAL LISBON // POPULATION 10.8 MILLION // AREA 92,090 SQ KM // OFFICIAL LANGUAGES PORTUGUESE & MIRANDESE

Portugal

Edge, charisma, good looks and pure Atlantic light – capital city Lisbon has the lot. Here *miradouros* (viewpoints) perch like birds' nests on its seven hills and vintage trams screech past *azulejo*-tiled houses, old-school shops, retro bars and pearl-white Age of Discovery monuments, affording tantalising glimpses of the Rio Tejo. Venturing north brings you to the surf-lashed coast of the Estremadura, Coimbra and the gravitas of its 500-year-old university, and the soulful city of Porto, with its grand parade of port lodges, strollable medieval centre and high-spirited nightlife. Further north, granite peaks and river valleys unfold, while the rural, foodie Alentejo and the cliff-backed beaches and whitewashed villages of the Algarve entice further south. Portugal's lushly volcanic islands – Madeira and the Azores – are hiking heaven.

Best time to visit
March to June and September, July and August to bake on the Algarve's busy beaches

Top things to see
- The raw, windswept, end-of-the-world beauty of Cabo de São Vicente
- The uplifting and extraordinarily intricate Mosteiro dos Jerónimos in Lisbon's Belém quarter – the zenith of Manueline style
- World-class modern art, Moorish architecture and fairy-tale palaces in Sintra
- Coimbra, the Cambridge of Portugal, with a medieval heart and live fado in student-rammed bars
- Walled 14th-century Évora, a Unesco World Heritage site

Top things to do
- Uncover dinky boutiques down dusty alleys and a heady mix of bars, restaurants and clubs in chilled-out Lisbon
- Poke around the Alfama quarter, Lisbon's castle-topped Moorish old-timer
- Explore dramatic cliffs, gold-sand beaches and scalloped bays on the Algarve
- Tour a port-wine lodge and taste Portugal's legendary tipple in popular Porto
- Hike rugged peaks in the Parque Nacional da Peneda-Gerês

Getting under the skin
Read: the funny 18th-century love story *Memorial do Convento* by Nobel Prize–winner José Saramago
Listen: to Mariza, whose album *Terra* fuses traditional fado with world sounds
Watch: *Night Train to Lisbon,* in which Jeremy Irons travel to the Portuguese capital in the footsteps of a mysterious woman
Eat: *cataplana* (seafood and rice stew in a copper pot); *pastéis de nata* (Portuguese custard tarts)
Drink: Sogrape's Barca Velha *vinho* (wine) with your meal, followed by vintage port from the Douro Valley

In a word
Bom dia (Hello!)

Trademarks
Fado; football; *pastéis de nata;* salted cod; the Algarve; cork; port wine

Random fact
The sleeves-up people of Porto recite an old saying about the country's biggest cities – 'Porto works, Coimbra studies, Braga prays and Lisbon plays'

1. A vineyard in Portugal's colours of red and green
2. Beautiful, historical Porto, Portugal's second-largest city
3. Lisbon's photogenic fortress, Torre de Belém
4. A goat herder takes the high ground in the Parque Nacional da Peneda-Gerês

P

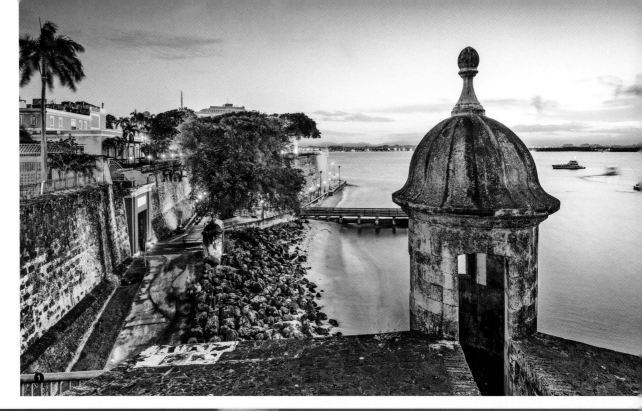

1. Paseo de la Princesa, a 19th-century esplanade in San Juan

2. The whole of Palomino island is a private luxury resort

3. Cobblestones pave the streets of Old San Juan

P CAPITAL SAN JUAN // POPULATION 3.6 MILLION // AREA 9104 SQ KM // OFFICIAL LANGUAGES SPANISH & ENGLISH

Puerto Rico

Old Spain lives on in Old San Juan, the centuries-old walled seaside town within the vast urban sprawl that makes up the island's capital. Here cobblestone streets buzz with some of the Caribbean's best shopping, eating and entertainment – as befits an island that has long been one of the main overseas vacationing spots for Americans. While it will take time for the island to heal from the devastating hurricane season of 2017, Puerto Rico's feisty Latin spirit holds firm. Bars bounce to home-grown salsa and bomba, rum cocktails flow amid mural-splashed streets, and you only have to stop by the roadside come weekends to sample the archetypal island leisure activity of sharing *lechón* – whole roast pig, cooked on a spit, eaten animatedly, and washed back by a few cold ones.

Best time to visit
November is lovely and crowds are few; December to April is the most popular time

Top things to see
- Old San Juan, the 500-year-old centre of the nation and an engrossing, vibrant window into the past
- Ponce, a colonial gem known for its criollo architecture and a centre for traditional dance
- The myriad fauna in the dry forests of Bosque Estatal de Guánica
- The 'cathedral of rum' at the Bacardi factory

Top things to do
- Listen to the silence in the nature reserves of the island of Vieques
- Follow the bouncing frogs in El Yunque, the island's surviving tropical rainforest
- Burrow like a turtle into the warm, and turtle-friendly, sands of Culebra
- Surf on and dive below the waters of laid-back Rincón, with its '60s hippie vibe

Getting under the skin
Read: Rosario Ferre's revisionist stories in *Sweet Diamond Dust;* or Hunter S Thompson's *The Rum Diary*
Listen: to the sounds of Tito Puente and Willie Colon
Watch: the acclaimed *West Side Story* representing stateside Puerto Ricans of the day; also Rachel Ortiz's heartfelt documentary *Mi Puerto Rico*
Eat: plantain dishes like *mofongos* and *tostones; tembleque* (coconut pudding); *comido criollo* (an ever-changing stew)
Drink: piña coladas; phenomenal coffee produced by the haciendas in the Central Mountains

In a word
Qué pasa? (What's happening?)

Trademarks
Living *la vida loca;* surfing; Bacardi rum cocktails; baseball players

Random fact
The island's future veers between the extremes of independence and statehood: a discussion about the pros and cons will always result in raised voices

SEAN PAVONE | GETTY IMAGES // JEAN DU BOISBERRANGER | GETTY IMAGES // DOMINIK DABROWSKI | GETTY IMAGES

Q CAPITAL DOHA // POPULATION 2.1 MILLION // AREA 11,586 SQ KM // OFFICIAL LANGUAGE ARABIC

Qatar

Qatar's rulers seem determined to put the country firmly on the international map as a regional financial capital and rival to Dubai for oil-rich glitz and Gulf glamour. The nation's ambitious vision is plain to see in Doha, where cultural developments, swanky hotels and iconic skyscrapers are springing up across the city and a huge investment has been made in art galleries and museums. Those looking for a more traditional Gulf experience here will not be disappointed either – there's a renovated souq (don't miss the falcon area), desert excursions out among the sand dunes, ancient rock carvings and, of course, plenty of places to stop for a traditional pour of bitter Arabic coffee.

Best time to visit
November to March, to avoid the fierce heat and humidity

Top things to see
- Al-Corniche: Qatar in a nutshell along 7km of waterfront with innovative architecture and old-style dhows
- Palm Tree Island: Doha's answer to Dubai's feats of modern engineering in the Gulf waters
- The sensational Museum of Islamic Art in Doha, designed by architect IM Pei
- Al-Wakrah: with fine mosques, glorious beaches and shallow waters where flamingos wade
- Rock carvings dating back thousands of years at Jebel Jassassiyeh

Top things to do
- Sleep overnight in Khor al-Adaid, a lovely stretch of water surrounded by sand dunes
- Pass the evening eating wonderfully well in the restaurants of Al-Bandar in Doha
- Engage in some retail therapy at the glitzy luxury shopping malls of Doha
- Go birdwatching in the mangroves and gardens of Al-Khor
- Explore the country's northern tip with lovely beaches and evocative abandoned villages

Getting under the skin
Read: *Arabian Time Machine: Self-Portrait of an Oil State,* a collection of interviews with Qataris and a window on local society
Listen: to Ali Abdel Sattar, Qatar's enduringly popular musical export
Watch: *Qatar: A Quest for Excellence,* exploring Qatari culture and music

Eat: *labneh* (a type of yoghurt cheese made from goats' milk)
Drink: strong black coffee; fruit juices; alcohol in top-end hotel bars and restaurants

In a word
Salaam (Hello)

Trademarks
Old wind-towers alongside sleek modern

architecture; fierce summer heat; Arabian oryx

Random fact
Foreign maps of Arabia drawn before the 19th century didn't show Qatar

1. The futuristic skyline of Doha

2. Souq Waqif in Doha, a cleverly redeveloped 19th-century souq

3. Traditional lanterns at a market stall

4. The exceptional Museum of Islamic Art in Doha

(R) CAPITAL BUCHAREST // POPULATION 21.8 MILLION // AREA 238,391 SQ KM // OFFICIAL LANGUAGE ROMANIAN

Romania

Transylvania is hands-down Romania's best-known region, and Count Dracula its best-known resident. But Romania has a great deal more to it than vampire legends. With a mighty section of the Carpathian Mountains, a white-sand stretch of Black Sea coast, bucolic vistas wherever you turn your gaze, Orthodox churches and a clutch of medieval walled cities, Romania is more picturesque than Bram Stoker would have you believe. And the country now boasts fresh cultural draws, like Cluj-Napoca's art collective, the Fabrica de Pensule; Bucharest's nerve-jangling escape games; and acclaimed film festivals in Braşov and beyond. Romanians are convivial, always willing to stop for a lengthy chat under blossoming pear trees, to move with the rhythms of the seasons and to make the most of the sun while it shines.

Best time to visit
May to June and September to October

Top things to see
- The wooden churches of Maramureş, with their intricate carvings and Gothic spires
- The world's second biggest building, Ceauşescu's imposing Palace of Parliament in Bucharest
- Dazzling icons and frescoes full of Biblical scenes, allegories and cautionary tales in Bucovina's painted monasteries
- Fairy tales and macabre myths portrayed in stained glass within Târgu Mureş' stunning Hall of Mirrors
- The Merry Cemetery in Săpânţa, where colourful tombstones tell irreverent tales of the interred

Top things to do
- Uncover the medieval delights of Braşov, centre of bucolic Transylvania, home to Gothic churches and Europe's narrowest street
- Check over your shoulder as you tour so-called Dracula's Castle in Bran or venture to the real deal, Vlad the Impaler's citadel in Poenari
- Enjoy the views from the medieval citadel of Sighişoara, perched on a hillock and ringed with 14th-century towers
- Push a rowboat out into the Danube delta to tour an expansive wetland teeming with birdlife
- Soak up the sun on the golden sand of the most popular Black Sea resort, Mamaia

Getting under the skin
Read: *Along the Enchanted Way* by William Blacker, an account of life in rural Romania and a doomed love affair with a Roma girl
Listen: to the inspirational, upbeat, improvised Romany mayhem of Taraf de Haidouks
Watch: *12:08 East of Bucharest*, a deadpan look at the decline of the communist regime; *Gadjo Dilo* by Tony Gatlif, a tale of a Frenchman pursuing a Romany musician
Eat: *mămăligă* (a cornmeal staple); *sarmale*, cabbage rolls crammed with mincemeat; or *ciorbă de burtă* (tripe soup that allegedly cures hangovers)
Drink: local wines, including Murfatlar, Odobeşti and Târnave; *ţuică,* a brandy potent enough to knock your socks off

In a word
Buna (Hello)

Trademarks
Count Dracula and all that Transylvanian business; rolling countryside; the tyranny of Ceauşescu; sturgeon from the Danube delta; handicrafts including wooden spoons, painted eggs, embroidery and leatherwork

Random fact
In 1884, Timişoara became the first European city to have electric street lighting

1. The snow-dusted village of Bran in Transylvania

2. Bucharest's massive Palace of Parliament, symbol of Ceauşescu's excesses

3. Dairy farmers in Maramureş, Romania's folkloric heart

1. St Petersburg's lavish Church on the Spilled Blood

2. Moscow's GUM department store, with fancy shops, restaurants and architecture

3. Snow piles high in the Siberian town of Tynda

R CAPITAL MOSCOW // POPULATION 142.5 MILLION // AREA 17,098,242 SQ KM // OFFICIAL LANGUAGE RUSSIAN

Russia

Stretching from the Baltic to the Bering Sea, Russia is a country of epic proportions. The original kingdom of Rus grew up along the western borders of Europe, where royal cities such as Moscow and St Petersburg still stun with their elegance and sophistication. After the extravagance of the tsars came the austerity of the Soviet Union, which created its own set of imposing tourist attractions. Nevertheless, hints of Russia's golden age endure in lavish palaces and opera houses that host some of the world's finest opera and ballet companies. That is one Russia; the other is a land of endless forests, silent lakes and humble cottages, where the welcome from ordinary people is as warm as the heat of the fire. Come with an open mind and at all times be ready to toast Mother Russia with a glass of vodka.

Best time to visit
May to October

Top things to see
- The Kremlin in Moscow, home to towering cathedrals, the treasures of the tsars and the institutions of the Russian state
- St Petersburg's awe-inspiring Hermitage Museum, an 18th-century palace holding one of the world's finest art collections
- Kamchatka, the remote 'land of fire and ice' with its snow-covered volcanoes and reindeer herds
- Russians with their guard down on the Black Sea coast, the nation's summer and winter playground

Top things to do
- Experience the rural side of Russia, in graceful country towns like Suzdal and the island of Kizhi
- Wander through the fortress of Veliky Novgorod, followed by a Volkhov River boat ride
- Take a 9289km journey on the Trans-Siberian Railway from Moscow to Vladivostok

Getting under the skin
Read: *War and Peace* by Leo Tolstoy, given new vigour by Pevear and Volokhonsky's celebrated translation
Listen: to Rachmaninov piano concertos; Tchaikovsky's lyricism; and Stravinsky's modernism
Watch: *Russian Ark,* a mesmerising journey through St Petersburg's Winter Palace, shot in a single take
Eat: *pelmeni* (meat dumplings); or borsch with *smetana* (sour cream)
Drink: vodka; Baltika beer; and piping hot tea poured from a *samovar*

In a word
Zdrastvuyte (Hello)

Trademarks
Vodka; free-spending oligarchs; Soviet symbols; massive military parades; *matryoshka* dolls; fur hats; caviar; cabbage and potatoes; the Cold War

Random fact
The Hermitage in St Petersburg is home to a crew of more than 70 cats, who keep the palace rodent-free, as they have since the time of Catherine the Great

1. Fishing boats with three hulls and long prows for attaching nets at work on Lake Kiva

2. A family of mountain gorillas plays in Volcanoes National Park

3. A Rwandan man performs a traditional dance

(R) CAPITAL KIGALI // POPULATION 12 MILLION // AREA 26,338 SQ KM // OFFICIAL LANGUAGES KINYARWANDA, ENGLISH & FRENCH

Rwanda

Rwanda, *Le Pays des Milles Collines* (The Land of a Thousand Hills), is draped with life: mountain gorillas play in pockets of virgin rainforest; patchwork fields cling to steep slopes; and Rwandans radiate the unfathomable strength and endurance of the human spirit. The beauty of it all shatters preconceptions, just as the stories of the genocidal past can break hearts. Travels here are incredibly rewarding, taking visitors to new highs as well as leading them on an introspective trip into the depths of the human condition. Meanwhile Rwandans, on a remarkable journey of their own, have regained their feet and continue to stride forward to a peaceful future.

Best time to visit
Mid-May to mid-March, to avoid the long rains

Top things to see
- The National Museum in Butare, with one of Africa's best ethnographical exhibits
- Papyrus gonolek and other rare bird species in the rich Nyabarongo wetlands
- Elephants, buffalo and giraffes on Akagera National Park's open savannah

Top things to do
- Share a gleeful hour with mountain gorillas in the rainforests of Volcanoes National Park
- Travel the length of Lake Kivu, sampling unspoilt beaches every step of the way
- Contemplate humanity's darkest side at the Kigali Memorial Centre, a haunting tribute to those lost in the genocide
- Track chimps, L'Hoest's monkeys and colobus troops beneath the Afromontane forest's canopy in Nyungwe Forest National Park

Getting under the skin
Read: *We Wish to Inform You that Tomorrow We Will Be Killed with Our Families* by Philip Gourevitch, which delves into the horrors of the 1994 genocide
Listen: to Jean-Paul Samputu, an international award-winning recording artist famous for his neo-traditional Rwandan music
Watch: *Gorillas in the Mist,* based on Dian Fossey's autobiography about her life's work with gorillas
Eat: grilled *tilapia* (Nile perch)
Drink: *icyayi* (sweet, milky tea)

In a word
Muraho (Hello, in Kinyarwanda)

Trademarks
Gorillas in the mist; the apocalyptic 1994 genocide; forgiveness; volcanoes; *Le Pays des Milles Collines*

Random fact
Once defined by their respective tribes, Rwandans were asked to shed this aspect of their identity after the genocide; with no more Hutus and no more Tutsis – only Rwandans

R

S CAPITAL BASSETERRE // POPULATION 51,134 // AREA 261 SQ KM // OFFICIAL LANGUAGE ENGLISH

Saint Kitts & Nevis

Driving around the northern reaches of St Kitts, you pass mile after mile of sugar cane gone wild. The once all-encompassing lifeblood of the nation is no more and the huge plantations have been abandoned. Meanwhile beaches across the island rattle with the percussion of construction as a new economy based on tourism takes hold. Even the train once used for hauling cane now hauls tourists. But if change is coming fast to this classic eastern Caribbean island, it is managing to retain its essential qualities: a laid-back culture given to loud, boisterous celebration and an utter contempt for stress. Nevis is much the same albeit in a package that's almost impossibly alluring: circumnavigating the island on a two-hour drive is one of life's meandering pleasures.

Best time to visit
Year-round, although the hurricane season (June to October) has more storms

Top things to see
- Basseterre, the capital of St Kitts: equally thriving and shambolic
- St Kitts' Brimstone Hill Fortress, a rambling 18th-century fort and a Unesco site
- Historic Charlestown, the small main town on Nevis with a mellow vibe that makes you want to settle back on a park bench
- Plantation houses with sweeping sea views on St Kitts
- Frigate Bay on St Kitts, with a string of fun beach shacks serving lobster for dinner and drinks till dawn

Top things to do
- Ride one of the ferries linking the two islands
- Sip a cocktail as you trundle around the coast on the Kitts Scenic Railway
- Take a guided hike on the lush mountainsides of Nevis
- Windsurf on Nevis' Oualie Bay, a world-class site
- Dive in Sandy Point Bay far below the ramparts on Brimstone Hill

Getting under the skin
Read: *Only God Can Make a Tree* by Bertram Roach: part love story, part historical romance, with plenty of insight into island life
Listen: to Christmas music; there's a strong local tradition to set old chestnuts to calypso and other Caribbean beats
Watch: out for some film talent as St Kitts is spending big money to establish film production facilities
Eat: breakfast on saltfish and coconut dumplings, the national dish, with a side of spicy fried plantain
Drink: CSR (Cane Spirit Rothschild), a potent potion made from sugar cane and most often mixed with Ting, a grapefruit soda

In a word
Menono (I don't know)

Trademarks
Snorkelling; laid-back attitude; old sugar plantation estates; fine beaches; cricket

Random fact
The federation of the two islands forms the smallest nation in the Western Hemisphere

1. Cockleshell Beach on St Kitts has great views across the water to Nevis

2. Basseterre waterfront in the evening light

3. Hauling in the catch at Oualie Beach, Nevis

Best time to visit
Enjoy perfect weather with plenty of other visitors from December to May; at other times, you get rain, humidity and solitude

Top things to see
- Pigeon Island, a former hangout for pirates with evocative names like Wooden Leg de Bois
- The St Lucia parrot, a rainbow-plumed bird that only lives on the island
- Soufrière, an authentic fishing town that's welcoming yet unaffected by tourists
- The buzzing markets of Castries, the capital, which are windows into island life
- Gros Islet, a genial mix of loafers, Rastas and beach bums

Top things to do
- Dive in Anse Chastanet, a marine park that's also ideal for snorkelling
- Climb the jagged Pitons, two volcanic formations towering over the island
- Crew one of the many transiting yachts on the glass-smooth waters of Marigot Bay
- Avoid becoming lunch for the boa constrictors of the Frigate Islands Nature Reserve
- Catch the breeze with kite-surfing on the south coast

Getting under the skin
Read: Derek Walcott's *Collected Poems, 1948–1984,* an anthology by the St Lucian Nobel Prize winner
Listen: to the local version of the banjo called the *bwa poye*
Watch: various films that use St Lucia for palm-tree scenes, such as *Dr Doolittle* (1967), *Superman II* (1980) and *White Squall* (1996)
Eat: 'saltfish and green fig', salted cod cooked with unripe banana
Drink: Piton, a locally brewed lager

In a word
Bon jou (Good day, in Kwéyòl, which the French Creole islanders sometimes use)

Trademarks
Pirate hideouts; impenetrable jungles; bananas aplenty

Random fact
Although the British invaded in 1778 and the French ceded the island for good in 1814, old traditions linger: most people speak a French-accented patois, are Catholic and live in towns with French names

1. The quaint fishing village of Canaries nestled on the beautiful and scenic winding West Coast Road

2. The wreck of the *Lesleen* freighter off Castries is now a coral garden delight

3. The sky-scraping Pitons overlook Soufrière

S **CAPITAL** CASTRIES // **POPULATION** 162,781 // **AREA** 616 SQ KM // **OFFICIAL LANGUAGE** ENGLISH

Saint Lucia

The colour wheel is simple on St Lucia: rich green for the tropical land, pure white for the ring of beaches and brilliant blue for the surrounding sea. And, if you look closely, you can fill out the rainbow. Yellows, oranges and reds emerge once you spot the flowers in the lush forest and take in the jaunty little villages with their brightly painted homes. (Yellow also gets help from the many banana plantations dotting the hilly countryside.) Take time for all the pleasures of surf and sand while tasting the cultural stew of loud reggae, piquant food and rum-fuelled escapades. Away from the coast, there are hikes amid the towering limestone Pitons that are alive with the echoes of waterfalls.

S CAPITAL KINGSTOWN // POPULATION 103,220 // AREA 389 SQ KM // OFFICIAL LANGUAGE ENGLISH

Saint Vincent & The Grenadines

Caribbean fantasies converge on this collection of 32 islands at the south end of the Leeward Islands. Party like a rock star in the fabled $150,000-a-week estates on Mustique; hang out with reggae-addled locals and itinerant fishers on St Vincent; or live your own pirate fantasy amid Tobago Cays. In fact SVG (as it's known) might be the ideal place to finally live out that dream of owning a yacht, as you can avoid the commitment by simply renting one and lazing your way about the islands, letting the winds and your moods guide you from one perfect spot to the next. Or indulge your inner sailor and catch a ride aboard somebody else's yacht – the ultimate in carefree wanderlust.

Best time to visit
Most people arrive December to May but the wet summer months can be nice and uncrowded

Top things to see
- Tobago Cays, a five-spot of tiny islands that could be a model of Caribbean perfection
- Kingstown, the buzzing Vincentian capital with its maze of porticoed stone alleyways
- St Vincent's Windward Hwy, a seemingly scripted mix of wave tossed shores, placid coves and pastel-hued villages
- Fort Charlotte, an 1806 Kingstown edifice with commanding views of a dozen islands
- Port Elizabeth on the sweep of Bequia's yacht-dotted Admiralty Bay

Top things to do
- Trek through montane and cloud forest to the crater-topped La Soufrière volcano
- Go Bequia-bound to buy a model boat, hit the beach or explore the quirky Moonhole community
- Hunt for treasure amid the myriad variations of coral reefs and shipwrecks
- Claim your sandy patch on Mayreu's Saltwhistle Bay, a beach so fine it needs a sixth star
- Cruise to the Tobago Cays and Mustique in luxury under the sails of the *Friendship Rose*

Getting under the skin
Read: about village life in St Vincent in Cecil Browne's *The Moon is Following Me*
Listen: to reggae; steel bands; and local boy made good, Kevin Lyttle

Watch: the *Pirates of the Caribbean* movies, which used SVG as a principal location
Eat: *bul jol:* saltfish with tomatoes and onions, served up with roasted breadfruit
Drink: the locally distilled Sunset Rum

In a word
Check it? (Do you follow what I'm saying?)

Trademarks
Rock stars and royalty; yachts; volcanoes; pirate movies

Random fact
The British dreamed of making the islands a plantation paradise for growers after the French were expelled in 1783, but volcanic eruptions, hurricanes, the abolition of slavery and more thwarted the scheme

1. Admiralty Bay is often packed with yachts from the world over

2. Black Point, Windward Coast, St Vincent

3. A model boat maker in his workshop on Bequia

S CAPITAL APIA (S); PAGO PAGO (AS) // POPULATION 195,476 (S); 54,343 (AS) // AREA 2831 (S); 199 (AS) SQ KM // OFFICIAL LANGUAGE SAMOAN

Samoan Islands

Slow down, way down, to Samoan time. Hardly anything disturbs the balmy peace except for the occasional barking dog or passing pick-up truck. All the attributes of an island paradise are here – cascades, jungles and endless blue lagoons – but without all the usual tourist hoopla. While resort experiences are few, authentic cultural experiences abound. Music is everywhere: exuberant drumming resounds through the *fiafia* dance nights, choral music emanates from churches on Sundays while Samoan hip hop is played day and night. Comprising two entities, independent Samoa and the US territory of American Samoa, the Samoan Islands share a history of being one of the strongest cultural forces in the Pacific.

Best time to visit
Between May and October, the dry season when many major Samoan festivals are held

Top things to see
- The Robert Louis Stevenson Museum in the author's former home, lovely Villa Vailima
- The eerie desolation of the Saleaula Lava Field
- An edge-of-the-world sunset at Cape Mulinu'u
- A game of *kirikiti*, Samoan-style cricket where dancing is as important as catching the ball
- Gorgeous, geometric Pe'a (traditional male tattoos) against bronze skin

Top things to do
- Gaze at the sky while floating in the To Sua Ocean Trench giant swimming hole
- Drift through the spectacular coral colonies of the Palolo Deep Marine Reserve
- Bathe in the jungle pool at Afu Aau Falls before standing atop pyramidal Pulemelei Mound
- Soak up the island vibe while strolling around the island of Manono
- Stride along Tutuila's mountainous spine to the top of Mt Alava

Getting under the skin
Read: Gavin Bell's *In Search of Tusitala,* which retraces Robert Louis Stevenson's South Sea voyages
Listen: to locally grown Samoan hip hop – Mr Tee or New Zealand-based Samoan artists King Kapisi and Scribe
Watch: *O Le Tulafale* (The Orator), the slow-burning 2011 drama shot on Upolu
Eat: local favourites such as *oka* (raw fish in lime juice and coconut milk) and *palusami* (taro leaves cooked with coconut cream)
Drink: a crisp, ice-cold Valima, one of the best beers in the Pacific

In a word
Fa'a Samoa (The Samoan way)

Trademarks
Tattoos; Robert Louis Stevenson; paradisiacal swimming holes, Polynesian-style hip hop; *fiafia*

dances; 2009 tsunami

Random fact
The blue-green vermicelli-shaped palolo reef worm emerges like clockwork the same time every year to mate; these salty treats are said to be a potent aphrodisiac prized by Samoans

1. Swimming in the fairy grotto of the To Sua Ocean Trench
2. Children in a *fale*, a house without walls to let the breeze pass through
3. Return to Paradise Beach, named after the 1953 movie filmed here
4. The clocktower in central Apia

Best time to visit
May, June and September; July and August get crowded

Top things to see
- Palazzo Pubblico with its richly decorated facade
- The relics of Saint Marinus inside the neoclassical Basilica del Santo
- A 13th-century prison, 8m deep, in the darkest depths of the Montale tower
- Skinning devices, knee breakers and other ghastly torture devices at the Museo della Tortura

Top things to do
- Revel in pure unadulterated kitsch in San Marino's overdose of souvenir shops
- Take snaps of the republican soldiers, track down local euro coinage (or buy a souvenir set) and send a postcard home using a San Marino stamp
- Get your passport stamped at the tourist office – there are no border controls between San Marino and Italy
- Climb up to all three towers pictured on the national flag: the Guaita, Cesta and Montale, for sweeping coastal panoramas; on a clear day, you can even spy Croatia

Getting under the skin
Read: *A Freak of Freedom,* an evocative portrait of San Marino penned in 1879 by English explorer James Theodore Bent
Listen: the sonatas and choral works of Cesare Franchini Tassini, the most famous of modern Sammarinese composers
Watch: Darryl Zanuck's *The Prince of Foxes* – the American director 'rented out' the entire republic to film the 16th-century period drama
Eat: *zuppa di ciliege* – a 'soup' made from cherries, sugar and wine, served with local bread
Drink: a full-bodied Brugneto red, dry white Biancale or sweet dessert Oro dei Goti from San Marino's steeply terraced vineyards

In a word
Ciao (Hello/Bye)

Trademarks
Stamp and coin collecting; fortresses; Mount Titano; rampant postcard production; gaudy army uniforms

Random fact
San Marino had to wait until 2004 to celebrate its first success in international football: a 1-0 defeat of Liechtenstein (this remains its only victory to date)

1. The *funivia* to the hilltop Città di San Marino

2. The oldest and largest of San Marino's castles, Torre Guaita

3. Palace guards outside the Palazzo Pubblico

S CAPITAL CITTÀ DI SAN MARINO // POPULATION 32,448 // AREA 61 SQ KM // OFFICIAL LANGUAGE ITALIAN

San Marino

The world's oldest republic, and Europe's third-smallest state, San Marino is a living quirk of history that today packs in the tourists. An island of sovereignty in the tempests of Italian politics since AD 301, it has its own constitution (dating to 1600 – the world's oldest), army and currency, and attracts millions of tourists each year to the stunningly picturesque Città di San Marino, its capital and a Unesco-protected medieval hill town atop 750m-high Monte Titano. Beyond this lie its stunning Appenine territories and Sammarinese *castelli* (communes) such as Serravalle, Borgo Maggiore and Domagnano.

1. The 16th-century fort of St Sebastian, São Tomé town

2. Children play on a fishing boat on the Príncipe beach of Praia das Burros

3. Locals walk through a plantation called Rio do Ouro (river of gold) in the north of the island of São Tomé

S CAPITAL SÃO TOMÉ // POPULATION 186,817 // AREA 964 SQ KM // OFFICIAL LANGUAGE PORTUGUESE

São Tomé & Príncipe

Life is beautiful, and this nation is full of it: rainforests blanket rolling hills and backdrop spellbinding beaches; tropical birds circle stark volcanic rock formations; and aquatic life aplenty patrols immaculate shores. Paradise it is, but this has not always been the case for the people who've called it home. Uninhabited when discovered by Portuguese seafarers in 1470, the fertile islands were soon inhabited by African slaves and *degredados* (undesirables sent from Portugal), all of whom were forced to work new sugar plantations. While travellers can't help but notice the colonial vestiges – the Portuguese language, Roman Catholicism and magnificent architecture – it is the peaceful, easygoing São Toméan vibe that will stick with them forever.

Best time to visit
June to September (the dry season)

Top things to see
- Turtle hatchlings poking their noses out of the sand and hurrying down the beach to the great blue sea
- Cão Grande, a massive volcanic tower rising from the jungle floor
- Distinctive forests, orchids and birds as you hike up Pico São Tomé
- Pristine reefs, clear waters and more aquatic life than bubbles leaving your diving regulator

Top things to do
- Slide into a São Tomé cafe and savour each and every sip of your *bica* (tiny cup of coffee)
- Pinch yourself on Príncipe's Banana Beach
- Peruse the aged architectural remains of Roça Agostinho Neto, the most elaborate colonial plantation estate

Getting under the skin
Read: Miguel Sousa Tavares' novel *Equador (Equator)*, an enchanting story about the governor of the islands' life turning upside down following his arrival from Portugal
Listen: to *Vôa Papagaio, Vôo!*, the seminal work of Gilberto Gil Umbelina
Watch: *Extra Bitter: The Legacy of the Chocolate Islands*, Derek Vertongen's exploration of slavery
Eat: *calulu* (smoked fish with a sauce of *oca* leaves, palm oil, local chillies and fresh herbs)
Drink: palm wine

In a word
Lévé lévé (Easy, easy) – it's a mellow 'hello', and the motto of São Tomé

Trademarks
Cocoa; *roças* (plantation estates); sublime beaches; warm Atlantic water; *motoqueiros* (motorcycle taxis); *bicas*

Random fact
It was on the island of Príncipe where Albert Einstein's theory of relativity was proven in an experiment by Arthur Stanley Eddington on 29 May 1919

Best time to visit
November to February

Top things to see
- Madain Salah, the rock-hewn Nabataean city in an otherworldly desert landscape
- Saudi Arabia's most beguiling city, Jeddah, with souqs and a wood-and-coral old quarter
- Najran's echoes of Yemen with its forts and multistorey mud homes
- Audacious modern architecture in glamorous Riyadh
- Hejaz Railway's old stations and tracks made famous by Lawrence of Arabia

Top things to do
- Dive or snorkel the Red Sea with scarcely another diver in sight
- Take the cable car down the cliff to the hanging village of Habalah
- Venture into one of the world's most famous deserts, the Rub' al-Khali, or Empty Quarter
- Journey back to the 19th-century origins of Wahhabi Islam and al-Saud ruling dynasty in Dir'aiyah
- If you're Muslim, fulfil your religious duty and make the pilgrimage to Mecca

Getting under the skin
Read: *Arabian Sands* by Wilfred Thesiger, a travel literature classic about journeying through the Empty Quarter with the Bedouin
Listen: to the call to prayer; or to Abdou Majeed Abdullah, the closest thing Saudi Arabia has to a rock star
Watch: National Geographic's *Inside Mecca* (the only way for a non-Muslim to see inside this city is via photographs or footage)
Eat: *khouzi* (lamb stuffed with a chicken that is stuffed with rice, nuts and sultanas)
Drink: cardamom-flavoured coffee

In a word
Allahu akbar (God is Great)

Trademarks
Oil-rich sheikhs and Bedouin nomads; Mecca and Medina, Islam's holiest cities; vast shopping malls

Random fact
During Bedouin feasts, excessive conversation among the normally chatty Bedouin is considered a sign of poor manners

1. A stone-carved tomb at Madain Saleh

2. A shepherd leads his flock in the Eastern Province

3. Pilgrims walk anti-clockwise around the Ka'ba in Mecca, pictured before recent development work

S CAPITAL RIYADH // POPULATION 26.9 MILLION // AREA 2,149,690 SQ KM // OFFICIAL LANGUAGE ARABIC

Saudi Arabia

Reclusive and yet an influential player on the world stage, Saudi Arabia is a land shrouded in mystery for outsiders. Tourist visas are almost impossible to get, but somehow countless expats and millions of Muslim pilgrims flood into the country from all corners of the earth every year to visit the birthplace of Islam and its holiest cities – Mecca and Medina. The prizes for those who do make it here also include an ancient Nabataean city to rival Petra, world-class diving and avant-garde architecture alongside cities built of coral.

S CAPITAL EDINBURGH // POPULATION 5.2 MILLION // AREA 78,772 SQ KM // OFFICIAL LANGUAGE ENGLISH

Scotland

What a luxuriant oil painting Scotland is: a beguiling mix of sophisticated city and brooding landscape, no place quite eats into the traveller's soul like this. True, the weather – buckets of rain and wind-whipped cloud – is hardly Mediterranean. But tramp beneath castle-crowned crags and cinematic skies mirrored in lonely lochs, and it doesn't matter. This is one of Europe's last great wildernesses, serenaded by an island-laced coastline with waltzing seals, dolphins and whales. Cosmopolitan capital Edinburgh appeases culture fiends with wonderful museums, festivals and arts; while traditional rival Glasgow cuts the grain with innovative architecture, dining and nightlife. Pour yourself a nip of fine Scottish malt whisky, sit back and savour...

Best time to visit
May to September; August for the Edinburgh festival season

Top things to see
- The fine view of the Firth of Forth from Edinburgh Castle
- Ben Nevis, a true taste of the magnificent Scottish Highlands
- Skara Brae, a Neolithic stone village built in 3100 BC in the Orkney Islands
- The deserted beaches and walking trails of the inspirationally remote Outer Hebrides
- Festival antics: Edinburgh's Hogmanay and Fringe and Shetland's Up Helly Aa are favourites

Top things to do
- Get a hole in one on the world's oldest golf course in St Andrews
- Hike spectacular cliff tops on the northern islands of Orkney
- Catch salmon, visit castles and enjoy lazy forest walks in Royal Deeside – the British Royal family has their country retreat, Balmoral, here
- Admire Victorian architecture and shop in Glasgow, Scotland's most bustling city
- Get a taste of Glasgow's vibrant music scene at King Tut's or the Barrowland

Getting under the skin
Read: Alasdair Gray's *Lanark,* a dark, passionate fantasy about Scotland, Glasgow and storytelling
Listen: to the Corries for real McCoy Scottish folk

Watch: *Trainspotting* by Danny Boyle – a Scottish youth tries to wean himself away from Edinburgh's druggie underworld
Eat: haggis with *neeps 'n' tatties* (turnips and potatoes)
Drink: a dram of single malt whisky; to get the better of a hangover, knock back Barr's Irn-Bru, a bubble-gum-scented, radioactive-orange-coloured soft drink

In a word
Slàinte mhath (Cheers!)

Trademarks
Haggis; malt whisky; smoked salmon; Sean Connery; caber-tossing; kilts; bagpipes; Hogwarts; the Forth Rail Bridge; writers Robert Louis Stevenson and Robert Burns; the Loch Ness monster

Random fact
Bevvied, blootered, hammered, fleein', fou, steamin', stotious, plastered and just plain pished… all these words mean 'drunk' in Scotland

1. Princes St in enticing Edinburgh

2. Highland cows roam the Scottish moors

3. The atmospheric ancient standing stones of the Ring of Brodgar

(S) CAPITAL DAKAR // POPULATION 13.3 MILLION // AREA 196,722 SQ KM // OFFICIAL LANGUAGE FRENCH

Senegal

Devout yet dedicated to having a good time, Senegalese make their country one of West Africa's most rewarding. The soundtrack of their lives is an exciting one, a rich and wild tapestry of tunes created by some of the continent's top musicians – and the beats will pull you (happily) to the dance floors of Dakar. The terrain here also tells a diverse story, from coastal beaches and mangrove forests to savannah woodland and the dusty Sahel of the interior. It all provides the backdrop for attractions that are just as varied, everything from poignant monuments to slavery, the elegance of French and African cultural fusion, and unparalleled birdwatching (millions of birds pass through Senegal on their migratory path between Africa and Europe).

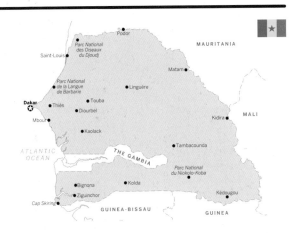

Best time to visit
November to February – the dry season and relatively cool

Top things to see
- Francophone West Africa's most lively and compelling capital, Dakar
- The car-free and tranquil island, Île de Gorée, with its monuments to Africans cast into slavery
- Touba, home to the Mouride Sufi brotherhood and the extraordinary Grand Mosque
- The mangroves, forests and wildlife of Parc National du Delta du Saloum
- Cap Skiring, among West Africa's most beautiful beaches

Top things to do
- Sink into the sublime beats of the St-Louis Jazz Festival, one of the continent's best music events
- Listen to Gregorian chants in Wolof at the Keur Moussa Monastery
- Watch millions of migratory birds in the Parc National des Oiseaux du Djoudj
- Take a pirogue through the bird-rich Parc National de la Langue de Barberie
- Traverse the wilderness and look for threatened wildlife in the Unesco-listed Parc National du Niokolo-Koba

Getting under the skin
Read: *God's Bits of Wood* by Ousmane Sembène, a classic tale of colonial West Africa; or Mariama Bâ's *So Long a Letter,* a window on the world of Senegalese women
Listen: to Youssou N'Dour; or Orchestra Baobab

Watch: *Moolaade,* directed by Ousmane Sembène, a beautifully told tale about female circumcision
Eat: *tiéboudieune* (rice cooked in tomato sauce with chunks of fish, vegetables and spices); *yassa poulet* (grilled chicken marinated in a thick onion and lemon sauce)
Drink: hibiscus *bissap* (hibiscus juice); *gingembre* (ginger beer); *bouyi* (baobab juice)

In a word
Asalaa-maalekum (Greetings, peace – in Wolof)

Trademarks
The Wolof and Mandinka peoples; migratory birds in their millions; internationally renowned music scene; *marabouts* (holy men)

Random fact
Touba is the site for one of Africa's largest pilgrimages – 48 days after the Islamic New Year, two million people descend on the town for the Grand Magal pilgrimage

1. Fula women in the Desert de Lompoul

2. A fishing boat ferries locals in St-Louis

3. Minarets of the Grand Mosque of Touba, one of the largest mosques in Africa

4. Salt is extracted from the pink waters of Lac Rose (Lac Retba)

S **CAPITAL** BELGRADE // **POPULATION** 7.2 MILLION // **AREA** 77,474 SQ KM // **OFFICIAL LANGUAGE** SERBIAN

Serbia

Former Yugo-mates Croatia and Montenegro may have nabbed the coastlines, but for character, culture and conviviality, little landlocked Serbia is hard to beat. From the rollicking nightclubs of Belgrade to the hushed monasteries of Fruška Gora, the green mountains of Zlatibor to the arid towers of Djavolja Varoš, endearing village cottages to the communist blocks of the cities, this is a land which celebrates – and revels in – its delicious differences. The people are almost frighteningly welcoming: visitors should brace themselves for a hearty three-kiss hello, endless exhortations to eat, and glasses of potent spirits thrust into their hands. EU-bound and on the up, Serbia is a stunning surprise.

Best time to visit
Between May and September

Top things to see
- Kalemegdan Citadel in Belgrade, over the confluence of the Danube and Sava
- The bucolic rolling hills of Fruška Gora, a realm of vineyards, orchards and Orthodox monasteries
- Art nouveau architectural treasures in Hungarian-influenced Subotica
- The well-preserved churches and frescoes of Studenica Monastery, one of the most sacred sites in Serbia
- The more than 200 creepy, cryptic stone towers of Djavolja Varoš (Devil's Town)

Top things to do
- Party until dawn (and beyond) on Belgrade's bacchanalian river-barge nightclubs (splavovi)
- Mosh at the EXIT festival in Petrovaradin Fortress on the Danube
- Hit the piste at Kopaonik, Serbia's premier ski resort, or take on the trails of Tara National Park
- Release your inner nerd with sci-fi-ish interactive elements and learn about the great scientist's inventions at the Nikola Tesla Museum in Belgrade
- Dance and drink like there's no tomorrow at the Dragačevo Trumpet Assembly in Guča, a frenetic festival like no other on earth

Getting under the skin
Read: *The Serbs: History, Myth and the Destruction of Yugoslavia* by Tim Judah, a nonpartisan observation of the Serbs and their history
Listen: to *trubači,* wild, haunting brass sounds influenced by Turkish melodies and Austrian military music
Watch: the films of Emir Kusturica, including *Black Cat, White Cat,* a shambolic, comic, colourful Romany tale; or *Underground,* the surreal story of seemingly never-ending Balkan conflicts
Eat: *ćevapčići* (grilled kebab) or *pljeskavica* (spiced beef patties)
Drink: *rakija,* a fiery spirit made from fermented fruit

In a word
Živeli (Cheers!)

Trademarks
Brass bands; river-barge clubs and restaurants; spicy, grilled meat; three-kiss hellos; tennis world number-one Novak Djoković; Orthodox monasteries

Random fact
The Serbs use both the Cyrillic and Latin alphabets, switching between them without a second thought

1. River barges dock along the River Sava in Belgrade

2. Rolling fields outside Novi Sad in the foothills of Fruška Gora

3. Competitors take a break at the Dragačevo Trumpet Assembly in Guča

3

Best time to visit
March to May and September to November

Top things to see
- Thunderous clouds of feathers flocking in the skies over Bird Island
- Anse Source d'Argent, a heavenly stretch of white sand and crystal-clear water punctuated by naturally sculpted granite monoliths
- The rare and ever-so-suggestive coco de mer palms growing in primordial Vallée de Mai on Praslin Island
- The remote raised corals of Aldabra Atoll, the spellbinding home to 150,000 giant tortoises
- A perfectly prepared plate of succulent seafood being placed in front of you

Top things to do
- Forget *Jaws* and share the depths with sea creatures big and small at the aptly named Shark Bank
- Satisfy any *Robinson Crusoe* fantasies on the shores of the Outer Islands
- Set your pace to slow and sink into the laid-back vibe on the beautiful granite island of La Digue
- Unleash your inner Indiana Jones hiking in the jungle-clad hills of Morne Seychellois National Park
- Nothing (as long as you're planted on one of the planet's most astounding beaches)

Getting under the skin
Read: *Seychelles Since 1770: History of a Slave and Post-Slavery Society* by Deryck Scarr
Listen: to Jean-Marc Volcy, who's fused modern Creole pop with traditional folk music
Watch: *Le Monde de Silence,* Jacques Cousteau's ground-breaking documentary, much of which was filmed at Seychelles' Assomption Island
Eat: *trouloulou* and *teck teck,* two local varieties of shellfish
Drink: *calou* (a palm wine that will put a bounce in your step)

In a word
Bonzour (Good morning, in Kreol Seselwa)

Trademarks
Aldabra giant tortoises; coco de mer palms; picture-postcard beaches; coral atolls

Random fact
Weighing up to 20kg, the seed in the famously erotic fruit of the Seychelles' female coco de mer palm is the plant kingdom's largest

1. An ox-drawn cart wends its way across La Digue Island

2. Granite rock formations on Anse Source d'Argent

3. The stunning seascape and landscape of Mahé Island

S CAPITAL VICTORIA // POPULATION 90,846 // AREA 455 SQ KM // OFFICIAL LANGUAGES ENGLISH, FRENCH & CREOLE

Seychelles

A hundred million dollars' worth of pirate treasure may lurk nearby, but you won't care. When you're in this tropical Indian Ocean paradise, surrounded by white-sand beaches, intoxicating waters and swaying palms laden with exotic fruit, you'll already feel like the richest person on the planet. And who wants to get dirty digging on holiday? Hewn seductively from granite or grown from corals, the Seychelles' 115 islands were uninhabited until the 18th century – many still are. The burgeoning society is primarily African in origin, though it's infused with touches of French, Indian, Chinese and Arab influence. The only thing known to test the Seychellois' renowned pacific nature is their long-standing government.

Best time to visit
November to April

Top things to see
• Busy Freetown, perhaps no better symbol of the nation's resilience
• Bunce Island, an important landmark in the tragic history of slavery
• Outamba-Kilimi National Park, a beautiful, peaceful refuge for elephants, leopards and hippos
• Turtle Islands, a small slice of rarely visited paradise off the Sierra Leonean coast
• The town of Sulima, a timeless place to kick back and rest from life on the African road

Top things to do
• Laze on beautiful beaches within striking distance of Freetown
• Search for pygmy hippos and primate species in the Tiwai Island Wildlife Sanctuary
• Hike through lowland rainforest and spot 333 bird species in the Gola Forest Reserve
• Climb to the summit of Mt Bintumani, watching for wildlife along the way

Getting under the skin
Read: *The Devil that Danced on the Water* (memoir) and *Ancestor Stones* (novel) by Aminatta Forna for their fascinating insights into modern Sierra Leone
Listen: to palm wine music (or *maringa* as it's known locally), whose finest exponent was the late SE Rogie
Watch: *Blood Diamond,* directed by Edward Zwick, a brutal yet uplifting civil-war tale with Leonardo DiCaprio; or the disturbing documentary *Cry Freetown* by Sorius Samura
Eat: rice served with *plasas* (a sauce of pounded potato or cassava leaves, palm oil and fish or beef)
Drink: Star, the top-selling beer; light and fruity *poyo* (palm wine)

In a word
Owdibody (How are you? – literally 'How's the body?')

Trademarks
Civil war; blood diamonds; war amputees; an impressive return to peace; Ebola; resilience

Random fact
On Valentine's Day in 1972 miners in the Koidu area discovered the Star of Sierra Leone, a 968.9-carat diamond – it still ranks as the largest-ever alluvial diamond discovered

1. Colourful Kent Harbour on Freetown Peninsula

2. A plate of cashew fruits ready for selling in Tombo

3. Surf's up on the remote and dreamy Turtle Islands

S CAPITAL FREETOWN // POPULATION 5.6 MILLION // AREA 71,740 SQ KM // OFFICIAL LANGUAGE ENGLISH

Sierra Leone

After the dark days of the 1990s, when brutal conflict – fuelled by warlords' exploitation of diamond reserves – ravaged Sierra Leone, the nation's resilient people began picking up the pieces and rebuilding their country and lives in 2002. The results were impressive enough to entice intrepid travellers, and they soon began to enjoy the sublime beaches, rainforest-clad mountains and terrific wildlife-watching opportunities. What also enthralled visitors was the people of Sierra Leone themselves, ever friendly, open and honest. Tragically the Ebola outbreak, which spread from neighbouring Guinea in 2014, pushed Sierra Leone to the brink yet again. With peace and renewed health, the future of the country (and its tourism industry) should be a bright one – its people want and deserve nothing less.

Best time to visit
Year round – February to October tends to be drier, but skies are hazy from June to October

Top things to see
- Gardens by the Bay, Singapore's most show-stopping green space
- National Gallery Singapore, the new star in Singapore's fantastic museum and gallery scene
- Colourful temples and elaborate mosques in Chinatown, Little India and Kampong Glam
- Tiong Bahru, a revived 1930s housing estate, packed with cafes and boutiques
- A menagerie of exotic beasties at the Singapore Zoo and Night Safari

Top things to do
- Light a joss stick at the historic Thian Hock Keng, Singapore's oldest Hokkien temple
- Take a bumboat to Pulau Ubin for some monkey and monitor-lizard spotting in a natural setting
- Feast your way around the Straits in one of Singapore's legendary hawker centres
- Sip a Singapore sling at Raffles, the famous hotel where the cocktail was invented in 1915
- Join in the fun of one of Chinatown's colourful festivals

Getting under the skin
Read: *Foreign Bodies,* Hwee Hwee Tan's gripping tale of young people on the wrong side of the Singapore justice system
Listen: to local and international DJs man the decks at iconic Singapore nightclub Zouk
Watch: Woo Yen Yen and Colin Goh's *Singapore Dreaming* or Tay Teck Lock's *Money No Enough* for insights into the Singapore psyche
Eat: hawker food – top treats include Hainanese chicken rice, *roti prata* (fried flat bread with curry dipping sauce) and the world-famous Singapore laksa
Drink: Tiger beer (the national brew), *kopi* (strong coffee with condensed milk), *teh tarik* (strong, sweet 'pulled' tea with condensed milk

In a word
Kiasu (Fear of losing) – a Hokkein/Singlish term for one of the defining traits of the competitive inhabitants of Singapore

Trademarks
Raffles; Changi Airport; Tiger beer; the dynasty of Lee Kuan Yew; 'No Durians' signs; fines for littering and spitting, Chingay; expensive alcohol; the city's 'garden city' vision

Random fact
Singapore is the world's largest exporter of exotic aquarium fish

1. A monk chants at the Buddha Tooth Relic Temple in Chinatown

2. Tasty treats can be found at Lau Pa Sat hawker centre

3. Twin pagodas are doubled in reflection at the Chinese Garden in Jurong East

4. 'Supertrees' at futuristic Gardens by the Bay are illuminated at night

S CAPITAL SINGAPORE // POPULATION 5.5 MILLION // AREA 697 SQ KM // OFFICIAL LANGUAGES ENGLISH, MALAY, MANDARIN & TAMIL

Singapore

Some travellers knock Singapore for its corporate mindset, draconian laws and high prices, but this Southeast Asian metropolis can no longer be accused of lacking redeeming features. Fans of the city-state rave about its amazing green spaces, great shopping, fabulous food and the intoxicating blend of Indian, Chinese and Malay culture that has shaped the national identity. With an increasing edginess that can now compete with that of Bangkok and Hong Kong, there's plenty to see, from quirky ethnic neighbourhoods and world-class museums and galleries to historic temples where the air is thick with incense. To top it off, the city is fabulously well-organised, and perfect for families.

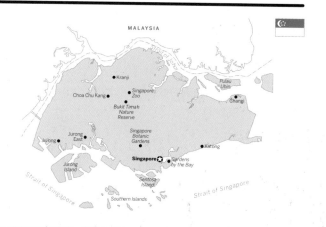

S CAPITAL BRATISLAVA // POPULATION 5.5 MILLION // AREA 49,035 SQ KM // OFFICIAL LANGUAGE SLOVAK

Slovakia

This small, proud and dramatically mountainous nation at the heart of Eastern Europe is still remembered by much of the outside world as the less famous half of the act formally known as Czechoslovakia. Indeed, since independence Slovakia has retreated into itself rather than embracing the European mainstream – folk traditions still hold sway, family life is paramount and nature is king. Slovakia's natural world includes the High Tatras mountains, which attract passionate hikers and skiers, and the wonderful raw nature of the Malá Fatra and Slovenský Raj National Parks. Unpretentious Gothic cities, stately castles and picturesque villages complete the scene, while the quiet but friendly Slovaks will welcome you warmly to their fascinating land.

Best time to visit
May to September for hiking, December to March for skiing

Top things to see
- Bratislava's charming Old Town, with its magnificent castle overlooking the Blue Danube
- The sprawling, rocky mass of Spiš Castle, Europe's biggest fortress
- Neat pastel facades on the Gothic-Renaissance burghers' houses in Bardejov
- The precipitous peaks and pine-topped ridges in the Malá Fatra National Park
- Prickly spires and battlements on Bojnice Castle, the most visited chateau in Slovakia

Top things to do
- Plunge into a thermal pool, breathe 'seaside' breezes in a salt cave, or be wrapped naked in hot mud at a Piešťany thermal treatment
- Dip your toes over the edge of a *plte* (wooden raft) down Dunajec Gorge
- Clamber up the ladder and chain ascents to the precipice in Slovenský Raj
- Crunch through the snow on the walking trails of the High Tatras

Getting under the skin
Read: the straightforward tales of feisty Slovakian women in *That Alluring Land: Slovak Tales* by Bozena Slancikova-Timrava
Listen: to wailing *gajdy* (bagpipes) and *fujara* (shepherd's flutes) that are central to much Slovakian folk music
Watch: internationally acclaimed *Krajinka*, directed by Martin Sulik: 10 vignettes of Slovakian rural life, landscape and ways throughout the 20th century
Eat: *bryndzové halušky* (potato dumplings with sheep's cheese and bacon)
Drink: local beers such as dark, sweet Martiner or full-bodied Zlatý Bažant; or very quaffable local wines

In a word
Ahoj (Hello)

Trademarks
Wooden churches; communist-era brutalist tower blocks; hearty food; folk arts and traditions

Random fact
Venus of Moravany, a headless female fertility symbol carved from mammoth bone found near Piešťany in 1938, is almost 25,000 years old

1. Ground out by ancient glaciers, Strbske Pleso lake in the High Tatras

2. A hiker descends from Kopa Kondracka (2005m) on the Slovakia–Poland border, High Tatras

3. Bratislava's picturesque castle and Old Town

Best time to visit
May to September

Top things to see
- The view over Ljubljana's old town and the bridges of the Ljubljanica River from the ramparts of Castle Hill
- Subterranean chambers and cave-dwelling salamanders in Postojna
- Shimmying dancers in shaggy sheepskin and masks at the Kurentovanje festival
- The sparklingly azure Adriatic Sea at Piran, with its Venetian ambience
- The snow-white horses of Lipica, bred for the Spanish Riding School in Vienna

Top things to do
- Ring the wishing bell in postcard-perfect Church of the Assumption on Bled Island, then return to shore in a piloted gondola
- Hike between mountain huts on well-marked trails in the Julian Alps
- Raft the foaming waters of the Soča River
- Sip wine at the source in Maribor, home to the world's oldest living grapevine
- Shop for remarkably detailed lace in former mercury-mining town Idrija

Getting under the skin
Read: *Forbidden Bread* by Erica Johnson Debeljak, a memoir of an American woman coming to terms with life in Slovenia
Listen: to traditional folk 'big band' music, featuring pan pipes and zithers alongside usual folk instrumentation; or try the electro-industrial stylings of Laibach, now infamous for being the first Western musical act to perform in North Korea
Watch: Damjan Kozole's *Rezerni Deli* (Spare Parts), a provocative and award-winning tale of the trafficking of illegal immigrants through Slovenia
Eat: *zlikrofi* (dumplings filled with cheese, bacon and chives), followed by *struklji* (sweet, cottage-cheese dumplings) or *palacinke* (pancakes)
Drink: wine such as peppery red Teran; or *zganje* (fruit brandy distilled from many fruits)

In a word
Dober dan (Hello)

Trademarks
Alpine sports; Lipizzaner horses; three-headed Mt Triglav; fairy-tale castles; forested mountains

Random fact
The national icon of Slovenia is the *kozolec* (hayrack) – there's now a museum in Sentrupert entirely dedicated to the craftsmanship of these well-loved farming tools

1. Dancers at the Kurentovanje festival, a spring and fertility rite performed in Ptuj

2. Summer in the Soča River Gorge, Triglav National Park

3. Predjama Castle, former lair of legendary robber baron, Erazem of Predjama

4. Bled Island and its Church of the Assumption, Lake Bled, Julian Alps

S **CAPITAL** LJUBLJANA // **POPULATION** 2 MILLION // **AREA** 20,273 SQ KM //. **OFFICIAL LANGUAGE** SLOVENIAN

Slovenia

Contrasts abound in tiny Slovenia. In this modern, forward-looking nation, myths of three-headed mountain gods live on, and nostalgia for the agrarian past remains strong. Slovenia is thoroughly Slavic yet displays obvious Italianate and Austro-Hungarian influences. It boasts a clutch of Alpine peaks where snow may last into summer, but where Mediterranean breezes may suddenly raise temperatures. With almost half of its total area covered in forest, it is one of the greenest countries on earth, something in which its residents – generally multilingual and suntanned, and always welcoming – take immense pride. Villages are orderly, churches picturesque and castles imposing, yet the pagan spirit of the people lives on in their raucous and colourful festivals.

Best time to visit
June to September has mild weather – good for hiking but rough seas mean the diving conditions aren't ideal

Top things to see
- Rusty WWII relics around Honiara
- The artificial stone and coral islands of Malaita's Langa Langa Lagoon
- The sensory overload, variety and bustle of Honiara's central market
- Leaf-mound nests of megapodes, birds that use volcanic heat to incubate their eggs
- Eerie skull caves, the final resting places of vanquished warriors and chiefs

Top things to do
- Dive the fantastic 'Iron Bottom Sound' WWII wrecks off Guadalcanal
- Assist rangers tag sea turtles on ecofriendly Tetepare Island
- Take a dip in the natural pools beneath Mataniko or Tenaru Falls
- Kayak, dive or snorkel through the marine-life-rich waters of Marovo Lagoon
- Surf the crowd-free point breaks off Pailongge on Ghizo

Getting under the skin
Read: *Solomon Time*, Englishman Will Randall's funny and insightful account of trying to start a chicken-farming business on Rendova
Listen: to Narasirato, a panpipe ensemble mixing traditional Malaita sounds with contemporary beats
Watch: Terrence Malick's *The Thin Red Line*, the gritty epic based on James Jones' 1963 novel about the WWII battle for Guadalcanal
Eat: *ulu* (breadfruit), the Solomon Islands' staple
Drink: SolBrew pale lager, the local brew

In a word
No wariwari (No worries)

Trademarks
Spear-fishing; animist beliefs; blond-haired Melanesians; shark calling; skull caves; underwater volcanoes; sunken WWII warships; deep-sea fishing; snorkelling and scuba diving

Random fact
There are 67 indigenous languages in the Solomons so, even though English is the official language, Pijin is what's used for day-to-day communication

1. Young islanders on Sandfly Island

2. The dramatic 60m drop of Tenaru Falls, Guadalcanal

3. Islanders gather around a cruise ship to sell their produce

S CAPITAL HONIARA // POPULATION 597,248 // AREA 28,450 SQ KM // OFFICIAL LANGUAGE ENGLISH

Solomon Islands

Want to get off the beaten path? That's easy: there is no beaten path in the Solomon Islands. It's just you, the ocean, dense rainforests and traditional villages, and it feels like the world's end. With a history of headhunting, cannibalism and (more recently) civil unrest, the islands are much safer than their past reputation suggests and are now an ecoadventurer's dream. The volcanic, jungle-cloaked islands jut up dramatically from the tropical Pacific and are surrounded by croc-infested mangroves, huge lagoons, beaches and lonely islets. Islanders are laid-back, friendly and still practice ancient arts and till their village gardens the way they have for thousands of years.

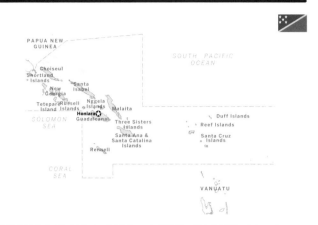

S — CAPITAL MOGADISHU (SOMALIA), HARGEISA (SOMALILAND), BOSASSO (PUNTLAND) //
POPULATION 10.3 MILLION // AREA 637,657 SQ KM // OFFICIAL LANGUAGE SOMALI

Somalia

A tale of two cities? Try a story of two nations and an autonomous state. This problematic patchwork is made up of Somalia, Puntland and Somaliland. The former has dominated the press for more than 20 years, with armed conflict, warlords and Mogadishu hotel bombings, while Puntland (autonomous since 1998) has become associated with the piracy plaguing the Indian Ocean. The golden child has been Somaliland, a self-proclaimed republic since 1991 that is wedged between Ethiopia and the Gulf of Aden. With a record of maintaining both peace and order, it lured bold travellers with astounding archaeological sites, epic beaches and the welcoming Isaq clan of Somalis. The risk of terrorism and kidnap, however, has now also risen within Somaliland to a point where it, too, is unsafe to travel.

Best time
December to March, when it is coolest

Places of interest
- The inconceivable treasures of Las Geel, a series of caves containing hundreds of the world's best preserved Neolithic rock art
- Sheekh, the site of a 13th-century necropolis
- The blissful white sands of Baathela Beach on the outskirts of Berbera
- An unheralded wealth of aquatic life along the island reefs north of Zeila
- The atmospheric livestock market in Burcao

Local customs
- Bonfires and dancing at the annual festival of Neeroosh, held each July in celebration of the start of the solar year
- Widespread use of the narcotic leaf *qaat*, with some of those interested in Sufi spiritualism using it to reach a trance-like state as a way of communing with Allah
- Celebrating a vibrant musical heritage that focuses on Somali folklore

Getting under the skin
Read: *The World's Most Dangerous Place* by James Fergusson
Listen: to *The Journey* by Maryam Mursal, the first woman to sing Somali Jazz (Peter Gabriel sings back-up in this effort)
Watch: *Black Hawk Down*, Ridley Scott's dramatic take on the US military's disastrous 3 October 1993 combat mission in Mogadishu
Eat: *anjeero* (local flatbread) topped with sheep liver and onions
Drink: *shaah* (Somali black tea) with *heel* (cardamom) and *qarfe* (cinnamon)
In a word
Ma nabad baa? (A greeting, literally meaning 'Is it peace?')

Trademarks
Pirates; civil war; Islamic militias; warlords; delayed elections (Somaliland); narcotic *qaat* leaves; Las Geel; some of the planet's longest beaches

Random fact
At its height piracy generated nearly US$200 million in annual income, making it Somalia's biggest industry

1. Camel herders draw water from a well in the Ogaden region

2. Vivid Neolithic rock art at Laas Geel, Woqooyi Galbeed, Somaliland

3. Traditional dance is an important part of Somali culture

❶

❷

S CAPITAL PRETORIA (ADMINISTRATIVE), BLOEMFONTEIN (JUDICIAL), CAPE TOWN (LEGISLATIVE) // **POPULATION** 48.6 MILLION // **AREA** 1,219,090 SQ KM // **OFFICIAL LANGUAGES** ZULU, XHOSA, AFRIKAANS, SEPEDI, ENGLISH, TSWANA, SESOTHO, TSONGA, SWATI, VENDA & NDEBELE

South Africa

The 'Rainbow Nation' moniker doesn't cover the half of it. The astonishing diversity of South Africa is not just seen in its vibrant people, but in everything. Landscapes and wildlife collide to offer incredible sights and activities – beachgoers share sand with penguins on the Cape's beaches, divers encounter whales (and great whites), safari cognoscenti watch iconic species in the bushveld, and hikers eye vultures soaring over the snowy peaks of the Drakensberg. The historical sites, ranging from the Cradle of Humankind to the Apartheid Museum, are no less compelling. And South Africa's human drama – its pain, its injustice and its hopeful spirit – is palpable. The result is sobering and challenging, fascinating and inspiring – alluring enough to keep most visitors returning time and time again.

Best time to visit
Year-round, with spring (September to November) and autumn (April to May) ideal almost everywhere

Top things to see
- Cape Town and the distant Robben Island alone in Table Bay, viewed from the top of Table Mountain
- Namakwa's vast, colourful carpets of spring flowers
- Cape Agulhas, the southern tip of Africa, where the Indian and Atlantic Oceans meet
- Stark and solitary landscapes of shifting sands in Kgalagadi Transfrontier Park
- Stunning panoramas from almost anywhere amid the peaks and valleys of the Drakensberg

Top things to do
- Bush walk at dawn past elephants and zebras in Kruger National Park
- Spend time in Soweto, Johannesburg's sprawling, turbulent, hope-filled soul
- View dolphins, crashing waves and waterfalls while trekking along the Wild Coast
- Discover Cape Town, with its lively vibes and cosmopolitan rhythms
- Explore the beauty and birdlife of lovely iSimangaliso Wetland Park

Getting under the skin
Read: *Long Walk to Freedom* – Nelson Mandela's inspirational autobiography
Listen: to 'Nkosi Sikelel' iAfrika' (God Bless Africa) – part of the South African national anthem of unity
Watch: *Amandla! A Revolution in Four-Part Harmony*, which uses music, song and the voices of political activists and other prominent South Africans to document the anti-apartheid struggle
Eat: *biltong* (dried and cured meat); *mealies* (maize); and *boerwors* (sausages)
Drink: wines from the Cape Winelands; or *rooibos* herbal tea

In a word
Howzit?

Trademarks
Table Mountain; Springboks rugby team; Nelson Mandela; Kruger National Park; wildlife; whales; surf; *braai* (barbecue)

Random fact
There are more than 2000 native species of plant on Table Mountain, more than are found in the entire United Kingdom

1. There are thought to be more than 12,000 elephants in Kruger National Park

2. Just south of Cape Town is Llandudno and its popular surf beach

3. A San woman from the Kgalagadi region

4. The distinctive streets of the Bo-Kaap district, Cape Town

❸

❹

Best time to visit
September to November, for spectacular autumn colours

Top things to see
- Markets, museums and medieval city gates in the bustling capital, Seoul
- Acres of tombs, temples and ruins in historic Gyeongju
- The royal mausoleums of the Baekje dynasty at Gongju and Buyeo
- Traditional Korean life on the islands of Dadohae Haesang National Park
- Mountains, forests, hot springs, temples and plenty of serenity at Seoraksan National Park

Top things to do
- See strange denizens of the deep on sale in Busan's fish market
- Feast on *chimaek* (fried chicken and beer) in Seoul's trendy Hongdae neighbourhood
- Ski and snowboard on Olympic slopes at Alpensia and Yongpyong Ski Resorts
- Stand as close as you safely can to the world's most volatile border between North and South Korea on a tour of Panmunjom and the Demilitarized Zone (DMZ)
- Hike the stunning south coast of Jeju island and the country's highest peak, Hallasan, along the Jeju Olle Trail

Getting under the skin
Read: *A Geek in Korea* by Daniel Tudor and *I'll Be Right There* by Shin Kyung-sook
Listen: to *pansori* – musical story-telling, often described as the Korean equivalent of the blues
Watch: Kwak Jae-yong's romantic-comedy smash *Yeopgijeogin geunyeo* (My Sassy Girl); or Hong Sang-soo's poignant *In Another Country*
Eat: *kimchi* (fiery pickled cabbage with chilli) and *galbi* (a variety of grilled dishes)
Drink: *soju* (local rice spirit); or *bori cha* (warming tea made from roasted barley)

In a word
Jeong (Emotional attachment bordering on love)

Trademarks
Korean barbecue; taekwondo; K-pop; ginseng; *kimchi*; hot springs; free-trade zones; high-tech cities

Random fact
South Korea has an entire holiday dedicated to its writing system: Hangeul Day, celebrated on 9 October

1. Destroyed first by fire then by the Japanese, Gyeongbokgung Palace in Seoul is now being slowly restored

2. Lanterns decorate Cheonggyecheon stream, an urban renewal project in Seoul

3. Downtown Seoul, overlooked by N Seoul Tower

S CAPITAL SEOUL // POPULATION 49 MILLION // AREA 99,720 SQ KM // OFFICIAL LANGUAGE KOREAN

South Korea

South Korea is a North Asian beacon of progress and modernity, second only to Japan in its enthusiasm for scientific breakthroughs, gadgets and gizmos. Korean expats have spread the cuisine of their homeland across the globe, but surprisingly few travellers have explored this ultramodern but deeply traditional corner of Asia. For every high-tech metropolis, South Korea boasts a medieval fortress or a verdant national park where locals come to escape the hubbub. Even after two millennia, the teachings of Confucius still resonate in Korea, and Koreans are famous for their national pride, which rises to a crescendo in support of the national soccer and taekwondo teams.

Best time
October to March (the dry season)

Places of interest
- The endless lagoons, tortuous channels and lush papyrus fields of the Sudd, one of the world's largest wetlands
- The resting place of John Garang de Mabior (or Dr John, as he's known locally), a South Sudan rebel and former First Vice-President of Sudan, who was instrumental in ending that country's civil war
- The southern swamps, where 800,000 white-eared kob and half a million topi and Mongalla gazelles take part in what is possibly the largest mass movement of animals on the planet

Local customs
- There are many important traditional dances, such as the Dinka's leaping, the Beja's sword dance and the Halfa's *barabrah*
- Eating sweet Maridi honey, which is known for its healing properties
- Dinka people use cattle urine to wash, as well as to dye hair

Getting under the skin
Read: *Dinka: Legendary Cattle Keepers of Sudan* by Angela Fisher and Carol Beckwith, a vibrant book full of powerful images of the Dinka culture
Listen: to Emmanuel Jal's *Ceasefire*, an album that calls for peace across his land, which he fittingly created with Abdel Gadir Salim, a singer and composer from northern Sudan
Watch: *Lost Boys of Sudan*, a documentary film by Megan Mylan and Jon Shenk, following two Dinka boys who escaped Sudan's civil war (and lion attacks) to live an altogether different life in America
Eat: *asida* (porridge made from sorghum) – it's served with a meaty sauce or vegetables
Drink: *aradeab* (tamarind juice)

In a word
Salaam aleikum (Peace upon you)

Trademarks
The world's newest nation; oil; the Sudd; civil war; Dinka people

Random facts
Bulls are so important in South Sudan that many people are actually named after them; white bulls (the most prized) are sacrificed for celebrations and peace (or most recently, after the naming of the Cabinet)

1. A Dinka man prepared for a traditional wrestling match

2. Dinka herders from the Bahr al Ghazal region tend to their zebu cattle

3. A traditional Toposa settlement near Riwoto in Eastern Equatoria

S CAPITAL JUBA // POPULATION 11.1 MILLION // AREA 644,329 SQ KM // OFFICIAL LANGUAGE ENGLISH

South Sudan

Born out of more heartache and bloodshed than any other nation on the continent, South Sudan quietly came to be on 9 July 2011. The half-century of civil war – Africa's longest-running conflict – that preceded the 2011 independence referendum was fuelled by oil riches, and pitted Islam against Christianity, Arab against black African and central government against regional autonomy. Although tourist infrastructure wasn't even at the embryonic stage, peace at the nation's birth meant the door was open to adventurous souls keen to experience the world's newest country. The alluring attractions – both cultural and natural – included the intriguing Dinka people and what may be the planet's largest animal migration. Sadly, just 17 months after inception, civil war broke out and the door to travellers was slammed shut.

Best time to visit
May, June, September and October

Top things to see
- The Alhambra, the exquisite highpoint of Andalucía's Islamic architecture
- Córdoba's Mezquita, perfection rendered in stone
- Gaudí's Barcelona, the astonishing architectural legacy that came to define a city
- Madrid's golden mile of art, three of the world's best art galleries
- Santiago de Compostela's cathedral, Spain's most sacred corner and a flight of architectural extravagance

Top things to do
- Go on a foodie crawl sampling San Sebastián's world famous *pintxos* (Basque tapas)
- Hike the Pyrenees in Catalonia or Aragón
- Drive along the dramatic Galician coastlines of Rías Altas or the Costa da Morte
- Laze on a secluded and perfect beach on Ibiza or Formentera
- Escape the modern world in inland Spain's stone-and-timber *pueblos* (villages)

Getting under the skin
Read: *Don Quijote de la Mancha* by Miguel de Cervantes; or *Roads to Santiago* by Cees Nooteboom, a fascinating journey through modern Spain
Listen: to El Camarón de la Isla, Paco de Lucia, Enrique Morente and Chambao for the essence and evolution of flamenco
Watch: any film by Pedro Almódovar, especially *Volver* (Return) or *Los Abrazos Rotos* (Broken Embraces)
Eat: tapas; wafer-thin slices of *jamón ibérico de bellota;* and paella (especially in its birthplace, Valencia)
Drink: *vino tinto* (red wine) from La Rioja wine region; *vino blanco* (white wine) from Galicia; or *fino* (sherry) from Jerez de la Frontera

In a word
¿Qué pasa? (What's happening?)

Trademarks
Flamenco; paella; bullfighting; football; fiestas; Picasso, Dalí and Goya; summer invasions of vacationing northern Europeans on the Costa del Sol; Camino de Santiago pilgrimage route

Random fact
Spaniards spend more on food per capita than anyone else in Europe

1. Park Güell, one of Barcelona's many Gaudí masterpieces

2. The ruin of Cortijo del Fraile in Almeria, scene of a violent crime of passion

3. Creating human towers has been a Catalan tradition for more than 200 years

4. The idyllic bay of Bahía de La Concha and Isla de Santa Clara, San Sebastián

S CAPITAL MADRID // POPULATION 47.4 MILLION // AREA 504,782 SQ KM // OFFICIAL LANGUAGE CASTILIAN SPANISH

Spain

Spain is Europe's most exotic country, a heady mix of often curious traditions and a relentless energy that propels Spaniards into the future. You see it in Spain's architecture: the Islamic confections of Al-Andalus and soaring Gothic cathedrals share the territory with avant-garde creations by Gaudí and Santiago Calatrava. Or you taste it in the food: you're just as likely to find three generations of the same family in the kitchen as you are chefs with three Michelin stars honouring the innovations of new Spanish cuisine. There are jagged sierras, wild coastlines, soul-stirring flamenco and world-class art galleries that span the centuries. But for all this talk of past and future, Spaniards live very much in the present where life is one long fiesta.

S **CAPITAL** COLOMBO // **POPULATION** 21.7 MILLION // **AREA** 65,610 SQ KM // **OFFICIAL LANGUAGES** SINHALESE & TAMIL

Sri Lanka

Blessed by the sun, buffeted by the spice-scented trade winds of the Indian Ocean, and scarred by civil war, Sri Lanka is slowly rebuilding its reputation as the southern gateway to South Asia. While investigations continue into the bloody final years of the conflict, ordinary Sri Lankans are looking to a new future of peace and prosperity, in which returning tourists will play a major role. The attractions of this land of sand and cinnamon are the same as they ever were – blissful beaches and barrelling surf breaks, Buddhist stupas, ruined kingdoms, wild elephants, lofty lookouts, graceful tea plantations in the hills and some of the most monumental religious sculptures the world has ever seen. Now picture all this crammed into a compact tropical island that swims with the flavours, smells and sounds of the Indian subcontinent.

Best time to visit
December to March, to avoid the southwest monsoon

Top things to see
- Museums, monuments and colonial trim in the frenetic capital, Colombo
- Ruined palaces and super-sized Buddhas in the old royal capital of Polonnaruwa
- A forest of stone columns and *dagobas* (stupas) in Anuradhapura
- Elaborate gardens and exquisite frescoes in the ancient fortress at Sigiriya
- A very different side of Sri Lanka in the Tamil city of Jaffna

Top things to do
- Kick back on the sparkling sands of Sri Lanka's southern beaches
- Watch the rising sun cast its rays over the island from Adam's Peak
- Search for leopards and elephants in the foliage of Yala National Park
- Surf the wild breaks at Arugam Bay
- Make the pilgrimage to the Temple of the Tooth in World Heritage–listed Kandy

Getting under the skin
Read: Shyam Selvadurai's unconventional love story *Funny Boy*; or Romesh Gunesekera's coming-of-age drama *Reef*
Listen: to *baila* (Sri Lankan dance music); the Sri Lanka calypso of La Ceylonians; or the quirky metal rock of Stigmata
Watch: the antiwar films of Asoka Handagama – his *Aksharaya* (A Letter of Fire) was banned in Sri Lanka, but copies are circulating online

Eat: 'hoppers' (or more properly *appa*), delicious pancakes made from fermented rice and coconut milk
Drink: *toddy* (a local wine made from fermented palm sap); or *arrack,* the same thing but distilled and bottled

In a word
Ayubowan (May you live long)

Trademarks
Bendy palm trees; sun-kissed beaches; sacred stupas; Ceylon tea; fishermen on poles; colonial hand-me-downs; jumbos in the jungle; fresh coconuts; short eats; batik; cricket-obsessed locals; Tamil Tigers

Random fact
Sri Lanka gave the world cinnamon – the island has been trading the spice since at least 2000 BC

1. Although a famous image of Sri Lanka, the practice of stilt fishing is only 70 years old

2. Tea is a major Sri Lankan export; women harvest leaves near Nuwara Eliya

3. The ruins of a 5th-century palace sit atop Sigiriya (Lion Rock) in the Matale District

4. A market vendor from Dambulla, Matale District

S CAPITAL KHARTOUM // POPULATION 34.8 MILLION // AREA 1,861,484 SQ KM // OFFICIAL LANGUAGES ARABIC & ENGLISH

Sudan

There is no other country on earth that travellers are as apprehensive to visit as they are pained to leave. Sudan stretches over swathes of the Sahara to the singed shoreline of the Red Sea, and is dotted with impressive relics of civilisations dating back to pre-Pharaonic Egypt. Yet for visitors its greatest treasures are the Sudanese – diverse as they are mysterious, generous as they are welcoming. The world often wrongly paints the entirety of Sudan in the same perilous shade even though its conflicts have been restricted to the west in Darfur and to the south in what is now Africa's newest nation, South Sudan. The peaceful northeast, a region exuding the country's true nature, offers travellers both incredible solitude and hospitality.

Best time to visit
October to March (the dry season)

Top things to see
- The colossal 3500-year-old remains of the kingdom of Kerma's capital
- Whirling dervishes stirring up more than dust at Omdurman's Hamed el-Nil Mosque
- A shiver of hammerhead sharks circling above you in the Red Sea – their silhouettes are eerily unmistakable
- The holy mountain of Jebel Barkal and the vestiges of the Temple of Amun, the centre of the kingdom of the Kush

Top things to do
- Let your eyes wander in the fascinating souqs (markets) of Kassala before letting your legs take over in the extraordinarily shaped Taka massif
- Witness colourful fluid dynamics in action as the two Niles, Blue and White, meet and meld in Khartoum
- Wade through the ancient sands enveloping the astounding pyramids at the royal cemetery of Begrawiya, the resting place of the Meroitic Pharaohs
- Board a barge and voyage south up the White Nile from Kosti

Getting under the skin
Read: *Emma's War* by Deborah Scroggins, not only a compelling, real-life tale of a British aid-worker marrying a Sudanese warlord, but also a great introduction to the nation and its civil war
Listen: to *Stars of the Night*, Abdel Gadir Salim's album laced with songs of his homeland
Watch: *The Devil Came on Horseback*, a powerful documentary exposing the war crimes in Darfur
Eat: *fuul* (stewed brown beans) for a traditional breakfast, complete with cheese, egg, salad and flatbread
Drink: sweet black *shai* (tea); or coffee infused with cinnamon and cardamom

In a word
Salaam aleikum (Peace upon you)

Trademarks
Hospitality of the highest order; the meeting of the Niles; ancient pyramids; Nubia; civil war; ethnic cleansing in Darfur

Random fact
Sudan is dotted with more ancient pyramids than Egypt

1. Nuba women from Nyaro village in the Kordofan region carry water

2. The pyramids of Meroë were built on the banks of the Nile by the ancient Kingdom of Kush

3. A Bedford bus carries passengers from Khartoum to Shendi, a centuries-old market town on the Nile

4. Worshippers enter the Great Mosque of Khartoum

1. The ornate Hindu temple of Arya Dewaker in Parimbo

2. Creole women in *kotomisi* dresses; originating during the slavery era *kotomisis* were intended to discourage sexual interest

3. The splendid male Guianan cock-of-the-rock

S CAPITAL PARAMARIBO // POPULATION 566,846 // AREA 163,820 SQ KM // OFFICIAL LANGUAGE DUTCH

Suriname

One of South America's smallest countries, Suriname packs in a surprising jumble of cultures. The heavily forested nation is home to a mix of people descended from West African slaves; Javanese, Chinese and Indian labourers; native Amerindian groups; and Dutch, Lebanese and Jewish settlers. Paramaribo, where half the population resides, is a blend of synagogues and mosques, Indian roti shops and Chinese dumpling houses spread among Dutch colonial buildings. Outside the capital, dirt tracks and meandering rivers lead to Suriname's natural wonders, which include African-like savannahs, vast swathes of protected rainforest and remote beaches that are a major breeding site for endangered sea turtles.

Best time to visit
February to April, and August to early December

Top things to see
- Paramaribo, Suriname's vivacious capital and Unesco World Heritage site with its fantastic blend of cultures (and cuisines)
- The Central Suriname Nature Reserve, a staggering 1.6 million-hectare reserve of diverse ecosystems and incredible wildlife
- The Amerindian village of Palumeu, offering a locally run ecotourism experience on the remote banks of the Boven Tapanahoni River

Top things to do
- Take an incredible boat journey along the Upper Suriname River stopping off at Maroon villages
- Stand watch over the sands of Galibi Nature Reserve as giant leatherback turtles emerge from the sea to lay their eggs on the beach (April to August)
- Spy howler monkeys in the jungle canopy of the Brownsberg Nature Reserve

Getting under the skin
Read: *Tales of a Shaman's Apprentice* by Mark Plotkin, about an ethnobotanist's surprising discoveries living among Amerindians in Suriname and Brazil
Listen: to flautist Ronald Snijders' mix of jazz, beatbox, classical melodies and indigenous sounds
Watch: Pim de la Parra's *Wan Pipel*, which provides a fascinating glimpse into Surinamese society
Eat: *bami goreng* (fried noodles); or *pom* (a casserole of chicken and elephant ear root)
Drink: ice-cold Parbo beer

In a word
Fa waka? (How are you?)

Trademarks
Pristine rainforest; bauxite

Random fact
Although Dutch is the official language, the lingua franca is Sranan Tongo, an English-based creole with African, Portuguese and Dutch roots that emerged from the plantations, where it was spoken between slaves and slave owners

DANIÏTA DELIMONT | GETTY IMAGES // FRANS LEMMENS | GETTY IMAGES // WIM SMEETS/ BUITEN-BEELD | GETTY IMAGES

Best time to visit
March to November

Top things to see
- Rare black rhinos in lovely Mkhaya Game Reserve
- The annual Umhlanga (reed dance) in Swaziland's royal heartland
- Preparations for the sacred Incwala ceremony around the royal kraal at Lobamba
- Rolling hill panoramas around Piggs Peak in northern Swaziland
- Brilliant orange flame trees and lavender jacarandas dotting the woodlands of the Ezulwini Valley, with its abundance of comfortable lodges and fine craft shops

Top things to do
- Hike or birdwatch in wild Malolotja Nature Reserve
- Shop for Swazi candles, wood carvings and other traditional crafts around Malkerns and in the Ezulwini Valley
- Shoot the rapids on the Usutu River
- Explore the forests and rugged scenery in and around Ngwempisi Gorge
- Walk amid the wildlife in tranquil Mlilwane Wildlife Sanctuary or the large Hlane Royal National Park

Getting under the skin
Read: *The Kingdom of Swaziland* by D Hugh Gillis – a look at the influences shaping modern-day Swaziland
Listen: to the songs and traditional rhythms of Bholoja's 'Swazi Soul' music
Watch: the mix of performers at the annual Bushfire Festival, with theatre, music, poetry and more
Eat: *sishwala* (maize porridge)
Drink: *tjwala* (home-brewed beer), often served by the bucket

In a word
Yebo (Yes) – also an all-purpose greeting

Trademarks
Black rhinos; sugar cane; Swazi crafts; HIV/AIDS; King Mswati III; *amahiya* and spear

Random fact
During preparations for the Incwala ceremony, young Swazi men harvest branches of the *lusekwane* bush and bring these to the royal kraal at Lobamba; a wilted branch is interpreted as a sign that the young man bearing it has had illicit sex

1. Young Swazi men mix traditional dress with contemporary touches

2. Sibebe, or Bald Mountain, is the world's second-largest monolith

3. An African bush elephant charges a safari vehicle at Hlane Royal National Park

CAPITAL MBABANE // POPULATION 1.4 MILLION // AREA 17,364 SQ KM // OFFICIAL LANGUAGES SWATI & ENGLISH

Swaziland

In Swaziland – Africa's last remaining absolute monarchy – traditional culture is strong. You're just as likely to see a man garbed with an *amahiya* (traditional robe) and spear as with jeans and a brief case, and traditional crafts and customs abound. Mbabane – the capital – has a Western gloss at first glance, but get away from the malls and central area, and you'll be treated to the laid-back hospitality, pride and vibe for which tiny Swaziland is renowned. Whether it's hiking in the hills, watching wildlife in a small but stellar collection of parks and reserves, trying to catch a glimpse of the king or shopping for crafts, this quirky country offers a wealth of surprises to anyone who lingers long enough to discover its secrets.

CAPITAL STOCKHOLM // **POPULATION** 9.6 MILLION // **AREA** 450,295 SQ KM // **OFFICIAL LANGUAGE** SWEDISH

Sweden

For a small, far-flung country, Sweden has long punched above its weight. First it was Vikings, then the contagious Scandi-pop of ABBA, then Ericsson phones and Ikea's flat-pack revolution, then Sweden's darker side, brought to life in *Wallander* and *The Girl with the Dragon Tattoo*. Indeed, the real-life locations for Sweden's silver-screen outings have become tourist attractions in their own right, alongside more established sights such as graceful Stockholm and the scenic Bohuslän coast. In the countryside, Sweden still meets expectations: scattered islands, forests full of berries, villages of red weatherboard houses, in short, a playground for lovers of the great outdoors. But the cities are changing fast as Sweden manages an unprecedented influx of refugees that is changing the nation's own perception of itself.

Best time to visit
May to August if you're after sunshine, December to March if you want to ski

Top things to see
- The glittering beauty of Stockholm from Söder Heights
- A manageable portion of the 24,000 islands of the Stockholm archipelago, ideally on a boat cruise
- The midnight sun above the Arctic Circle, preferably from Abisko National Park, deep in the heartland of the Sami people
- Glass blown to perfection in the glassworks of Glasriket (the Glass Kingdom)
- Rocky islands and idyllic fishing villages of the picturesque Bohuslän coast

Top things to do
- Celebrate Midsummer in the story-book villages surrounding lovely Lake Siljan
- Throw yourself into the great outdoors, kayaking around Bohuslän, cycling around Gotland, or cross-country skiing and hiking in frozen Norrland
- Bed down for a night in the supercool Icehotel at Jukkasjärvi
- Dig into history in Stockholm's Djurgården, home to the Skansen open-air museum and the Vasamuseet
- Hang out with verified Vikings at the Foteviken Viking Reserve

Getting under the skin
Read: crime-busting novels courtesy of Stieg Larsson's blockbuster *Millennium Trilogy,* or Henning Mankell's Kurt Wallander series; or the sweet tales of *Pippi Longstocking*
Listen: to ABBA or Roxette, if that's your thing; or give the Hives or Millencolin a spin
Watch: any of the 62 films directed by the great Ingmar Bergman; the acclaimed *My Life as a Dog*; or the sublime, subtle vampire film *Let the Right One In*
Eat: *lax* (salmon) in its various guises; game such as elk and reindeer; and the requisite *köttbullar* (Swedish meatballs), served with mashed potatoes

and lingonberry sauce
Drink: *kaffe* (coffee); Absolut vodka; or the beloved *aquavit* and *öl* (beer)

In a word
Jättebra! (Fantastic!)

Trademarks
ABBA; Ingmar Bergman and Greta Garbo; blond hair; dark dramas; cool design; expensive drinks; the midnight sun; Ikea; meatballs; Saabs and Volvos; tennis players; Vikings

Random fact
The best-known Swedish inventor is Alfred Nobel, who discovered dynamite and also, ironically, founded the Nobel Institute (giver of peace prizes)

1. Västerbotten in northern Sweden: long winters and endless evergreen forests

2. A fishing village on the notoriously windy Weather Islands

3. Stockholm's historical Soder Malarstrand, a 'beach street' with ship berths

3

S CAPITAL BERN // POPULATION 8 MILLION // AREA 41,277 SQ KM // OFFICIAL LANGUAGES GERMAN, FRENCH, ITALIAN & ROMANSCH

Switzerland

Few places invite self-indulgence quite as much as Switzerland. Whether you're into Alpine action, hip urban cities, lakeside pursuits or hiking through green fields, you'll find a way to treat yourself here. Roam its picture-postcard castles and villages, soak in mountain spa waters, pause for a schnapps or hot chocolate in a chalet strewn with geranium boxes, admire the views on a mountain train between pine wood and glacial peak, or glide silently on skis around the pyramid-shaped Matterhorn. This small, landlocked country of four languages was an essential stop on every 18th-century Grand Tour, it was the place where winter tourism was born and where Golden Age mountaineers scaled new heights, and it has continued to captivate travellers ever since.

Best time to visit
Year-round

Top things to see
- The majestic Matterhorn dominating the chic ski resort town of Zermatt
- Lake Geneva: whether you paddle board on it or dine alfresco by its side
- Europe's largest glacier, the Aletsch, sticking out its iced serpentine tongue for 23km
- The might and power of the thunderous Rheinfall; best admired from the viewing platform Känzeli in Schloss Laufen
- The medieval chateau-village of Gruyères and its working cheese dairy

Top things to do
- Shop for urban fashion and dance until dawn in Europe's hippest city, Zürich
- Wallow, quite literally, in modern architecture at the spa of Therme Vals
- Hike through flower-dotted meadows and larch woodlands past shimmering blue lakes and rocky outcrops in the high-altitude Swiss National Park
- Check out live jazz lakeside at the legendary Montreux Jazz Festival in July
- Take a train trip through some of the most magnificent Alpine scenery in the world

Getting under the skin
Read: *At Home,* a collection of short stories by Zürich cabaret artist Franz Hohler
Listen: to folk band Sonalp – a fusion of Swiss yodelling, cow bells and world sounds; or Bern-born singer-songwriter Sophie Hunger
Watch: the James Bond 1960s classic *On Her Majesty's Secret Service* for action-packed shots of Bern, Grindelwald and snowy Saas Fee
Eat: *rösti* (a shredded, oven-crisped potato bake) and *würste* (sausages) in German-speaking Switzerland and a cheesy fondue or raclette when there's snow
Drink: prestigious Calamin or Dézaley *grand cru* from the Unesco-protected vineyards of Lavaux facing Lake Geneva

In a word
Grüezi ('Hello' in Swiss German)

Trademarks
Matterhorn; *Heidi;* yodelling; clockwork efficiency; chocolate; cows; private banks; luxury watches; Swiss Army knives; Sigg water bottles

Random fact
Müsli (muesli) was invented in Switzerland at the end of the 19th century; the most common form around the globe now is the ever-popular *Birchermüsli*

1. The 13th-century Aigle Castle commanding vineyards and its eponymous town
2. Cross-country skiers in the Upper Engadine valley, Grison Alps
3. The scene of many mountaineering epics; the Matterhorn from Zermatt
4. Lake Geneva and Jet d'Eau's 140m plume of water

S CAPITAL DAMASCUS // POPULATION 17 MILLION // AREA 185,180 SQ KM // OFFICIAL LANGUAGE ARABIC

Syria

Currently in the grip of unspeakably brutal conflict, it's impossible to imagine what the future holds for Syria; it's cold comfort to say that this once-glorious civilisation has survived the horrors of war many times before throughout the ages. The country has always stood at history's crossroads - its Roman ruins, Crusader castles and truly ancient cities are still testament to that, though many of these are under threat. However, the indestructible traditions of the Syrian people, among them warm hospitality, storytelling, sweet tea, a wonderful cuisine and a rich artistic culture, still endure.

Best time
March to May (spring)

Places of interest
- The extraordinarily beautiful old city of Damascus, with abundant signposts to the Middle East's great civilisations
- The norias, or historic wooden waterwheels, of Hama
- Crac des Chevaliers, the stunning hilltop Crusader castle with a labyrinth of rooms and panoramic views
- Bosra's 15,000-seat Roman theatre and citadel
- The historic Euphrates River, the longest in Western Asia

Local customs
- Haggling for textiles, spices and other goods in local souqs
- Visiting the peerless Umayyad Mosque in Damascus after sunset
- Smoking flavoured tobacco through a waterpipe, called a *nargilah*
- Wandering through Qala'at Samaan, where St Simeon Stylites once sat
- Sitting in cafes in the Bab Sharqi quarter of Damascus' Old City

Getting under the skin
Read: *The Dark Side of Love* by Rafik Schami, a beautifully written love letter to his troubled nation
Listen: to Lena Chamamian's *Shamat*
Watch: *Out of Coverage,* directed by Abdellatif Abdelhamid, a nuanced study of Syrian society that somehow satisfied Syrian censors
Eat: *booza,* an elastic, melt-resistant ice cream, rolled in pistachio nuts
Drink: *shay na'ana* (mint tea), the essential complement to Syrian hospitality
In a word
Ahlan wa sahlan (Welcome)

Trademarks
Larger-than-life posters of the Assad dynasty that has ruled in Syria since 1970; two of the oldest continuously inhabited cities on earth (Damascus and Aleppo)

Random fact
One out of every three Syrians is under 15 years old

1. The central courtyard of Khan As'ad Pasha, a caravanserai in the Old City of Damascus

2. The rose-gold relics of ancient Palmyra (known in Arabic as Tadmor) prior to their destruction by Isis in 2015

3. Aleppo's famed Al-Madina Souq, much of which is thought to have been destroyed in the Syrian Civil War

1. The volcanic peak of Maupiti and its coral atoll

2. Riding a monster wave at terrifying Teahupo'o

3. A traditional wedding priest from the Tuamotu Islands

(T) CAPITAL PAPE'ETE // POPULATION 277,293 // AREA 4167 SQ KM // OFFICIAL LANGUAGE FRENCH

Tahiti & French Polynesia

Seductively tranquil and lushly gorgeous, French Polynesia offers much more adventure than its jet-set reputation suggests. From the vast lagoons of the Tuamotu atolls, to the culturally intense Marquesas Archipelago, the country's 118 islands are spread over a marine area almost twice the size of Australia and hold an impressive amount of diversity. Divers will find clear-water nirvana, hikers steamy-jungle bliss and foodies a delicious French cuisine with Polynesian flavours. Whether you're lounging or surfing, the scent of *tiare* (gardenia) flowers is ubiquitous and a warm tropical softness caresses the skin. Splurge at luxury resorts or stay with locals in rustic abodes or boutique-style bed and breakfasts – the French Polynesian dream isn't just for movie stars.

Best time to visit
The cooler, drier months between May and October

Top things to see
- Ra'iatea's Taputapuatea *marae* (ancient temple), considered one of the most important in the Pacific
- The county's best dancers shaking their hips at the Heiva i Tahiti festival (July)
- Shell necklaces, woven hats and colourful *pāreu* (sarongs) at Pape'ete's market
- The outrageous view over Mo'orea's two bays from the Belvédère lookout
- The best (and craziest) surfers in the world carving through cavernous tubes at Teahupo'o

Top things to do
- Learn to love sharks while diving the passes of immense Rangiroa atoll
- Hike rugged Nuku Hiva with its razor-edged cliffs, timeless valleys and dramatic waterfalls
- Live luxe at one of Bora Bora's opulent resorts
- Snorkel with humpback whales in Rurutu's waters

Getting under the skin
Read: *The Miss Tutti Frutti Contest* by Graeme Lay – tales from the South Pacific, including Paul Gauguin's shocking Tahitian secrets
Listen: to the hypnotic, omnipresent ukulele
Watch: *Kon-Tiki*, which retraces Thor Heyerdahl's epic voyage from South America to Polynesia
Eat: raw fish in its many forms: coconut-milk *poisson cru*, Mediterranean-influenced carpaccio and Asian-inspired sashimi
Drink: a Hinano, the country's signature beer

In a word
Haere maru (Take it slow)

Trademarks
Tiare flowers; Tahitian pearls; Paul Gauguin; Mutiny on the *Bounty*; over-water bungalows; surfing

Random fact
The letter 'b' doesn't exist in Tahitian language, so Bora Bora should actually be called Pora Pora, but Captain Cook misheard the name when he came here

(T) **CAPITAL** TAIPEI // **POPULATION** 23.3 MILLION // **AREA** 35,980 SQ KM // **OFFICIAL LANGUAGE** MANDARIN

Taiwan

One of the four Asian tigers, the island of Taiwan is divided from the Chinese mainland by the Taiwan Strait – and by a yawning political divide. Politically known as the Republic of China (ROC), Taiwan has been ruled by the nationalist government founded by Chiang Kai-shek since 1945, although the island is nominally claimed by the People's Republic of China (PRC). Politics aside, this is a land where skyscrapers rub shoulders with misty mountains and rugged coastlines. Away from the futuristic capital, Taipei, Taiwan is a tapestry of forested peaks, giant Buddhas, hot springs, basalt islands and tribal villages. No wonder the island was christened *Ilha Formosa* (Beautiful Island) by Portuguese sailors when they passed by in the 1540s.

Best time to visit
September to November, for ravishing autumn colours, and January or February for the annual lantern festival

Top things to see
- The view over Taipei from the 509m-high Taipei 101 tower
- A staggering array of Chinese artefacts in Taipei's National Palace Museum
- Historic temples and gourmet dining in Tainan, the ancient capital
- Stunning roadside scenery while cycling the South Cross-Island Hwy or Hwy 11
- Basalt outcrops and delightfully sculptural stone fish traps on the Penghu islands

Top things to do
- Trek through marble canyons beside a jade-green river in Taroko Gorge
- Learn to drink tea the Taiwanese way in the tea gardens of Pinglin
- Hike to hidden waterfalls and hot springs in the jungles around Wulai
- Learn about Taiwan's aboriginal heritage among the Yami tribal people on lovely Lanyu island
- Test your commitment to adventurous eating at one of Taipei's legendary night markets

Getting under the skin
Read: Hsiao Li-hung's classic love story *A Thousand Moons on a Thousand Rivers*
Listen: to the slickly packaged Mandopop of Jay Chou, F4, Fahrenheit and S.H.E
Watch: *Seediq Bale,* an epic film about the Wushe Rebellion, and Ang Lee's *Eat Drink Man Woman* for an insight into Modern Taiwanese culture

Eat: *chòu dòufu* ('stinky tofu'), marinated in a brine made from decomposing vegetables and shrimps
Drink: Ali Shan tea, a delicate oolong grown at high altitude in Taiwan's central mountains

In a word
Chīfàn le ma? (Have you eaten yet?)

Trademarks
The Taipei 101 tower; nationalist founding father

Chiang Kai-shek; oolong tea; bubble tea; night markets; sky lanterns; instant noodles

Random fact
Both instant noodles and bubble tea (also known as 'boba' or 'pearl milk' tea) were invented and popularised in Taiwan

1. Taiwan's dry September winds are perfect for drying persimmons
2. The ornate facade of Bao'an Temple, Taipei
3. Taipei 101 and the city skyline from Elephant Mountain
4. A lantern-maker relaxes outside his shop

T

Best time to visit

June to September (mountains), March to May, October to November (Dushanbe and lowlands)

Top things to see

- Pamir Hwy, one of the world's great road trips, linking Khorog and Osh
- The Wakhan Corridor, a gloriously scenic valley of Silk Road forts, Buddhist stupas and 7000m peaks on a remote border of Tajikistan and Afghanistan
- Marguzor Lakes, a string of seven turquoise lakes and homestays near Penjikent
- Istaravshan, a small town with a great bazaar, mosques and madrasas hidden in its side streets

Top things to do

- Fasten your seatbelt on the scenically outrageous flight from Khorog to Dushanbe, the only route in the former Soviet Union where pilots were awarded hazard pay
- Trek the Fann or Pamir Mountains, up there with the world's best mountain scenery
- Stay overnight in a mountain homestay or yurtstay to experience the region's humbling hospitality
- Stroll among the neoclassical facades of Rudaki, Dushanbe's main drag, which owes more to St Petersburg than Central Asia
- Dangle across a rushing river on a makeshift cable car at Jizeu

Getting under the skin

Read: *Land Beyond the River* by Monica Whitlock, for a rundown of recent history; *The Hundred Thousand Fools of God* by Theodore Levin for insights into Tajik musical culture

Listen: to a folk singer belting out a Rudaki poem to the tune of a six-stringed *rubab* (Persian lute) in the western Pamir

Watch: Bakhtyar Khudojnazarov's *Luna Papa*; or Jamshed Usmonov's *Angel on the Right*

Eat: a communal bowl of Pamiri *kurtob* (a deliciously cool and creamy mix of flat bread, yoghurt, onion, tomatoes, chives and coriander)

Drink: a locally brewed Sim-Sim *piva* (beer) at the fountains of Dushanbe's Ayni opera house

In a word

Roh-i safed (Have a good trip)

Trademarks

Bazaars; warm hospitality; Marco Polo sheep; skullcaps; Persian poetry; 'roof of the world' ; Silk Road fortresses; wrestling

Random fact

Ancient Sogdian, the language of the Silk Road, is still spoken in the more remote parts of Tajikistan's Yagnob Valley

1. A family ride their donkey cart through the historical city of Penjikent

2. The monumental entrance to Hisor Castle in western Tajikistan

3. Rushan on the Panj River is part of the Gorno-Badakhshan Autonomous Region

T **CAPITAL** DUSHANBE // **POPULATION** 7.9 MILLION // **AREA** 143,100 SQ KM // **OFFICIAL LANGUAGE** TAJIK

Tajikistan

A Persian speaker in a Turkic world, tucked in a mountain cul-de-sac at the furthest corner of the former USSR, Tajikistan is an adventure travel destination whose potential is still largely unexplored by tourists. Aside from bustling Silk Road towns and colourful bazaars, Tajikistan's main pull is the Pamir Mountains, an awesomely beautiful high-altitude plateau of intensely blue lakes, Kyrgyz yurts and rolling valleys that has impressed everyone from Marco Polo to Francis Younghusband. If your favourite places include Tibet, Bolivia or northern Pakistan, chances are you'll be blown away by little-known Tajikistan.

Ⓣ CAPITAL DODOMA // POPULATION 48.3 MILLION // AREA 947,300 SQ KM // OFFICIAL LANGUAGES SWAHILI & ENGLISH

Tanzania

Some countries make noise. Tanzania makes music. Its largest soundstage – the vast Serengeti plains – hosts earth's most spectacular natural show, the great migration. Not only do grasses sway to the millions of wildebeest hoof beats, but so do the lucky visitors who drop in each year. Melodies of different sorts, whether the chants of leaping Maasai warriors, the lilting songs of Kilimanjaro guides or the rhythmic lapping of turquoise waters on Zanzibar's shores, are as intrinsic to travellers' experiences as Tanzania's epic visuals – dramatic Rift Valley landscapes, colourfully clad locals and spellbinding wildlife. Although the nation is home to one of Africa's most diverse populations, tribal rivalries are almost nonexistent. As you'd expect from a great maestro, harmony reigns.

Best time to visit
June to October or December to January

Top things to see
- A stream of countless wildebeests risking life and limb as they cross the Serengeti's croc-infested Grumeti River
- Dawn breaking over the African savannah from your spot atop Kilimanjaro
- Turquoise waters cresting Zanzibar's reefs and flowing over the white sands
- Thousand-strong buffalo herds on Katuma River's wild floodplain in Katavi National Park
- The interior of Kilwa Kisiwani's Great Mosque lit by a sun low on the horizon

Top things to do
- Paint a rippled picture on a glassy canvas while sailing in a traditional dhow
- Drop into the wildlife-laden depths of Ngorongoro Crater
- After chimpanzee tracking, calm your racing heart on a tropical beach in Mahale Mountains National Park
- Weave slowly past brass-studded, intricately carved Swahili doors while taking in the intoxicating air of Stone Town in Zanzibar
- Kayak past hippos, elephants and smaller species in Selous Game Reserve

Getting under the skin
Read: *Empires of the Monsoon: A History of the Indian Ocean* by Richard Hall, for an understanding of the country's past
Listen: to Bongo Flava, a form of Swahili hip hop incorporating Afrobeat and arabesque melodies
Watch: *Kilimanjaro – To the Roof of Africa,* a stunning IMAX documentary by David Breashears
Eat: *ugali* (maize and/or cassava flour); or *mishikaki* (marinated meat kebabs)
Drink: *mbege* (banana beer); or *uraka* (a brew made from cashews)

In a word
Hakuna matata (No worries)

Trademarks
Serengeti; the great migration; Kilimanjaro;

Zanzibar; Maasai people

Random fact
The Anglo-Zanzibar conflict on 27 August 1896 stands as the world's shortest war – it lasted a grand total of 38 minutes

1. The piercing and stretching of earlobes, as displayed by this chief-in-waiting, is common among the Maasai

2. An idyllic beach on Unguja island, Zanzibar Archipelago

3. Mothering is tiring work; a yawning eastern chimpanzee at Gombe National Park

(T) CAPITAL BANGKOK // POPULATION 67.5 MILLION // AREA 513,120 SQ KM // OFFICIAL LANGUAGE THAI

Thailand

When it comes to traveller appeal, Thailand ticks all the boxes: perfect beaches, emerald jungles, ancient ruins, exotic islands, golden temples, captivating coral reefs, friendly locals, bustling cities, cascading rice terraces, tranquil traditional villages, steamy tropical weather, phenomenal food, five-star extravagance and indulgence on a shoestring. Despite the nation's political instability, people just keep coming back to Thailand, lured by a wealth of travel experiences and an anything-goes attitude that finds its best expression in the hedonistic beach parties of the southern islands.

Best time to visit
November to April, to escape the main rainy season

Top things to see
- Culture, chaos and Buddhist temple splendour in Bangkok, Thailand's energetic capital
- The atmospheric ruins of the old Thai capitals at Sukhothai and Ayuthaya
- Pristine rainforests teeming with wildlife at Khao Yai and Khao Sok National Parks
- Humbling relics from the Thailand–Burma Railway at Kanchanaburi
- Idyllic islands, from party-ready Phi-Phi to the more castaway-style isles of Ko Tarutao National Marine Park

Top things to do
- Conjure up a Thai feast on a cooking course in Bangkok, Phuket or Chiang Mai
- Test your head for heights by climbing the awesome karst outcrops at Krabi
- Visit atmospheric tribal villages around Chiang Rai and Mae Hong Son
- Dive with magnificent megafauna off Ko Tao or around the Similan Islands
- Dance barefoot on the sands at a full-moon bash on Ko Pha-Ngan

Getting under the skin
Read: *Monsoon Country* by Nobel Prize–nominated Thai author Pira Sudham
Listen: to the jazz compositions of His Majesty King Bhumibol Adulyadej, including the classic *Sai Fon* (Falling Rain)
Watch: Chatrichalerm Yukol's historical romp *Legend of Suriyothai;* or the unconventional, arthouse films of Apichatpong Weerasethakul

Eat: *tom yam kung* (hot and sour prawn and lemongrass soup); or Thailand's eponymous noodle dish, *pàt tai*
Drink: Singha and Chang beer; or Sang Som whisky, successor to the infamous and now banned Sang Thip

In a word
Sanuk (Fun) – the cornerstone of the Thai psyche

Trademarks
Golden stupas; floating markets; colour-coded curries; orange-robed monks ; flamboyant lady boys; Thai silk; hill tribes; elephants; backpacker beach parties; Khao San Road

Random fact
No Thai would think of building a new house without erecting an accompanying *san phra phum* (spirit house) for the animist spirits dwelling on the site to live in

1. The work of generations: rice terraces in Chiang Mai Province
2. The 19m-high seated Buddha of Wat Phanan Choeng temple, Ayutthaya
3. The tropical paradise of Loh Samah Bay, Phi Phi islands
4. Traditional Thai treats freshly handmade at a floating market

③

④

(T) **CAPITAL** LHASA // **POPULATION** 5.6 MILLION // **AREA** 1,228,400 SQ KM // **OFFICIAL LANGUAGES** TIBETAN & MANDARIN

Tibet

Tibet is without doubt one of the most beautiful, tragic and uplifting corners of Asia. Life in this Buddhist nation was forever altered in 1950, when Chinese forces invaded to claim the independent kingdom of Tibet for the 'motherland'. So began a story of cultural cleansing that has claimed nearly a million lives, yet amazingly, the traditional culture of the Tibetan people still endures, even though migrants from the rest of China are fast remodelling Tibet in their own image. You'll feel its spirit at shrines and monasteries, at herders' markets and village dances, and at the sacred mountain of Kailash, where pilgrims perform a ritual *kora* (circumambulation) to absolve themselves of sin. To join the Tibetans, even for a short time, is to be humbled by the triumph of the human spirit over adversity.

Best time to visit
Mid-May to September

Top things to see
• Potala Palace, the empty former home of the exiled Dalai Lama, now bustling with tourists
• Mt Everest, the literal high point of Tibet, shared with Nepal but a vision of majesty when viewed from the Tibetan side
• Nam-tso, a breathtaking high-altitude lake home to hardy nomads and rich birdlife
• Buddhist doctrine in technicolour in the magnificent murals at Gyantse Kumbum
• Tibet's second city Shigatse, and Tashilhunpo Monastery, home of the Panchen Lama

Top things to do
• Watch maroon-cloaked monks at Sera Monastery debate Buddhist dialectics with a slap and a shout
• Hire a 4WD for the classic overland route along the Friendship Hwy from Lhasa to Kathmandu
• Take the world's highest train ride across the Tibetan plateau to Lhasa
• Trek over 5200m passes from Ganden to Samye, two of Tibet's finest monasteries
• Cleanse a lifetime of sins by pacing a circuit around Mt Kailash, Asia's holiest peak

Getting under the skin
Read: *The Story of Tibet: Conversations with the Dalai Lama* by Thomas Laird for a mix of history and insight from Tibet's spiritual leader; or *Trespassers on the Roof of the World* by Peter Hopkirk for superbly readable accounts of early European travels into this secret world
Listen: to *Chö* or *Selwa* by Choying Drolma, the sublimely spiritual Tibetan nun
Watch: John Bush's *Vajra Sky Over Tibet* for a beautiful cinematic journey; or the challenging *Windhorse*, the first ever Tibetan-made feature film
Eat: *momos* (dumplings); a sizzling yak steak; or *tsampa* (ground roasted barley)
Drink: salty *bo cha* (yak butter tea) at a remote monastery; or sip sweet milky *cha ngamo* tea in a bustling Tibetan teahouse

In a word
Tashi Delek! (Hello, literally 'Good fortune')

Trademarks
The Dalai Lama; the 'roof of the world'; the Land of Snows; yaks; mass migration from China; cultural cleansing; riots and immolations; monks with prayer wheels; pilgrims; butter lamps and butter tea; juniper incense

Random fact
Yak tails from Tibet used to be exported to the US to make Father Christmas beards

1. Tibetan girls ham it up for the camera, Barkhor, Lhasa

2. The former residence of the Dalai Lama, Potala Palace, Lhasa

3. A monk holds a 1000-year-old Buddhist text at Po Dang Gompa, Sadeng

4. Sacred Yamdrok Lake is en route from Lhasa to Mt Everest

1. Just east of Dili is Cape Fatucama and its Christo Rei statue

2. Women bathe at the colonial-era Marobo hot springs

3. A villager from Liurai, south of Dili

T · CAPITAL DILI // POPULATION 1.2 MILLION // AREA 15,000 SQ KM // OFFICIAL LANGUAGES PORTUGUESE & TETUN

Timor-Leste

Becoming the first sovereign state of the 21st century was no small victory for Timor-Leste, which fought hard for its independence from a 24-year occupation by Indonesian forces. But while the first years of freedom were tumultuous, this impoverished former Portuguese colony is steadily rising to its feet. Stunning natural wonders, from mist-shrouded mountain peaks to rugged, deserted beaches, await those ready to challenge the lack of tourism infrastructure and diabolical – but improving – roads. Outside the buzzing capital Dili, many people live in traditional dwellings as they have for centuries. Pristine dive sites are still being discovered. Everywhere you go, you'll meet proud, friendly locals curious to find out what brings you to this long-forgotten corner of the world.

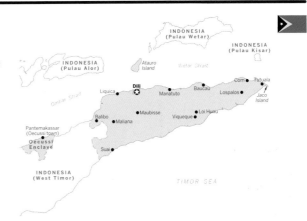

Best time to visit
It's hot all year, but May to November is driest

Top things to see
- Atauro Island, a starkly beautiful isle off Dili that beckons divers, hikers and beach bums
- Traditional architecture, including the iconic stilted Fataluku houses in the nation's east
- The sun sinking below the sea with a cocktail in hand at the recently-restored Balibo Fort
- Local life on the beaches of Dili, from spirited soccer matches to fishermen hauling in their loads

Top things to do
- Strap on a tank and explore the excellent dive sites that dot the nation's north coast
- Learn about Timor-Leste's tortuous history at Dili's excellent Resistance Museum
- Spend an afternoon lazing on the powder-white sands of uninhabited, sacred Jaco Island
- Hike to the summit of Mt Ramelau, the nation's highest peak, to watch the dawn break over Timor

Getting under the skin
Read: Luis Cardoso's *The Crossing: A Story of East Timor*, a lyrical memoir of growing up under Portuguese and Indonesian rule
Listen: for *tebe,* festive folk music
Watch: *Balibo,* the confronting feature film about a group of Australian-based journalists executed while reporting on Indonesia's activities in Timor in 1975
Eat: 'fish on a stick' served at makeshift roadhouses along the coast
Drink: rich Arabica coffee grown in the hills above Dili

In a word
Bom dia! (Good morning!)

Trademarks
Xanana Gusmão; José Ramos-Horta; resistance fighters; colourful woven *tais* (traditional cloth)

Random fact
A small patch of Timor-Leste (the Oecussi exclave) sits about 80km from the rest of the country, sharing all its land borders with Indonesian West Timor

Best time to visit
Mid-July to mid-September

Top things to see
- The Unesco World Heritage–listed area, Koutammakou, famous for its fortified Tamberma compounds
- Lomé's extraordinary Musée International du Golfe de Guinée, with busy markets and fine beaches nearby
- Badou, located in the heart of picturesque mountains and a base for good hiking
- The once-threatened Parc National de Fazao-Malfakassa, with elephants and great birdwatching
- The crossroads town of Dapaong, which has a stunning cave settlement nearby

Top things to do
- Hike through the cocoa and coffee plantations around Kpalimé
- Journey by pirogue to Togoville, then immerse yourself in voodoo traditions
- Swim in the bug- and croc-free lagoon of Lac Togo
- Wander Lomé's Marché des Féticheurs and observe everything from porcupine skins to warthog teeth
- Catch a glimpse of Muslim Togo in pretty countryside in the peaceful town of Bafilo

Getting under the skin
Read: *The Village of Waiting,* the first book by George Packer (who now writes for the *New Yorker*) about his time as a Peace Corps Volunteer in a Togolese village
Listen: to drums, *lithophones* (stone percussion instruments), then more drums
Watch: Togolese director Anne-Laure Folly's *Femmes aux Yeux Ouverts* (Women with Open Eyes)
Eat: *pâte* (a dough-like substance made of corn, manioc or yam) accompanied by sauces such as *arachide* (peanut and sesame) or *gombo* (okra)
Drink: *tchoukoutou* (fermented millet), the preferred tipple in the north

In a word
Be ja un sema (How are you? in Kabyé)

Trademarks
Castle-like clay houses of the Tamberma; the ruling Eyadéma dynasty; the Sparrow Hawks (Togo's national football team) and Emmanuel Adebayor

Random fact
Togo is one of only two countries in Africa where more than 40% of its land is suitable for agriculture

1. Local colour in the northern city of Kara

2. A voodoo sculpture from a Lomé fetish market

3. Earthern cones used as granaries sit outside a mud hut in the village of Tamberma, Atakora Mountains

T CAPITAL LOMÉ // POPULATION 7.3 MILLION // AREA 56,785 SQ KM // OFFICIAL LANGUAGE FRENCH

Togo

Togo could have been designed to cram as much of Africa as is geographically possible into one small space. For a start, its palm-fringed beaches are a world away from the verdant hills and savannah of the north. Its human geography, too, boasts a diversity way out of proportion to the country's size: a staggering 40 ethnic groups live within its borders. Thanks to intermittent unrest and four decades of rule by the same family, Togo's once-thriving tourism industry has taken a battering, but in its stead have come little guesthouses and small-scale ecotourism projects. And the appeal of the attractions that once drew tourists here in droves – wildlife, stunning natural beauty and intriguing cultural traditions – remains undiminished.

(T) CAPITAL NUKU'ALOFA // POPULATION 106,322 // AREA 748 SQ KM // OFFICIAL LANGUAGES TONGAN & ENGLISH

Tonga

Say goodbye to tourist hype – the Kingdom of Tonga is pure Polynesia. You won't find resorts selling packaged fun and you won't have to look too hard for authentic experiences because they're everywhere. From the monarchy, to Christian church services, feasts and traditional dancing, Tonga pulsates with cultural identity. The backdrop to this vibrant way of life is sublime: pristine beaches, rainforests, soaring cliffs and underwater caves; and migrating humpbacks are frequently spotted from July to November. Go with the flow and let the Tongan way of life carry you away on island time.

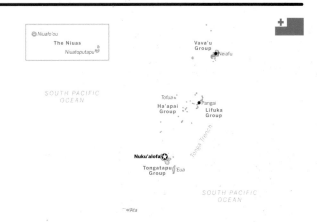

Best time to visit
May to October when it's cooler and drier

Top things to see
- The 13th-century Ha'amonga 'a Maui trilithon – the 'Stonehenge of the South Pacific'
- Tongan arts, crafts and pyramids of tropical fruit at the Talamahu Market
- Captivating fire-dancing inside Hina Cave while feasting on Tongan fare
- Hundreds of Mapu'a 'a Vaea blowholes spurting at once along a 5km stretch of coastline
- A colourful Sunday church service with magnificent, booming choirs

Top things to do
- Swim with or watch humpback whales that come to breed in Tongan waters
- Kayak around Vava'u's turquoise waterways and islands to deserted beaches
- Explore the remote doughnut-shaped volcanic isle of Niuafo'ou
- Hike through low-key 'Eua's limestone caves and tropical forests to dramatic cliff edges
- Laze on Uoleva's spectacular beach and, if you're lucky, watch whales breaching offshore

Getting under the skin
Read: *An Account of the Tonga Islands,* by Dr John Martin, which vividly retells the story of William Mariner, who was adopted by the Tongan royal family in the early 19th century
Listen: to *Dance Music of Tonga* by Mālie! Beautiful!

Watch: *My Lost Kainga,* the story of a Tongan woman raised in Australia who returns to the islands to discover her own culture
Eat: a feast prepared in an *umu* (earthen oven): taro and yam, roast suckling pig, coconut, fresh fish and shellfish
Drink: kava, the murky forget-your-cares-and-stare-at-the-sunset tipple that's a part of the Tongan experience

In a word
Ha'u 'o kai (Come and eat!)

Trademarks
Polynesian monarchy; migrating humpback whales; *tapa* (bark cloth); deserted white-sand beaches; packed churches on Sunday

Random fact
From midnight on Saturday Tonga closes down for 24 hours; the Sunday day of rest is so enshrined in Tongan culture that it is illegal to work

1. Humpback whales migrate south to breed in the warmer waters of the South Pacific Ocean

2. Play Robinson Crusoe for a week; a coral atoll in the Vava'u group

3. Rugby is a national obsession on Tonga; a game on Tongatapu

1. Queen's Royal College is the oldest and most prestigious secondary school in the islands

2. A classic palette of tropical colours on Maracas Beach, Trinidad

3. Colourful costumes are the order of the day during the Parade of Bands, Port of Spain

T · CAPITAL PORT OF SPAIN // POPULATION 1.2 MILLION // AREA 5128 SQ KM // OFFICIAL LANGUAGE ENGLISH

Trinidad & Tobago

Like a perfect *callaloo* (a thick green stew), Trinidad and Tobago are a rich hotpot of flavours, cultures and influences. You can hear it in the music, which combines everything Caribbean (calypso, soca, steel pan, parang, reggae and much more) and see it in the locals, a melange of African, Spanish, Asian and Amerindian peoples. Half of the capital, Port of Spain, is falling apart while the rest buzzes with an energy that can overwhelm; often you can't separate the two. Oil and gas production are Trinidad's economic engine, so tourism can be an afterthought – good news if you hate well-trodden paths. Tobago is more visitor-oriented, but the beaches still throng with as many locals as tourists. Trinidad and Tobago are always authentic.

Best time to visit
It is slightly wetter May to September; the real joy is at Carnival in February

Top things to see
• Trinidad's remote northeast coast with its deserted, wave-tossed beaches
• Queen's Park Savannah, where all of Trinidad comes to sip fresh coconut water and people-watch
• Brasso Seco, the rainforest village in the green heart of Trinidad
• Trinidad's Asa Wright Nature Centre, where a full list of bird species tops 430

Top things to do
• Lose yourself at Port of Spain's world-class annual Carnival, the Caribbean's biggest and best
• Surf Mt Irvine Bay on Tobago and wheedle out tips on secret spots from locals
• Snorkel the shallow coral gardens around Speyside in Tobago
• Dip into waterfalls and hike through the rainforest in Trinidad's coastal Northern Range

Getting under the skin
Read: *White Woman on a Green Bicycle* by Monique Roffey – Trinidad's history through an emigre's eyes
Listen: to Lord Kitchener's classic calypsos or rapid-fire soca from Machel Montano
Watch: *Pan! Our Music Odyssey:* the lowdown on the national instrument
Eat: *callaloo* (a thick green stew made with dasheen leaves, okra, pumpkin and local seasonings)
Drink: sorrel (made from a type of hibiscus, mixed with cinnamon and other spices)

In a word
You limin' tonight? (Are you hanging out tonight?)

Trademarks
Carnival; cricket matches; party culture; birdwatching

Random fact
Trinidad's Grande Riviere is one of the world's top turtle-watching spots, with up to 500 giant leatherbacks visiting nightly at the peak of the season

(T) CAPITAL TUNIS // POPULATION 10.8 MILLION // AREA 163,610 SQ KM // OFFICIAL LANGUAGE ARABIC

Tunisia

Wedged between two reclusive North African giants, Tunisia has for decades been proudly open to the world. Despite the horrendous terrorist attacks of 2015, the country remains a deeply welcoming place, whose people prize visitors more than ever. From ancient times when the Carthaginians controlled much of the Mediterranean's seagoing trade, Tunisia has always turned its face towards Europe, and it's from there that until recently many sun-starved Europeans flocked to Tunisia year round. Elsewhere you'll find the wondrous dunes and landscapes of the Sahara, some extraordinary troglodyte and Berber architecture, Roman cities of antiquity, clamorous medinas and one of the best-preserved Roman colosseums in the world.

Best time to visit
November to April

Top things to see
- El Jem, the world's third-largest colosseum, one of Africa's most impressive Roman sites
- Jerba's whitewashed buildings, a rare synagogue in the Arab world, fortress architecture and beaches
- The charming old town of Mahdia, untouched by Tunisia's coastal tourism explosion
- Sweeping views from Roman city Dougga's capitol, theatre and other fine monuments
- Sidi Bou Saïd, the whitewashed and blue-doored clifftop village that is among the Mediterranean's prettiest

Top things to do
- Trek into the dunes of the Grand Erg Oriental for a deep-desert experience
- Imagine yourself in a *Star Wars* movie amid the architecture of the Ksour region
- Lose yourself in the labyrinth of Tunis medina
- Haggle for carpets amid the glorious architecture and mosques of Kairouan
- Wander through Tozeur, a lovely oasis town in the heart of some stunning country

Getting under the skin
Read: Mustapha Tlili's novel *Lion Mountain*; or *Pillar of Salt* by exiled Tunisian Jewish writer Albert Memmi
Listen: to Dhaffer Youssef's *Electric Sufi*, a ground-breaking fusion of contemporary jazz and traditional instruments
Watch: the original 1977 *Star Wars*: Southern Tunisia was the location for Tatooine, the home planet of Luke Skywalker
Eat: harissa (a fiery red-chilli paste); *brik* (deep-fried pastry filled with egg and other delights); seafood; couscous
Drink: Celtia (a local lager); Turkish coffee with orange blossom or rose water

In a word
Shukran (Thank you)

Trademarks
Ancient Carthage (close to modern Tunis); Island of the Lotus Eaters (Jerba); *Star Wars* film sets; troglodytes

Random fact
George Lucas was influenced in many ways by Tunisia during his time filming there: Obi-Wan Kenobi's distinctive robe was directly taken from traditional Berber clothing, and the Sandcrawler used by the Jawas to cross Tatooine was directly inspired by the strange shape of the Hotel du Lac in Tunis

1. The fortified granary of Ksar Ouled Soltane, Tataouine district

2. Much loved by artists, the town and port of Sidi Bou Saïd

3. Tunisian cafes are generally all male with four simple coffee options

Best time to visit

April to June, and September to October

Top things to see

- The soaring interior domes of İstanbul's Aya Sofya and the Blue Mosque
- The glassy blue waters of Ölüdeniz lagoon and nearby, the untouched Butterfly Valley
- A glimpse of Turkey as it once was in the elegant Ottoman-era konaks (mansions) of Safranbolu
- Ephesus, the best-preserved Roman city in the eastern Mediterranean
- Captivating landscapes, from the memorial-lined sands of the Gallipoli peninsula to the rugged crags of Mt Ararat

Top things to do

- Wander among the 'fairy chimneys' and rocky outcrops of Cappadocia, or float over them in a hot-air balloon.at dawn
- Get pummelled, soaped and rinsed on the marble in a hammam (Turkish bath)
- Watch the sunset amid the monumental stone heads on Nemrut Dağı
- Haggle for carpets, cushions, copperware or ceramics in İstanbul's Grand Bazaar
- Abandon yourself to the winds and tides on a Blue Voyage from Fethiye

Getting under the skin

Read: *Istanbul: Memories of a City* by Nobel Prize– winner Orhan Pamuk; and Barbara Nadel's İstanbul whodunits featuring detective Çetin Ikmen
Listen: to the pop of Tarkan; or Anatolian-folk infused albums from Sezen Aksu
Watch: *Uzak* (Distant), an observation of Turkey's modern dilemmas by Nuri Bilge Ceylan; and *Crossing the Bridge: the Story of Music in Istanbul* by Fatih Akin
Eat: Turkey's delicious kebaps: try the rich southern *adana*, prepared with ground lamb and spices, or *testi*, from the Black Sea, cooked in a sealed earthenware pot
Drink: *çay* (tea) in tulip-shaped glasses; *rakı* (aniseed-flavoured grape brandy); or *ayran* (a refreshing yoghurt drink)

In a word

Hoş geldiniz (Welcome)

Trademarks

Domes and minarets; kebaps; carpet sellers; Turkish delight; Mediterranean beaches; blue-glass eye amulets; prayer beads; political stand-offs; hammam

Random fact

Van cats, native to southeastern Turkey, have different coloured eyes (one blue, one green) and love swimming

1. Ultramarine and turquoise blend at Ölüdeniz and its lagoon

2. A cornucopia of wares: Instanbul's Grand Bazaar

3. The Ortaköy Mosque on the Bosphorus in Istanbul

4. Dawn breaks over the surreal rock formations of Cappadocia

T | CAPITAL ANKARA // POPULATION 80.7 MILLION // AREA 783,562 SQ KM // OFFICIAL LANGUAGE TURKISH

Turkey

The story of Turkey is like a Turkish meal: endless courses and oh so many flavours. Sun, sea and sand are the obvious drawcards, but this is backed up by a full hand of cultural riches: ruins from ancient empires; forts and castles forged by sultans and crusaders; basilicas and mosques that recall Byzantium; medieval bazaars and caravanserais. In culture as well as geography, Turkey straddles the boundary between Europe and Asia, and its people oscillate between the two. Despite periodic disagreements, conservative traditionalists and modern progressives both find space to flourish in one of the Middle East's most dynamic economies. For visitors though, the main appeal is still the balmy climate, the romantic ruins and landscapes, and the lavish, carnivorous cuisine.

Best time to visit
April to May, and September to November

Top things to see
- The wacky monuments of Ashgabat, including the world's largest carpet, and empty streets lined with impressive white marble ministry buildings
- The ancient Seljuq capital of Merv, once the world's largest city until it was captured by Genghis Khan
- Konye-Urgench, the 13th-century ruined capital of the Khorezmshahs
- The views of the capital from the Turkmenbashi Cableway
- Kow-Ata Lake, an underground thermal pool on the southern fringes of the Karakum desert

Top things to do
- Search for dinosaur footprints at Kugitang Nature Reserve
- Ride an Akhal-Teke horse across the foothills of the Kopet Dag mountains
- Take a 4WD trip through the desert to the burning Darvaza Gas Crater, also known as the 'Doorway to Hell'
- Splash in the Caspian Sea in the resorts near port city Turkmenbashi before catching a ferry to Azerbaijan

Getting under the skin
Read: *Unknown Sands: Journeys Around the World's Most Isolated Country* by John Kropf, which chronicles travels through Turkmenbashi-era Turkmenistan
Listen: to *City of Love* by Ashkabad, a lilting five-piece Turkmen ensemble
Watch: Waldemar Januszczak's undercover documentary *Travels with My Camera: The Happy Dictator*; or *Karakum*, a sweeping adventure about a boy in search of his father in Turkmenistan
Eat: *dograma*, a traditional Turkmen meal of pieces of bread, meat and onions
Drink: a cooling cup of *chal* (sour fermented camel's milk) as the sun rises over the Karakum desert

In a word
Siz nahili? (How are you?)

Trademarks
Turkmenbashi statues; golden horses; desert; natural gas; tribal carpets; shaggy hats; fiery craters; camels; cotton production

Random fact
At 1375km, the Karakum Canal – used to irrigate the Karakum desert for agricultural production, especially cotton – is one of the longest water supply canals on earth

1. Turkmen school girls in traditional costume

2. Turkmen statues in front of the Independence Monument in Ashgabat

3. Darvaza Gas Crater in the Karakum Desert is a natural gas field that's been burning since 1971

CAPITAL ASHGABAT // POPULATION 5.1 MILLION // AREA 488,100 SQ KM // OFFICIAL LANGUAGE TURKMEN

Turkmenistan

Largely isolated from the rest of the world since independence from the USSR in 1990, Turkmenistan's first two decades were dominated by eccentric late President 'Turkmenbashi' (Father of the Turkmen), who set about recreating the country in his own image, using as funds one of the world's largest reserves of natural gas. The result is a fascinating fiefdom of oddball sights and quirky historical remains. Gasp at the huge Turkmenbashi Ruhy Mosque, stare in awe at the Ministry of Fairness, and be one of the few people to have glimpsed the strangest corner of Central Asia.

(T) CAPITAL COCKBURN TOWN // POPULATION 49,070 // AREA 430 SQ KM // OFFICIAL LANGUAGE ENGLISH

Turks & Caicos

The oddly named Turks and Caicos are a group of 40 low-lying coral islands dotting their own patch of turquoise water on the edge of the Caribbean Sea, just a 90-minute hop from Miami. Despite the islands being firmly established favourites with the wintering masses, it's still easy to escape the resorts and find your own slice of the old Caribbean here. Providenciales, the main island, is renowned for its silky smooth white sand and is dominated by a long stretch of flashy hotels and resorts. However, get off Provo (as locals call it), and you'll find a different world of pastel villages, proudly kept churches and languid, reef-protected shores. Locals (called 'belongers') are Caribbean through and through and will welcome you to a world that can be found surviving in few other Caribbean islands.

Best time to visit
December to July

Top things to see
- Grace Bay, the setting for the best resorts and the most vivid sunsets
- Grand Turk, a world away from the development of Provo, is a charming old-world Caribbean island
- Mudjin Harbor, a hidden beach on Middle Caicos reached by stairs amid the cliffs
- Chalk Sound, a vibrant blue, almost neon in its intensity
- Caicos Conch Farm, where you can find out everything you could hope to know about great pink molluscs

Top things to do
- Dive the superbly clear waters almost anywhere, discovering rich marine life can be spotted everywhere
- Spot humpback whales off Salt Cay
- Delight in conch-everything at seafood shacks in Blue Hills on Providenciales
- Spot flamingos and iguanas on West Caicos
- Catch the balmy breezes while windsurfing off Grand Turk

Getting under the skin
Read: J Dennis Harris' *A Summer on the Borders of the Caribbean Sea*, a classic 19th-century travelogue
Listen: to ripsaw music, a local style combining conga drums, concertina and actual saws; top talents include Lovey Forbes, and Tell and the Rakooneers
Watch: *Turks and Caicos*, a 2014 BBC thriller based around murky business dealings in the islands
Eat: golden brown, moist and chewy conch fritters or have conch curried, sautéed, in ceviche, perched on a salad
Drink: any of several kinds of Turks Head beer

In a word
All right, all right (Hello)

Trademarks
Tax haven 'residents'; lavish resorts;

birdwatching; diving

Random fact
Canadians love holidaying in Turks and Caicos so much that there has long been talk of making the islands a province of Canada, something for which local support waxes and wanes

1. Caribbean beach bliss on Grand Turk
2. Men playing dominoes in a local tavern on Providenciales, Caicos
3. The sea around Turks and Caicos is famed for its rich marine life

1. Tuvaluan boys skylark in the ocean

2. The white and green strip of Funafuti, the only island with a road

3. Classic Tuvaluan fare: coconuts and fish for dinner

T CAPITAL FUNAFUTI // POPULATION 10,698 // AREA 26 SQ KM // OFFICIAL LANGUAGES TUVALUAN & ENGLISH

Tuvalu

Tuvalu is one of the smallest, remotest and most low-lying nations on earth: its highest point is only 4.6m (15ft) above sea level. Approaching the island by plane after endless ocean, a dazzling smear of turquoise and green appears, ringed with coral and studded with coconut palms. On the ground, experience the slow pace of the unspoiled South Pacific: stroll around town, chat with the locals at the airport if the plane is arriving or float in the sparkling lagoon. The most energetic activity is to motorbike up and down the country's only tarmac road on Funafuti with the local boy racers. Unfortunately, Tuvalu's very existence is threatened by rising sea levels, an effect of climate change.

Best time to visit
May to October, the dry season, when cooling trade winds provide natural air conditioning

Top things to see
- A *fatele*, a Tuvaluan dancing song with building percussive rhythms and crescendo singing
- *Te ano*, a sport unique to Tuvalu, where two balls get hit around by co-ed teams
- Sublime sunsets while floating in the luminous waters of Funafuti Lagoon

Top things to do
- Realise your desert-island fantasies on the sparkling islets of the Funafuti Conservation Area
- Experience traditional life on a remote island with the few remaining families of Funafala Islet
- Hire a bicycle and explore the length of Fongafale
- Maroon yourself on the outer islands where the supply ship might (or might not) pick you up again in a few weeks

Getting under the skin
Read: *Where the Hell is Tuvalu?*, a comic tale by Philip Ells about being in Tuvalu as 'the people's lawyer'; *Time and Tide: The Islands of Tuvalu*, a photographic essay by Peter Bennetts and Tony Wheeler
Listen: to Te Vaka, a mesmerising group of dancers and musicians fusing traditional Pacific and contemporary sounds
Watch: *The Disappearing of Tuvalu: Trouble in Paradise*, a frank documentary on rising sea levels
Eat: a streetside snack of chicken curry or fish roti
Drink: coconut water straight from the nut

In a word
Fifilemu (To be very peaceful, quiet)

Trademarks
Fine-sand beaches on clear seas; 'dot tv' millionaires; isolation; rising sea levels; outrageous *fatele* dances

Random fact
The top-level domain internet suffix for Tuvalu is '.tv' – in 2002 the country sold the rights to their suffix to VeriSign for US$45 million, and renewed the contract in 2012 for another nine years

Best time to visit
January to February, or June to September

Top things to see
- Cheetahs giving chase in the incredible mountain-fringed savannah of Kidepo Valley National Park
- Candlelit vegetable stalls punctuating the darkness on Kampala's backstreets
- A narrow gorge trying to strangle the powerful Nile at Murchison Falls – the result is rather extraordinary
- Lush terraced hills flowing down to the serenity of Lake Bunyonyi

Top things to do
- Do the unthinkable – penetrate Bwindi's Impenetrable Forest and come face-to-face with mountain gorillas
- Endure the cold and wet to reach mystical highs in the glaciated 'Mountains of the Moon' (Rwenzoris)
- Listen to the chorus of chimp calls while following in their actual footsteps in Kibale Forest National Park
- Stir the Nile with your paddle before it shakes you (and your raft) to the core

Getting under the skin
Read: *Waiting* by Goretti Kyomuhendo, one of Uganda's pioneering female writers – it tells of the rituals of rural life as well as the omnipresent fear during the fall of Idi Amin
Listen: to the rumba sounds of Afrigo Band, one of Uganda's longest-running groups
Watch: *The Last King of Scotland*, Kevin Macdonald's adaptation of Giles Foden's novel about the emotional whirlwind surrounding Idi Amin's physician
Eat: *matoke* (cooked plantains) and groundnut sauce; *rolex*, a chapatti wrapped around an omelette
Drink: Bell Beer, infamous for its 'Great night, good morning!' ad jingle – hangover-free it's not, but it's tame in comparison to *waragi* (millet-based alcohol)

In a word
Habari? (What news? In Swahili)

Trademarks
Gorillas; Lake Victoria; anti-gay legislation; Idi Amin; 'Mountains of the Moon'

Random fact
Winston Churchill was one of Uganda's earliest tourists – his 1907 visit had a lasting impact, with his 'Pearl of Africa' description becoming one of the nation's monikers

1. Half the world's critically endangered mountains gorillas live in Bwindi Impenetrable National Park

2. Uganda's third largest export is tea and the best tea is hand plucked

3. At the top of Murchison Falls the Nile surges through a gap 7m wide

4. Organised chaos: Kampala mini bus station

U | **CAPITAL** KAMPALA // **POPULATION** 34.8 MILLION // **AREA** 241,038 SQ KM // **OFFICIAL LANGUAGE** ENGLISH

Uganda

Emphatically fecund, this petite nation punches well above its weight in terms of nature. Its lush forests reverberate with life, their dense canopies shielding the playground of hundreds of bird and mammal species, including half the planet's mountain gorillas. Its savannahs, nestled in some of Africa's most stunning settings, nurture classic safari wildlife, and the Rwenzoris, Africa's highest mountain range, are clad in endemic plant species and topped with equatorial glaciers. Although controversial anti-gay legislation has cast a shadow on the entire nation, most Ugandans are open, eloquent and polite – their warmth of spirit is palpable.

U CAPITAL KYIV // POPULATION 44.6 MILLION // AREA 603,550 SQ KM // OFFICIAL LANGUAGE UKRAINIAN

Ukraine

Ukraine is the birthplace of Eastern Slavic civilisation, with a capital at least 1500 years old, and home to seminomadic Hutsuls who still inhabit the rugged Carpathian Mountains. Experiencing this enormous country can mean anything from gleaming Orthodox churches to craggy mountain passes, fine-sand beaches or pulsating nightlife. In 2014 Russian troops advanced into Crimea, the peninsula jutting from Ukraine's southeast, commencing another turbulent chapter to a region already marked by invasions. Certainly, Ukraine's story is far from concluded. In a country where headscarf-clad babushkas rub shoulders with Kyiv fashionistas and sports cars share road space with horse-drawn carts, there's simply no telling what Ukraine's next chapter may hold.

Best time to visit
May to October

Top things to see
- The caverns with mummified remains of monks at Kyevo-Pecherska Lavra
- Nostalgic folk art, windmills and traditional village huts at the open-air Museum of Folk Architecture in Pyrohovo
- The fortress of Kamyanets-Podilsky in a majestic setting above the Smotrych River
- Carpathian National Park, Ukraine's largest wilderness preserve and home to lynx, bison, brown bears and wolves

Top things to do
- Hop aboard a boat tour in the Danube Delta Biosphere Reserve, a haven for great white pelicans, red-breasted geese and other feathered friends
- Stroll the seaside promenade in Odesa, taking in elegant 19th-century buildings and the cinematic icon of the Potemkin Steps
- Lose yourself in the atmospheric back lanes of pretty Lviv, a Unesco World Heritage site, with buildings dating back to the 14th century and intimate coffee houses
- Delve into Kyiv: marvel at 1000-year-old St Sophia Cathedral, shop along cobblestone Andriyivsky Uzviz and catch a show at the National Opera Theatre

Getting under the skin
Read: *Death and the Penguin* by Andrey Kurkov, an absurdist and socially incisive novel about a man and a penguin living in modern-day Kyiv

Listen: to the fast-paced dance melodies of traditional folk-music ensemble Suzirya
Watch: Oksana Bayrak's *Avrora*, the evocative story of a 12-year-old orphan and aspiring dancer who witnesses the Chornobyl disaster
Eat: tasty *varenyky* (boiled dumplings served with cheese or meat); borsch (beetroot soup); and *salo* (salted or smoked pork fat)
Drink: vodka; *kvas* (a sweet beer made from fermented bread)

In a word
Vitayu (Hello)

Trademarks
Cossacks; *pysanky* (hand-painted eggs); costumed folk singers; ice fishing; Chornobyl; Soviet architecture; Orthodox churches; *shapkas* (fur hats)

Random fact
The exclusion zone left uninhabited since Chornobyl's nuclear meltdown is turning into an offbeat tourist attraction, with guided tours bringing curious visitors and photography enthusiasts inside the abandoned Soviet-era town of Pripyat

1. A traditional Ukranian wooden church south of Kiev

2. Ballet has a long heritage in the Ukraine, which is home to the famed Kiev Ballet company

3. Floral motifs on tanks outside the Museum of the History of Ukraine in World War II, Kiev

1. Camel polo can only be played in Dubai, where the game was invented

2. Children visit one of the world's largest mosques, Sheikh Zayed Grand Mosque in Abu Dhabi

3. Like a giant 110m-high headlight: Aldar's headquarters in Abu Dhabi

U　CAPITAL ABU DHABI // POPULATION 5.5 MILLION // AREA 83,600 SQ KM // OFFICIAL LANGUAGE ARABIC

United Arab Emirates

Welcome to one of the greatest shows on earth, an astonishing blend of Arabian tradition and race-for-the-future innovation. Few countries have undergone such an extraordinary transformation as the seven emirates of the UAE. A century ago, this was an impoverished Bedouin backwater and Dubai and Abu Dhabi were quiet little villages huddled by the water's edge. But fabulous oil wealth, wedded to sharp business nous, have made these two of the world's most energetic and architecturally exciting cities that together represent the future of the Gulf. Scratch beneath the surface and you'll discover the proud Bedouin traditions that provide the foundation for UAE society, not to mention date-filled oases, stirring sand dunes, dramatic mountains and coral rich waters.

Best time to visit
Late October to late February

Top things to see
- The National Museum, old-style souqs, wind towers and modern architecture of Dubai
- Hatta, a Dubai getaway with a wonderfully reconstructed heritage village
- Dubai's Burj Khalifa, the world's tallest building
- Abu Dhabi, one of the richest cities on earth with an extravagant modern skyline
- Khor Fakkan, the most beautiful port in the UAE with a long corniche and fine beaches

Top things to do
- Enjoy early-morning camel racing in Dubai
- Head out into the sand dunes of Liwa Oasis, the first ripples of the Rub' al-Khali (Empty Quarter)
- Discover the other UAE in the oasis town of Al Ain with busy souqs and a fort
- Dive and snorkel at the world-class sites off Badiyah
- Drive from Fujairah to Oman's Musandam Peninsula between the mountains and Arabian Sea

Getting under the skin
Read: *Dubai: The Story of the World's Fastest City* by Jim Krane
Listen: to *Ahlam*, the eponymous album by UAE's first lady of song
Watch: contemporary Arab cinema at the prestigious Dubai International Film Festival
Eat: *khuzi* (a stuffed whole roast lamb); *Umm Ali* (a pudding with raisins and nuts)
Drink: dark muddy *qahwa* (coffee)

In a word
Al-Hamdu lillah (Thanks be to God)

Trademarks
Oil wealth; wadi-bashing (four-wheel-driving around UAE's oases); shopping; Burj al-Arab; a cultural mix of Arab, Western and Asian expats

Random fact
Dubai's police fleet includes vehicles made by Aston Martin, Bentley, Ferrari, Lamborghini and McLaren

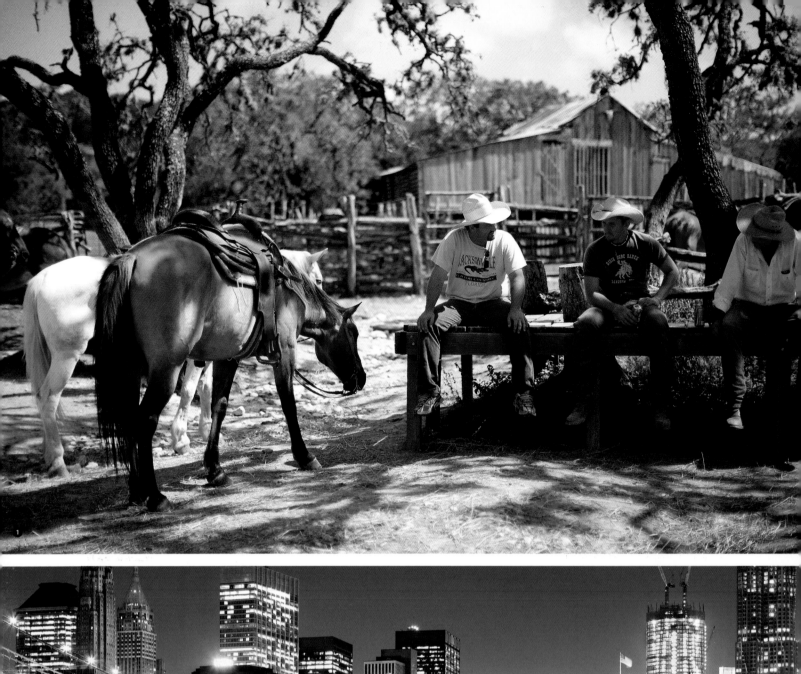

U **CAPITAL** WASHINGTON, DC // **POPULATION** 316.4 MILLION // **AREA** 9.8 MILLION SQ KM // **OFFICIAL LANGUAGE** ENGLISH

United States of America

There can be no activity more American than travelling in America. Residents of the USA think nothing of moving thousands of kilometres for a job, on a whim, because of love or simply due to boredom. An eternal optimism fuelled by the hope of better times around the next curve is coupled with the promise of discovery. The culture is ever-changing and this vast nation has a corner for every taste. Extraordinary beauty is bound together by commercial squalor, cities beguile and horrify, while franchised taste seems to be the national fabric even as individual creativity is celebrated. The variations are myriad, find your own adventure from New York to California, Alaska to Florida, Chicago to New Orleans.

Best time to visit

Year-round

Top things to see

- New York City, which locals already assume you know is the centre of the universe
- California, which combines boundless beauty with the world's eighth-largest economy
- The jaw-dropping vistas of the Grand Canyon stretching into infinity
- New Orleans, where America meets France, Africa and the Caribbean
- The natural fireworks of autumn leaves in New England

Top things to do

- Hit the museums and splendid government buildings of Washington, DC
- Escape the hordes on a back trail of Yellowstone National Park
- Joyfully join the smiling masses at the real Disneyland
- Road trip through the South, land of blues and barbecue
- Bike across San Francisco's iconic Golden Gate Bridge

Getting under the skin

Read: three great American road-trip books: John Steinbeck's *Travels With Charley*; William Least Heat-Moon's *Blue Highways*; and Jack Kerouac's *On the Road*
Listen: to Bob Dylan's poetic *Highway 61 Revisited*; country great Johnny Cash's *Live at Folsom Prison*; *King of the Delta Blues Singers* by blues legend Robert Johnson
Watch: American epics: *Gone With the Wind, Citizen Kane, The Godfather, A River Runs Through It, Forest Gump, 12 Years a Slave, Boyhood*
Eat: New York pizza, Chicago hot dogs, Southern barbecue, Maine lobster, Tex-Mex burritos, apple pie
Drink: craft beers; Californian reds; regional soft drinks like Moxie, Cheerwine and Dr Brown's

In a word

Yo! Howdy! Hi!

Trademarks

Cheeseburgers; red, white and blue everything; oversized cars; oversized houses; oversized portions; national parks; guns; Hollywood; vast, open spaces

Random fact

In January, the average low in Boston is -6°C, the average high in Miami is 24°C

3

1. Cowboys and the Wild West loom large in American culture; Dixie Dude Ranch, Texas
2. City of dreams: Brooklyn Bridge and Manhattan's vast skyline, New York
3. Jazz originated in New Orleans; Daniel Farrow plays Preservation Hall in the French Quarter
4. Bison graze near the steaming Mud Volcano, Yellowstone National Park

4

U

Best time to visit
December to March (summer)

Top things to see
- Montevideo, Uruguay's culturally rich capital with 19th-century neoclassical buildings and a photogenic Old Town
- The picturesque cobblestone streets of Colonia del Sacramento, beautifully set above the Río de la Plata
- Cabo Polonio, a fishing village that attracts a staggering amount of wildlife – sea lions, seals and penguins, with whales spotted offshore
- The beguiling, laid-back surfing and fishing village of Punta del Diablo

Top things to do
- Discover Uruguay's cowboy culture at the Fiesta de la Patria Gaucha (March) in Tacuarembó, featuring rodeos, parades and folk music
- Join the international party crowd at the dance clubs in Punta del Este
- Tour the gloomy ruins of the infamous Fray Bentos meat-processing factory, recently given Unesco World Heritage status
- Enjoy a soak in the thermal baths of Termas de Daymán
- Feast on steak at a *parrilla* (steakhouse) inside Montevideo's Mercado del Puerto

Getting under the skin
Read: any of Juan Carlos Onetti's short stories or novels set in the fictional town of Santa Maria
Listen: to the talented singer-songwriter and Academy Award winner Jorge Drexler
Watch: *The Last Train*, Diego Arsuaga's comedy-drama about a group of train aficionados who decide to steal an old train in order to prevent its sale to Hollywood
Eat: huge steaks cooked over a sizzling barbecue
Drink: maté, the smooth tea made from the leaves of yerba maté, sometimes served in a hollow gourd with *bomba* (metal straw)

In a word
¿Me estás jodiendo? (Are you kidding me?)

Trademarks
Football (soccer); Fray Bentos meat pies; beach resorts; beef; tango; gauchos (cowboys)

Random fact
In late 2014 Uruguay became the world's first country to legalise the cultivation and sale of marijuana – it even has 'pot clubs', greenhouses where members can grow cannabis plants

1. The elegant dome of the 18th-century Montevideo Metropolitan Cathedral

2. Riders celebrate gaucho culture at Fiesta de la Patria Gaucha in Tacuarembó

3. The Uruguayan Clásico between Montevideo football clubs Peñarol and Nacional is the year's most important fixture

U CAPITAL MONTEVIDEO // POPULATION 3.3 MILLION // AREA 176,215 SQ KM // OFFICIAL LANGUAGE SPANISH

Uruguay

By almost every quality of life index – high literacy, low corruption, freedom of press and a host of other civil liberties – ultra-liberal Uruguay is a Latin American leader. This verdant nation shares with its bigger neighbours Brazil and Argentina a passion for football, a proclivity for juicy home-grown steak and a thriving gaucho culture (horsemen, cattle ranches and big open skies). Peaceful and prosperous, Uruguay and its rolling farmland rear up in a charming coastline of wondrous colonial towns, lonely fishing villages, surf-pounded beaches and – in Punta del Este – probably South America's liveliest beach party capital.

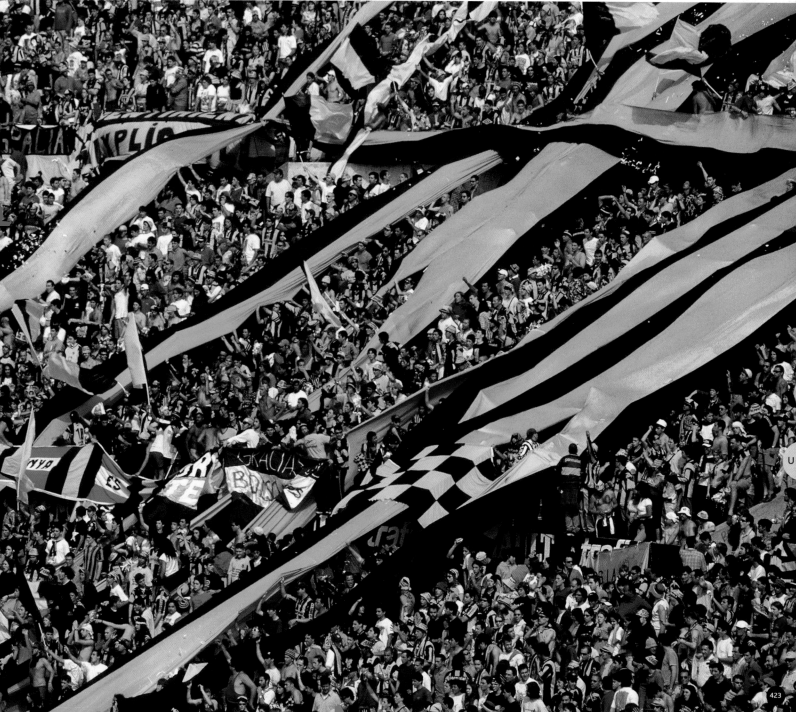

1. Elaborate Timurid tilework on the necropolis of Shah-i-Zindi, Samarkand

2. The Tian Shan or 'Celestial Mountains' near the ski resort of Chimgan

3. Glazed-bricks ornament a tower of the Muhammad Amin-Khan Madrassa in Khiva

U // CAPITAL TASHKENT // POPULATION 28.7 MILLION // AREA 447,400 SQ KM // OFFICIAL LANGUAGE UZBEK

Uzbekistan

Any Silk Road romantic who's daydreamed of travelling the Golden Road to Samarkand or the desert tracks to Bukhara will already have their sights firmly set on Uzbekistan. As the cultural and historic heart of Central Asia, the country's Islamic architecture of floating turquoise domes and towering minarets easily ranks among the region's greatest sights, while in the foreground old men with white beards and stripy cloaks haggle over melons in the bazaar or savour a pot of green tea beside a crackling kebab stand. Despite an authoritarian government and strong police presence, travel through this essential slice of the Silk Road is dripping with epic history at every turn.

Best time to visit
April to June, September to October

Top things to see
- Samarkand's Registan Square, one of the world's great architectural ensembles
- Shah-i-Zinda, Samarkand, a necropolis that marks the highpoint of Timurid tilework
- The old slave-raiding walled city of Khiva, frozen in time and surrounded by desert
- The Savitsky Museum, an incredible collection of Russian avant-garde art in the remote city of Nukus
- The scattering of ruined palaces built by Timur (Tamerlane) in his hometown of Shakhrisabz

Top things to do
- Explore the desert citadels of Khorezm
- Haggle for *suzani* carpets, embroidery and striped silks in backstreet bazaars
- Ride the beautiful Tashkent metro with its lavishly decorated stations
- Get lost in the mosques, mausoleums and madrasas of Bukhara's backstreets

Getting under the skin
Read: Peter Hopkirk's *The Great Game* to gem up on the region's imperial shenanigans
Listen: to *Yol Boisin*, by world-music diva Sevara Nazarakhan; or try something by the Tashkent-taxi-cab favourite Yulduz Usmanova
Watch: Michael Winterbottom's *Murder in Samarkand*, about a controversial British ambassador sidelined by his own government
Eat: *plov*, a dish of rice, meat, and carrots (the oil from which is rumoured to an aphrodisiac)
Drink: *kok choy* (green tea) at a traditional teahouse

In a word
Yol boisin (May your travels be free of obstacles)

Trademarks
Timur; blue-domed mosques; minarets; desert; *plov*; the Silk Road; skullcaps; white beards

Random fact
Uzbekistan is one of the world's two countries to be double land-locked (two countries from the sea)

ROBERT PRESTON PHOTOGRAPHY | ALAMY // MISONNTE | GETTY IMAGES // LUIS DAVILLA | GETTY IMAGES

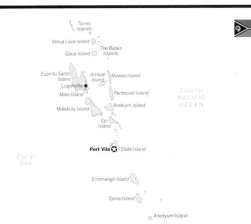

V | CAPITAL PORT VILA // POPULATION 261,565 // AREA 12,200 SQ KM // OFFICIAL LANGUAGES BISLAMA, ENGLISH & FRENCH

Vanuatu

An ancient living culture, accessible volcanoes, world-class diving and some of the best cuisine in the Pacific make Vanuatu an extraordinary place to visit. Despite a history of indentured labour (known as blackbirding) and conjoint colonising by the French and British, islanders still welcome visitors with authentic warmth. Smiles are as easy to come by as *laplap* cooked in a pit oven, crusty French bread or fresh fish flavoured with herbs and coconut. Port Vila, the compact capital and tourist centre, is colonial-cool with glorious views of the harbour. From here set off to the outer islands for perfect beaches and crystal-clear waters – as well as black magic, fiery eruptions of lava and authentic Melanesian *kastom* (custom).

Best time to visit
April to October (the southern winter), when temperatures aren't too stifling

Top things to see
- The explosive volcanic fireworks of Mt Yasur
- The land divers of Pentecost, who leap from man-made wooden towers
- The Dog's Head cannibal site, complete with dismemberment tables and fire pits
- *Rom* dances, sorcery and cultural demonstrations at one of north Ambrym's festivals
- The chambers, tunnels and underground lake of Valeva Cave from a kayak

Top things to do
- Camp in the active caldera of Mt Marum surrounded by lava beds, jungle and cane forests
- Swim through an underwater world of sunken luxury liners, caves and coral gardens off Luganville
- Keep your eyes peeled for dugongs while snorkelling in Epi's Lamen Bay
- Relax 'resort style' at the delightful Oyster Island on Santo
- Abseil down the 35m Mele Cascades for a dip in an aquamarine freshwater pool

Getting under the skin
Read: *Getting Stoned with Savages*, a witty account of J Marten Troost's misadventures in Vanuatu and Fiji
Listen: to *Best Of* by the ni-Vanuatu singer Vanessa Quai, a 'living cultural icon'
Watch: the 2015 movie *Tanna*, a heartfelt tale shot in Vanuatu and starring the indigenous Yakel tribe
Eat: *laplap*, taro paste cooked with coconut and meat in an earthen oven
Drink: *aelan bia* (island beer), otherwise known as kava, a becalming non-alcoholic but narcotic brew

In a word
Tank yu tumas (Thank you very much)

Trademarks
Live volcanoes; drumming; friendly locals; land diving; wild boar; carvings; spears; French-inspired cuisine; snorkelling and scuba diving; black magic

Random fact
The last recorded act of cannibalism in Vanuatu was in 1969 by the Big Nambas tribe on Malekula who are also said to be the last islanders to convert to Christianity

1. Port Resolution on Tanna Island was named by Captain Cook after his ship, the HMS *Resolution*
2. The classic colours of a tropical paradise: Port Vila and Iririki Island, Efate
3. Black magic practitioners from the village of Fetukai, Tanna Island

V POPULATION 839 // AREA 0.44 SQ KM // OFFICIAL LANGUAGES LATIN & ITALIAN

Vatican City

It is quite extraordinary to find a fully functioning city-state in the middle of a modern European capital. The chaos and attitude of Rome ends at the walls of the Vatican, where medieval traditions and arcane rituals take the place of coffee-shop culture and Vespas. This – the world's smallest nation – is the seat of the Catholic Church, ruled with absolute authority by the Pope, from a palace with over a thousand rooms, protected by a squadron of single Swiss men in flamboyant red, yellow and blue uniforms. You don't have to be Catholic to appreciate the Vatican; the city-state is also one of the world's great repositories of architecture, culture and art.

Best time to visit
April and June (the low season); Wednesdays when the Pope meets his flock

Top things to see
- Michelangelo's Sistine Chapel – his ceiling frescoes and *The Last Judgement* are awe-inspiring
- The pope, who turns up consistently at 10.30am on Wednesdays (get there early to get a seat!)
- The Swiss Guard – all male, Swiss and single – and their marvellous, Renaissance-styled skirt pants
- One of the world's greatest collections of sacred art inside the Vatican Museums

Top things to do
- Hike the 320 steps up St Peter's Basilica, the world's largest dome – the panorama is dizzying and dazzling
- Zigzag around Doric columns and absorb the extraordinary air of St Peter's Square
- Kiss or rub for luck the right foot of bronze St Peter inside the basilica
- Take a tour of the 'City of the Dead' and see St Peter's tomb beneath the basilica
- Experience a calmer side to the Vatican in the Vatican Gardens, a lavish sprawl of lawns, grottoes, fountains and topiary

Getting under the skin
Read: *A Season for the Dead* by David Hewson for a fast-paced thriller about a serial-killer cardinal
Listen: to papal speeches and news from the city on Radio Vatican (live-streaming or podcasts in English) at www.radiovaticana.org
Watch: Tom Hanks flit around the Vatican City in Ron Howard's film adaptation of Dan Brown's *Da Vinci Code* sequel, *Angels and Demons*
Eat: Roman pasta such as creamy carbonara (egg yolk, parmesan and bacon); and fiery *alla matriciana* (tomato, bacon and chilli)
Drink: wines such as Frascati and Torre Ercolana (the Vatican consumes more wine per person than any other country)

In a word
Amen

Trademarks
The Pope and the Popemobile; Catholicism; St Peter's; the Sistine Chapel and Michelangelo; Swiss Guards; pilgrims; saintly souvenirs

Random fact
The Popes' previous pad was in Avignon, southern France; the clergy moved to the Vatican City in 1377

1. Symbol of the church's great wealth: the vast dome of St Peter's Basilica

2. *Apollo and the Muses*, a fresco by Tommaso Conca in the Museo Pio-Clementino

3. The Pontifical Swiss Guards of the Holy See are responsible for the Pope's safety

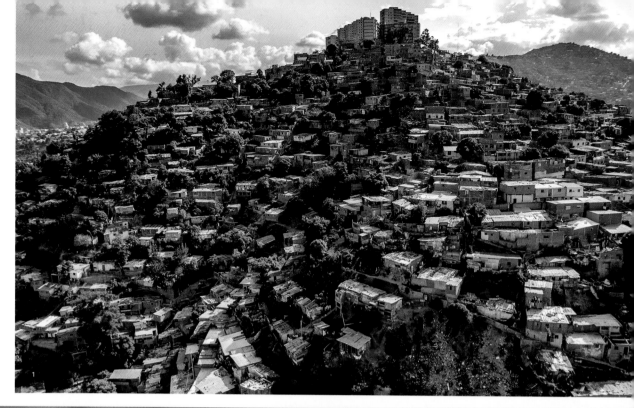

1. Chaos meets human habitation: a Caracas hill slum

2. Angel Falls drops 807m from Auyán-tepui, Canaima National Park

3. Tasty parcels: Piaora people from Amazonas State consider tarantulas a delicacy

V CAPITAL CARACAS // POPULATION 28.8 MILLION // AREA 912,050 SQ KM // OFFICIAL LANGUAGE SPANISH

Venezuela

Venezuela is a showstopper: almost nowhere in the world has physical beauty in such abundance or variety as this stunner, and its warm and friendly people are a joy to be among. Sadly though, the political situation here has made travel quite challenging: hyperinflation, long lines for basic consumer goods and spiralling crime, particularly in the capital Caracas, mean that visitors need to be forearmed with information and careful about where they go. That said, it's South America's cheapest destination, and its main attractions are still largely safe: head for the beaches of Los Roques, the waterfalls of Gran Sabana or the fantastic scenery of Mérida, Venezuela's Andean activities and extreme-sports capital, to best appreciate this wonderful, if challenging nation.

Best time to visit
December to April (the dry season)

Top things to see
- Angel Falls, the highest waterfall on earth, which drop over 300 storeys in Parque Nacional Canaima
- Los Roques, tiny islands with a friendly vibe
- Los Llanos, a savannah with anteaters, capybaras, anacondas, caiman and astounding birdlife
- Puerto Colombia in the Parque Nacional Henri Pittier, with its magnificent selection of beaches
- Gran Sabana's table mountains, roaring rivers, gushing waterfalls and wilderness

Top things to do
- Paragliding, canyoning, mountain climbing and hiking in the mountain town of Mérida
- Dive the pristine waters of Los Roques archipelago
- Hike to the top of Roraima, a massive table mountain with a wild landscape
- Explore the waterfalls, beaches and rainforests along the meandering Río Caura
- Discover the magnificent and largely undeveloped beaches of the Península de Paria

Getting under the skin
Read: the *Doña Bárbara* by Romulo Gallegos
Listen: to *The Venezuelan Zinga Son* by the indie-rock favourite Los Amigos Invisibles
Watch: *The Revolution Will Not Be Televised*, a documentary about the failed coup to oust Chavez
Eat: *pabellon criollo* (shredded beef, rice, black beans, cheese and fried plantain)
Drink: *guarapita*, sugar-cane spirit and fresh juices

In a word
Como esta? (How are you?)

Trademarks
Oil; beauty queens; *tepuis* (table mountains); Simon Bolívar; Angel Falls

Random fact
Sir Arthur Conan Doyle's book *The Lost World* was inspired by the table mountain of Roraima, where plant and animal species found nowhere else on earth were discovered in the 1890s

(V) CAPITAL HANOI // POPULATION 92.5 MILLION // AREA 331,210 SQ KM // OFFICIAL LANGUAGE VIETNAMESE

Vietnam

The story of Vietnam is a tale of two cities: poetic, dignified Hanoi and zestful, have-a-go Ho Chi Minh City. The slender arc of land strung out between these former wartime rivals has been the setting of some of Asia's greatest dramas, and some of its greatest tragedies, but Vietnam has moved on from battlefield tourism to become an essential stop on the overland trail. The geography dictates a linear trajectory – flying into Hanoi or Ho Chi Minh, then meandering from paddy fields to white-sand beaches and on to jungles, hill-tribe villages and sculpted limestone islands, or vice versa. En route, you may get whiplash from the pace of change in Asia's latest technological hub.

Best time to visit
March and April, September to November

Top things to see
- Hanoi's Hoan Kiem Lake, particularly when lined with morning exercisers at 5am
- Ho Chi Minh Mausoleum in the capital, Hanoi
- Dragon-shaped mountains and jade-green waters in Halong Bay
- The citadel and royal tombs along the Perfume River in Hué
- Terraced rice fields, mountains and traditional homes in Sapa

Top things to do
- Eat *pho* (noodle soup) on a tiny plastic stool at a sidewalk eatery
- Boat through the Mekong Delta
- Learn to make your own *goi cuon* (soft summer rolls) and *banh xeo* (crispy Vietnamese pancakes) on a cooking course in Hoi An
- Explore the backwaters by motorcycle, and see a gentler, calmer side to Vietnam
- Experience the great outdoors – on foot, by mountain-bike or on your hands and knees in the tunnels excavated by the Viet Cong

Getting under the skin
Read: *Dumb Luck* by Vu Trong Phung, a fun 1936 tale of Red-Haired Xuan, a Charlie Chaplin–type character
Listen: to the symphony of motorbike engines, honking horns and street vendor calls from a street cafe in Ho Chi Minh City
Watch: a film having little to do with war, Tran Anh Hung's *The Vertial Ray of the Sun*, showing life in modern Hanoi
Eat: as much local food as you can; Vietnamese treats like *pho* and *banh cuon* (steamed rice rolls with minced pork) are doubly delicious at source
Drink: *bia hoi* (draught beer), particularly at Hanoi's infamous '*bia hoi*' corner in the Old Quarter: a hundred stools, 101 drinkers and cheap beer

In a word
Troi oi! (Oh my!)

Trademarks
Conical hats; pyjamas; wartime relics; Halong Bay; cyclos; scooter gridlocks; smartphones and tech; Ho Chi Minh

Random fact
Superglue was reputedly invented as an emergency wound dressing in the Vietnam War

1. Junks cruise among the ethereal limestone isles of Halong Bay

2. Cascading rice terraces near the hill station of Sapa

3. Black Hmong from Bo Lu village; the Hmong are an ethnic minority from northern Vietnam

4. Ringed by ramparts and a moat, the Imperial Citadel sits on the banks of the Perfume River in Hué

Best time to visit
The weather is fine all year, November and May see less crowds

Top things to see
- Virgin Islands National Park on St John (USVI), with perfectly preserved beaches
- Devil's Bay (BVI), a natural beach play land surrounded by grottos, boulders and more
- Christiansted on St Croix (USVI), with a vast 18th-century fort and an appealing waterfront
- Buck Island Reef National Monument off St Croix (USVI), a haven for sea turtles
- The Baths on Virgin Gorda (BVI), a collection of volcanic boulders forming pools

Top things to do
- Deaden your pain with a trademark Painkiller cocktail at White Bay (BVI)
- Laze away your cares on the hideaway of Anegada (BVI)
- Dive sites like the sunken *RMS Rhone* (BVI) and the wall at Cane Bay (USVI)
- Hike St John's vista-rich Reef Bay Trail
- Kayak through the mangroves on the wild end of St Thomas (USVI)

Getting under the skin
Read: St Thomas native Tiphanie Yanique's island epic *Land of Love and Drowning*; or Alice Hoffman's *Marriage of Opposites*, set in the Jewish community of 1800s St Thomas
Listen: to *quelbe*, a blend of local folk music; a top group is Stanley and the Ten Sleepless Knights
Watch: *Christopher Columbus: The Discovery*, a 1992 epic featuring the Italian explorer washing ashore in the New World
Eat: *fungi* (boiled cornmeal and okra); *callaloo* (a stew of meat and local greens); johnnycakes
Drink: a debilitating range of fruity rum drinks

In a word
Limin' (Universal West Indian slang for hanging out)

Trademarks
Huge cruise ships; reggae rhythms; Cruzan and Pusser's rums; yachties; flamingos

Random fact
The USVI is an unincorporated territory of the USA; the BVI is a Crown Colony of the UK

1. The granite boulders and private pools of the Baths, Virgin Gorda (BVI)

2. Despite their fierce appearance, the local iguanas are herbivores

3. Somewhere to rest awhile; Cruz Bay, St John (USVI)

CAPITAL ROAD TOWN (BVI), CHARLOTTE AMALIE (USVI) // **POPULATION** 31,912 (BVI), 104,737 (USVI) // **AREA** 505 SQ KM **OFFICIAL LANGUAGE** ENGLISH

Virgin Islands

Although considered one archipelago, the Virgin Islands are divided between two countries: the British Virgin Islands (BVI) and the United States Virgin Islands (USVI). And the curiosities don't stop there. St Thomas on the USVI can be mobbed by tourists (cruise ships larger than some islands dock here by the dozen) yet at the other end of the island, you'll find peaceful stands of mangroves. Its siblings, St Croix and St John, are much quieter and feature beaches and wild places as beautiful as any in the Caribbean. Meanwhile the 40 islands of the BVI are more than content to remain as quiet as possible, except for requisite island rhythms.

W CAPITAL CARDIFF // POPULATION 3 MILLION // AREA 20,764 SQ KM // OFFICIAL LANGUAGE WELSH & ENGLISH

Wales

Wales at its best is tramping in splendid isolation across magnificent green hills and purple-heather moors, valleys ringing with the song of male voice choirs and poetry of 6th-century bards, local pubs beckoning with a pint of Best Bitter. This raw, underrated land of heady, rough-cut landscapes, mighty stone castles and lyrical morning mists is enriched by myths, literature and the fiercely patriotic, rugby-loving, song-mad Cymry (Welsh) themselves. Rejuvenated modern cities and a grand industrial heritage lie alongside all that natural beauty, while an ever-increasing range of adventure sports opportunities and some fine festivals keep this small, damp, glorious nation buzzing.

Best time to visit
May to September

Top things to see
- The towering, elegant, 200-year-old aqueduct at Pontcysyllte
- Snowdon, Wales' highest and headiest peak at 1085m
- The Six Nations Rugby Championships in Cardiff
- Conwy, Caernarfon, Harlech and Beaumaris castles
- The Brecon Beacons National Park – rugged hills, moors and fantastic pubs

Top things to do
- Hike, mountain bike, camp, trampoline and surf artificial waves in Snowdonia National Park
- Shop for china in Portmeirion, a whimsical vision of Italian classicism
- Listen to male voice choirs at Llangollen's International Eisteddfod and folk and rock at Crickhowell's Green Man
- Follow the Pembrokeshire coastal path through quaint fishing villages and around secluded coves
- Frolic across sandy beaches and limestone cliffs on the Gower Peninsula

Getting under the skin
Read: *Random Deaths and Custard* by Catrin Davydd, one of Wales' best contemporary creative writers
Listen: to operatic arias by Welsh tenor Aled Wyn-Davies
Watch: *Solomon and Gaenor*, a turn-of-the-20th-century tale of forbidden love set against South Wales' coalfields
Eat: *bara brith* (tea-soaked fruit loaf); a Welsh cream tea (fruit scone with strawberry jam and whipped cream); or a lunchtime plate of Welsh rarebit (an 18th-century version of beer-soaked Cheddar cheese on toast)
Drink: a pint of Cardiff-brewed Brains or ale from a local microbrewery

In a word
Bore da (Hello, good morning)

Trademarks
Mountains; sheep; coal mines; male voice choirs; rugby; tongue-twisting place names starting with double L; King Arthur and Merlin; leeks; the Welsh red dragon

Random fact
Genuine Welsh products: Richard Burton, Anthony Hopkins, Laura Ashley, Roald Dahl, Tommy Cooper, Peter Greenaway, Alfred Sisley, Gareth Bale

1. Tryfan in Snowdonia requires an easy scramble to get to the summit

2. The home of the arts in Wales: Millennium Centre, Cardiff

3. There's surfing in Wales? A surfer emerges from the chilly waters of Langland Bay

W

Y   CAPITAL SAN'A // POPULATION 25.5 MILLION // AREA 527,968 SQ KM // OFFICIAL LANGUAGE ARABIC

Yemen

Yemen's history reads like the retelling of legends – to the Romans, the country was Arabia Felix (Happy Arabia), Noah is said to have launched his ark from here, the Queen of Sheba once ruled the land and there was dazzling wealth from the frankincense trade. Today, Yemen's fortunes are about as distant from those stories as it's possible to be, with civil war taking its toll on an already poverty-stricken population. With none of the oil wealth of its neighbours, parts of Yemen seem like a time capsule to old Arabia, including mud 'skyscrapers', stunning mountain scenery, San'a's historic rammed-earth houses, and the weird and wonderful landscapes of Socotra Island.

Best time
October to March

Places of interest
- San'a, the 2500-year-old Unesco World Heritage–listed city with 14,000 ancient buildings
- Wadi Hadramawt's otherworldly mud villages, especially Shibam which has been dubbed the 'Manhattan of the Desert'
- Shaharah, the ancient mountain village with a 17th-century suspended bridge and fantastic scenery
- Thilla, the historic fortified village with stone walls and lovely architecture
- Socotra Island with its strange and unique dragon's blood trees

Local customs
- Shopping for dried fruits and spices in San'a's Souq al-Milh
- Dancing with daggers in a performance of *bara*, a traditional folk dance
- Tucking into one of Yemen's many varieties of flatbread, served fresh from the tandoor
- Burning frankincense to savour the richly perfumed smoke
- Chewing *qat*, the leaves of a mildly narcotic plant

Getting under the skin
Read: *Yemen: Travels in Dictionary Land* by Tim Mackintosh-Smith, wry observations of Yemeni life from a long-time San'a resident
Listen: to *Habibi Ta'al* by Ahmed Fathey, a renowned Yemeni oud player and singer
Watch: Pier Paolo Pasolini's *Arabian Nights*, a racy adaptation of the age-old collection of stories that includes scenes shot in Yemen; or *A New Day in Old Sanaa'a*, the first-ever Yemeni film by Bader Ben Hirsi
Eat: *saltah* (a piping-hot meat stew with lentils, beans, coriander and fenugreek)
Drink: tea scented with cardamom; or coffee with ginger

In a word
Mumkin ithnayn shay (Two teas please)

Trademarks
Frankincense; Queen of Sheba; mud skyscrapers in the Wadi Hadramawt; Bedouin tribesmen with *jambiyas* (ceremonial daggers); chewing *qat*

Random fact
Despite having been unified for centuries, modern Yemen was actually divided into two countries – South Yemen and North Yemen – until 1990

1. San'a is one of the world's oldest continuously inhabited cities
2. Sometimes called the 'Madagascar of the Arabian Sea': Socotra island
3. A woman wearing a traditional conical hat, Al Hajjarin village, Wadi Dawan
4. The distinct canopy of the dragon blood tree, so called because of its dark-red resin

Z CAPITAL LUSAKA // POPULATION 14.2 MILLION // AREA 752,618 SQ KM // OFFICIAL LANGUAGE ENGLISH

Zambia

Although copper and cobalt run through Zambia's veins, its heart is made of anything but heavy metal. The people, who've long been encouraged to embrace their varied cultural backgrounds and traditions, are perfect examples – they're easy-going, incredibly welcoming and open. The vast swathes of untapped wilderness, many of which are national parks, also stand in contrast to the all-important mining industry. Home to an incredible diversity of wildlife and landscapes (and some of Africa's best-trained guides), the parks offer just as a wide a variety of phenomenal safari experiences – walk through South Luangwa, paddle a canoe in the Lower Zambezi or 4WD deep into Kafue. In Zambia visitors don't just see wildlife, they get to know it.

Best time to visit
May to early October, when skies are dry, temperatures are cool and all the safari camps are open

Top things to see
- Your white-water raft after one of the Zambezi's Class-V rapids
- Eight million fruit bats flocking into Kasanka National Park in late October
- The wildlife of the 'Emerald Season' in Kafue National Park (December to April)
- The Lozi king leading his people's retreat from the annual floods in the Ku'omboka ceremony
- Cheetah chasing puku on the Busanga Plains

Top things to do
- Delicately dodge hippos and crocs while canoeing in Lower Zambezi National Park
- Bungee jump into the abyss from the Zambezi bridge
- Wade across the Luangwa River on a safari walk in South Luangwa National Park
- Venture into the wilderness of Liuwa Plain National Park to witness the other wildebeest migration
- Peek over the edge of Victoria Falls while swimming in the Zambezi's precariously placed Devil's Pool

Getting under the skin
Read: *A Point of No Return* by Fawanyanga Mulikita; *Kakuli* by Norman Carr; *The Unheard* by Josh Swiller
Listen: to *kalindula* music – Ricki Ilonga and Larry Maluma are both great options
Watch: *The Death of Tyson*, a short documentary on the life of an AIDS orphan
Eat: *nshima* (porridge made from ground maize) with *chibwabwa* (pumpkin leaves) and *nkuku mu chikasu* (village chicken)
Drink: the local beer, Mosi

In a word
Muzuhile? (How are you? in Bemba)

Trademarks
The Zambezi; Victoria Falls; walking safaris; wild dogs; the Copper Belt; Luangwa leopards; bat migration

Random fact
One cheeky monkey relieved himself on President Rupiah Banda during a televised press conference in the State House gardens in 2009 – Banda laughed, looked up at the tree and jokingly scolded: 'You have urinated on my jacket!'; later that year the State House's wild primates were all evicted (coincidence?)

1. Young women from Livingstone in traditional dress

2. Carmine bee-eaters nest in the banks of the Luangwa River

3. The luxury *Royal Livingstone Express* takes in Zambezi Falls

4. An African elephant mother and calf in Lower Zambezi National Park, one of the most pristine parks in Africa

1. Modern Harare: the city began as a fort built by the Pioneer Column, a force raised by Cecil Rhodes

2. Mighty Victoria Falls, locally known as Mosi-oa-Tunya (the smoke that thunders)

3. A hippopotamus and friend at Mana Pools National Park

Z // CAPITAL HARARE // POPULATION 13.7 MILLION // AREA 390,757 SQ KM // OFFICIAL LANGUAGES ENGLISH, SHONA, NDEBELE, XHOSA, VENDA, TSWANA, TONGO, SOTHO, SHANGANI, NDAU, NAMBY, KOISAN, KALANGA, CHIBARWE, CHEWA & SIGN LANGUAGE

Zimbabwe

Treasures – Zimbabwe is full of them. Yes, really. It's only because the nation's politics and economic woes have provided such fodder for the international press over the past couple of decades that more isn't known of them. However, once visitors are on the ground here the true rewards of travel still take centre stage. The national parks offer some of the most rewarding wildlife encounters on the continent and protect diverse landscapes, which vary from the wonders of Victoria Falls and the depths of the lush Zambezi Valley to the craggy heights of the Eastern Highlands. In the heart of the country mythical rock formations play canvas for ancient rock-art and intricate vestiges of Great Zimbabwe tell of a Medieval African kingdom. The only thing Zim is missing is you.

Best time to visit
May to October (the dry season)

Top things to see
- Endangered African wild dogs hunting en masse in Hwange National Park
- Victoria Falls thundering below from the seat of a microlight aircraft
- The medieval city of Great Zimbabwe, once a religious and political capital
- Fossilised skeletons of dinosaurs while hiking on the Sentinel estate
- The 'wilderness of elephants', otherwise known as Gonarezhou National Park

Top things to do
- Canoe the Zambezi in Mana Pools National Park
- Sense the spirit of the sacred Matobo Hills, a dramatic showroom of 3000 ancient rock-art sites
- Fly like a superhero across Batoka Gorge on the 'Zambezi Swing'
- Walk into the Eastern Highlands' mists and wonder how you ended up in Scotland
- Track black rhino along the edge of Lake Kariba in Matusadona National Park

Getting under the skin
Read: *The Fear: Robert Mugabe and the Martyrdom of Zimbabwe* by Peter Godwin
Listen: to *Viva Zimbabwe,* a compilation ranging from catchy political anthems to *sungura* guitar melodies
Watch: *Mugabe and the White African,* a documentary following a farmer's fight to save his land
Eat: *sadza ne nyama* (maize-meal with meat gravy)
Drink: Bohlinger, a Zimbabwean-brewed lager

In a word
Mhoro (Hello, in Shona)

Trademarks
Victoria Falls; Zambezi River; Robert Mugabe; hyperinflation; Great Zimbabwe; Cecil, the lion

Random fact
While visitors can no longer legally spend Zimbabwe dollars, they are entitled to use nine other currencies

Dependencies, Overseas Territories, Departments & Administrative Divisions/Regions

Australia
- **Ashmore & Cartier Islands** (northwest of Australia in the Indian Ocean)
- **Christmas Island** (south of Indonesia in the Indian Ocean)
- **Cocos (Keeling) Islands** (south of Indonesia in the Indian Ocean)
- **Coral Sea Islands** (northeast of Australia in the Coral Sea)
- **Heard Island & McDonald Islands** (southwest of Australia in the southern Indian Ocean)
- **Norfolk Island** (east of Australia in the South Pacific Ocean)

China
- **Hong Kong** (see p175)
- **Macau** (see p231)

Denmark
- **Faroe Islands** (east of Norway in the North Atlantic Ocean)
- **Greenland** (see p155)

France
- **Bassas da India** (west of Madagascar in the Mozambique Channel)
- **Clipperton Island** (southwest of Mexico in the North Pacific Ocean)
- **Europa Island** (west of Madagascar in the Mozambique Channel)
- **French Guiana** (see p141)
- **French Polynesia** (east of Tahiti in the Pacific Ocean)
- **French Southern & Antarctic Lands** (southeast of Africa in the southern Indian Ocean)
- **Glorioso Islands** (northwest of Madagascar in the Indian Ocean)
- **Guadeloupe** (see p159)
- **Juan de Nova Island** (west of Madagascar in the Mozambique Channel)
- **Martinique** (see p249)
- **Mayotte** (in the Mozambique Channel between Mozambique and Madagascar)
- **New Caledonia** (see p281)
- **Réunion** (see p445)
- **Saint Pierre & Miquelon** (in the North Atlantic Ocean, south of east coast of Canada)
- **Tromelin Island** (east of Madagascar in the Indian Ocean)
- **Wallis & Futuna** (see p446)

Netherlands
- **Aruba, Bonaire and Curaçao** (see p444)
- **Saba, Sint Eustatius, and Sint Maarten** (in the eastern Caribbean Sea, to the east of Puerto Rico)

New Zealand
- **Cook Islands** (see p95)
- **Niue** (see p445)
- **Tokelau** (see p446)

Norway
- **Bouvet Island** (southwest of South Africa in the South Atlantic Ocean)
- **Jan Mayen** (east of Greenland in the Norwegian Sea)
- **Svalbard** (see p446)

UK
- **Anguilla** (see p17)
- **Bermuda** (see p49)
- **British Indian Ocean Territory** (see p445)
- **British Virgin Islands** (see p435)
- **Cayman Islands** (see p77)
- **Falkland Islands** (see p133)
- **Gibraltar** (see p445)
- **Guernsey** (northwest of France in the English Channel)
- **Jersey** (northwest of France in the English Channel)
- **Isle of Man** (Irish Sea)
- **Montserrat** (see p445)
- **Pitcairn Islands** (see p313)
- **St Helena** (includes Ascension, Tristan da Cunha, Gough, Inaccessible and the three Nightingale Islands)
- **South Georgia & the South Sandwich Islands** (see p446)
- **Turks & Caicos Islands** (see p411)

USA
- **American Samoa** (see p335)
- **Baker Island** (North Pacific Ocean)
- **Guam** (see p161)
- **Howland Island** (North Pacific Ocean)
- **Jarvis Island** (South Pacific Ocean)
- **Johnston Atoll** (southwest of Hawaii in the North Pacific Ocean)
- **Kingman Reef** (North Pacific Ocean)
- **Midway Islands** (west of Hawaii in the North Pacific Ocean)
- **Navassa Island** (west of Haiti in the Caribbean Sea)
- **Northern Mariana Islands** (see p161)
- **Palmyra Atoll** (North Pacific Ocean)
- **Puerto Rico** (see p319)
- **Virgin Islands** (see p435)
- **Wake Island** (North Pacific Ocean)

Other Places of Interest to Travellers

The following destinations don't fit neatly elsewhere in this book. They are officially dependencies of other nations, but they are not large enough or on a road well enough travelled to warrant a full and separate entry. Despite this, at Lonely Planet we believe that these destinations are of special interest, whether that be due to wildlife or history or geography, and they are generally considered to have a strong independent identity and to be quite different from their parent countries. Tony Wheeler, Lonely Planet's founder and perennial explorer, compiled this section.

Aruba, Bonaire & Curaçao

CAPITAL ORANJESTAD (A), KRALENDIJK (B), WILLEMSTAD (C)
POPULATION 110,663 (A), 15,800 (B), 227,000 (N)
AREA 180 SQ KM (A), 294 SQ KM (B), 444 SQ KM (C)
OFFICIAL LANGUAGES DUTCH, SPANISH, ENGLISH, PAPIAMENTU

It's possible that the 'ABC Islands' are the most concentrated area of multiculturalism in the world. Papiamento, spoken throughout the islands, is testament to this fact – the language is derived from every culture that has impacted on the region, including traces of Spanish, Portuguese, Dutch, French and local Indian languages. The islands are diverse: upmarket Aruba is the most touristed island in the southern Caribbean, Bonaire has an amazing reef-lined coast, and go-go Curaçao is a wild mix of urban madness, remote vistas and a lust for life.

Diego Garcia – British Indian Ocean Territory (UK)

POPULATION 4000
AREA 60 SQ KM
OFFICIAL LANGUAGE ENGLISH

Diego Garcia and the islands of the Chagos Archipelago make up the British Indian Ocean Territory. Technically it's uninhabited: in the 1970s the island's British administrators deported the population and most of them now live on Mauritius. They were replaced by military personnel as Diego Garcia became a military base, a stationary aircraft carrier handy for US B52s to set out on bombing missions to Iraq or Afghanistan. Don't plan on visiting the territory's islands, atolls and reefs; visitors are definitely not welcome.

Gibraltar (UK)

POPULATION 29,258
AREA 7 SQ KM
OFFICIAL LANGUAGE ENGLISH

Strategically situated guarding the Straits of Gibraltar, the narrow entrance to the Mediterranean from the Atlantic Ocean, the Rock of Gibraltar makes an interesting stumbling block for British-Spanish relations. The Spanish want it back and the British would probably be happy to hand it over, but there's no way the citizens of Gibraltar will go. They like their curious little corner of England on the shores of the Mediterranean. Towering over the town, the upper Rock offers spectacular views, and houses the colony of Barbary macaques – Europe's only primates. If they ever depart, so the legend goes, so will the British.

Montserrat (UK)

CAPITAL PLYMOUTH
POPULATION 5241
AREA 100 SQ KM
OFFICIAL LANGUAGE ENGLISH

In 1997 a volcanic eruption devastated Montserrat. Despite plenty of warning that after 400 sleepy years the Soufrière Hills Volcano was about to wake up, there were still 19 deaths and the capital, Plymouth, was buried. Reconstruction is still going on over two decades later, but despite this there's a certain magnificent desolation about the place. Montserrat's few visitors come for volcano-related day trips. Those who stay longer will relish the solitude and enjoy the chance to become part of the island's rebirth.

Niue (New Zealand)

CAPITAL ALOFI
POPULATION 1190
AREA 259 SQ KM
OFFICIAL LANGUAGES
NIUEAN & ENGLISH

Midway between Tonga and the Cook Islands, which makes it a long way from anywhere, Niue is a classic example of a makatea island, an upthrust coral reef. It rises often vertically out of the ocean so there's very little beach, but in compensation there are amazing chasms, ravines, gullies and caves all around the coast. Some of them extend underwater, giving the island superb scuba-diving sites. Like a number of other Pacific nations, the world's smallest self-governing state has been suffering a population decline: today there are more Niueans in New Zealand than on 'the Rock of Polynesia'.

Réunion

CAPITAL ST DENIS
POPULATION 844,994
AREA 2517 SQ KM
OFFICIAL LANGUAGES FRENCH

Réunion is so sheer and lush, it looks like it has risen dripping wet from the sea – which it effectively has, being the tip of a massive submerged prehistoric volcano. The island is run as an overseas department of France, and French culture dominates every facet of life, from the coffee and croissant in the morning to the bottle of Evian and the carafe of red wine at the dinner table. However, the French atmosphere of the island has a firmly tropical twist, with subtle traces of Indian, African and Chinese cultures.

South Georgia (UK)

CAPITAL GRYTVIKEN
POPULATION 10-20
AREA 3755 SQ KM
OFFICIAL LANGUAGE ENGLISH

Aptly described as looking like an Alpine mountain range soaring straight out of the ocean, South Georgia's topography is matched only by its equally spectacular wildlife. The remote island's human population, scientists of the British Antarctic Survey, may drop as low as 10 during the long Antarctic winter. But there are two to three million seals, a similar number of penguins and 50 million birds, including a large proportion of the world's albatrosses. Add industrial archaeology in the shape of the island's half a dozen abandoned whaling stations, plus South Georgia's role in the final act of Sir Ernest Shackleton's epic escape from the ice, and it's no wonder this is one of the most popular destinations for Antarctic tourists.

Svalbard (Norway)

CAPITAL LONGYEARBYEN
POPULATION 1872
AREA 61,229 SQ KM
OFFICIAL LANGUAGE NORWEGIAN

Far to the north of Norway, the archipelago of Svalbard has become a popular destination for Arctic travellers, keen to cruise the ice floes in search of whales, seals, walruses and polar bears. Apart from wildlife there are also some terrific hiking possibilities on the main island where you might encounter reindeer and Arctic foxes. The main town, the engagingly named Longyearbyen, has a long history of coal mining.

Tokelau (New Zealand)

POPULATION 1337
AREA 12 SQ KM
OFFICIAL LANGUAGE TOKELAUN,
ENGLISH, SAMOAN

Tokelau consists of three tiny atolls, each of them laid out on classic atoll design principles: a necklace of palm-fringed islands around a central lagoon. Off to the north of Samoa, the islands are not only a long way from anywhere, but also a long way from each other; it's 150km from Atafu past Nukunonu to Fakaofo. They're also very crowded: there may be less than 1400 people but they've got very little land to share; none of the islets is more than 200m wide and you've got to climb a coconut tree to get more than 5m above sea level. Getting there is difficult even for yachties, as none of the lagoons has a pass deep enough for a yacht to enter.

Tristan da Cunha (UK)

CAPITAL EDINBURGH
POPULATION 267
AREA 98 SQ KM
OFFICIAL LANGUAGES ENGLISH

Officially a dependency of St Helena, over 2300km to the north, Tristan da Cunha is frequently cited as the most remote populated place in the world. The island is a simple, towering volcano cone, and an eruption in 1961 forced the complete evacuation of the island. The displaced islanders put up with life in England for two years but most of them returned as soon as the island was declared safe in 1963 and went straight back to catching the crawfish that are the island's main export. Nightingale, Inaccessible and two smaller islands lie slightly southeast of the main island.

Wallis & Futuna (France)

CAPITAL MATA'UTU
POPULATION 15,613
AREA 274 SQ KM
OFFICIAL LANGUAGES FRENCH

This French Pacific colony is made up of two islands, separated by 230km of open ocean and remarkably dissimilar. Wallis is relatively low lying with a surrounding lagoon fringed by classic sandy motus (islets), while Futuna is much more mountainous and paired with smaller Alofi. The populations are equally dissimilar: Futuna has connections to Samoa while the Wallis links were with Tonga. Wallis has one of the Pacific's best archaeological sites at Talietumu and an unusual collection of crater lakes, while both islands are dotted with colourful and often eccentrically designed churches.

Authors

Carolyn Bain	Anthony Ham	Lorna Parkes	Matt Phillips	Lee Slater	Stephen Lioy
Joe Bindloss	Anita Isalska	Luke Waterson	Robert Reid	Jess Lee	Tom Masters
Celeste Brash	Catherine Le Nevez	Sarah Reid	Regis St Louis	Kerry Christiani	Megan Eaves
Paul Clammer	Emily Matchar	Polly Thomas	Ryan Ver Berkmoes	Mara Vorhees	
Mary Fitzpatrick	Helen Elfer	Bradley Mayhew	James Smart	Megan Eaves	
Will Gourlay	Kate Morgan	Carolyn McCarthy	Hugh McNaughtan	Tamara Sheward	

This edition

Cartographers
Corey Hutchinson
Alison Lyall
Anthony Phelan
Anita Bahn

Wayne Murphy
Julie Sheridan
Shahara Ahmed
Mark Griffiths
Diana Von Holdt

This edition was
fact-checked by
Lonely Planet's
team of Destination
Editors in offices in

the UK and USA,
including:

Bailey Johnson
MaSovaida Morgan

Alexander Howard
Laura Crawford
Sarah Reid
Megan Eaves
Joe Bindloss

Tasmin Waby
Helen Elfer
Matt Phillips
Gemma Graham
Kate Morgan

Anna Tyler
Brana Vladisavljevic
James Smart
Lorna Parkes

THE TRAVEL BOOK
A JOURNEY THROUGH
EVERY COUNTRY IN THE WORLD

3rd Edition

Managing Director, Publishing Piers Pickard
Associate Publisher Robin Barton
Coordinating Editor Bridget Blair
Editor Ross Taylor
Art Direction and Design Daniel di Paolo
Coordinating Cartographer Wayne Murphy
Pre-Press Production Ryan Evans
Print Production Larissa Frost, Nigel Longuet,
Jean-Pierre Masclef
Thanks Dora Ball, Brendan Dempsey, Barbara
di Castro, Lyahna Spencer, Florian Poppe, Matt
Phillips, Shahara Ahmed, Jennifer Carey

Published in 2018 by
Lonely Planet Global Limited
CRN 554153
www.lonelyplanet.com

Lonely Planet Offices
Australia The Malt Store, Level 3, 551 Swanston St,
Carlton, Victoria 3053 T: 03 8379 8000

Ireland Digital Depot, Roe Lane (off Thomas St),
Digital Hub, Dublin 8, D08 TCV4

USA 124 Linden St, Oakland, CA 94607
T: 510 250 6400

UK 240 Blackfriars Rd, London SE1 8NW
T: 020 3771 5100

Stay in touch lonelyplanet.com/contact

ISBN 978 1 78701 763 4
10 9 8 7 6 5 4 3 2 1

Text & maps © Lonely Planet Pty Ltd 2018
Photos © as indicated 2018
Printed in Malaysia

Cover images: © Matt Munro, Jonathan Gregson, Joe Windsor-Williams, Lottie Davies, Justin Foulkes, Kris Davidson, Mark Read, Philip Lee Harvey, Catherine Sutherland, Eric Lafforgue, Pete Seaward